The Prairie Gardener

PUBLICATIONS BY H. F. HARP

Hardy Chrysanthemums for Manitoba Gardens
Manitoba Department of Agriculture, no. 421, 1965.

Hedges for the Prairies
Canada Department of Agriculture, no. 1153, 1962.

Peonies for the Prairie Garden
Manitoba Department of Agriculture, no. 420, 1965.

Winter Storage of Tender Bulbs, Tubers and Corms
Manitoba Department of Agriculture, no. 422, 1965.

The Prairie Gardener

H. F. Harp

HURTIG PUBLISHERS
EDMONTON

Hurtig Publishers
10560 105 Street
Edmonton, Alberta

Printed and bound in Canada

ISBN: 0-88830-093-X

Preface

Gardening is one of the purest expressions of human joy in life and living things and, in one form or another, can be enjoyed by those who live in apartments, in urban homes and in rural areas where space is almost unlimited. Gardening books are plentiful enough, but most have been written by gardeners who live in the milder parts of Canada, in England and in the United States. There has long been a need for a comprehensive book on gardening dealing with the special problems of the prairie gardener, who has to cope with a short growing season and extremes of heat and cold.

To make the best kind of garden we have to know what plants are most likely to succeed. Time and money are wasted when trees and shrubs too tender for the prairies are planted. There is a temptation to buy plants from the descriptions and beguiling pictures in modern nursery catalogues but, unless the plants are fully hardy, they soon die in a prairie garden.

This book is written by a prairie gardener who has gleaned his knowledge from forty years of practical experience. It is directed both to those who are only starting to be gardeners and to those who, by trial and error, have already gained some knowledge. The first section of the book is a discussion of techniques basic to the care of all growing things on the prairies; it is there for the novice, and as a background reference for each of the chapters that follows. The second section is a detailed guide to those plants which thrive in the prairie garden.

Acknowledgments

I am grateful to Dr. W. R. Leslie, former superintendent of the Morden Experimental Farm, for the opportunity he gave me to improve my knowledge of horticulture and to pursue the fascinating field of plant breeding. This resulted in modest achievement and made it possible for me to write this book. I wish to thank Mr. Brian Andrews, gardening editor of the *Edmonton Journal,* for his valuable help as technical editor and Mr. Jan Vandenberg, who did all the illustrations. To my publisher, to Miss Susan Kent, who helped to make the book more readily understood by the novice gardener, and to Mrs. Dawn Martinook, who typed the original manuscript, I am also deeply indebted.

Contents

PART TWO

Credits for Illustrations
Photos of alpine fir and dwarf mugho pine, facing page 193 courtesy the Department of Plant Science, Faculty of Agriculture, University of Alberta.
Line illustrations by Jan Vandenberg, Edmonton.

Part One

One

Planning the Prairie Garden

Garden Design

There have been radical changes in garden design since the first settlers came to the Great Plains regions a hundred years ago. The need for shelter is as great as it ever was on the windswept prairies but, in built-up areas, windbreaks of caragana hedges are no longer a necessity. Everything starts from an idea: good design is the proper arrangement of trees and shrubs, walks and special features that fit into an environment to create unity, variety and harmony. Unity is achieved when all parts of the garden are seen as being part of the whole and not as three separate gardens. The front garden, the utility area and the back garden are three distinct parts, yet they are all part of one garden. Variety is the happy accommodation of as many plants as possible, effective only when we can grow them all well and make them appear to belong in their particular spot. Harmony results when we are able to fit into a pattern the many different sizes, shapes and colors of plants to make a pleasing picture. A tree planted in the wrong place — too near the house wall, for example — not only spoils the picture; it becomes a nuisance and sooner or later will have to be removed.

In the small garden it is not easy to make the front area, middle and back area a single unit joined by lawns and walks. Variety is necessarily limited in a small garden: one or two specimen trees may be all there is room for; shrubs have to be used sparingly or they soon take up room that should be reserved for perennial and annual flowers. To make a garden peaceful and harmonious we must be sure to have the right plants in the right places. We can take certain liberties in the perennial border by using a few woody plants here and there, but we must keep in mind, for instance, that hybrid tea roses and bedding geraniums have no place in the perennial border.

Good design is, in fact, a matter of personal taste, though there are accepted principles of design which, if moderated to suit the particular piece of property and the taste of the homeowner, will give satisfaction. The wise gardener will tend to follow a few basic rules without feeling he is tied down; rather, he will feel he is free to create the kind of garden best suited to the plot of land he is working with and to the needs of his family.

Where does one start when making a new garden and what does one do first when renovating an old one? By the time a new home is ready to live in, the contractor has cleaned up the building rubbish, rough-graded the front area and laid turf. The chances are the sods were lifted from a pasture of native grass, tough enough to stand plenty of wear and tear but quite unsatisfactory for a first-class lawn. In some areas, where native trees have been left standing, they can be used to great advantage providing they are suitable: oak, ash and elm are useful only if you have sufficient room; boxelder or Manitoba maple, poplar and native willow have no place in the average-sized garden.

There are three main areas, front, middle and back, to be considered when planning a garden and this kind of arrangement has a basic application to all properties regardless of size; we may call these areas the approach area, the utility area and the pleasure garden.

The Approach Area

The approach area or front garden should complement the house, enhancing its best features by using plants that seem to belong in their surroundings. There must be a balance on either side of the entrance, yet this does not necessarily mean two pyramidal cedars guarding the front door. Balance can be created by planting one upright-growing evergreen on one side, a bank of low, dense evergreens on the other. The aim is to make a frame for the picture which is the façade of the house, setting it off to the best advantage by using trees and shrubs that are not too colorful nor yet too drab. The first and most basic consideration in designing this area is the lawn, which will form the backdrop to the entire scene.

Lawn design – On small properties it is best to slope the lawn from the front of the house to the sidewalk rather than to make it into two levels.

Grass banks are difficult to keep green when the weather is hot and dry for long periods. Low forms of juniper will make a better cover for a bank, but one will still have a two-level lawn and this tends to make the house appear to be closer to the sidewalk than it really is. The way to go about making a lawn and the best kinds of grass to use are discussed fully in chapter ten.

The foundation planting – When the lawn is in, you can pay attention to the foundation planting, to what will seem to frame the house so that it looks to be part of its surroundings and not as though it had suddenly been dropped, ready made, into a foreign environment. First of all, there are the boundary lines to be considered; hedges, fences and shrub borders do much to make or mar the appearance of the house. If ornamental fences are too ornate or too colorful they detract from the house. The same can be said for hedges, and there is no place in the approach area for shrubs with highly colored leaves.

Before you do anything with the front of a town property, take a look at the house from across the street; visualize what certain shrubs will look like when planted in certain areas. Modern houses often extend well across the lot, leaving only a few feet available for planting trees and shrubs. But bare walls can be screened with suitable shrubs and the front corners tied to the landscape with low, dense foliage. If the house is two-storied and the lot narrow, it is more difficult to tie the house to the landscape; the best effect is obtained with spreading shrubs such as villosa lilac and bush honeysuckle.

The bungalow-style home calls for low shrubs with formal, rounded or pyramidal heads, or branches that spread horizontally and are slow to grow. Both evergreens and deciduous shrubs can be used to good effect. Dwarf mugho pines and certain junipers, such as Skandia and Arcadia, are a good choice. They can be planted on the south- and west-facing fronts, whereas the dwarf cedars, or arborvitae as they are properly called, had better be planted on the east or north side. The well-known blue spruces, Kosters and Hoopesi, are sometimes mistakenly planted in the foundation border where, after a few years, they outgrow their surroundings to spoil the landscape plan. There are dwarf forms of the Norway spruce *(Picea excelsa)* which may safely be planted• in the foundation border without fear of overcrowding. These dwarf spruces may suffer some browning on a south- or west-facing border; otherwise, they emerge fresh and green in the spring. The hardiest ones are the nest spruce *(P. excelsa nidiformis)* and repens *(P. excelsa repens)*. Both are spreading evergreens, slow growing – ten-year-old plants will not be much more than a foot high. They will give contrast to the broad-leaved, deciduous shrubs and, if they are under a cover of snow, they will not suffer any winter injury.

The low, prostrate junipers make useful ground covers when planted between the shrubs and are ideal where an all-evergreen bed or border is required. They grow equally well in sun or shade, needing little attention beyond a light pruning now and again to keep any stray shoots within bounds. There are several suitable kinds; most of them are selections of the native prostrate juniper *(Juniper horizontalis)* with varying shades of green and silvery blue.

To relieve the monotony of an all-evergreen foundation planting, spring-flowering bulbs can be used effectively. Tulips are best, choosing the late-blooming Darwins and Cottage tulips, planting them in bold groups, using varieties with bright colors. Tulips will not succeed, though, if planted too close to the foundation wall in the shelter of a wide roof overhang. The soil is often poor in these areas, due, in most instances, to subsoil being mixed with the topsoil when the basement was excavated. The area seldom gets sufficient water as the wide roof shelters the ground from rain. The tulips will make a colorful show in May and early June but, from then on, the foundation border will look drab unless you follow the tulips with lilies or patches of bright annuals.

The most effective foundation planting will have year-round interest provided by evergreens, plus added color changing and continuing through the growing seasons. To provide summer color, plant a patch or two with bright red geraniums or scarlet salvias; don't overdo it or you draw too much attention to the gaudy flowers and the whole picture of a house amid pleasant surroundings is disrupted.

The foundation border should never be planted with a collection of mixed annuals, nor is there any place for herbaceous perennials in the foundation border. The only exception permitted would be a specimen peony or two, but only if the border is wide enough to allow room for a full-grown peony and the soil rich enough to keep the plants thrifty. The peony flowers last but a few weeks and there is a danger of damage to the young, tender shoots of peonies when the plants are set out in a foundation planting. If the border faces either south or west, the soil warms early in the spring, exciting the dormant shoots into growth only to be damaged by a late spring frost. By spreading a thin layer of peat moss over the crown of a peony in October you insulate the dormant buds against sun heat and the shoots are retarded, to grow when danger of frost is past.

Lawn plantings – When the final plans for the foundation border have been made, some thought should be given to the front lawn – what to plant here? Do I need trees? shrubs? is there room? and, if so, what do I plant and where should it go?

To face up to the problem squarely, first ask yourself: is there need for a tree, or should there be a shrub border somewhere out front? Is there a place for perennials? When you decide you have room for a tree in the front yard make sure you plant the right kind, in the right place. There are trees that soon get too big, trees that have bad habits — scattering seeds, shedding twigs after a summer storm, bearing fruit which may be attractive to children. Trees that rightly belong in the natural forest can be used in parks or on large estates, but they have no place in a small garden; where such are mistakenly planted they become a nuisance, crowding out shrubs and flowers.

The flowering crabapples are esteemed as ornamental trees and most of them are suitable for small gardens, though some are better adapted than others. The ideal ornamental crabapple or rosybloom is fully hardy, makes a shapely, long-lived tree and will put on a show of bloom every year. Some varieties bloom profusely one year but sparsely the next; some have fruits that are attractive to children who may break down the branches in their attempts to get at the crabapples. The best kind of rosybloom will have medium-sized crabapples, brightly colored, that will remain attractive for a long time in the fall and persist on the tree through the winter to provide food for birds.

The mountainash and the birch may be considered as suitable trees for the front area where their special requirements of soil, shelter and moisture can be met. Both do best in neutral or slightly acid soil that is moist and well drained.

The front lawn should not be cluttered up with flower beds or single specimen shrubs, or the whole area will appear to be smaller than it really is. Furthermore, flower beds cut into the turf need a lot of care to keep their edges neat and tidy. Keep the front area simple in design and it will not only take less time in maintenance care; it will take on more character than an area of small flower beds and narrow strips of turf.

Before you plant a hedge along the front of the property, ask yourself whether or not it will add anything to the look of the place — will it be a thing of beauty and will it serve a useful purpose? Front hedges are kept low or they obstruct the view from the sidewalk. There are any number of hedge plants hardy and reliable, deciduous and evergreen, and some can be clipped to make two-foot hedges that can be maintained with a minimum of care year after year. Hedges, their uses and how to plant and maintain them in good condition are dealt with in chapter nine.

The Utility Area

When the front area has been made presentable, attention can be given to the middle or service area where there is space for growing vegetables and possibly for a reserve garden, where flowers such as gladioli and other sorts useful for cutting can be grown. In this area also will be found the garden frames and, perhaps, a small greenhouse.

The utility area must be well planned so that every foot of space is put to the best use. The vegetable garden may not be as important as it once was when winter supplies of potatoes and other root crops were grown and stored in prairie home gardens. But every garden has room for a small plot where salad plants can be grown and enjoyed fresh. Salad plants and herbs should be planted close to the back door where they can be gathered quickly if needed in a hurry.

Space reserved for clothes lines stretched up and down the back garden is no longer necessary since indoor drying is done with machines. But an umbrella-type clothes line, set up near the back door, is a useful thing in the summer and provision should be made for it when planning the middle section or service area. A secluded spot for the garbage cans should also be found in this area, where they can be handy, yet out of sight.

Hedges and fences separate this area from the front and the back or private garden. Hedges take up more room than fences and they can be more costly to maintain in good shape as they may need to be trimmed several times through the growing season. Fences can be pleasing to look at as well as being functional and they require little or no maintenance. A plain board fence, unpainted and out of line, will be an eyesore; a fence made of louvered plywood or woven slats will add much to the look of the property as well as give privacy and shelter from wind.

The choosing of a fence may be just as important as choosing the drapes for the living room; it must harmonize with the house and look as though it belongs where it is. The design should complement the architectural style of the house: for example, a louvered fence, painted brown, will harmonize with a low, bungalow-style house painted pale green. On the other hand, a white picket fence would be very much out of place in those surroundings. There are many designs and many kinds of materials available as screens and fences: the most natural looking are made of wood; those made of filigreed concrete blocks are used most effectively in formal areas against the background of a modern building.

The Pleasure Garden

The pleasure garden or living-out area is the most important and interesting part of the whole landscape plan. It is here that you create an area for the comfort and enjoyment of the whole family and it is here you can express your own individual personality. There are no hard and fast rules to follow in making a pleasure garden or living-out area; its design will depend on what interests you most in gardening and how much time and money you are prepared to spend on making and maintaining it. There are styles in garden design as there are in architecture, home furnishings and fashions. The English and Italian styles have influenced garden design in this country with a certain Spanish style which has come to Canada by way of California.

The English style evolved from the quaint Elizabethan formal gardens, enclosed in walls and hedges, to the more natural garden designs of William Robinson, Gertrude Jekell and other apostles of nature. Today the English garden tends to be simple and restful, with a quiet charm of its own.

The continental style is distinguished by terraces, formal areas with statues, summerhouses, pergolas, and arbors surrounded by hedges of clipped yew or box. In the eighteenth century and up until Victorian times, the practice of clipping evergreens to represent birds, animals and other figures was elevated to the level of an art. In one famous English garden, chessmen of clipped golden yew guarded an area described as the Italian Garden. The French style favored a series of formal flower beds, laid out in a geometric pattern, which came to be known as carpet bedding or parterre, making use of urns, statuary, fountains and trellises. This style was once popular in England, where the affluent made homes and gardens in the style of Louis XIV.

There has been a strong influence of the Californian style in our gardens lately, a style that originated in Spain and the countries of the Near East. This style emphasizes the use of walls and fences, pools and restful areas where shade and water provide relaxation.

In small gardens, it is not possible to have sweeping stretches of lawn flanked by trees and shrubs grouped in a natural-looking manner, with running streams, pools and outcrops of rock. But we can give even the smallest garden a more natural look when we leave the grass areas open and group the shrubs along the boundaries. The boundary plantings should be varied or the effect of informality will be lost. A group of dense shrubbery on one side can be balanced by a specimen tree or a smaller group of shrubs with colorful leaves. The boundary plantings should lead the eye to an interesting focal point where a special feature is dominant. The view from the patio or living-out area should take in the whole of this area, with the eye coming to rest at a distant spot on a garden seat, arbor, pool, sundial or bird bath.

The owner of a small garden will have to be most discriminate in his choice of trees and shrubs. Overplanting must be guarded against or flowers will be crowded out in a forest of rank growth. The boundary plantings on small properties will consist mostly of shrubs — some tall, some medium and some dwarf; there will be room for trees of only moderate size and they should be carefully chosen for their height at maturity, for their hardiness, showiness and long season of interest. (Check closely the varieties of trees and shrubs described in chapter eight.)

These boundary plants should grow tall enough to screen from view any unsightly objects and be dense enough to keep out unwanted animals. At the same time, they should be arranged tastefully so that they will look attractive. Shrubs can make a background for the rest of the garden — the flower beds are seen to better advantage against a backdrop of greenery — but flowers must not be in competition for soil moisture with the roots of trees or shrubs.

In deciding what kind of shrubs to use in the boundary planting to obtain an informal or natural effect, keep in mind that harmony of texture, form and leaf color is important. Shrubs with small, bright green leaves should be planted towards the front; shrubs with large, dark green leaves, farther back. To give the illusion of distance, use shrubs with misty gray foliage. Shrubs with large leaves such as villosa lilac *(Syringa villosa)* will tend to make a small garden appear smaller, so choose medium- and smaller-leaved plants to keep things in better proportion.

It is poor landscaping, in the pleasure garden as well as the approach area, to plant specimen shrubs here and there — cut into the lawn or along the edge of a walk. This arrangement is never satisfactory; the shrubs may thrive well enough but the overall design will be ruined.

On small city properties where the lot may be too narrow for shrub borders, a narrow hedge can be substituted to give shelter and privacy. There are plenty of good hedge plants, some deciduous, some evergreen. Here again, you must consider costs and the work involved in maintaining a hedge in good condition. Before deciding on the kind of hedge best suited to your needs, refer to chapter nine for a detailed discussion. And remember that a hedge may well be a second choice when considering screens for the back garden or living-out area.

Climbing plants on wire fences will take less room and require less work to maintain in good condition than either shrub borders or hedges. Consider the climbers when planning a narrow garden; there are a number of suitable sorts useful for this purpose. Some grow fairly rapidly to cover the whole fence in greenery; some have showy bloom, interesting seeds or leaves which turn red in the fall. There is no merit in covering walls with climbers unless the walls or the building itself are ugly. On the other hand, it may be possible to grow a Jackman clematis on a house wall, whereas the same plant set out in the open on a pergola would not succeed. When you plant a clematis against a house wall it will not only get shelter; it will benefit from the extra heat in the soil around the foundation of the house.

Good garden design means the pleasing arrangement of a variety of suitable trees, shrubs and flowers, giving consideration to their functional and aesthetic value. Hedges and fences should serve the dual purpose of providing privacy and shelter, at the same time pleasing the eye. In a well-planned garden, trees and shrubs, hedges and fences, flower beds and borders will be admired as individual features that unite to make up an interesting landscape.

Two

How Plants Grow

Light

The process by which plants use light to convert gases from the air and water in their roots into stored energy is one of the miracles of nature. Gardeners, perhaps more than anyone else, are aware of this; even the novice knows that plants in poor light grow spindly and soon become emaciated. The green cells in the leaves manufacture sugars from carbon dioxide and water by a process called photosynthesis. Light from the sun or from an artificial source supplies the motivating power, and only when light is present can the process continue.

The duration of light, its intensity and its quality all influence the rate of growth and the initiation of flower buds on certain plants. The duration of light normally means the number of hours of continuous daylight, but the period of light in relation to the period of darkness in a twenty-four-hour cycle has a marked effect on some plants. Some plants only initiate their flower buds when the days and nights are about equal in length. The best-known examples are chrysanthemums, poinsettias and kalanchoes which, under natural light, flower during the autumnal equinox. The commercial flower growers take advantage of this to produce chrysanthemums every month of the year by shading the plants to speed up flowering or retarding the process by providing additional light with fluorescent lamps. The home gardener can, with some simple equipment, achieve the same results; refer to chapter seven. Some plants flower best when the days are long; the petunia and tuberous begonia are good examples. A number of plants are not noticeably affected by the length of the day; roses, carnations and African violets are in this group.

In the most northerly settled parts of Canada, where the season of frost-free days is extremely short, it is still possible to produce good specimens of leafy vegetables, potatoes and other root crops as well as a selection of annual flowers. In these areas, growth is phenomenal because of the long days of summer.

When we grow plants in growth cabinets or in special areas indoors, we must consider the kind of light we provide and its intensity. Outdoor plants are assured of a balanced light from the rays of the sun, though, if certain plants are set in the shade, the amount of natural light may not be enough to sustain healthy growth.

Temperature

The speed of plant growth is regulated by its environment; the temperature of the air and the soil plays an important part. When the soil first warms in the spring, green shoots appear and the rate of growth accelerates as the sun's rays become more intense. The optimum temperature for corn, a warm-weather plant, is said to be eighty-six degrees Fahrenheit but, though growth slows down at higher temperatures, the process does not stop. Different groups of plants grow best in a temperature range to which they have long been accustomed. The brassica tribe, for example, a plant family which includes the cabbages and turnips, thrives in cool climates; the tomatoes, sweet corn and melons revel in heat.

It is possible to control temperatures to a limited extent and to make wise use of temperature variations, even in a small garden, in order to accommodate a variety of plants. On the north side of buildings or hedges the soil will stay cooler than on the south side; plants should be set out accordingly. Hedges and screens can provide shelter from cold winds; by thus trapping sun heat you create areas where warm-weather crops will do best. By laying on a mulch of granulated peat or some other suitable material, a process described fully in chapter four, you can insulate the soil against the torrid heat of summer, conserve moisture and create conditions that are more favorable for the cool-weather crops. Temperature can also be controlled by constructing a greenhouse, or with garden frames heated by electric cables or heat lamps which have largely replaced the fermenting material used formerly.

Water

Water is the soul of the garden; without it, plants die. The immediate revival of vegetation when rain has soaked the soil after a period of drought is refreshing to man as well as plants. Water makes up most of the bulk in living plants. It comprises about fifty percent of mature wood, sixty-five percent of the green weight of leaves and succulent twigs, seventy percent of the roots, eighty percent of the weight of herbaceous plants, eighty-five percent of the fruit of apples and strawberries and ninety percent of the edible parts of leafy vegetables. Through their fine roots, plants suck up water from the soil to distribute it to the topmost branches and leaves. It is from this water that plant food is taken up and used in the growing process. The level of water in the soil is therefore reflected in the appearance of the plant: at low levels the leaves may wilt; at a sudden and excessively high level, fruits may crack and the dense heads of cabbages split open.

The natural rainfall cannot be regulated and a sudden excess can leave the soil in a soggy state. If this unhealthy condition persists, the roots die from lack of air. To assist excess water to get away quickly, drainage tiles or pipes are sometimes used. To conserve moisture, the gardener can put on a mulch of peat, chopped hay or other materials which may be more readily available. The loss of water through transpiration can be curbed when the leaf surface is reduced by pruning. This is the normal procedure when making greenwood cuttings.

The home gardener who may spend a good deal of time watering his lawn and plants should understand the basic principles of watering so that he can gauge the plants' requirements, and water accordingly. Once it has been decided that water is needed, be sure to put on enough to soak the soil a foot deep. How are you to tell when a plant needs water? The lawn gives you your first clue when it loses its fresh green color. Grass uses enormous quantities of water in July and August when dry weather and low humidity are most likely to occur. When the leaves of cabbage and other broad-leaved plants lose their greenness and take on a bluish tinge, when the leaf edges of the sweet corn start to curl, the chances are that these plants are dry at the root.

When, how and how much to water lawns and various plants are dealt with more specifically in chapter four but, as a general rule, not less than the equivalent of an inch of rain is needed weekly through periods of drought. Daily dribblings do more harm than good by inducing the development of surface roots, which are in more constant need of watering. Large trees growing in well-drained soil will have adequate supplies of moisture all the year round in areas where the total amount of precipitation is twenty inches or more. Trees in dryland areas, where the rainfall may be only half that amount, will be stunted unless they are watered from dugouts or tap water.

The method used by gardeners to determine the state of the soil regarding moisture is to dig down with a trowel or shovel, examining a soil sample at the six-inch level. If the soil crumbles when squeezed, it needs water; otherwise, the watering can be postponed for a few days longer. Generally, it is better to delay watering your plants for a few days than to apply water too soon. But to defer watering until the plants show definite signs of distress is to subject them to serious shock, which may end in permanent damage. Experienced gardeners can tell by the appearance of a plant if watering is necessary, but the novice had best be guided by the soil test.

Three

Soil

Soil is the home for the roots of plants. It acts as a reservoir for the mineral nutrients, as a sponge from which the plant draws water and as a source of oxygen. Soils vary in composition, but all soils must be worked properly and their various mineral deficiencies corrected if they are to nourish plant life. Infertile soil is the cause of physiological disorders — aberrations in the normal growth of plants — and is as dangerous to plant health as disease organisms or pests.

Soil Types

The solid portion of soil is a mixture of weathered rock and organic material. The rock can be igneous, which is produced by the action of intense heat, or limestone, which results from chemical precipitation or an accumulation of shells. The organic material is the remains of plants in various stages of decomposition.

The gardener classifies soils as sandy, loamy clay, silt and muck soils. Sandy soil is composed of coarse particles which allow water to pass through quickly, leaching or washing out plant nutrients. Sand may be alkaline, if formed from calcareous rock, or neutral when obtained from a lakeshore. All sand is porous; some coarse sand, or sharp sand as the gardener calls it, is much more porous than fine, powdery sand. Sand contains no plant nutrients but it aids in aerating the soil so that the plant's roots can move around freely in search of food. It needs generous applications of humus, compost, peat or rotted barnyard manure to improve its water-holding capacity and productiveness.

Fertile loam has the good qualities of sandy soil — it is easy to work — and the productiveness and water-holding capacity of heavier soils.

Clay soil is made up of tiny particles of mineral matter that stick together to bind the soil and reduce the amount of air it holds. Its texture is therefore too compact to be worked successfully while it is wet. Clay soil is slow to warm in the spring, so early crops are best sown in lighter soil.

Muck soil is made up entirely of decaying plants and has no mineral content; it is made fertile by adding chemicals and draining off excess water, and used extensively to grow truck or market-garden crops.

Silt is fine soil deposited by rivers, streams and the lapping water of lakeshores. Silt loams are made up of particles not so fine as clay nor so coarse as sand. They are usually fertile, easy to work and, with some modification, can be made highly productive.

The home gardener will be modifying and improving his soil by digging it deeply in the fall, adding humus in the form of granulated peat, barnyard manure, leaf mould and garden compost. Clay soils are the most difficult to manage and the most resistant to change. To get them in the best physical condition you must work them at the right time: if you attempt to cultivate a heavy soil while it is still wet, it dries hard and lumpy, making it difficult to rake to a fine tilth; you can, however, prevent the tiny particles of clay from cementing themselves together if you add organic matter or humus. When no organic material is added to land which is in crop year after year, it loses its fertility and productiveness. On larger acreages, soil is improved by planting cover crops of legumes such as alfalfa which gather and store nitrogen from the air. Legumes have deep, penetrating roots with nodules that store the nitrogen.

The bacteria and other micro-organisms that live in the soil feed on decomposing vegetation to make ammonia; from the ammonia, nitrites and finally nitrates are produced, important elements in plant nutrition. Before the micro-organisms can start their manufacturing processes, though, the soil has to warm up. In the meantime, quick-acting, high-nitrogen fertilizers are applied to grass and vegetable crops to speed up growth.

Fertilizers

The chemical fertilizers are becoming even more important in the home garden. They should only be regarded, however, as supplemental; they can never take the place of good soil management, which maintains the soil in good heart by adding organic matter as required and by digging and cultivating.

Nitrogen, phosphorus and potash are the major elements required by plants. These elements must be available in sufficient quantities for the plant to stay healthy and in vigorous growth. Chemical fertilizers are sold in bags of various sizes with the amounts of nitrogen, phosphate and potash plainly shown on the bags. The amounts are always given in the same order — for example, a fertilizer marked 11.48.0 contains eleven percent nitrogen, forty-eight percent phosphate and no potash; one marked 10.52.17 will have ten percent nitrogen, fifty-two percent phosphate and seventeen percent potash.

Nitrogen promotes leaf and shoot development, maintaining a deep green color. Too much stimulates lush growth which may delay seed making and the ripening process of woody plants. Plants that are starved of nitrogen are a sickly, yellowish green; the leaves are smaller than normal and the stems weak. Nitrogen is available as ammonium nitrate, which contains up to thirty-three percent nitrogen. Ammonium sulphate contains about twenty-one percent.

Phosphorus promotes flower and fruit development, stimulates root growth and is essential to the plant's health and vigor. Phosphorus deficiency is manifest in stunted plants with purplish leaves. On some plants, the leaves are mottled dark green with overlaid patches of dull reddish bronze; on others, the undersides of the leaves are purplish. Bone meal, formerly used extensively as a phosphate fertilizer, is slow acting and the effect is long lasting. Superphosphate, which is made by treating rock phosphate with sulphuric acid, is available in highly concentrated forms with up to forty-eight percent phosphorus, and is available in a starter solution with fifty-two percent phosphorus.

Potash is vital to healthy plant growth. It is responsible for the movement of carbohydrates within the plant. Potatoes, corn and root crops generally, as well as peas and beans, respond to potash fertilizer when grown on sandy soils. Prairie gardens are well supplied with potash as a general rule, especially in areas where the soil is heavy. Soils rich in vegetable matter may be deficient; the peat soils of the north are an example. Potassium deficiency is associated with the marginal discoloration and final necrotic condition of the edges of the leaves. Muriate of potash (potassium chloride) contains up to sixty percent potash, according to its degree of refinement. Old-time gardeners have long used wood ashes as a satisfactory source of potash, especially valuable for legumes (peas and beans). The high alkaline content of wood ashes is, however, detrimental to plants that are subject to lime-induced chlorosis — mountainash, Japanese rose, Amur maple. Wood ashes are not recommended for potatoes since the presence of alkali favors the development of scab.

Minor Elements

Other elements necessary to healthy plant growth are calcium, magnesium, sulphur, iron, and the trace elements, boron, manganese, copper, zinc and molybdenum. Though these minor elements are not needed in large amounts, their complete absence in the soil can lead to a serious breakdown in the health of a plant.

Calcium is required in varying amounts by most plants. Some soils contain too much for certain plants, which may cause a condition known as chlorosis, a physiological upset that causes leaves to yellow while the veins remain green. Vegetable plants, particularly those belonging to the cabbage tribe, are lime lovers and a deficiency results in stunted plants. The stems of carnations are weak in a lime-starved soil. Prairie soils, however, are generally high in lime and, except in the wooded areas of the north, liming the soil is rarely necessary. Liming does have the effect of breaking down certain clay soils to make them easier to work.

Sulphur is needed to make the proteins, chlorophyl and hormones that regulate plant growth. Its acidity is useful in neutralizing alkaline soil but large quantities are necessary for it to be of much use. Two pounds to one hundred square feet, applied in the spring by raking it into the topsoil, will help to neutralize soil with an excessive lime content.

Iron is as essential to good health in plants as it is to humans. Most soils contain an adequate amount for the plant's needs but, in heavy soils that are high in lime, it may not be in a soluble form. Certain plants show the effect of iron deficiency readily. Leaves turn yellow although the veins remain green and, unless the unsuitable soil condition is corrected, the whole leaf dies to weaken the plant, lessening its chances of winter survival. Iron sulphate can be sprayed on the leaves to help correct the chlorotic condition. Iron citrate crystals can be inserted under the bark of trees and shrubs to give immediate response, but the chelated or soluble forms of iron added to the soil have the best long-term results.

Magnesium is needed for the production of chlorophyl and combines with phosphate as a magnesium-phosphate compound. Deficiency signs are similar to those manifest by plants lacking iron, but the affected leaves are usually found on the lower part of the plant, whereas iron deficiency is first manifest in the top growth. Magnesium can be added to the soil in the form of magnesium sulphate (Epsom salts).

The amount of boron needed by most plants is very small but the lack of it causes a number of physiological disorders to vegetables and fruits, notably stem splitting in celery, browning of cauliflower, internal blackening in carrots, crown rot of beets, brown heart of turnips and cork disorders of apples. Boron deficiency is said to be responsible for twenty or more physiological disorders of plants. Boron in the form of Borax is sometimes applied as a spray by orchardists and market gardeners.

Manganese functions with iron in the synthesis of chlorophyl. Legumes are supposed to be more susceptible to manganese deficiency than some other plants. Manganese chlorosis first appears as areas of yellow or reddish tissue between the veins of leaves. The recommended treatment for soil showing manganese deficiency is an application of manganese sulphate. Barnyard manure, formerly used to correct the deficiency, has become scarce; this may account for the increase in manganese deficiency which has been noted in recent years.

Copper is present in most plants in minute quantities and is thought to be an oxidizing agent. Dieback (a disorder fatal to trees, in which the outer or topmost parts die first) in citrus fruits is considered to be caused by a copper deficiency. It is more likely to be lacking in soils that are high in organic matter. Copper sulphate is commonly applied in truck gardens where plants have shown symptoms of copper deficiency.

It is only recently that zinc has been recognized as an important minor element in soils. Most soils have sufficient zinc but its availability declines as the soil increases in alkalinity. Zinc appears to be necessary for normal growth and the production of chlorophyl. It is said that better zinc assimilation occurs when tomato plants are grown under reduced light. Zinc deficiency causes rosette of apples, little-leaf of plums and grapes and a mottling of the leaves of citrus fruits. Application of zinc sulphate as a spray is more reliable than soil treatment.

Four

Gardening Skills

To become proficient in the various skills of gardening you need practice. Some are simple and not difficult to learn but other skills require deft fingers and considerable experience. We learn to do by doing, and the more time you spend gardening, the more skilful you will become in the use of the tools of the trade.

Soil Care

Digging — Digging is a simple operation done with a spade, shovel or fork, turning over the topsoil to a depth of a foot or so. Skilled workers will turn under the weeds and trash so that it rots, making humus to increase the fertility of the soil, and will keep the surface level to make a finished job. The best time to dig is in the fall, leaving the soil rough; the gardener will feel a sense of exhilaration working in the autumn air, and the soil benefits by being exposed to frost and the weather through the winter months. The deeper you dig, the better, except that the infertile subsoil should not be brought to the surface.

Double digging, which improves the depth of fertile soil, is sometimes practical for special crops and is an effective way of preparing the soil for sweet peas, asparagus and other deep-rooting plants. The easiest way to go about it is to dig a trench two feet wide and one foot deep, carrying the soil to the far end of the patch to be trenched. Loosen the subsoil with a square-tined fork, adding a layer of barnyard manure or garden compost.

Use a garden line to mark off another two feet and dig the surface soil forward to the first trench. A garden line can be made of any heavy cord; it should be long enough to stretch across the garden. You can buy ready-made garden lines with a metal reel attached. Repeat the work until the plot is finished and the last trench filled with the topsoil taken from the first.

When you dig in the spring you may use a fork, which is better for breaking up lumps than a shovel or spade. Ground that was dug in the fall and allowed to lie rough through the winter may not require forking over but, if it does, use a flat-tined fork to turn it over lightly.

Raking – To prepare a seedbed for vegetables, to make the soil smooth and level for a lawn, to clear stones and rubbish from areas where plants are to be set out, you need to rake. Like digging, raking is a simple operation but it requires a certain skill to keep the work level and the soil worked to the finest tilth – that is, the rough portions broken down into fine granules – for sowing seed. Special care is taken in preparing the soil for carrots and onions: carrots need deep, well-pulverized soil free of stones and hard lumps; onions need firm soil which is best prepared by deep digging, treading, raking, treading and raking a second time. The skilled gardener uses a crisscross motion to put a fine tilth on a seedbed. For this work, a rake with twelve tines is best. Wider rakes with curved tines are more suitable for raking off rubbish and stones.

Hoeing – Hoeing is a regular summer chore which is necessary to kill weeds and to create a good growing condition for young plants by conserving soil moisture. In periods of dry weather, or in gardens where no means of water is available, you can make a dust mulch by regular hoeing which will be of benefit in retarding rapid evaporation. The surface of the soil is cultivated or stirred to a depth of an inch or so between the rows of seedlings and between the young plants in the annual border. This loosening of the topsoil prevents it from baking to form a hard crust around the young plants. Regular hoeing will keep the soil friable or granular and create the best possible conditions for good growth. Several kinds of push hoes do these jobs very well. Where weeds have been allowed to grow tall, the draw hoe or chop hoe is used; the same tool is used to earth up potatoes.

Making a compost heap – Compost – vegetable growth in a state of decomposition – is made by rotting down organic matter. All kinds of garden refuse, from lawn clippings to hedge trimmings, from the leaves of vegetables as they are prepared for use in the kitchen to fish waste, can be used. When properly decomposed, compost smells sweet and is a fertile and an economical substitute for barnyard manure. It improves the water-holding capacity of sandy soil and the aeration of heavy clay. Every garden, both big and small, accumulates quantities of waste material which can be rotted down into rich, nutritious humus to build soil fertility.

A heap four feet square enclosed in chicken wire will be big enough for a small garden. Choose a site in a far corner where it will not be seen from the sitting-out area. Make the pile in six-inch layers of material as it becomes s available — if you have a grass catcher on your lawn mower, use the grass to make compost; when you clip your hedge put the trimmings on the compost heap, with weeds and vegetable waste from the kitchen. Each layer of material can be dusted with a pound of ammonium sulphate and sprinkled with water to keep it moist. A bacterial composition sold under the trade name Acto speeds the decomposition when added to the heap; a five-pound bag is sufficient to convert up to two and one-half tons of garden refuse into rich, soil-building humus. In dry weather it may be necessary to water down the heap but it should not be kept soggy wet. If the material used for composting is made up largely of grass clippings and the trimmings of hedges, there is a likelihood it will generate too much heat, so fork it over, rebuilding the heap after it has stood for a month or so.

It takes a year completely to decompose garden refuse, so, by starting a pile with leaves and other material in the fall and adding to it through the summer months, it will be ready for use a year hence.

Mulching — The importance of mulching plants in prairie gardens cannot be stressed too much. In July and August temperatures can soar and humidity can be very low. The hot, dry atmosphere saps moisture rapidly from the soil unless it is insulated by a mulch.

Mulching is done by spreading a few inches of vegetative material on the bare soil to conserve moisture, kill weeds, reduce the soil temperature and prevent the soil from being blown or washed away. The choice of material is wide but the home gardener will be using the kind that is readily available and not too expensive. First choice is granulated peat moss: a bale containing six cubic feet covers a large area when it is spread two inches deep. Mulches of sawdust, grass clippings, either cereal or flax straw and marsh hay are more limited in their usefulness. Summer mulches are put on in early July when the ground has warmed: if put on too soon, warm weather crops such as tomatoes can be checked; on the other hand, if you wait until the ground is dried out, the mulch will do little, if any good. Winter mulches of straw will protect tender roses and other plants. Whatever you use as a mulch should be put on evenly, making a neat job. Peat is far less unsightly than straw or sawdust and in most prairie gardens, where the soil may tend to be alkaline, the peat will have a beneficial neutralizing effect.

Manuring and fertilizing — Ground that is being cropped regularly will also need to be manured regularly to keep it fertile. Organic manure, which is obtained from the residue of plants and animals, makes humus to enrich the soil. Mineral or inorganic fertilizers do nothing to improve the physical condition of the soil but can supply nutrients to stimulate plant growth when they are used in the right amounts and at the right time.

Barnyard manure is the best soil builder, though it is not so readily available these days. It will vary in quality according to its source and to how it has been processed and stored. Half-rotted, strawy horse manure gives bulk to heavy clay soil; mixed barnyard manure is more effective on lighter soils. Dig in a three-inch layer in October, then fork over the ground in the spring to mix it thoroughly. Poultry manure is high in ammonia and nitrogen as well as phosphate and potash, but it lacks the bulk of horse or cow manure and contains less humus. Litter from chicken and turkey barns should be stored in a dry place and mixed with equal parts of soil or peat before it is used, since it gives off concentrated fumes of ammonia which will burn the lower leaves of roses and other plants when used as a mulch.

Where barnyard manure is not obtainable, use granulated peat which has been fortified with chemical fertilizer. A cupful of 27.14.0 or 11.48.0 in a pailful of peat is dug into the soil in October, at the rate of a pailful to the square yard. Baled, granulated peat from the sphagnum moss is best suited to prairie soils. Its fairly acid reaction helps neutralize prairie soils which tend, for the most part, to be alkaline.

Sawdust can improve the texture of heavy soil but in itself has little value as a fertilizer. When sawdust decomposes, it uses nitrogen, drawing it in the process from the soil to deplete the supply for the plants. If you store sawdust for a year or so before you use it to mix with the soil, it will not deplete the nitrogen supply to the same extent it would if used fresh. To prepare it for use, add a pound of ammonium sulphate (21.0.0) to a wheelbarrow full of coarse sawdust. Dig it into the soil in October after you have spread it evenly two inches deep.

Garden compost (which has been discussed earlier in this chapter) is as good or better than barnyard manure. It contains nutrients in a form that is readily available to the plants and is long lasting in its effect. It can be spread among perennial plants in the spring and dug into the ground in October. In the vegetable garden, it should be dug or ploughed in in the fall.

Plant Care

Planting — Trees and shrubs with bare roots and dormant tops can be planted as soon as the soil thaws out in April or early May. The same plants, grown by nurserymen in containers of one kind or another, can be planted in June but there is no special advantage to setting out these plants in the torrid heat of July or August. Evergreens are planted in May

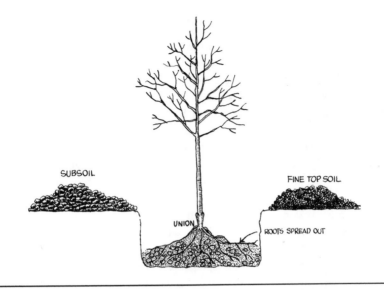

The young tree is set on a mound of soil with the roots fully extended and the union of scion and understock just below soil level.

or August; the latter date is generally preferred as the warm soil induces new roots to form rapidly. Moisture may be a controlling factor in August though, unless you have plenty of water on tap. May can be dry and windy — conditions that are particularly trying for evergreens.

When you transport a tree from a nursery row to its permanent home in the garden, dig a hole big enough to hold the roots when fully extended and deep enough to loosen the subsoil. Barnyard manure, at the rate of a pailful to each tree, can be worked into the subsoil but should not be mixed with the topsoil. Make a mound of well-pulverized soil in the hole, setting the young trees upon it in order to keep the roots apart as the soil is filled in. Two persons, working together, can do a better job of planting a tree than one working alone. As the soil is filled in, the tree is adjusted to its proper height, which should be only slightly deeper than it grew in the nursery. If the tree is gently shaken and pulled up, the soil will find its way among the roots. Tread the soil firmly with the heel of your boot, leaving a depression around the base of the tree to facilitate watering. In dry areas where facilities for watering are limited or nonexistent, you may dig holes for trees in the fall, leaving them open over winter to catch snow and spring run-off water.

Herbaceous perennials, except for the bearded irises, peonies and bleedinghearts, are planted in the spring. Most of them will transplant readily and, where failure occurs, it is usually due to setting out plants that have too much top growth — in other words, too-late planting and not firming the soil about the roots or watering the plants adequately.

Lilies and other bulbs planted in September or later should be watered only if the soil is dry. Tulips will not make roots in dry soil, however, and the bulbs should be watered in to ensure good rooting.

Sowing seeds — In the vegetable garden, seeds are sown in rows, using a garden line to keep the rows straight. Annual flowers are sometimes raised from seed sown in patches where the plants are intended to bloom. The depth of sowing is important; if you bury the seeds too deep they rot before they germinate, especially if the soil is wet for long periods. If you fail to cover the seeds with sufficient moist soil and keep the soil moist by watering it as required, germination will not take place. Depth of sowing is regulated by the size of the seeds; the carrots and other small-seeded vegetables are sown one-half inch deep; beets, cucumbers and melons slightly deeper, but not more than an inch; corn, peas and beans about two inches. If the soil is light and sandy, slightly deeper sowing is advisable.

Most of the root vegetables are spaced eighteen inches between rows. In a small garden, they can be fifteen inches to save space but, in the farm garden, with a large area in vegetables, the rows should be two feet or wider to accommodate mechanical cultivators. Use a triangle hoe or an ordinary hoe to make the seed trenches after you have stretched the line across the plot to be sown. Measuring sticks eighteen inches long or whatever distance you intend to space the rows are thrust into the soil. The line is stretched to the measuring sticks as tightly as possible, then, using the corner of the hoe, the trench is opened at the right depth. When this is done, the line is removed and the seeds sown by scattering them evenly and thinly along the trench.

A common mistake.is to sow seeds too thickly. If the seeds you sow are up to the standard germination requirements, seventy-five or more out of every hundred will grow. When you sow too thickly you waste seed and the seedlings, being overcrowded, are drawn and weak. Moreover, you make a lot of extra work for yourself when it comes time to thin the seedlings.

Cover the seeds with fine soil, using the back of the rake to push the soil into the trench. Firm the soil by walking on the rows, then put a finish to the seedbed by lightly raking the soil level. Rake in the same direction as the rows, in other words, parallel to the rows and not at right angles to them. If the topsoil is dry and you have no means of watering it, draw back the dry soil between the rows before you make trenches in the moist soil. Later on, starting when the seedlings are a few inches high, you can gradually level the soil without harming the young plants.

When you sow patches of Shirley poppy, candytuft, California poppy, calendula, nasturtium, mignonette, larkspur and other annuals that flower satisfactorily from seed sown outdoors, have the soil in good tilth. Make the patches not less than two feet wide in circular or irregular shapes. Draw trenches across the patches six inches wide for the candytuft, California poppy or other low plants and a foot for the tall larkspurs. Sow the seed thinly; cover it with fine soil made firm by treading, then rake the patch level. Cover the patches with several layers of newspaper to insulate the soil from drying winds.

Pruning – Pruning is one of the least understood of garden operations, as evidenced by the bad examples of pruning in many gardens. Why do we prune? To cut out the dead wood, which is not only an eyesore but a hindrance to healthy growth. Dead wood permits entry of disease organisms which can spread to the healthy portions of the tree. Pruning is also done to build or maintain a shapely tree or shrub, to open the centre to let the sunlight in and to keep the trees and shrubs within reasonable bounds. Sunlight gives health and, when it cannot penetrate to the centre of the trees and shrubs, branches that become crisscrossed in the centre are liable to become unthrifty.

When do we prune? In the spring before the leaves unfold is the best time for deciduous trees and shrubs, except that some flowering shrubs are best pruned right after they have done blooming; the lilacs and the early summer-flowering spireas are in this group. Evergreens should be pruned when they have completed their seasonal growth in July. To prune in the fall is to expose the wounds to drying winds and is likely to result in winter injury. To prune deciduous trees and shrubs in June when growth is lush is also detrimental, as the tip growth is the most beneficial to the plant and to remove it is to check growth severely.

Use the secateurs, which are hand pruners, to make clean cuts on wood up to an inch in diameter. When you cut off a twig, make the cut close to the branch; when you cut off a branch, make it close to the main trunk. If you leave stubs they die back to admit disease; when you cut close and paint the wounds with tree paint, they heal to leave no noticeable scar. A waterproof surgical dressing called Braco tree emulsion is easy to apply and not expensive. A fast and effective pruning paint is obtainable in a pressurized can; it provides a protective coating against disease entering pruning wounds, stops the flow of sap from maples and other trees that bleed readily in the spring and repels insects. When you prune with a saw or tree loppers, chamfer, or cut the edge of the bark with a knife to make a slanting surface, before you apply tree paint.

Watering – The natural water supply, which comes from rain and snow, is sometimes in excess of a plant's requirements; sometimes the soil is parched. In most urban gardens water is laid on; in farm gardens, dugouts catch rain and run-off water in the spring, storing it for summer use. When plants are in full growth they need an inch of rain a week, so, when rains are not forthcoming, water from the garden hose supplements the natural supply.

Watering should begin before the plants are in distress from drought. If you let the soil become bone dry, it will take enormous quantities of water to restore adequate soil moisture and much of the water will be wasted in the process. It is important to know just when to water your lawn, flower borders, trees and shrubs. Too much, too soon may be more harmful to the plants than too little, too late. The knowledgeable gardener tells by looking at a plant whether or not it needs watering. The appearance of the leaves gives a clue, but it takes years of experience to learn the art of watering plants. Potted plants can be checked for water by tapping the side of the pot with the knuckles. A dry plant has a ringing sound; a wet one sounds dull. By lifting the pot and examining the bottom opening you can also estimate the state of the soil.

When a plant needs water, you must give it sufficient but no more. You can gauge appropriate amounts by the kind of soil — light or heavy — and by the size of the plant and the spread of its roots. In sandy loam, an inch of water will penetrate the soil a foot deep. To get the same penetration in heavy clay soil, you will need to double that amount. As for lawns, about four and one-half gallons of water per square yard will approximate the weekly inch of rainfall prairie lawns require. A rough estimate of the amount of water you put on your lawn can be made by placing a straight-sided can where the sprinkler is working. Be sure the can is straight sided; if it is flared only slightly the gauge will not record accurately. An inch of water in the can indicates that approximately an inch of water is on the lawn.

Water is usually most necessary in July and August, but May can be a dry month and sometimes a hot, dry spell in June will make watering a steady chore, especially for the newly set annuals and other plants set out earlier. Deciduous trees and shrubs as well as evergreens that were planted in the spring may need frequent waterings to keep the soil moist, but you must keep in mind that new roots will not be produced in soil that is constantly wet; in fact, overwatering can cause newly planted trees to die.

Various kinds of sprinklers are available as well as a perforated plastic hose. The oscillating type of sprinkler is most popular for the home garden; it sprays the water in an even pattern. Trees and shrubs are sometimes watered by means of hollow pipes sunk into the ground. The lower end of the pipe has holes to distribute water down to the roots. The perforated hose is useful for narrow strips of grass and other places where water is required in a confined area. A slow-running hose is best for giving a thorough soaking to established peonies and other vigorous perennials and is also one of the best ways to water evergreens. Hybrid tea and other tender roses are best watered by letting the garden hose run slowly among the plants; overhead watering creates conditions that are conducive to the spread of black spot, a serious fungal disease. By watering in the early morning or early evening hours, the plants get the full benefit from the water; during the heat of the day, up to thirty percent can be lost by evaporation when you use an overhead sprinkler. You water most efficiently and economically when you allow the garden hose slowly to trickle water in furrows, trenches or shallow depressions made around individual plants.

Weeding — Weeds are unwanted plants that sap the soil moisture, smother cultivated plants and may be host plants for insects and diseases. Weeds are killed by chemicals, by stirring the soil with a hoe or some kind of cultivator, and by mulching.

In the home garden, broad-leaved weeds on the lawn are easy to kill with selective herbicides. In the vegetable garden, the early and regular use of the push hoe is the most effective way of killing weeds. By keeping the soil stirred between the rows you create the best possible growing conditions for the vegetables. Weeds growing in the rows are pulled by hand before they grow large enough to shade the cultivated plants and rob the soil of moisture. Hand weeding is best done as the ground dries following a rain and while the soil is still moist. In dry soil, the weeds break off to grow again when you attempt to pull them. Succulent weeds such as purslane should never be allowed to thrive or they have to be raked off and carried away after hoeing — otherwise, they grow again. Moreover, they will have made a million seeds and scattered them far and wide. Manure, used as a mulch on herbaceous perennial plants, usually contains viable weed seeds which can be a nuisance when the seeds germinate to choke the cultivated plants. If the manure is used as a winter mulch, it can be forked in lightly the following spring, destroying the weed seeds as they start to germinate.

Weeding, like a lot of other garden chores, is most effective when you do it at the right time . . . which is *as soon* as the weed seedlings emerge.

Spraying and dusting — We spray or dust plants with various poisons to control pests and diseases. Many kinds of chemicals are used as contact sprays, stomach poisons and systemic pesticides. A contact spray kills pests by penetrating their skin immediately upon spraying or after they have walked on plants which have been sprayed. Insects with chewing mouth parts (caterpillars, etc.) eat leaves treated with stomach poisons and die. Certain insects with sucking mouth parts are not easy to kill with sprays but can be controlled by systemic pesticides. The chemical used in this case is absorbed by the plant through its roots, making its sap poisonous to insects. The new shoots and buds have immediate protection and the spray is not washed off by rain.

The gardener must first of all identify the pests present in his garden, then decide how to rid the plants of them. Spray calendars are obtainable from provincial departments of agriculture; choose the recommended chemical and use it strictly in accordance with the directions on the container.

Pesticides can be pure chemicals, or compounds with the active ingredient mixed with other substances to bring it to a useable form. Emulsified concentrates are prepared in an oily liquid with an emulsifier added so that the two will mix, they may contain up to seventy-five percent active insecticide by weight. These compounds make a milky substance when mixed with water and uniform coverage is only possible when the spraying is efficient. Some slight agitation in the sprayer is needed to ensure good mixing. Wettable powders are fine clays to which have been added the pesticide and a wetting agent, to ensure rapid mixing with water. Wettable powders are kept in suspension by agitation. All-purpose garden dusts are obtainable in hand applicators. They have a lower active ingredient content than wettable powders but are effective in controlling small outbreaks of pests and diseases. Any number of garden dusts are on the market for the control of insects and diseases. Some are safe to use on vegetable crops as they contain only pyrethrum powder or Derris, which is nontoxic to humans. Other more dangerous dusts containing DDT, Chlordane or some other highly toxic chemical are used to kill cutworms, ants, the larvae of the June bug and similar insects, although these poisons are gradually being restricted since they have been demonstrated to be long-term pollutants. General purpose dusts for controlling common insects and diseases of ornamental plants are obtainable. They contain a mixture of chemicals to kill aphids, spider mites, leaf-hoppers and many other insects as well as controlling black spot and powdery mildew.

Gardeners should bear in mind that some pesticides are extremely toxic to warm-blooded animals and to humans. As a general rule, the herbicides are less poisonous than the pesticides, and the fungicides are in between.

Much has been written about poisons but today, more than ever, warnings must be heeded as more potent poisons are on the market. In spite of repeated warnings to wear protective clothing, users of Parathion, an extremely poisonous pesticide, have been taken to hospitals suffering from organophosphate poisoning. Children are often the victims of careless handling of insecticides by adults. Keep your insecticides locked up; make sure you know what is in the bottle and how much is required to kill the pests.

Don't smoke when mixing poisons and don't breathe in dusts and fumes. Skin contamination may occur if you spray in hot weather, because the skin absorbs the poison more readily when it is wet with perspiration.

Many bees are killed for no good reason when gardeners use poisons carelessly. Avoid spraying fruit trees when the blossoms are open and bees are working at pollinating. Malathion is highly toxic to bees, so use Derris or Kelthane, which are both nontoxic to bees.

The safety rules are simple to follow: before you do anything, read the label — then read it again. Use the correct amounts of chemicals, as directed — don't guess. Never smoke while you work with poisons; wear protective clothing when necessary, and wash your hands and face when the job is done.

Five

Gardening Tools and Machinery

The number, kind and quality of gardening tools you buy will reflect the extent of your interest in gardening, but both novice and professional gardeners will wisely choose tools of good design and quality. Cheap tools are a poor investment and, while there may be some truth in the saying that "only a poor workman grumbles about his tools," it is ultimately more economical to buy the best tools obtainable.

The basic tools are spade, shovels, forks, hoes, rakes, cultivator, pruning tools, trowels, hand weeders and a garden line. Mechanical equipment will include a suitable lawn mower and, perhaps, a garden tiller.

Hand Tools

Spades — The spade is not much used in prairie gardens; shovels seem to be preferred by most home gardeners. A modern high quality spade, however, is a fine tool for deep digging. Some have stainless steel blades and shaft fitted to wooden handles. Some have shafts of Plastim, a special polypropylene moulding which encases a selected wooden core combining strength and durability with a weatherproof finish. Two sizes are available and both are light in weight, one weighing about four and one-half pounds, the other about three and one-quarter pounds. A good quality spade should be in every gardener's stock of tools. Trained gardeners prefer it to a shovel for digging and it is the best tool for lifting trees and shrubs as well as deep-rooted perennials such as peonies.

Shovels – Good quality shovels are braced high on the handles to give strength. Round-nosed shovels are obtainable with either short or long handles; long-handled shovels may be easier on the back but not so practical as short-handled ones for digging small flower beds. The number two round-nosed shovel is standard for general use in the home garden. A square-mouthed shovel is of no use for digging but is the best tool for mixing soil and gathering up rubbish.

Forks – Forks are designed for loosening soil, for moving hay and manure and for digging potatoes. Some have flat tines or prongs; some are square and some are round and slightly curved. The flat-tined fork is sometimes called a potato fork; it usually has four tines or prongs and is useful for digging in soil that is not too hard. Square-tined forks with four or five tines are called digging forks and are used to dig beds and borders to leave the soil in good workable condition. Heavier square-tined forks are used in trenching to loosen the subsoil, and are of little use in home gardens. Forks with either two or three round tines are used for moving hay. Manure forks with four or five round tines are useful in gathering up garden refuse as well as moving manure. The tines are curved to keep the material from falling off. In most home gardens, a flat-tined potato fork and a manure fork will serve for digging and gathering up rubbish, and may be the only forks needed.

Hoes – There are many kinds of hoes; some are specially designed for certain jobs, but two general-purpose hoes are basic tools for the home garden: push hoes and draw hoes. Both come in a variety of shapes and sizes.

Among the push hoes, the Dutch hoe is favored for stirring the soil between the rows of newly emerging seedlings and among newly set annuals. It has a blade four, six or eight inches wide and about two inches deep attached to the handle by a stirrup-shaped piece of round iron. The Dutch hoe is not so practical in areas where weeds have grown tall as they tangle in the blade. Another type of push hoe has a solid blade attached to the handle by a single piece of round iron. One of the best push hoes for killing weeds on large, open areas is called the Orchard hoe. It has cutting edges back and front as well as at the sides. When set at the proper angle, it can be used while standing in an upright position which lessens fatigue.

The most popular type of draw hoe, or chop hoe, as it is sometimes called, has a six-inch blade attached to the handle by a curved piece of round iron. The draw hoe is used where the ground is hard and the weeds too big for the push hoe. Smaller- and larger-bladed draw hoes are available but, if you're only buying one, the six-inch size is most useful. The Warren hoe is shaped like a shield, sharp pointed for making furrows;

a triangular hoe is used for the same purpose but furrows can be made with equal facility with the ordinary draw hoe. Square and pointed hoes with two- or three-pronged cultivators attached are obtainable but they are not more efficient than a draw hoe and cultivator as separate tools.

Rakes — There are many kinds of garden rakes; the one most useful to the home gardener is the fifteen-inch, fourteen-tooth steel rake with either straight or curved teeth. This is the all-purpose garden rake used for raking grass or raking the seedbed to a fine tilth. The curved-tooth model does a better job of lawn raking because it cleans out the grass when it is pushed forward. Some gardeners prefer a twelve-inch, twelve-tooth rake for making a fine seedbed or for raking between rows of seedlings where a wider rake cannot be used. A smaller rake about seven inches wide has ten teeth and may have some practical use for getting into odd corners of the rock garden. The blades of these rakes are attached to the handle by a single piece of iron. Others, called bow rakes, are attached to the handle by two pieces of iron which are joined to the outer edges of the rake. Bow rakes work well enough on the lawn but are not so easily manipulated when making a fine seedbed.

A dandelion rake is specially designed to remove dandelion heads as well as plantains and other broad-leaved plants in the lawn. It has twenty-six teeth on a piece of curved steel about sixteen inches wide and is a useful tool for cleaning up the lawn in the spring. Another kind of rake for leaves and grass is called a lawn sweep. It has twenty-two flat and flexible teeth of spring steel and is about eighteen inches wide. A similar rake made of bamboo is not so durable; otherwise, it serves the same purpose.

Cultivators — Garden cultivators are available in several designs, some with three tines, others with five and some with weeders or hoes attached. The most practical ones have five detachable tines that can be arranged in combinations of two, three, four or five tines. Small cultivators for working among rock garden plants have a single flat, pointed tine. A fork with the tines bent at a ninety-degree angle to the handle makes a suitable cultivator for stirring the soil under low-growing shrubs. The home gardener can get along very well with an ordinary three- or five-tined cultivator.

In the farm garden, where long rows of vegetables may be grown, a Planet Junior combined cultivator, seeder and "hiller" will be a good investment. A single- or double-wheel hoe made by the same firm will enable the gardener to cultivate a large area rapidly and easily.

Knives — Several kinds of knives are used by gardeners. Some are designed for special propagating jobs such as grafting and budding, others as pruners and as general purpose knives. Grafting and budding knives have fine steel blades; the budding knife has a handle tapered to a thin wedge shape which is used to lift the bark to facilitate the insertion of a bud. Pruning knives have a curved blade made of heavy steel. The handle, too, is curved to enable the user to keep a firm grip. Good quality knives are made by Saynor in England and Tina in Germany.

Pruning tools — Pruning is an important job in the garden and one that is often badly done with poor tools. Good quality tools make clean cuts, but it takes a skilled gardener to know when and how to prune. For pruning roses and shoots of other plants of up to finger thickness, the pruning shears or secateurs are used. The wise gardener will buy the best. Swiss-made secateurs sold under the trade name of Felco, made of aluminum with steel blades and plastic-coated handles, are among the best pruners. The handles are shaped to fit the hand to make the pruning job more comfortable. A neat catch keeps the blades closed when the shears are not in use. The Rolcut secateurs have a single steel blade that is squeezed against a brass plate to make a clean cut without bruising the wood. Some gardeners prefer the Rolcut secateurs for pruning hybrid tea roses and other plants with soft stems.

For pruning trees and shrubs, several kinds of heavy pruners or lopping shears are available. Some are mounted on ten-foot poles and are useful for pruning high branches of not more than an inch or so in diameter. Heavy pruners capable of cutting through two-inch branches are useful for cutting down old hedges and lopping the branches off trees and shrubs. The Forester pruner, one of the best, cuts through wrist-sized wood with ease; the handles are thirty-four inches long. The Disston lopping shear is one of the best general-purpose heavy pruners; it cuts through wood an inch and a half in diameter and is useful for all sorts of pruning jobs where the work is a bit too heavy for the secateurs.

The home gardener will get along well enough with a Disston pruner and a pair of Felco secateurs. When tree lopping or other heavy pruning has to be done, a saw can be used.

Pruning saws come in a variety of shapes and sizes: some have straight blades; some are curved and some are fitted with long handles for reaching high branches. Pruning saws with curved blades work with a pull, not a push movement, and are useful in places where straight-bladed saws are not easy to manipulate. A good pruning saw made by the Disston Company has a curved blade that folds into the handle. The blade is tightened up by a thumb screw which, when loosened, allows the blade to fold, making the saw easy and safe to carry. An English-made pruning saw designed like a meat saw has a detachable blade fourteen inches long and is useful for some pruning jobs where the branches are not too thick.

Grass or hedge shears — Hedge shears with seven-, eight- or nine-inch blades are available; the nine-inch size is a bit heavier than those with a shorter blade but speeds up the operation of hedge clipping considerably. High quality shears are made by Disston in America and by Brades, an English company.

When you buy a pair of hedge shears, see that they have a notch at the base of the blades for cutting through finger-sized branches. Certain fine-twigged and small-leaved hedges can be rapidly trimmed with electric hedge trimmers but, unless you have such a hedge and enough of it to make the use of an electric hedge trimmer practical, use the hand shears. The hedge shears are also used to trim grass from around trees and other places not accessible to the lawn mower. Long-handled grass shears with the blades set at right angles to the handles are used to edge grass around flower beds and driveways.

Miscellaneous small tools — A number of small hand tools are useful for planting, weeding and cultivating. For setting out annuals, a trowel is a useful tool. High quality trowels are obtainable in stainless steel; others, made of ordinary steel, are cheaper and quite satisfactory. Some trowels, poorly made of light metal, are not a bargain at any price. The ordinary trowel is about three inches wide and about a foot long with a wooden handle. A narrow, sharp-pointed trowel is obtainable for transplanting small seedlings.

Small hand cultivators with three sharp tines are useful among rock garden plants and for stirring soil in window boxes, planters and other places where larger tools cannot be used.

Sharp-bladed dandelion weeders with a notched blade are obtainable in various lengths. They are used to dig out solitary plants of dandelions or plantains that pop up in the lawn.

Dibbles are pointed pieces of wood of various sizes used for transplanting seedlings into plant boxes or young plants to the open ground. Some, made of steel, are offered for sale by seedhouses. One has a hollowed stem to remove soil and is useful for planting bulbs.

Garden Machinery

Lawn mowers — Since the introduction of rotary lawn mowers powered by gasoline engines or electricity, every backyard gardener with a pocket handkerchief-sized lawn has had to have one. Power lawn mowers take a lot of the drudgery out of grass cutting but, in urban areas especially, they add to the noise and pollute the air with fumes when they are run by a gasoline engine. Rotary mowers beat off the blades of grass, sometimes bruising the ends to leave them grayish and shabby. However, a well-sharpened rotary mower operated at the right speed, which should be a brisk walking pace, can do an acceptable job of grass cutting. A reel-type mower, in first-class shape, will do a better job and make less noise.

The Toro and Lawn Boy mowers, both rotary and reel-type, are good makes that give years of service if properly maintained. The eighteen- or nineteen-inch width is suitable for the average-sized home garden lawn; see that it has a four-cycle motor and recoil starter. Two-cycle motors, which operate on a mixture of gasoline and engine oil, are more noisy than four-cycle engines and often give off smoke from burning oil.

The reel-type lawn mower cuts the grass with a scissors-like action as the blades of the reel come in contact with the stationary blade, which can be adjusted to the required height by set screws. An eighteen-inch reel-type mower powered by a two-horsepower four-cycle engine will cost more than a rotary mower of the same size and with the same engine but, for first-class lawn maintenance, it is hard to beat and may be cheaper in the long run. The mower should be sharpened once a year, the oil in the crankcase changed as required and always maintained at the right level.

Power tillers and cultivators — Mechanical power-driven tillers can take a lot of the drudgery out of preparing the soil for making a lawn or sowing seeds. The selection of machines is wide and varied and, even in a small garden, there may be a place for a mechanical tiller. A small unit capable of tilling to a depth of six inches and adjustable to widths of from twelve to twenty-eight inches is a good general-purpose tiller for the average home garden. It can be used for cultivating and killing weeds as well as for preparing the soil for a lawn or for a seedbed in the vegetable garden. Rotary tillers with six-horsepower motors and two-speed transmissions will meet the requirements of a large farm garden. For convenience of handling, these larger machines have a reverse gear which comes in handy for backing away from walls, fences, trees and shrubs.

There is a tendency for the home gardener to use the rotary tiller as a cultivator, stirring the soil too deeply with the result that the soil moisture is lost. Rotary tillers are fine for pulverizing the soil to obtain a good tilth but, unless they are adjustable to till at a shallow depth, you had best use a wheel hoe.

The Merry Tiller, Choremaster and the Ariens Super Jet are useful machines. They do a good job of preparing the soil for planting seeds, aerating the soil and rotovating mulches of leaves and compost to improve the texture of the soil and kill the weeds.

Six

The Home Garden Greenhouse

There is keen interest in home greenhouses these days as we have more money and more leisure time, and more people are living in retirement than ever before. Home gardeners in the prairie provinces, where spring is so eagerly awaited, dream of owning a small greenhouse which may be operated at reasonable cost all the year round, or just for a few months in spring and summer.

Building the Home Greenhouse

During the past twenty years or so there have been tremendous advances in the design and management of greenhouses. The modern greenhouse is completely automatic; ventilators open and close as temperatures rise and fall, with heat supplied by hot water or hot air fuelled by gas, oil or electricity. It is also possible to install a thermostatically controlled extractor-fan which will reduce the greenhouse temperature by ten degrees or so during the torrid summer days.

Wherever you live, it is possible to grow plants in the dead of winter if you have a greenhouse. Seed can be started early, to supply vegetables for salads and bedding plants for transplanting to the open ground in June. House plants can be set out in a shaded greenhouse during the summer months and, in the fall, chrysanthemums will continue to bloom until

Christmas. These flowers can be kept in bloom during other seasons too if the plants are shaded or given supplemental light, according to the natural daylight of the particular time of year.

The most economical greenhouse for the novice gardener is the lean-to, placed either on the south or east side of the house. Where space and initial costs are important factors, a lean-to greenhouse seven feet wide, running the whole length of the house wall, is practical. In this kind of greenhouse there is room for one bench about three feet wide, a series of shelves attached to the house wall, several hanging baskets or flower pots and a walk wide enough to allow easy access to the plants. The cheapest construction material is wood; Western red cedar *(Thuya plicata)* is durable and requires little painting, supplemented by applications of linseed oil every four to six years. Aluminum is more costly to start with, but involves no long-term costs for painting or additional maintenance.

The lean-to greenhouse needs a solid foundation to prevent it separating from the adjoining building when the ground heaves in winter. Concrete blocks or clay bricks are suitable; build them thirty inches above ground level. The blocks or bricks should be built on a foundation of concrete about two feet deep and nine inches wide.

The even-span greenhouse gives more growing space; the smallest practical size is about ten feet wide with room for two forty-inch benches and a thirty-inch walk. Models with room for three benches and two walks have a minimum width of fourteen feet. When attached to a building, these span-roof greenhouses are a bit cheaper to heat than when the same house is detached or free-standing.

The latest design has walls that slant outward for extra light, and continuous vents; it is automatically operated and is all metal. Automatic ventilators and heat controls allow the gardener to leave his greenhouse unattended for long periods. Without these modern conveniences, he must be on hand to regulate temperatures by opening and closing the vents and by adjusting the heat controls as required. You may be able to heat your greenhouse with an extension from the home heating system; otherwise, a separate unit, either hot water, hot air or electricity, is installed.

Heaters — When selecting a greenhouse heater, make sure it is large enough to maintain the required temperature even in the coldest weather. It is false economy to use one that barely generates sufficient heat when a larger size costs but little more, with something in reserve for cold, windy nights. You can heat a home garden greenhouse efficiently with various kinds of heating equipment fuelled by gas, oil or electricity. Years ago it was thought that hot water was the most efficient heat for a greenhouse. Nowadays, warm-air heating systems are entirely satisfactory for small greenhouses. It was thought that warm-air heaters dried out the air excessively, but this is not so; modern warm-air heaters recirculate the moist air from the greenhouse where frequent dampening of walks and benches keeps the humidity sufficiently high for optimum plant growth. It is also possible to install a wet-pad humidifier to keep the air moist if the greenhouse is left unattended for long periods. If your home is heated with a warm-air furnace, it may be possible to extend it to heat your greenhouse; this is most practical if the greenhouse is attached to the dwelling. Separate thermostat controls, operating independently of the residence thermostat, are required.

There are automatic gas heaters for small greenhouses with the combustion chamber entirely sealed off outside the greenhouse. These have built-in blower fans that distribute warm air evenly. The cabinet of these gas heaters is welded throughout to ensure against gas leaks — most important, as some gas fumes are deadly to plants.

For the small greenhouse, used only from March until November, an all-electrical heating system may be practical. An electric blower-type heater with directional louvers and safety fan guard will provide a complete heating unit for a small greenhouse at reasonable cost.

Glazing — There is no completely satisfactory substitute for glass, though the initial cost is much higher than the various plastic materials now available. In the long run it will pay to use glass, especially if the greenhouse is of solid construction and first-class materials are used. A heavy grade of polyester film called Mylar will last up to seven years when properly fitted and secured to a solidly constructed frame. The chief advantages of polyester film are low cost, light weight and the need for less structural support. It transmits light at about the same rate as glass but does not gather as much dust and grime as lapped panes of glass. There are lighter grades of polyester film which are cheaper than Mylar but these tend to sag with temperature changes. A more expensive glass substitute made of fibreglass is available in either corrugated or flat sheets two or four feet wide. It costs about fifty cents a square foot, whereas the heavy-duty Mylar polyester film costs twenty-five cents for the same quantity. The corrugated fibreglass sheets should be considered for roofing the home greenhouse in areas where hail is liable to break glass.

Operating the Home Greenhouse

Once the gardener has acquired a greenhouse, the next problem is operating it successfully. It takes considerable skill and knowledge to manage a greenhouse filled with a mixture of plants differing somewhat in their general requirements of heat, light and humidity. Space becomes a problem in the spring when seedlings are transplanted to flats, and bulbs and tubers for summer flowering are started into growth. All available space must be used profitably without overcrowding the plants. Shelves, erected close to the glass, can be useful for starting seeds sown in pots or seed pans. They should be placed within a foot of the glass and not made too wide or they cast considerable shade on the plants below. Plants and seed pots, placed on shelves, will need frequent attention; otherwise, they dry out. Shallow metal trays containing an inch of moistened gravel can be used to hold pots containing seedlings, to lessen chances of drying out. The shelves should be placed to allow easy access to the plants for watering.

Some plants require more heat than others: tuberous begonias, gloxinias and African violets, for example, should be given the warmest spot. Besides heat, these plants must have subdued light; full sunlight, even in the early part of spring, will damage the leaves.

A propagating case, electrically heated, will be useful for starting the cuttings and seeds of long-season annuals that need to be planted early. A propagating case can be made the width of the greenhouse bench and as long as required. It is made of lumber in the shape of a garden frame — the front is about a foot high and the back a bit higher. The top is glass; an electric cable is laid in the bottom of the case and covered with a mixture of peat and sand.

The impulse to crowd a small greenhouse with a whole conglomeration of plants should be restrained; it becomes difficult to water them properly and the dangers of disease and insect pests are increased.

Watering — The art of watering plants is mastered through experience; the greenhouse gardener who knows when to water potted plants and seedlings and how much to give them is well on his way to successful greenhouse operation. Potted plants in full growth use water rapidly during the long days of summer but, in winter, they can go for a week or longer without water. Rubber plants, bowstring hemp and aspidistra are examples of plants that should be watered sparingly, especially in periods of short daylight. Potted bulbs in full bloom take daily waterings and so will hydrangeas. Newly potted plants are watered sparingly until the roots are growing freely in the new soil; too much water makes the soil sour and cuts off the supply of oxygen from the roots. Seedlings need daily care; a few hours without water can be ruinous. Pots containing seedlings are best watered by placing them in a bowl half filled with water, allowing them to remain until they are saturated.

Temperatures — During the winter months when plant growth is at a low ebb, there should be no attempt to maintain minimum night temperatures over fifty-five degrees Fahrenheit. In very severe weather it is best to keep the night temperature at fifty degrees and the plants on the dry side, rather than strive to keep more heat and humidity. Excessive heat and moisture with low light intensity weakens the plants and creates conditions favorable to disease. In the spring, as the sun increases in power, the temperatures under glass rise rapidly and seedlings can be burnt off if they are neglected at this time. When the sun heat raises the temperature above seventy-five degrees, the greenhouse must be ventilated.

Ventilating the greenhouse — The ventilators should be opened on every possible occasion as long as the outside temperature in the sunlight is above freezing and the air reasonably calm. Draughts from cold air are harmful to plants, so the ventilating must be done carefully. When the temperature under the glass rises to seventy-five degrees and outside conditions are mild and sunny, open the ventilators a crack, increasing the amount of air as the sun increases in power. The closing of the ventilators is also done gradually, starting in the middle of the afternoon by reducing the amount of air until the house is finally closed an hour or so before sundown.

Supplies for the Home Greenhouse

To operate the smallest greenhouse efficiently, you need a supply of soil, peat, sand, flower pots and boxes for transplanting seedlings. A watering can, sprayer and a supply of chemicals for controlling insects and plant diseases are also necessary, as well as two sizes of sieves.

The potting shed — Attached to the greenhouse is a potting shed where the necessary supplies are kept. It will have a strong bench about table height and three feet wide. Under the bench, in separate bins, the soil, peat, sand, leaf mould and rotted manure are stored. Flower pots and pans, seed flats and boxes for transplanting will be stacked neatly. The clay pots are best stored in racks where they are safe from breakage. A locked cupboard will be useful and safe for storing chemicals used for killing insects and controlling diseases.

Soil — Rotted sod makes the best base for soil used in the greenhouse. The home gardener may use turf edgings from the lawn or he may buy a quantity of turf from a landscape gardener. A pile of turf stacked grass-side down will rot in six months to make a fibrous loam. It may be necessary to water the pile occasionally to speed up the rotting process.

Peat — Granulated peat is an excellent soil conditioner, increasing the water-holding capacity of the mixtures used for sowing seeds and potting plants. Its pH value of about 4.5 neutralizes alkaline soil, but too much peat may cause injury to root tips.

Sand — Sand should not be too coarse nor too fine. Clean, gritty sand of one-eighth-inch grist is best for rooting cuttings. Sand from pits may be highly alkaline; sand from lakeshores may be more satisfactory.

Flower pots — Clay pots have been used since the early days of gardening and are still preferred by some to plastic pots. All kinds of plants can be grown well in both clay and plastic pots if proper consideration is given to watering. Clay pots, being more porous, dry out quicker than plastic pots; during the short days, this is an advantage. All sizes are available in both kinds, ranging from two and one-quarter inches to eight or ten inches, including azalea pots which are not so tall as the standard flower pot.

Boxes and flats — Shallow flats for sowing seeds or pricking out seedlings can be made from builder's lath and one- by two-foot lumber. The flats are sixteen inches long, one foot wide and two inches deep. The laths are spaced one-quarter of an inch apart to provide drainage. Boxes for transplanting annuals should not be made too large or they are cumbersome when filled with soil; a box fifteen inches long, one foot wide and three inches deep is suitable. The size can be modified to suit the width of the greenhouse benches and save space.

A GARDEN FRAME

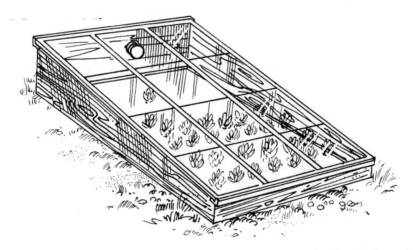

The garden frame — A garden frame will be useful for hardening off bedding plants, tomatoes and other early vegetable crops. The frame should be made of two-inch lumber — either pine or fir is preferred to spruce — and should measure about six feet by three feet for the average home gardener's requirements. From a height of about fifteen inches at the back, it should slope to a front height of ten inches. A good frame will be airtight, with a well-fitted sash glazed with panes of glass or covered with heavy plastic. It should be placed in a sheltered part of the garden, either facing south or set against the house wall. Provision should be made for extra covering on frosty nights; a double thickness of burlap with a sheet of heavy paper between the two layers will keep out ten degrees of frost if the frame is well made and airtight. A frame six feet by three heated with one two hundred-watt lamp will keep out twenty degrees of frost; it is safe to transfer bedding plants to such a frame in mid-April. On the other hand, if there is no heat provided except that generated by the sun, it is not safe to put tender plants in a cold frame until the first week of May.

Watering cans and sprayers — The high-grade English-type watering can (Haws can) is a costly item but is a good investment for a gardener with a greenhouse. Plastic cans in various shapes and sizes are obtainable but they are not provided with sprinklers fine enough for watering small seedlings. A medium-sized English-type watering can, complete with two sprinklers, one coarse, one fine, and holding a gallon of water costs about twelve dollars. A galvanized can of the same size but inferior in design costs about three dollars.

A two-gallon galvanized sprayer is also recommended for greenhouse work. Smaller tin-plated sprayers cost less but are not durable.

Sieves — Two sieves for screening soil and sand are needed; one should have a quarter-inch mesh, the other a half-inch mesh.

Control of insects and diseases — The control of pests is greatly simplified by using smoke generators and systemic insecticides as well as ordinary sprays and dusts. If routine methods of eradication are started before the outbreak of an epidemic, serious damage to your plants can be avoided. Diseases are not so easily controlled, but much can be done to prevent the spread of disease by practising sanitation. Use clean pots and flats, sterilized soil and keep the atmosphere in the greenhouse buoyant with fresh air as far as this is possible.

A Calendar of Operations for the Home Greenhouse

March — Start the heating system around the middle of the month, then clean up flats, flower pots, any rubbish, and wash down the walls and benches. By starting off with a clean greenhouse, you lessen chances of pests and disease. Soil for seed sowing is made ready by mixing two parts loam, one part peat and one part sand. The soil is then treated with Panodrench, a sterilant, to ward off fungal diseases. Boxes, flats and seed pans should be scrubbed clean before use. Seed of snapdragons, petunias, stocks and other annuals requiring a long growing season should be sown now. Tuberous begonias and cannas can be started into growth as soon as the house has warmed up and a night temperature of sixty degrees can be maintained.

April — Seedlings of early-sown annuals are ready for transplanting to flats. Geraniums, tuberous begonias and cannas are ready for larger pots. Seed of tomatoes should be sown early in the month; the quick-growing annuals — zinnias, marigolds — may be sown after mid-April. By the end of the month the hardiest plants, such as pansies, snapdragons and chrysanthemums, can safely be moved to a garden frame. Space becomes a problem as seedlings are transplanted, but the room for later-sown annuals like marigolds and zinnias will be provided once the hardier plants are moved to the garden frame.

May — By the middle of the month all the bedding plants, potted geraniums, tuberous begonias and cannas can be moved to a garden frame, where exposure to air and lower temperatures will harden them off in readiness for transplanting to the open ground. Hardening off is a process whereby greenhouse plants which have been grown under ideal conditions of uniform heat and moisture are gradually inured to outdoor conditions. They are removed first to a garden frame with a well-fitting glass top or sash to protect the plants from frost and chilling winds. By removing the sash on warm sunny days and replacing it at night, then later on removing it altogether, the plants can be set out in the open ground without a setback.

June — Tomato plants, started from seed sown in early April, can be transplanted to nine-inch pots or boxes a foot square and ten inches deep. Half a dozen such plants will provide ripe fruit several weeks before plants that are grown outdoors. When the last of the bedding plants have been removed, wash down the walls and benches before the potted tomatoes are set up in the warmest part of the house.

House plants, including ferns, foliage plants, begonias and other flowering plants, will thrive during the summer months in a shaded greenhouse. Amaryllis, hydrangea and fuchsias, though, are best plunged in the soil outdoors, preferably on the east side of the house. They must be watered regularly in periods of drought.

The glass must now be coated with a shading compound to reduce the light intensity. Commercial preparations are available but a suitable shading can be made by mixing green or white latex paint with water. The shading is put on before the house plants are moved in; otherwise, even a few hours exposure to full sunlight in an unshaded greenhouse will be ruinous. The shading is removed in mid-September, but certain plants which are extrasensitive to light, such as ferns, gloxinias and African violets, may need to be shaded for a few weeks longer if the weather is warm and sunny.

July — Watering, ventilating and control of insects, particularly thrips and mites, are regular chores. Tomatoes in pots will be producing ripe fruit, so they need fertilizer and plenty of water. The soil must be kept moist and fertile or the fruits will not reach full size. Irregular watering, allowing the soil to become bone dry, will greatly increase the chances of blossom-end rot. This is a physiological upset said to be caused by an imbalance of calcium due to the plant being checked in its normal growth. It appears first as a tiny black speck on the skin of the fruit at a point where the blossom was attached to the fruit. It increases in size and, finally, that portion of the fruit rots. Regular attention to dampening down the walks and benches will be needed to offset the usually hot, dry conditions outdoors.

August — As the first fruits of outdoor tomatoes are harvested, the greenhouse-grown tomatoes may gradually be moved outdoors or discarded to make room for potted chrysanthemums. Some of the outdoor chrysanthemums are just beginning to bloom but frost may be threatening; with a greenhouse, you can pot them and bring them in before they are harmed by the frost. Place them in seven-inch pots and shade them for a few days with newspapers, keeping the roots moist but not constantly saturated. Syringe the tops of newly potted chrysanthemums once or twice a day to keep the leaves from wilting.

September — Potted ferns, foliage plants and other house plants that have been thriving in the greenhouse may be repotted in September if their size warrants. Keep the humidity high by dampening the walks and benches and lightly syringe the ferns and foliage plants.

Tuberous begonias, planted outdoors in shaded beds, should be carefully lifted, transplanted into pots of suitable size and brought into the greenhouse before the plants are damaged by frost. Window boxes planted with tuberous begonias will continue to bloom for several weeks.

You can now take cuttings of geraniums that are growing outdoors in beds and planters. The best cuttings are young shoots about four inches long, taken from plants that have been growing in full sun. Geraniums that have been growing in half-shade and those that have been overwatered produce soft cuttings that are more likely to rot off in the process of rooting. Geraniums are very susceptible to a fungal disease called pythium, better known as blackleg, which well describes the appearance of the disease. It pays to select sturdy, short-jointed cuttings, removing one or two of the bottom leaves before you make a clean, horizontal cut across the base.

Put an inch of coarse gravel in each five-inch pot, covering this with an inch of rough soil. Fill the pot with sand to one-half inch below the rim of the pot to facilitate watering. The filled pots should be sterilized by baking them in a two hundred-degree oven for half an hour. When they are cool, set them in pans of boiled water until the surface of the soil is moist before you plant the cuttings. Dip the end of the cuttings in rooting powder before you insert them around the inner edge of the pots. Set the cuttings an inch or so apart and about an inch deep — a five-inch pot will hold a dozen cuttings. When you have given them a good watering, set the pots on a sunny window, shaded for a few days. Keep the sand moist but not saturated and, in a few weeks, the cuttings will take root. The young plants should not be disturbed until January.

Tulips, daffodils and hyacinths for late-winter and early-spring bloom are potted now. Set the potted bulbs out in a garden frame under a six-inch covering of peat moss or soil. Certain house plants, such as amaryllis, hydrangeas and fuchsias, which have been plunged in the soil outdoors since June, must now be brought into the greenhouse to finish ripening off the current year's wood.

October — Tuberous begonias, passing out of bloom, will need to be watered less frequently. When the leaves turn yellow, withhold the water to ripen off the tubers. Dahlias cut down by frost can be dug up after the tops are cut off. The roots can be dried off on the greenhouse floor. Gladioli corms can be dried off in the greenhouse by spreading them on a sunny bench.

November — Unless the greenhouse is to be operated through the winter months, November will bring to an end the year's activity. At little extra cost, the home greenhouse can be operated until Christmas but this is not warranted unless it is well stocked with chrysanthemums and other late-blooming plants. If the greenhouse is to be closed by the end of November, the house plants should be moved back to the dwelling house before the weather gets too cold. The potted Dutch bulbs will need to be taken to the basement to continue rooting, along with Easter lily bulbs, which are potted now. The tuberous begonias are dried off and stored in peat. House plants needing a midwinter rest, such as amaryllis, hydrangeas and fuchsias, should be taken to the basement. Amaryllis need no water after the leaves have dried off until it is time to start them into growth again in early February. The fuchsias and hydrangeas need only sufficient water to keep the wood from shrivelling.

December — Greenhouses operated all the year round can provide a constant supply of cut flowers if a proper program has been planned and executed. Dutch bulbs planted in September will not start to bloom until January, continuing until Easter or later as different varieties are brought from basement to greenhouse. But Easter lily bulbs, potted in November, will now need full sunlight, more water as the leaves develop and occasional doses of fertilizer, starting when the flower buds show.

January — The six-week period from the middle of December until the first week of February is the darkest and coldest time of the year. Greenhouse plants will be thriftier if kept a bit on the dry side in temperatures a little below rather than above their normal requirements. Deep snow on the greenhouse roof may cause damage to the structure besides shutting out the much-needed light. It pays to remove it.

By the middle of the month or early in February you can cut off the tops of the geranium cuttings, potted in September, to make more cuttings, treating them in the same manner as those taken from the plants growing outdoors. When new growth starts from the plants that you cut down you can pot them in three-inch jiffy pots.

Plant boxes, labels, soil and other materials soon to be needed can be made ready during the short days.

February — By the first week of February there is a noticeable lengthening of the daylight hours. Seeds of lobelia, pansies, sweet Spanish onions and some other long-season plants may be sown. Flowering bulbs passing out of bloom are discarded and the soil saved to fill boxes for transplanting annuals. Tulips are gradually dried off, the bulbs saved for replanting outdoors in September.

Seven

Growing Plants
under Artificial Light

Not so long ago chrysanthemums were only seen in bloom during the autumn months; nowadays one may obtain chrysanthemums, either as cut flowers or potted plants, all the year round. This has been made possible by the use of controlled lighting. In recent years there has been a tremendous increase in the use of electric light to aid plant growth and hobbyists as well as commercial growers are reporting remarkable results.

When scientists began studying plant growth in relation to flower bud initiation, they discovered that some plants have a regulating factor; the number of hours of continuous darkness in a twenty-four-hour period would determine the time of flowering. It was found that the regulation of light also affects the germination of certain seeds, the development of tubers and other growth processes. Light plays a most important part in plant growth; all plants need light to a greater or lesser degree and the most abundant and efficient source of light comes from the sun. It supplies the energy needed for the manufacture of starches and sugars, for the process of manufacturing carbohydrates from carbon dioxide and water in the presence of light which is called photosynthesis. Although artificial light cannot match the brilliance of the sun, nor does it have the same quality, it can be used effectively in the home to supplement daylight or to provide the whole source of light for certain plants.

About Artificial Light

Sources — There are many kinds of lamps available for growing plants indoors and, when used in proper combination, they produce light quality that is suitable for healthy plant growth. The tungsten filament and fluorescent tube are the most common lamps used for growing plants.

The tungsten filament or incandescent bulb is the ordinary light bulb; the current flows through the tungsten wire to heat it to incandescence. Lamp sizes and shapes vary from the ordinary sixty-watt household lamp to the high wattage reflector lamps that provide either flood or spot distribution. These lamps are used in greenhouses to provide uniform light on plants. Another type of incandescent lamp is made of thick, moulded glass and is useful outdoors to provide a more direct beam or wide-flood distribution.

Fluorescent lamps are altogether different from incandescent lamps. They give light of higher efficiency per watt of power and generate far less heat. There are several kinds; those best adapted for growing plants indoors are sold under the trade names of Daylight, Cool White and Gro-Lux.

Although the rates for electrical power vary from one place to another, the operating costs of indoor lighting for growing plants is not prohibitive. Mobile units fitted with fluorescent tubes are not expensive; a two-tube fixture complete with trays can be bought for about twenty-five dollars. Various kinds of planters are available which can be fitted with a canopy of two or four tubes.

Light quality — Sunlight gives ultraviolet and infrared rays in proper balance for healthy plant growth but, when plants are grown in areas where artificial light is the sole source of illumination, the quality of that light must be considered. Plant scientists have studied the problem of light quality and have discovered that light which is rich in reds tends to make stems grow taller. Blue light, on the other hand, produces a shorter plant with more vegetative growth. The white light given off by an incandescent lamp is rich in red and lacking in blue. To use ordinary electric light bulbs as the sole source of light for plants would result, therefore, in stems with long internodes (lengths of stem without flowers or leaves) and pale leaves. Fluorescent tubes, on the other hand, are rich in blues and will provide a healthy light source more closely approximating sunlight than incandescent bulbs. Furthermore, the fluorescent tube provides a high output of light per watt and, because the tubes are fairly cool, they can be placed closer to the plants than the incandescent lamps.

Light intensities — The standard unit for measuring the power of light is the foot candle; the sun at noon in summer has a power of ten thousand foot candles. Any room (size notwithstanding) with the ceiling covered with fluorescent tubes and the walls painted white would give about two thousand five hundred foot candles. For home use, a lighting installation that produces six hundred to eight hundred foot candles is satisfactory. Good vegetative growth of seedlings can be expected when artificial light of this intensity is available sixteen hours a day.

Some plants get along with far less light than others; aspidistra and bowstring hemp *(Sansevieria)*, for example, grow satisfactorily in sixteen hours of six hundred foot candles a day. Gloxinias require eight hundred foot candles for the same period of time to promote healthy growth and free flowering. African violets under six hundred foot candles for eighteen hours daily produce more bloom than when the same plants are under the same artificial light for twelve hours a day. The gardener can obtain bulletins specifying the light requirements of various house plants from the several electric companies which manufacture bulbs for growing plants indoors.

There are several kinds of meters used to measure the intensity of light; those used by photographers are most familiar. Some light meters are scaled in foot candles and measure fairly accurately the amount of light reaching the plants. When the home gardener installs a battery of fluorescent lamps, he should check the amount of light emitted by the tubes; while the light may diminish to some extent as the tubes age, there will be no radical change. Fluorescent tubes last for six or seven thousand hours before they need replacing. A standard fixture containing two forty-watt fluorescent lamps with a twelve-inch reflector gives an average over its entire area of 330 foot candles when the plants are from six to eighteen inches below the tubes. At six inches from the tube and in the centre of the fixture, the light intensity is seven hundred foot candles. At eighteen inches from the tube and at the extremity of the reflector, the light intensity is reduced to 290 foot candles.

The Benefits of Artificial Light

Photoperiodism — The response of plants to different periods of light and darkness is known as photoperiodism. It has been found by plant scientists that certain plants must have a certain number of hours of darkness in a twenty-four-hour period in order to initiate flower buds. Plants have been classified as short day, long day and indeterminate or day neutral. The chrysanthemum and poinsettia are short-day plants; the tuberous begonia, petunia and china aster are examples of long-day plants. The rose and carnation are day-neutral plants and are not affected by photoperiod or length of day.

The short-day plants must have about twelve hours of darkness in a twenty-four-hour period to initiate their flower buds. By extending the period of light by the use of fluorescent tubes, flowering can be retarded; by the proper manipulation of light and darkness, chrysanthemums can be brought into bloom at any season of the year. Home-grown poinsettias will continue to make only vegetative growth when the plants are subjected to extra light from an electric light bulb. Even the light from a street lamp, shining through a window, can cause a delay in the initiation of flower buds and bracts.

A new and far more economical method of delaying the initiation of flower buds is to apply cycles of light, switching it on for ten minutes and off for fifty minutes for a four-hour period in the middle of the night. This is called cyclic lighting; it has the advantage of reducing quite substantially the amount of electric current consumed and, if the light intensity is slightly higher than the continuously applied light, it is fully as effective. The poinsettia, for example, must have a complete and uninterrupted period of darkness for about twelve hours each day if the flowers are to form and the bracts color up. Tests have shown that a short period of light interrupting the period of darkness is sufficient to prevent the poinsetta from blooming. The tuberous begonias must have a short period of darkness and a long period of light to make flowers; to produce tubers for the next year's planting, however, the relative periods of light and darkness must be reversed. The length and intensity of the light can affect plants in other ways. The bright, decorative leaves of coleus are dulled if light intensity is reduced and the period of darkness extended. Bulbs such as tulips can be forced into bloom in low-light intensity; the flower buds are in the bulb and the main source of food reserve is supplied by the bulb itself.

House plants — In the home, fluorescent tubes are widely used to show off ornamental plants growing in special areas. Plants with large, shiny leaves can be effectively displayed by focussing light upon them. As a general rule, white light is preferred because it produces the most natural effect and will harmonize with the furnishings. Odd and sometimes attractive effects can be obtained with green- or pink-colored lights. Where colored lights supply most of the illumination, chances are they do not give sufficient light for healthy plant growth. If the home gardener desires such a display he should take care to move the plants around frequently, taking those from the display to an area where the light intensity is high enough to maintain good growth.

The young plants will make good headway under the fluorescent tubes when a light intensity of about eight hundred foot candles can be maintained. The Department of Horticulture of Ohio State University has given the following approximate values of light levels needed for some common house plants: African violet, six hundred foot candles; gloxinia, eight hundred foot candles; foliage plants such as philodendron, peperomia, Chinese evergreen, bowstring hemp and aspidistra, three hundred foot candles. Specimen plants of dieffenbachia, rubber plant and large-leaved philodendron can get along in a light intensity of one hundred foot candles when a reflector flood-type of incandescent lamp is used to direct a large portion of the light on the foliage.

African violets respond well to controlled light conditions; the plants are compact, requiring a minimum of bench space, and can be grown successfully in a windowless basement. The African Violet Society conducted tests at Ohio State University in which the sole source of light for the specimen plants was provided by Daylight fluorescent tubes; the check plants were grown in a greenhouse without supplement to the natural daylight. The African violets grown under the fluorescent lamps developed faster than those in the greenhouse. It was concluded that eighteen hours illumination per day at a light intensity of six hundred foot candles produced healthy, free-blooming plants in a period of up to four months from the time the young plants were potted.

The ordinary home basement can be suitable for many kinds of ornamental plants. The following plants thrive in home basement growth areas where fluorescent tubes can provide one thousand foot candles of artificial light:

Asparagus sprengeri, A. plumosa
Boston fern *(Nephrolepis exaltata)*
cacti in variety
cyclamen
Dutch bulbs: tulips, narcissi, hyacinths
Easter lily *(Lilium longiflorum)*
English ivy *(Hedera helix)*
kalanchoe
perpetual begonia *(Begonia semperflorens)*
poinsettia
shrimp plant *(Beloperone guttata)*
Wandering Jew *(Tradescantia tricolor)*
wax plant *(Hoya carnosa)*

Growing seeds under artificial light — Keen gardeners like to start their own tomatoes and bedding plants from seed sown indoors but, notwithstanding considerable experience, they often meet with failure. The seeds may not be viable; damping-off fungus may attack the seedlings or the light may be so poor that the plants grow weak and spindly. By using artificial light, the chances of success with indoor seeding are greatly improved.

While artificial light cannot restore life to seeds that have lost their viability, it can aid in germination and produce sturdy plants. Very little artificial light is needed to germinate seeds; even an incandescent sixty-watt lamp suspended two feet from the seed pots will provide sufficient light and give additional heat. Some of the house plants which may be grown from seed under artificial light are African violets, begonias (both tuberous and fibrous-rooted sorts), geraniums of the new Carefree varieties, abutilon or flowering maple, asparagus ferns, cacti, coleus, Jerusalem cherries, fuchsia, oranges, lemons, grapefruit and various primulas. The fact that plants do not come perfectly true from seed adds greatly to the interest of this method of propagation. Plants required for bedding purposes, though, such as petunias and marigolds, should be as uniform as possible; for this reason, F_1 hybrid seed is preferred.

Seed is sown in various materials; for indoor sowing, granulated sphagnum moss, vermiculite, perlite, sand and mixtures of these materials are used. The mixture must be well drained and free of contamination. A suitable soil mixture for sowing seeds is made by adding one part mixed sand and peat to one part loam; screen this through a quarter-inch sieve. A four-inch clay pot is large enough for all the seedlings of one variety likely to be required by the home owner; smaller sizes are not recommended as the small pots dry out too quickly. The hole in the pot is covered with a piece of crockery, faced with the hollow side down. Over this, place a handful of coarse gravel and cover it with an inch of the rough soil mixture. Fill the pot with the fine soil mixture, gently pressing it level with the lid of a tin. The surface of the soil should be one-quarter of an inch below the rim of the pot for the tiny seeds of African violet, begonia and gloxinia, about one-half inch for the larger seeds of tomato. Place the prepared pots in an oven heated to 180 degrees Fahrenheit and let them remain for half an hour. Stand the sterilized pots in a container of boiled water deep enough to reach the rim; when the water seeps through to wet the surface of the soil, remove the pots and drain off the excess water before you sow the seeds.

Small seeds should not be covered with the soil mixture; a piece of paper over a piece of glass is all the covering required. The seed pot can be placed in a polyethylene bag to keep in the moisture, but the bag must be removed at the first sign of germination. A constant temperature of sixty-five to seventy-five degrees will ensure satisfactory germination if the seed is viable.

Part Two

Eight

Trees and Shrubs

The woody plants are the most important in any garden plan. The perennial and annual flowers provide the summer color but the trees and shrubs, woody climbers and ground covers give year-round interest. All gardens may have room for a few trees and shrubs but the smaller the garden, the more discriminating must be the choice. Forest trees may look attractive while they are still young but sooner or later they outgrow their allotted space and usefulness in a small garden. Trees of any kind need room to develop to full stature and, where space is limited, no attempt should be made to grow large trees. Slender forms of certain trees are available and take less room. The prairie gardener may also have to make adjustments for hardiness by choosing special varieties of trees popular elsewhere. The Griffin poplar, for example, actually a hardy form of columnar aspen, substitutes for the Lombardy poplars which make a feature landscape tree in the milder parts of the country.

The early settlers planted the Manitoba maple or boxelder in boundary plantings and on the boulevards, where some remain to this day. It has nothing to recommend it except hardiness and rapid growth and, in most parts of the prairies, more attractive trees can be grown. The Manitoba maple is often plagued with aphids that drip honeydew to foul sidewalks and parked cars. There is no excuse for planting it except in windswept areas where it provides shelter for better trees.

There is not a wide choice of small trees that are hardy and suitable for a prairie garden and even those that are fully hardy and attractive are not widely used. The Ohio buckeye *(Aesculus glaba)*, for example, is rarely seen in prairie gardens, though good specimens exist in scattered areas across Manitoba, Saskatchewan and Alberta. The leaves are similar to the horse chestnut *(Aesculus hippocastanum)* but not so large. The flowers are creamy and quite attractive though not so showy as the horse chestnut. The flowers are followed by large, tawny-colored seed pods containing one and sometimes two chestnuts or "conkers." The leaves turn brilliant orange red in September and for a brief period are strikingly beautiful. The Ohio buckeye is a fine tree for a small garden and good specimens can be obtained from some of the prairie nurserymen. The true horse chestnut, on the other hand, is useless on the prairies. Where it has been tried it literally never got off the ground but remained a mass of basal shoots that tip-killed regularly.

Deciduous Trees in the Prairie Garden

Rosybloom crabapple — Rosybloom crabapples are the most popular small trees in the prairie garden. There are dozens of varieties and new ones are being introduced from time to time. Most of these rosybloom crabapples have descended from a form of *Malus pumila,* commonly called the redvein crabapple, crossed with the Siberian crabapple *(M. baccata).* The redvein crabapple has a distinct reddish purple pigment carried in leaves and stems, flowers and fruits, even to the very root of the plant. So potent is this redvein character that it is transmitted freely to seedlings of hardy crabapples used as understocks and is readily detected in the leaves. For the most part, rosybloom crabs are hardy all across the prairies, though there are some varieties not so well suited as others to areas where apple trees are difficult to grow. However, if you give these varieties a fair chance, providing them with the same shelter needed for apple trees, they will survive and grow well.

Prairie gardeners have long envied those in milder parts who sing of "cherry trees" and "seas of bloom," but rosybloom crabapples are "seas of bloom" equally beautiful and just as long lasting as the Japanese cherries. For a long time, the variety Hopa, introduced by Dr. Hansen of Brookings, South Dakota, held sway and there are many good specimens of this old variety to be found in Manitoba and elsewhere. Hopa is an upright tree with fine branches that tend to spread as the tree ages. The leaves are reddish purple, the flowers rosy mauve, fading rapidly in hot weather. The flowers are soon followed by a heavy crop of crabapples that falls to the ground before winter comes. Hopa is no longer popular as better varieties are obtainable, but it served to show the usefulness of rosybloom crabapples in prairie gardens and led the way to better varieties.

The variety Almey is a front-rank rosybloom introduced in 1945 by the Morden Experimental Farm and named for Mr. J. R. Almey of Winnipeg. It is said to lack full hardiness all across the prairies but good specimens are seen in all three provinces. It makes a vigorous tree with spreading branches that require careful pruning to keep the tree shapely. The branches tend to droop and spread to cover a large area, but the tree can be encouraged to grow upright by shortening the side branches while the tree is still young. Almey has the merit of initiating flower buds on young trees, whereas the process is long delayed with some other varieties. The leaves are first purple red, later bronzy green; the flowers are a rich carmine, red in the bud and deep rosy pink when fully open. Each petal carries a white blotch at the base which is in sharp contrast to the rest of the flower. When the weather at blossom time is cool and damp, there is no finer sight among the rosyblooms than a good specimen of Almey in full bloom. When the flowers fade, the tree is loaded with crabapples of medium size, bright orange red when ripe and long lasting on the tree. One of the joys of spring is the return of the birds, and watching them feed on the desiccated crabapples that remain on the Almey tree all winter.

The Morden Experimental Farm has added two more rosybloom crabapples called Garry and Selkirk. Garry is a splendid tree about twenty feet high, with slender branches and leaves that are first reddish, then bronze green. The flower buds are dark maroon red, opening to a good shade of rose, fading to pink. The flowers are borne in great profusion, arching the slender branches to give the tree a graceful outline. The fruits are a bit smaller than those of Almey but they are equally showy, long lasting and attractive to the winter birds. Selkirk is a vigorous tree, a bit taller than Garry, with bronzy dark green leaves and rosy pink blooms. The flowers are quite large with many clusters at the tip of the branches. The crabapples are bright red from August until they fall to the ground in November. Both varieties have been tested in various locations across the prairies and are recommended as worthy additions to the present list of rosyblooms.

Royalty is another new rosybloom raised by Mr. W. L. Kerr, who was superintendent of the Forest Nursery Station, Saskatoon. It has the darkest leaves of all the rosybloom crabapples and the flowers are dark red. Radiant is a Minnesota introduction with deep pink flowers and reddish fruits. It makes a neat, small tree with a roundish outline. Strathmore is an old variety with reddish purple leaves, rosy mauve flowers and purplish fruits. The tree growth is upright with many slender branches; it may be used effectively as an informal hedge. Rudolph is a very hardy rosybloom raised at Dropmore, Manitoba, by the late Dr.

Frank Skinner. The bright pink blooms hold their color well and make this variety one of the most attractive in bloom. There are many more to be found in the prairie nurserymen's catalogues and many new ones will be added in the future.

To avoid drabness, which can result from planting too many rosy-blooms, a few white-flowered crabapples should be included. In a small garden there may be room for only one and a variety named Snowcap, from the Beaverlodge Experimental Farm in Alberta, should not be overlooked. Snowcap produces an abundance of pinkish buds that open to pure white flowers, sharply contrasting with the rosybloom crabapples. The flowers are followed by small red fruits that show up well against the green leaves.

The species crabapple *(Malus baccata)* is worthy of consideration as an ornamental tree. A well-grown specimen, in full bloom, is a noble sight and the small red fruits are glossy and attractive at the end of the season. The Manchurian form of *M. baccata* is a hardy, vigorous tree with white flowers and tiny, berry-like fruit about the size of red currants. It is something of a rarity in prairie gardens but worthy of a place beside the more flamboyant members of the family. The Dolgo crabapple may not be fully hardy everywhere but, where it can be grown successfully, its usefulness as an ornamental should not be overlooked. The tree is shapely, requiring very little pruning, and the masses of white bloom show up well against the darker rosyblooms. The scarlet fruit is showy and useful in the kitchen.

Birch — The birches have a long season of interest: the slender branches are attractive when etched against the winter sky; the catkins are a feature before the leaves unfold and, in the fall, the golden yellow leaves are not excelled by any other tree. The white bark, attractive all through the year, is strikingly beautiful in winter.

There are several birches hardy and suitable for small gardens that are grown as single- or multiple-stemmed specimens. The European birch *(Betula pendula)* has several forms; Young's and the cutleaf weeping are most popular. Young's weeping birch makes a spreading tree with graceful branches that sweep the ground. The cutleaf weeping birch will grow to thirty feet or higher with finely cut leaves, pendulant branches and white bark. It needs a sheltered spot, lots of moisture and plenty of room to display its graceful lines. The native paper birch *(B. papyifera)* makes a splendid multiple-stemmed tree not so expensive as the select forms of the European birch which have to be grafted, but very attractive with pale green leaves and white bark.

The soil for birches should be rich in humus, neutral or slightly acid. They need plenty of water. One of the causes of failure is setting the young plant too deeply in badly drained soil. The birch has a rather shallow and wide-spreading root system, so it needs plenty of room and plenty of moisture. The birches, particularly the European forms, are susceptible to attacks by the bronze bark borer, which often ruins the tree before it reaches maturity.

Mountainash — The mountainash or rowan is a valuable tree for the prairie garden with a long season of interest in flowers, fruit and colorful leaves in the fall. The large compound leaves are handsome and usually healthy all through the season. The panicles or clusters of creamy flowers are showy in July and the bright red berries are a late summer and early autumn feature. The birds are fond of the fruit, gorging themselves to strip the trees and sometimes finishing the job before September is out.

There are several drawbacks to planting a mountainash. The main trunk may be damaged by sunscald unless you face the tree north or east of a building. Occasionally, fireblight will kill some of the young shoots and, if the soil is heavily charged with lime, you will have trouble with chlorosis. By digging in a pailful of acid peat and adding a small quantity of chelated iron, a bad soil condition can be put right. By choosing a species that has some resistance to fireblight and by rigorously pruning out infected branches of apples, crabapples, pears, cotoneaster and other related plants prone to the disease, you may not be in serious trouble.

There are several species that do well throughout the prairies, providing shelter and suitable soil are found. Green's mountainash *(Sorbus scopulina)* makes a round-headed, small tree with dark green leaves and bright red berries, and is highly resistant to fireblight. The showy mountainash *(S. decora)* makes a spreading tree with clusters of large fruit which are greatly relished by the birds. It is much like the American mountainash *(S. americana)*, which is found in some parts of the prairies growing wild. The European mountainash *(S. aucuparia)* is a taller and more slender tree with finer twigs and branches. It is quite susceptible to sunscald and fireblight.

Willow — Several willows are useful as multiple-stemmed trees but, as they grow rapidly, they must have plenty of room or be rejuvenated by hard pruning. Some are grown chiefly for the red or yellow bark of the young twigs, which is best when the plants are pruned back in April.

The silky white willow *(Salix alba sericea)* is sometimes called the Siberian silver willow. It makes an upright tree with narrow leaves of silver gray. The branches and twigs do not litter the ground after a summer storm in the manner of the golden willow. The redstem willow *(S. alba chermesina)* has brilliant bark on the young wood and is grown as a shrubby tree, or cut back annually when planted for winter and early spring color. The laurel leaf willow *(S. pentandra)* is a small tree with handsome, dark green, glossy leaves, much broader than most other willows. It is mostly seen as a shrubby tree but it can be grown as a shapely, single-stem specimen in well-sheltered gardens where soil moisture is adequate. The bark of the laurel willow is not so highly colored as that of the golden or redstem willows, but young shoots arising from cutback stubs are brilliant yellow green.

Weeping willows have long been esteemed for their distinctive charm but, in prairie gardens, many specimens have been planted with disappointing results. In favored areas, quite large trees are often seen but even those specimens are subject to severe injury from frost and drying winds. Shelter from the northwest is needed to ensure any kind of success and soil moisture must be replenished before freeze-up if the autumn weather is dry. There is much confusion in the identity of weeping willows; the best chance of success is to obtain a locally grown plant. The Wisconsin weeping willow, sometimes called Niobe, has made a thirty-foot tree in some prairie gardens but it is not long lived. It is a hybrid between the Chinese species *(S. babylonica)* and a European species *(S. fragilis).* Another willow with strikingly beautiful foliage is *S. exigua,* commonly called the coyote willow. The slender branches are clothed with narrow, silvery foliage which makes it a most distinctive willow. It suckers, or puts out numerous basal shoots when the plants are grown on their own roots; it should therefore be budded high off the ground, using some other nonsuckering sort such as the golden willow as understock.

Walnut — Walnut trees, such as provide the nuts sold commercially, are much too tender for the prairies but the black walnut, butternut and Manchurian walnut make respectable trees in favored spots. The butternut *(Juglans cinerea)* makes a spreading tree with huge leaves and low branches. The leaves are slow to open; the branches often appear to be dead early in the season — sometimes, they are. In the early fall the leaves yellow and soon drop but, in the summer, they provide welcome shade. The black walnut *(J. nigra)* is a large tree, fairly upright with a rounded head. The large compound leaves are handsome and the nuts may be eaten. The Manchurian walnut *(J. mandschurica)* is offered for sale by several nurserymen and, like the butternut and black walnut, is worth considering as a novelty tree in a well-sheltered garden.

Maple — In the farm garden there may be room for a few tall trees besides the birches and mountainash. The silver or soft maple *(Acer saccharinum)* makes a handsome tree in some parts of the prairies but in many places it has failed. The chief causes of failure are dry soil and a poor choice of stock. The hardiest Manitoba strains will make good trees in most parts of the prairies if they are sheltered and given plenty of water. In favored locations the silver maple grows rapidly and fifty-foot specimens are not uncommon where trees are near water. The leaves are deeply cut, medium green with a silvery underside. The young twigs are reddish on some specimens and the pendulant clusters of bloom are worth a close look.

When the blooms escape frost, enormous quantities of seed are produced and propelled to the ground. If the weather is damp for a few days, a forest of seedlings appears; otherwise, the seed quickly dies.

The sugar maple *(A. saccharum)* is not considered suitable for the prairies though it is not impossible to grow it reasonably well in some parts. Only the hardiest strains should be considered, sheltering the young trees from the northwest. The soil must be well drained and never dry for long periods. Good specimens exist at Morden, where hardy strains are being developed by the experimental farm plant breeders, and in Winnipeg there are several good specimens of hardy sugar maple, some twenty feet high.

The Norway maple *(A. platanoides)* is not suited to the prairies; even in the most favored locations it has failed to make a tree. Occasionally a specimen of the popular Crimson King survives for a few years, suffering annual winter damage that reduces it to a nondescript shrub, soon to die. The red maple *(A. rubrum)* is a magnificent tree in eastern Canada where it is esteemed for brilliant autumn foliage. It is not suitable for the prairies.

The Amur maple *(A. ginnala)* is more of a shrub than a tree, making a ten- to fifteen-foot specimen with fine leaves, showy bloom and ornamental seed pods, first green, then reddish. It is one of the most brilliant trees in September, with red or orange leaves. A similar tree, the Tatarian maple *(A. tataricum)* is not so colorful; the leaves are usually yellow in the fall. In some parts it may grow to twenty feet and is distinguished from the Amur maple by the leaves, which are not so deeply cut.

Native ash — The native ash or green ash *(Fraxinus pennsylvanica subintegerrima)* is grown extensively in windbreaks but is not greatly esteemed as a specimen tree. It leafs out late, dropping its leaves early in the fall, but occasionally puts on a magnificent show as the leaves turn brilliant yellow. Selected nonseeding or male clones should be planted and may be pruned to make shapely trees that provide shade when shade is most needed. The black ash *(F. nigra)* is not so well known nor so well adapted to the dry soil as the green ash. It is similar in general appearance but will grow taller where there is sufficient moisture.

Elm — The two elms generally planted in the prairie regions are the American elm *(Ulmus americana)* and the Dropmore elm or Manchurian elm *(U. pumila)*. The American elm is the most valuable shade tree and, in spite of the threat of Dutch elm disease wiping it out, thousands of trees are lined out on boulevards, in parks and, where there is room, in private gardens. At the present time the dread disease is slowly making headway in the general direction of the northwest but, if proper sanitation is practised and a sharp lookout is kept for the first signs of distress, there is no cause for alarm. Most of the specimens planted in prairie parks and gardens are seedlings which must be trained to make shapely trees. Trees of a select American elm with a shapely, upright habit are available. They cost more than seedling trees but are the best investment if a specimen shade tree is required and space is available.

The Dropmore elm is a smaller tree, used as a quick-growing hedge or windbreak or as a single specimen. The leaves are smaller than those of the American elm, dark green and long lasting. It is not unusual to see the Dropmore elm well clothed with leaves late in October when the American elm is bare. However, the American elm turns a rich, old gold color in September; the Dropmore elm has no autumn color.

Basswood, linden — The basswood or American linden *(Tilia americana)* makes a large, spreading tree where soil moisture is adequate. The leaves are large, medium green and sometimes infested with an insect that disfigures the surface with galls. The flowers are sweet scented and attractive to the bees.

The little-leaf linden *(T. cordata)* is not fully hardy all across the prairies, but in certain areas it makes a spreading tree with multiple trunks. The branches and twigs are rich brown in winter, the leaf buds prominent and slow to unfold. There is a wide difference in the strains of the little-leaf linden; a forty-year-old tree at the experimental station in Morden has made a shapely standard tree, but its trunk has been shaded from the sun. A similar tree, the Mongolian basswood *(T. mongolica)* is rare in cultivation but promises to be hardier and better adapted than the little-leaf linden.

The Planting and Care of Evergreens

The cone-bearing evergreens provide a variety of shapes and sizes in many shades of green. They have year-round interest but attract most attention in the winter when deciduous trees are bare. The spruces and pines produce quantities of cones when the trees mature and are picturesque when the male cones are developing in June. They are red on some of the spruces and produced in such profusion that they give the tree a reddish glow. When the male cones ripen, clouds of air-borne pollen float a considerable distance to fertilize the female cones.

In the heat of summer the blue needles of Kosters and other select spruces intensify their color, but in the winter, all are sombre green. In the home garden the smaller sorts are most useful and seen to the best advantage when planted in the foundation border, placing the taller ones at the corners of the house, the low ones under the windows.

Planting evergreens — There are two seasons when evergreens may be moved safely, although some may be moved successfully at other times if enough soil is moved with them. More depends on the kind of evergreen and the amount of soil on the roots than the time of year you do the job. May is a good time to transplant young plants, when the new buds are beginning to swell on spruce and pine. In September, when the soil is warm, transplanted spruce trees will soon make new roots if the soil is kept moist. The spruce trees move more easily than the pines and arborvitae. Large pines are difficult to transplant, so set out young plants in May, choosing a sunny spot. Pines prefer sandy soil that is neutral or slightly acid. If the soil is heavy, poorly drained and inclined to be alkaline, the plants soon sicken with chlorosis and die. The arborvitae grow well in shade; the pines do best in full sun. The Rockymountain junipers, too, are sun-loving plants. The dwarf forms of the Savin juniper will grow well facing in any direction; whichever way your house happens to be facing, you have a selection of evergreens which may be used as foundation plants.

Cultivating evergreens – Evergreens should be kept cultivated to kill weeds and to keep the soil surface from baking. When they are grown as lawn specimens, the turf must be cut back to just beyond the spread of the branches. Grass uses up soil moisture rapidly and evergreens will be stunted if they have to compete for soil moisture with turf. Cultivation should be shallow or the roots may be injured.

Fertilizing evergreens – In most parts of the prairies the soil is fertile and young trees will not need additional stimulants. Mature trees that seem to be growing poorly will benefit from a dose of fertilizer applied in the spring. Make holes with a crowbar or soil auger about a foot deep and spaced about two feet apart. Put a handful of 27.14.0 in each hole; replace the soil and give the whole area a good soaking. A summer mulch of rotted manure or compost, dug into the soil in the fall, will improve soil texture and slowly release plant food. The guide to fertilizing must be the appearance of the tree. If growth is satisfactory and the color of the needles normal, there is no need to apply fertilizer; on the other hand, if the color is poor and the tree stunted, fertilizer, properly applied in the right amounts, will do a lot of good. The roots of evergreens are sensitive to commercial fertilizers, so it is wise not to use fertilizer when young evergreens are transplanted.

Watering evergreens – Evergreens growing in the natural forest receive no moisture other than the rain, yet they manage to grow into large specimens. The reason is the deep pile of rotted leaves on the forest floor that insulates the ground against excessive heat and reduces evaporation. In the average home garden, there is no mulch to protect the ground from drying out and quite often evergreens are planted under a wide, overhanging roof where rain seldom falls. It is obvious that young evergreens in the home garden need special care until the roots have penetrated deep into the soil. Watering is most effective when the garden hose runs slowly to fill a shallow depression made around each plant. Sprinkling water on the surface is useless if the roots are in dry soil. In dry weather, a thorough watering every week or ten days will be needed; freshen the tops as well by forcibly spraying water on them after a hot day. This top spraying with water from the garden hose is of special benefit to evergreens near the house wall and under a wide roof overhang. In these areas there is more danger from attacks of spider mites, as they thrive and increase in numbers where the air is dry.

Pruning evergreens – Evergreens are pruned to keep them within reasonable limits of size, to remove twigs and branches which may have been injured or infected with disease and to maintain a shapely specimen. For the purpose of pruning, evergreens may be divided into two groups: those that develop their current year's growth from dormant buds and complete their annual growth early in the summer, and those that make their growth over a longer period. In the first group, the pines, firs and spruces are notable; the junipers and arborvitae are examples of evergreens with a more or less continuous habit of growth through the summer.

Specimen spruce trees are most attractive when they are allowed to grow naturally. Pruning should be restricted to the removal of a second "leader" or topmost shoot, if one appears, and of the occasional side shoot which may be out of line. The dormant bud on the top shoot may be damaged and fail to develop but lateral buds on the same shoot soon take over and, unless all except one are removed, the tree will be spoiled. The top of a spruce tree can be broken off by a violent storm but a new top will develop if one of the side branches is tied up in a vertical position. A broom handle or similar piece of wood is lashed to the main trunk of the damaged tree, projecting about two feet above the point of injury. The most vigorous branch from the topmost whorl is tied to the broomstick. It may not be possible to get the branch perfectly upright the first year, but it can be directed in the way it should grow and may be further adjusted to a vertical position a year later. The pruning of side shoots that tend to grow out of line must be done every year, since it is not possible for new shoots to develop from old wood. Once the tree becomes too large for its position, it should be taken out and a young one put in its place.

The arborvitae and the junipers require a somewhat different technique to keep them shapely and within bounds. The pruning is best done in early summer, using a pair of hedge shears. A pruning knife will make a better job; so will a pair of secateurs, but it takes more time. The tips of the young shoots are cut back to restrict growth and keep the plant compact; otherwise, it may soon become too large and outgrow its allotted space. Some forms of mugho pine tend to grow more rapidly than others and, where these have been used in the foundation planting, they need to be carefully pruned. In July, when the current year's growth is completed, reduce the young shoots by one-third their length. Use a sharp pruning knife or secateurs and make the cuts between the needles so that you avoid mutilating them. The judicious and regular use of the pruning knife will keep evergreens in good shape for many years.

Wintering evergreens — There is a big investment in evergreens; even the small sizes of blue spruce are expensive and, while the home gardener may have given his newly planted trees good summer care, they may suffer from winter drought. Since evergreens transpire moisture all the year round, they often suffer when water is cut off in the late summer. To overcome winter drought, soak the ground in October and lay on a cover of peat or leaves.

The arborvitae and small spruce trees will sometimes brown during the early part of spring if the sun strikes them on the southwest side. Excessive heat in April can do serious damage as the roots may still be frozen and not able to replace the high evaporation of moisture from the foliage. In 1952, temperatures around ninety degrees Fahrenheit were experienced for three days at the end of April in southern Manitoba. Evergreens that had looked well enough when the snow melted a month before soon turned brown and, in some instances, young plants died. It is a good plan to give the evergreens a thorough washing down with the garden hose when the weather turns warm in the spring. It will not only counteract high evaporation; it will wash off the accumulation of winter grime.

It may be necessary to shade young evergreens in October to protect them from the desiccation of drying winter winds; use burlap mounted on two stakes set out on the southwest side of the plant, quite close to but not touching it.

MULCH (IN WINTER ONLY)

Evergreens for the Prairies

The cone-bearing evergreens that are hardy enough for the prairies include a limited number of pines, spruces, firs, junipers and arborvitae, or cedars as they are erroneously called. The true cedars *(Cedrus)* are much too tender for the prairies. The larches are included as cone bearing though they are deciduous.

The evergreen conifers shed their needles by a gradual process, the older ones falling in August. The amount of leaf drop is related to the soil moisture. In periods of prolonged drought, the needle drop will be considerable.

Fir — The firs are not so well adapted to the dry air as the pines and spruces and, except for the odd specimen in parks and experimental gardens, very few are seen. The balsam *(Abies balsamae)* is distinguished by smooth bark, flattish needles and upward-facing cones. A dwarf form, *A. balsamae nana,* has been tried in some places but is not very satisfactory. A select form propagated by grafts is offered for sale by one nurseryman and is superior to the native balsam. It makes a compact, columnar tree with dark green needles.

Hardy strains of the Douglas fir *(Pseudotsuga taxifolia,* once called *Abies Douglasii),* are making good trees in some areas. As a young tree Douglas fir is most attractive, pyramidal in outline with branches reaching the ground. A thirty-foot specimen at the Morden Experimental Farm has never suffered winter injury and bears an annual crop of cones. The cones are distinctive, with a three-lobed appendage growing between the scales.

The white fir *(Abies concolor)* is a rare tree on the prairies and is not recommended. One specimen at Morden, thirty feet high, has been seriously damaged by sapsuckers and, on occasion, drying winds have browned the needles.

Spruce — The spruces are best known for the select forms of the Colorado spruce *(Picea pungens),* particularly the Kosters blue. The Norway spruce *(P. abies),* used as a shelterbelt tree in some areas, is not attractive as a specimen. The branches droop to give the tree a shaggy look and the needles tend to drop prematurely. The cones are light brown, quite large and provide a way of distinguishing the Norway from other spruces. Numerous dwarf forms of Norway spruce are available but they are not fully hardy. Good specimens of Maxwell, Ohlendorff and nest spruce have been grown in some parts of the prairies. At the Morden Experimental Farm, Maxwell spruce *(P. abies maxwelli)* makes a two-foot specimen occasionally browned by cold winds. The nest spruce *(P. abies nidiformis)* has been the most satisfactory and has seldom suffered winter injury. It makes a roundish plant with dense branches and tiny needles. A ten-year-old specimen, planted on the north side of a shrub border, is not much more than a foot high and attractive all the year round.

The white spruce *(P. glauca)* is a native tree extending in one form or another over the whole region and is used extensively as a windbreak. A variety called the Black Hills spruce *(P. glauca densata)* has shorter needles and is more desirable as a specimen tree. The black spruce *(P. mariana)* is common in swampy areas and has no special merit as a cultivated tree except in areas where the soil is poorly drained. A dwarf form of the Alberta white spruce *(P. glauca albertiana conica)* has fine, pale green needles and a compact pyramidal outline. It is not suitable for the open prairies except as a novelty evergreen. Several three-foot specimens remained healthy for a number of years at Morden in a rock garden shaded by tall trees and usually deep in snow from November to April.

The Colorado spruce *(P. pungens)* is probably the most widely planted spruce tree on the prairies. Seedling trees of the Colorado spruce are used extensively in windbreaks and hedges. Select seedlings are sold as specimens and named clones are propagated by grafts. The named sorts are most expensive; the grafting is a highly skilled technique and the young plants grow very slowly. The named clones are much alike with silvery or steely blue needles. Kosters, one of the first of the named varieties, is still the most popular; Morden Blue makes a denser tree but the color is essentially the same as Kosters. Hoopesi is a choice selection, with intensely blue needles and shapely branches. Young Colorado spruces, attractive for a time, may become a nuisance and a danger; as they grow larger, they tend to sap the soil moisture needed for other plants.

Montgomery spruce — There are a number of dwarf Colorado spruces which have originated in different parts of the world and are sold as grafted specimens. One called Montgomery is fully hardy, remarkably slow growing and as blue as Kosters. A twenty-year-old plant at Morden is four feet high and three feet across. Montgomery spruce makes several leaders, not one like a normal spruce. Little pruning is needed except to snip off the odd shoot that grows out of line. Montgomery spruce may be used in a mixed group of evergreens in the foundation planting with good effect.

Pine — The pines are distinguished by their long needles, borne in bundles of two to five and fastened at the base by a brown sheath. Several species and forms are grown in prairie gardens but not all are fully hardy.

The jackpine *(Pinus banksiana)* has little value as an ornamental tree except for those who are interested in growing a collection of pines. It has short needles, sometimes yellowish and unattractive. The cones are small, very hard and remain on the tree for several years.

The limber pine *(P. flexilis)* is out of its natural range in Manitoba but in sheltered areas it grows fairly well. The needles are borne in bundles of five; the young twigs are very pliable.

The white pine *(P. strobus)*, native to eastern Manitoba, is not well adapted to the plains area of the prairies and seldom grows satisfactorily. It belongs to the five-needle group and, in its native habitat, makes a picturesque symmetrical tree.

The western yellow pine or ponderosa *(P. ponderosa)* is an important timber tree in the western part of the continent but has little use in the home garden. The smaller and hardier *scopulorum* is native to southwestern North Dakota and has been used effectively in that area as an ornamental tree. Large specimens of the western yellow pine or bullpine as it is sometimes called are growing at the Morden Experimental Farm and, though the needles on the exposed side of the tree are browned occasionally, the trees have persisted in reasonably good health for forty years.

The mountain pine *(P. mugo)* and the various forms of the variety *mughus* are the most widely planted of the pines grown in prairie gardens. The mountain pine varies from low, spreading shrubs to small trees; the low-growing forms are most suitable in the home garden and are popular foundation shrubs. Some very dwarf, compact clones are offered for sale as grafted specimens but most are selected from seedling *(P. mugo pumillo)* and are kept dwarf by annual pruning.

The Scotch pine *(P. sylvestris)* is widely distributed in northern Europe, the hardiest strains being found in Finland. While it has no place in a small garden, it is esteemed for its picturesque outline and distinctive tawny orange bark. A grafted selection called *plumosa* makes a dense pyramid as a young tree, with long, dark green needles.

The red pine *(P. resinosa),* sometimes called the Norway pine, has no particular merit as an ornamental tree, although well-grown specimens are handsome and shapely.

The lodgepole pine *(P. contorta latifolia)* and the Austrian pine *(P. nigra)* are forest trees of no special value in prairie gardens. The lodgepole seems highly susceptible to chlorosis and occasionally suffers serious winter injury. The Austrian pine is not well adapted to the plains regions, although a specimen has grown to thirty feet at Morden while others have died.

One of the choice members of the tribe and one that can be grown successfully in sheltered gardens in a wide area of the prairies is the Swiss stone pine *(P. cembra)*. Mature specimens are growing well at Brandon and Morden and at least one prairie nurseryman offers young plants for sale. It belongs to the white pine group with needles in bundles of five. It makes a narrow, upright tree, pyramidal in outline, with fairly dense branches and dark needles. As the growth is rather slow, one foot a year or less, it makes an ideal pine for the home garden. It is worthy of a sheltered spot where the soil is well drained but not too rich.

The bristlecone pine *(P. aristata)* is native to the high mountains of the Sierra Range in the western United States, where the temperatures range from very hot to very cold. It is one of the oldest living things and for this reason alone it is worth including in a collection of evergreens. In some parts of the prairies, young plants are doing well and there seems to be a reasonable chance of success with this interesting species. It grows very slowly into a handsome, bushy shrub, with attractive needles sometimes studded with dots of resin.

Juniper — The junipers are another large group of evergreens ranging from prostrate forms that never get off the ground to tall, spreading trees. The low forms are most widely planted in prairie gardens and include varieties of the Savin juniper, Pfitzers and the Rockymountain juniper. The Savin juniper *(Juniperus sabina)* is one of the best for foundation planting or for the edge of shrub borders. It has fine-textured branches that flare out to four feet or higher in an attractive shade of green. Two dwarf forms called Arcadia and Skandia were selected from a number gathered in the Ural mountains; both are excellent low-growing junipers. Arcadia makes a spreading plant two to three feet high with bright green foliage. Growth is rather slow and the plant can be kept a bit lower by pruning. Skandia is more compact; the plants are two feet high and the foliage is tinged bluish green.

The Pfitzer junipers are not so well adapted as Arcadia, Skandia and the ordinary Savin juniper but, in favored spots, some are fairly satisfactory. The gold-tipped Pfitzer has green foliage tipped with yellow and is recommended for well-sheltered gardens.

The Rockymountain juniper *(J. scopulorum)* is native to the badlands of Montana, the Dakotas and Alberta. It is a dryland plant tolerant of intense cold and heat, drought and high wind. There are numerous clones available with gray or bluish foliage. Certain varieties seem to do better in some areas than in others; the local nurseryman's selection should be the guide. Medora, Grizzly Bear and Blue Haven are among the best. The Rockymountain juniper is subject to cedar-apple rust in areas where hawthorn, cotoneaster and other related plants are near to provide alternative host plants for the propagation of the disease.

The creeping juniper *(J. horizontalis)* is a native, prostrate species found over a wide area on sandy hillsides. It makes a dense mat of attractive foliage, either green or blue gray, creeping along the ground and making new roots as it goes. Like the Rockymountain juniper, the creeping juniper is a variable species and many selections have been made. These are offered by prairie nurserymen, each favoring certain varieties.

Douglasii and Dunvegan are two selections with blue foliage. Prince of Wales is green, turning purplish in the fall.

The eastern redcedar *(J. virginiana)* has grown fairly well in some parts of the prairies. A few large specimens did well at Morden for a number of years, but it is not so well adapted to the dry prairie conditions as the Rockymountain juniper, nor has it more ornamental value.

Arborvitae — The American arborvitae *(Thuja occidentalis)* is a variable species of many forms and colors. It is found wild in eastern Manitoba in areas where there is adequate moisture. Dry soil and cold winds are limiting factors in establishing the arborvitae but, given shelter from the northwest and an adequate supply of water in July and August as well as a final soaking just before the ground freezes, a number of varieties can be grown successfully.

The most popular shape is the pyramidal, used extensively in frontyard gardens. Many pyramidal forms are available but the only one so far that is dependable is the Brandon. The original tree has been growing at the Brandon Experimental Farm since the turn of the century and provided the cuttings for a local nurseryman who has propagated this hardy evergreen by the tens of thousands. The Brandon pyramidal arborvitae or cedar makes a slender pyramid with dark green foliage. It may be sheared once a year if required but it looks its best growing naturally. Older specimens may need to have the branches tied to prevent damage from heavy snow; the seed cones should be picked off while they are still green.

Tender strains of pyramidal cedar are offered for sale but these are useless in this part of the country. From the Lake St. John district of Quebec, a hardy, upright form was discovered by Dr. Skinner and made available a number of years ago. It has fine foliage, light to medium green, and makes a choice hedge. The Ware arborvitae *(T. occidentalis wareana),* sometimes called Siberian cedar, is considered one of the hardiest tall-growing forms. It makes a vigorous, broad shrub ten feet or higher with dense, dark green foliage that rarely browns in winter. A few low varieties have been tried and can be expected to grow satisfactorily in sheltered gardens: Little Gem is an example. If these dwarf varieties are planted on the north side of shelter, they remain under snow and reappear in the spring fresh and green. Many forms with variegated foliage, either golden or silvery, are available but these are collector's items that must be tried in favored spots and given special care.

Larch — The larch is a distinctive tree, cone bearing yet deciduous. It has little value as an ornamental tree in the home garden but it makes a fine hedge. The native tamarack *(Larix laricina)* is distinguished by its tiny cones and bluish green needles. The Siberian larch *(L. sibirica)* is similar to the tamarack; the needles are a brighter shade of green and the cones are much larger. A thirty-five-year-old specimen hedge at Morden is six feet high and still in quite good shape. The larches have a brief period of glory in September when the needles turn a brilliant gold.

Broad-leaf evergreens — Hardy evergreens suitable for prairie gardens are mostly conifers; the so-called broad-leaf evergreens are tender and only a few low-growing sorts are of any use in a prairie garden. Unless these low evergreens are under a cover of snow, they suffer winter injury.

In some areas, where snow is usually adequate, the canby pachistima *(Pachistima canbyi)* makes low mats of narrow, dark green leaves and sometimes a wealth of tiny, dull red flowers. It does best on a north-facing border; if facing south, it will often sunscald and soon die. At the Morden Experimental Farm it has persisted for twenty years, spreading to large mats and making an excellent ground cover.

The Japanese spurge *(Pachysandra terminalis)* has not been satisfactory, although it survived at Morden for several years. It needs an acid soil, plenty of moisture and a shady spot. Where these are provided and a deep cover of snow is kept on the plants until May, there is a reasonable chance of keeping the plants alive.

The Korean box *(Buxus koreana)* is the hardiest box and the only one liable to grow in prairie gardens. The English box was once popular in European gardens as a dwarf hedge but has fallen into disuse these days because of the increased costs of maintenance. The Korean box grows about two feet high with dense branches covered with tiny, roundish leaves. In a sheltered garden it thrives reasonably well, though occasional injury can be expected when snow cover is sparse. It needs shade, moisture and protection from drying winter winds. It is useless to try to grow it as a clipped hedge and only those who are collectors or wish to try and grow box for its old-world associations will be interested in making the attempt.

There are many forms of evergreen euonymus which are used as ground covers, wall plants and as specimen shrubs in eastern Canada and at the coast. These attractive plants cannot be grown on the prairies and it is a waste of time and money to try. Some attempts to grow the bigleaf wintercreeper as a ground cover have only succeeded in bringing the plant through the winter in poor shape.

The yew is one of the oldest trees in cultivation; specimens six or seven hundred years old are not uncommon in English churchyards, some of them healthy, some with hollow trunks. The native species *(Taxus canadensis),* commonly called the Canada yew, is growing fairly well in some favored spots on the prairies but, broadly speaking, even the hardiest yew is not very happy in the dry air. To preserve it from sunscald, plant it facing either east or north in soil that is well charged with humus. It gives year-round interest with its dark green foliage and sometimes produces translucent red fruit. The Japanese yew *(T. cuspidata)* makes a low, spreading plant, not fully hardy, but fairly good specimens are possible in shady, sheltered spots where the soil is neutral, well drained, cool and moist. A number of clones from a hybrid group have been tried at the Morden Experimental Farm but, although they sometimes manage to grow fairly well for a few years, sooner or later a hard winter kills them to ground level.

Ornamental Shrubs in the Prairie Garden

There is a wide variety of hardy shrubs suitable for the prairie garden: some are included in almost every landscape plan; others are not so common. In the small garden, the choice should be limited to medium and dwarf sorts with a few of the taller-growing ones for the boundary planting. A boundary planting of trees or tall shrubs will give privacy or hide an unsightly object from view; in selecting shrubs for the boundary planting, consideration should therefore be given to those with dense growth.

Shrubs can be used effectively to accent particular features of the landscape or to stand alone as individual specimens. A garden seat, sundial or some other special feature can be accented by flanking it with suitable shrubs. Special attention is given to colored foliage, showy flowers or attractive fruit when selecting shrubs for individual planting. There are shrubs with silvery gray leaves and some with yellow or reddish foliage but, in a small garden, such shrubs must be used sparingly. A small garden overplanted with trees and shrubs with golden, red or silvery leaves will appear to be smaller than it really is, because these bright colors seem to be nearer than the greens and browns of most trees. Shrubs with colorful leaves tend to dominate those with plain green foliage, so they should be used in proportion to the size of the garden. In the front area, the foundation planting is most important: low shrubs are used under windows, taller ones at the corners and a medium-sized shrub may be planted on either side of the entrance.

Before deciding which shrubs to plant in your garden, it will pay to study the recommended lists published by the provincial departments of agriculture. Some shrubs grow well in shade; some are suitable for hot, dry locations and some are tolerant of alkaline soil. There are also a number of species that demand an acid soil, and to attempt to grow these in soil high in lime will end in failure.

There are several native shrubs worthy of a place in the garden: the Saskatoon or serviceberry, the highbush cranberry, nannyberry, lead plant and false indigo. The commonest shrubs are lilacs, spireas, honeysuckles and potentillas.

Lilac – The lilacs are represented by dozens of varieties classed as French lilacs or common lilacs and a number of other species and hybrids. The French lilacs are the most popular; the common variety was planted as a windbreak by the early settlers and many miles of old lilac hedges can be seen today as well as decrepit bushes where farm homes once stood. The modern varieties have huge trusses of flowers in shades of blue and pink, deep purple and reddish magenta as well as pure white and deep cream. The plants do best in good soil that is well drained; some shade is tolerated but, for the best bloom, a place in the sun is necessary. The French lilac makes a rounded shrub up to ten feet high with dark green, leathery leaves that last on the bush well into October. The main feature is a profusion of bloom in early summer. The seed pods are not attractive nor are the leaves in the fall. The following list groups some of the best varieties in their color groups.

French lilacs in shades of blue:
   President Grevy, Emil Gentil, Maurice Barres, Condorcet
Reddish shades:
   Paul Thirion, Mrs. Edward Harding, Mme. F. Morel, Marechal Foch
Dark purples:
   Ludwig Spaeth, Rochambeau, Danton, Congo
Mauve shades:
   Leon Gambetta, Christophe Colomb, Olivier de Serres
Pink shades:
   Lucie Baltet, Mme. Antoine Buckner, Belle de Nancy, Esther Staley
White shades:
   Vestale, Edith Cavell, Ellen Willmott, Monique Lemoine, Primrose (cream)

In most parts of the prairies, all these varieties will give a good show of bloom if the plants are cared for properly. The spent flowers should be cut off, old wood removed from time to time and varieties that are prone to heavy suckering kept in bounds by ruthlessly digging out the suckers once a year. As soon as the flowers fade, cut off the whole truss down to that portion of the stem where two large buds are developing. If you cut beyond this point you destroy next year's bloom. Suckers can be cut out in October or in the early spring before the leaves unfold. Use a sharp spade to dig out the suckers, cutting them close to the main trunk of the plant.

A group of late-blooming lilacs which were first developed by Miss Isabella Preston of the Central Experimental Farm, Ottawa, has gained some prominence in Canadian gardens. Further breeding work done at Morden, Manitoba, and by Dr. F. L. Skinner of Dropmore, Manitoba, has improved on the early varieties. The new varieties have brighter flowers and the plants are not so coarse as some of the earlier sorts. With proper pruning these newer varieties will fit into a small garden where they prolong the display of lilac and make good background shrubs. Some of the popular lilacs in this group are Coral, Redwine, Royalty, Donald Wyman, Helen, Freedom and a new one with the brightest pink flowers called Miss Canada. Donald Wyman and Helen were raised by Dr. Skinner of Dropmore; the rest were developed at the Morden Experimental Farm.

A new group of lilacs from Dr. Skinner arouses a good deal of interest, especially in northern areas where the French lilacs are sometimes injured by frost. By crossing the Korean form of the early lilac *(Syringa oblata dilitata)* with selected varieties of the French lilacs, a new race of early flowering, hardy lilacs is now available called the American lilacs. They bloom a bit earlier than the French hybrids, do not sucker profusely and are hardy enough to grow all across the prairies. A few of the best are Asessippi (purple), Sister Justina (a pure white of rare beauty), Daphne (pink) and Pocahontas (a dark purple).

There is some confusion in a group loosely called Persian lilac. The true species *(S. persica)* is a fairly upright shrub five or six feet high with arching branches, narrow leaves and loose panicles of pale mauve or white flowers. A subspecies called *laciniata* is not so tall; the leaves are deeply lobed and the panicles of bloom are smaller. *S. chinensis,* a hybrid of

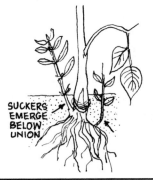

Lilac suckers should be removed with their roots attached.

persica, is sometimes called *rothamagensis* and is sometimes confused with the true Persian lilac. It grows up to eight feet in a spreading bush with slender branches and a profusion of lilac pink bloom a week or so later than the French or common lilac. It is occasionally severely damaged by winter winds that dry out the wood; when this occurs, it is necessary to hard prune the plant to restore its vigor, but bloom will be lost for two years.

The Hungarian lilac is similar to the Chinese or villosa lilac with large leaves and pale, lilac mauve flowers. The leaves are dark green and somewhat shiny, and the species has been used to produce hybrids with *S. reflexa.* It makes a splendid tall hedge, superior to villosa lilac, but it remains something of a rarity in prairie gardens.

A dwarf lilac with tiny leaves and loose panicles of sweet-scented mauve flowers is another rarity, though it is fully hardy and offered for sale by some prairie nurserymen. It is called the Meyer lilac *(S. meyeri)* and is a fine low shrub for foundation planting.

The Manchurian lilac *(S. velutina)* is worthy of consideration where there is room for a number of lilacs. The plants are about six feet high with a profusion of sweet-scented white flowers.

The Amur lilac and its variety, the Japanese tree lilac, make tall shrubs or small trees usually with multiple stems. The Amur lilac is not common in prairie gardens although it is hardy and not difficult to grow. It makes a fine background shrub either in full sun or partial shade; it takes longer to reach blooming size than most lilacs but has so much merit that it is worth waiting for. It has no bad habits of spreading by means of suckers and it is the last of the lilacs to bloom, extending the season to early July. The heart-shaped leaves are medium green, the flowers huge creamy panicles, billowy as a summer cloud and sweetly scented. The flowers are followed by sprays of elegant seed pods, first green, then tawny brown. The seed pods and the fine branches etched against the sky give the Amur lilac winter interest. The Japanese tree lilac grows taller; the leaves are darker green. Both the Amur and the Japanese tree lilac leaf out early and hold their leaves well into the fall.

Spirea – The spirea or meadowsweet is a large family of shrubs and herbaceous plants. The woody spireas provide some of the most showy shrubs. Most of them have white flowers and bloom early, though some are pink and bloom later. The garland spirea *(Spirea arguta)* is not fully hardy in prairie gardens; the fine twigs are sometimes dried out by winter winds. In favored spots, sheltered from the northwest wind and growing in soil that is moist, well drained and not too heavily charged with lime, the garland spirea can put on a magnificent show. The slender stems are covered with pure white blooms in late May; the leaves are narrow and pale green. Old wood is pruned out to ground level every three years or so; occasionally, winter injury is so severe that it pays to cut the whole plant down to the ground in April.

The Vanhoutte spirea *(S. vanhouttei)* is one of the most popular, though it is not fully hardy in prairie gardens. In some gardens where it has failed to flower well hardier sorts should be grown. The Vanhoutte spirea has attractive foliage and elegant stems of white flowers in early June. Regular pruning is important to keep the plant vigorous. Old wood tends to dry out; young shoots stand a better chance of good winter survival and will produce better blooms. Specimens five feet high are seen in favored spots but, like the garland spirea, it is not reliably hardy. The threelobe spirea is similar to the Vanhoutte with deeply lobed leaves of dark green and masses of white bloom. It makes a dense shrub three or four feet high, much hardier than Vanhoutte but with a tendency to produce suckers.

The Korean spirea *(S. trichocarpa)* blooms a bit later than the Vanhoutte, has graceful, arching stems and a profusion of bloom. The leaves are medium green and the plants are often six feet high. A dwarf and compact form of *S. trichocarpa,* which originated at the Forest Nursery Station, Indian Head, and is called Density, grows two to three feet high and bears flowers similar to those of the Korean spirea.

A hybrid between the Korean and the threelobe spirea, called Snowhite, makes a vigorous shrub about five feet high. It was developed at Dropmore by Dr. Skinner and combines the good qualities and hardiness of the parent plants. It blooms about the same time as the Korean spirea and is a valuable addition to the group, especially in areas where the Vanhoutte and garland spireas are unsuitable. Another hybrid spirea from Dropmore is a dwarf plant about two feet high with flat panicles of creamy white flowers in July. It is called Summersnow and is a fine spirea for foundation planting. The germander spirea *(S. chamaedryfolia)* is rather a coarse shrub six or seven feet high with off-white flowers. The Pikow spirea *(S. pikowensis)* is another hardy sort with arching branches and off-white flowers. It makes a five-foot shrub with medium green leaves and is a good choice where hardiness is of prime importance.

A number of pink-flowered spireas are suitable for prairie gardens, but not all are fully hardy. Two forms of the bumalda spirea *(S. bumalda)* are commonly grown. Froebeli has flat panicles of deep pink bloom in late summer. The plants are about two feet high and bear flowers on the young wood. Anthony Waterer is a similar plant, more compact and about eighteen inches high. The red flowers are showy from July until the end of the season. Like the Froebel spirea, it bears flowers on the young wood and occasionally kills back in winter. Spring pruning is recommended to encourage new shoots that bloom in the summer.

A new variety called Crispa *(S. bumalda crispa)* has attractive, deeply toothed leaves with wavy margins and deep pink flowers. A native pink-flowered species called Mensies spirea has spikes of deep rose on two- to three-foot plants. Like the other pink spireas, it prefers a neutral soil. The billiard spirea *(S. billiardi)* is another variety with spikes of pink blooms and rather dull foliage; it is quite susceptible to chlorosis. A new and attractive pink spirea called Rosabella is a dwarf plant less than two feet high. It is a hybrid of *S. betulifolia,* the birchleaf spirea, and was raised at Dropmore by Dr. Skinner.

Bush honeysuckle – The common bush honeysuckle *(Lonicera tatarica)* was widely planted as a windbreak and hedge as well as a specimen shrub. Older varieties tend to have pale pink flowers but new ones with bright red blooms are much more attractive. The bush honeysuckle is perfectly hardy all across the prairies, making a spreading bush ten feet high. In early June the bushes are a mass of flowers; later, the red- or orange-colored berries provide further interest. The appearance of the bush honeysuckle in winter is rather drab, with gray branches and an untidy outline.

There are several select forms; among the best are Arnold Red, Zabelli and Carleton. All have red flowers and fruits. Valencia and several others are grown for their abundance of brilliant orange berries. The Amur honeysuckle *(L. maackii)* is a distinctive honeysuckle with branches that spread more or less horizontally. The flowers are cream, darkening with age; the berries are deep crimson. A new honeysuckle called Clavey's dwarf makes a dense bush with gray green leaves and yellow flowers. It has some merit as a hedge plant in sheltered areas but is not showy enough for use as a specimen shrub.

The bush honeysuckles soon become decrepit and unshapely unless they are pruned regularly, cutting out old wood and reducing tall shoots to one-third their length to keep the bush neat.

Potentilla — The potentillas are a large group of plants, some woody, some herbaceous, that provide useful dwarf shrubs and a few hardy perennials. The woody plants are most important, the shrubby cinquefoil *(Potentilla fruticosa)* in its many improved forms being the most common. The primitive form is native to a wide area of the prairies, varying somewhat but generally a three- to four-foot shrub with dense foliage, medium to gray green, and yellow flowers. The improved forms are used freely in foundation plantings as hedges, specimens and group plantings. Near the house wall, where the soil and air tend to be dry, the cinquefoils will look rusty from infestations of spider mites but, where these insects are controlled and the plants are not allowed to suffer from drought, they have a long season of interest.

The five-part leaves are bright green on some varieties; the flowers vary a good deal in size and depth of color from the palest yellow to deep orange. Some of the popular varieties are Farreri, a two-foot plant with fine leaves and bright yellow flowers, Jackmanni, a taller but otherwise similar variety, and Coronation Triumph, a three-foot plant with yellow flowers. Moonlight and Primrose Beauty have pale flowers; Tangerine is orange yellow and tends to blanch with heat. There is some difference in the hardiness of these shrubby cinquefoils. All will be better adapted grown from native plants rather than from imported clones. A Manchurian species with white flowers is obtainable from some nurserymen; it makes a two-foot plant with large white blooms.

The potentillas are esteemed for their long season of bloom, which starts when the flush of spring-blooming spireas and lilacs is over and continues through the summer and fall. In full sun they can be depended on to flower freely; plants in shade will grow well but the flowers are not produced so freely.

Dogwood — The dogwoods range from lowly shrubs to stately trees. Some species found in the mild climate of the Pacific coast and in Florida have handsome, showy bracts, which are modified leaves, yellow or pinkish. These are not hardy on the prairies and, much as they are admired, there is no chance of their survival in a prairie garden. A number of hardy varieties make useful shrubs with showy, flat panicles of bloom and colorful bark. Some have variegated leaves, silvery or yellow, but the plants are not so robust as the plain-leaved kinds and in some areas, these variegated sorts are a failure.

The most widely planted variety is the Siberian dogwood *(Cornus alba sibirica)*, with brilliant bark color in late winter and early spring. The bark is a luminous coral red, contrasting sharply with the sombre green of spruce and pine and a ground cover of snow. The old wood is cut out every few years to encourage the development of young, colorful shoots. At the same time, a certain amount of pruning is necessary to maintain a neat bush.

A silver-leaved variety called Elegantissima *(C. alba argenta marginata)* is hardy in a partly shaded spot where the soil is moist but well drained. In open areas, it tends to suffer bark damage from sunscald and the top growth is desiccated by drying winds. Two golden variegated sorts, *C. alba gouchaulti* and *C. alba spaethii,* are not recommended for general use. In some favored spots they have both given some satisfaction. *Gouchaulti* seems hardier than *spaethii* but seems prone to attacks by leaf-rolling aphids.

A common species, the red osier dogwood *(C. stolonifera),* is not so attractive as the Siberian; the bark is dull red, the bush widely spreading and the foliage not attractive. The red osier dogwood is a useful filler shrub for full sun or partial shade. The yellowtwig dogwood *(C. stolonifera flaviramea)* has yellow green stems that light up the winter landscape in the manner of the Siberian dogwood. It seems to be quite hardy in a half-shaded spot where the soil is moist. The pagoda dogwood *(C. alternifolia)* makes a tall shrub with horizontal branches, a distinctive plant in the landscape although it has no colorful winter bark. In the eastern parts of its natural habitat it makes a fair-sized tree but in Manitoba, where it is extremely rare, it is a shrub.

Caragana — The Siberian peashrub *(Caragana arborescens),* or caragana as it is known to prairie gardeners, is one of the hardiest and most drought resistant of all shrubs. Millions have been planted since the prairie regions were first settled and millions more are needed in areas where even the hardiest trees need shelter. In its fresh greenery of spring, with handsome, bright yellow flowers, it is most attractive but, later on, it is usually dull and shabby. It has no special merit as a specimen shrub but the farm garden, in some areas exposed to high winds, will welcome the shelter of a caragana hedge.

The Sutherland caragana, which originated at the Forest Nursery Station, Sutherland, Saskatchewan, is an upright, slender form of the common caragana. It has merit as an accent shrub in the landscape because of its columnar form. A fern-leaf variety called Lorberg has fine leaves and makes a large, spreading shrub with graceful branches. *C. arborescens pendula,* a weeping form of the common caragana, has merit as an accent plant in the shrub border. It is grafted on stems of common caragana to make a cascade of branches that reaches the ground.

The pygmy caragana *(C. pgymaea)* is common in prairie gardens as a hedge and specimen dwarf shrub. It makes a neat, low hedge but the stems are wiry and hard to cut and the leaves are very susceptible to damage from spider mites. When used as a dwarf shrub in foundation plantings, it is often disfigured by mites and looks rusty by the end of the summer. In open, sunny positions, where the soil is well drained and where spider mites are not so likely to attack, it makes a spreading bush covered in early June with bright yellow flowers. The leaves are narrow, medium green; the branches are fine and liable to be flattened by heavy snow. A similar plant has more attractive foliage but is not so showy in bloom. This is the shortleaf caragana *(C. brevifolia).* The bright green leaves are very tiny and the plants have a fairly compact habit. Both the pygmy and the shortleaf caragana make neat edgings that can be close clipped to keep them a foot high; they make reasonably good substitutes for the box edging common in milder parts.

A select form of *C. microphylla* called Tidy originated at the Morden Experimental Farm. It is an improvement of the type plant, which tends to sprawl. Tidy has fine leaves and the plant is upright with a rounded head. A rare species called shagspire *(C. jubata)* is a dryland plant that is scarcely recognized as one of the tribe. It will grow on a dry mound in blazing sun where the soil is poor. The plant is unshapely, the branches clothed with long spines and shaggy hairs; the flowers are quite large and whitish. It has no merit as a garden plant except for those who are looking for collector's items. The Russian peashrub *(C. frutex)* has a deplorable suckering habit. The Globe caragana is a compact, nonsuckering form introduced by Dr. Skinner. It grows slowly into a neat, rounded bush and is a natural hedge plant as well as a fine specimen shrub for formal areas.

The Siberian salt tree *(Halimodendron halodendron),* a close relative of caragana, has leaves which are somewhat the same shape but tend to be gray green. The plants are seven or eight feet high, very spiny and, unless they are grafted on common caragana, they sucker badly. It is not uncommon to find young plants from suckers growing twenty feet from the old plant. The flowers are large and an attractive shade of soft rosy mauve. It has little merit as an ornamental shrub but its high tolerance of alkaline soil and usefulness as a hedge should not be overlooked.

Cotoneaster — The cotoneasters range from prostrate or decumbent plants to bushes and tall shrubs ten to twelve feet high. In some areas, fireblight has infected cotoneasters and occasionally the plants are severely injured but, in most parts of the prairies, the cotoneaster is generally accepted as one of the best of all hardy hedges. Its value as a specimen shrub is limited to one or two species with colorful berries. Cotoneasters lack the showy blooms of spirea and lilac but can be used sparingly as filler shrubs.

The species commonly used for hedges is the Pekin *(Cotoneaster lucida)*. It makes a dense bush that stands clipping to make a shapely hedge. The small leaves are dark green, glossy and quite colorful in the fall. The black fruits are not produced in any quantity when the plants are grown as a hedge but they add winter interest and provide food for the birds.

As a specimen shrub, the European red-berried cotoneaster *(C. integerrima)* has merit. It makes a more spreading bush than the Pekin, growing five feet high, with dull green leaves tending to be grayish on the undersides. It makes up for its 'poor foliage with a profusion of bright red berries in late summer. With careful pruning the bush can be shapely and fruitful to prolong interest in the shrub border or foundation planting.

Two showy cotoneasters, not fully hardy but of interest to the adventurous gardener, are the Sungary rockspray *(C. racemiflora soongarica)* and the multiflora *(C. multiflora)*. The Sungary has very large berries that ripen to a bright rosy red and arch the branches with their weight. The foliage is not attractive nor is it produced freely, but the species is worth trying in sheltered gardens if only for its showy fruit. The multiflora cotoneaster is one of the showiest in bloom; the flowers are freely produced on healthy plants and are followed by red berries. In the southern part of Manitoba, the multiflora may grow to six feet but it is considered too tender for most of the prairies. In the same hardiness class are several dwarfs which may be tried in well-sheltered gardens by those who like to experiment. The creeping cotoneaster *(C. adpressa)* has managed to stay alive and spread to cover an area of ten square feet in southern Manitoba and, although it occasionally kills back, it is attractive with small, glossy leaves and showy fruit. The rock cotoneaster *(C. horizontalis)*, which is admired in milder parts for its unique form, colorful leaves and berries and the herringbone pattern of the naked branches, will not succeed in prairie gardens.

All the cotoneasters do best in well-drained soil that is not too high in lime. Fireblight and scale insects may be troublesome occasionally but this should not deter you from using the hardiest ones for filler shrubs and hedges.

Mockorange — The mockorange *(Philadelphus),* or syringa as it is commonly called by some, encompasses a large group of shrubs ranging from two to twenty feet. Few are hardy enough for gardens all across the prairies but in most areas the hardiest sorts will grow reasonably well. Like the honeysuckle, the mockorange tends to be drab when not in bloom but, for old-world association, pure white blossoms and sweet scent, it is highly esteemed.

The many varieties of *P. lemoinei* include some of the most showy and sweet scented, but none are fully hardy. In well-sheltered gardens the enthusiast can look for them to bloom well occasionally when winter winds do not desiccate the branches. The hybrids of *P. coulteri,* a Mexican species, are far too tender for prairie gardens. They are greatly admired for their handsome, purple-blotched flowers and the sweetest scent of all the mockoranges. The virginal mockorange *(P. virginale)* is neither fully hardy nor especially attractive but in sheltered gardens it usually manages to produce its semidouble, sweet-scented flowers on wood that is below the snow line. The bush is unshapely, the large leaves dull, the winter appearance of the branches gray and cold.

The Manchurian mockorange *(P. schrenki)* and its variety *jackii* are the hardiest species and can be depended on to flower well if given reasonable care. In the milder parts of the southern prairies they grow six or seven feet high, bearing masses of creamy white, sweet-scented flowers in June. *P. lewisii* from the Rocky Mountain regions is fairly hardy and the variety Waterton is offered for sale by some prairie nurserymen. It makes a sturdy bush, six feet tall, with good foliage and a profusion of single white flowers in June.

Prairie plant breeders have produced a number of hybrid *philadelphus* which are hardy enough in most parts of the prairies. Several of these, raised by Dr. Skinner of Dropmore, Manitoba, make attractive shrubs with dense branches, good foliage and sweet-scented flowers. Galahad is one of the best, making a four-foot shrub with glossy leaves and pure white, scented flowers. Patricia, Mrs. Thompson and Purity are three more: Patricia has tiny, glossy leaves and creamy flowers very fragrant and profuse; Mrs. Thompson has medium, dark green leaves and white flowers; Purity has large, cup-shaped flowers freely produced and sweetly scented. Two hardy mockoranges developed at the Morden Experimental Farm, Audrey and Marjorie, are vigorous, tall-growing shrubs. Audrey makes a good background shrub eight feet high with fairly dense branches and masses of sweet-scented, creamy white bloom. Marjorie is taller and has limited use in the home garden. The vigorous branches produce a profusion of single white, scented blossoms in June. An earlier introduction from Morden called Sylvia is too tender except for a well-sheltered garden in the milder parts. At Morden it sometimes produces its sweet-scented, double flowers freely and its rich brown bark is attractive in winter. A variety from Minnesota called Snowflake is a more compact and upright form of virginal but it lacks full hardiness in prairie gardens.

The golden-leaved form of the sweet mockorange *(P. coronarius aureus)* is sometimes seen in prairie gardens but has little to recommend it. The plant is seldom vigorous, the bloom unattractive against the pale yellow leaves and, more often than not, it suffers severely in winter. The type plant, the common sweet mockorange, though not fully hardy is much preferred. A forty-year-old tree at Morden occasionally puts on a show of bloom to scent the evening air.

Ornamental prunus – Most of the members of the great tribe of prunus are cultivated for their fruit, but some have ornamental value and provide early interest in the shrub border. The commonest is the so-called double-flowering plum *(Prunus triloba multiplex),* which grows six or seven feet high and bears masses of pink flowers in late May. It is usually budded on wild plum, though plants on their own roots are obtainable. Unless the suckers from the plum stock, which are sometimes vigorous and prolific, are promptly removed, the double-flowering plum is liable to die. Plants on their own roots should be sought from prairie nurserymen. Imported plants may be grafted on tender understocks not suitable for prairie gardens. Those with aesthetic tastes will prefer the single form of *triloba;* some selections with glowing pink blossoms are choice though not often listed by nurserymen.

Select forms of the Russian almond *(P. tenella)* are available and recommended as the earliest pink-blooming shrub. The new forms are greatly improved and much preferred to the original Russian almond, which tends to spread rapidly by suckers and produces pale pink blossoms on sprawling plants. The new ones are upright, five feet high and bear masses of rich pink flowers in early May. The leaves are attractive through the summer and, if blooms have escaped frost, a quantity of ornamental fruit is produced. The plants are easy to grow on their own roots when softwood cuttings are taken in June using the modern methods of propagation. Suckers are no problem, though some are produced and may be dug out in the spring and replanted if required to increase stock. A hybrid with a select form of *P. tenella* as one of its parents and the Canada plum *(P. nigra)* as the other is called Muckle plum. It makes a lively show of bright pink blossoms in May, a few days later than the Russian almond. The leaves are halfway in size between those of the parents, dark green and free of blemish from insects or disease. There are no suckers, nor do the flowers produce fruit. Another hybrid *prunus,* Prairie Almond, has *P. triloba* as one parent and *P. pedunculata* as the other. It makes an attractive bush with masses of pale pink, darker-eyed flowers, and is fertile. Prairie Almond promises to be a stepping stone to better things but, like the double-flowering plum, it is best when grown on its own roots.

The redleaf plum *(P. cistena)* is not fully hardy; in favored areas it persists though it never gets very tall. Its chief merit is its reddish purple, shiny leaves, which are inherited from a purple-leaved form of the myrobalan plum. The other parent of the cross was the sandcherry.

The Shubert chokecherry *(P. virginiana Shubert)* has the peculiarity of turning its green leaves to purple, starting with mature leaves in June. By the end of July or sooner, all the leaves are purple. It makes a small tree unless it is regularly pruned, with rather coarse leaves and black fruit. It is not particularly handsome as the reverse side of the foliage is dull and, if it is budded on common chokecherry, suckers will be a nuisance.

The Mayday tree *(P. padus commutata)* makes a tree in favored areas, though it is sometimes seriously infected with black knot, a disfiguring fungus. A free-flowering form called Dropmore Mayday has long racemes of pure white flowers in mid-May.

The double-flowering pincherries, Stockton and Jumping Pound, have some merit as small trees but are not often planted. The Amur chokecherry *(P. maakii)* has a highly polished bark of rich coppery brown that is particularly attractive when the leaves have fallen and during the winter and early spring. It has no showy flowers or fruits nor are the leaves very handsome.

The Mongolian cherry *(P. fruticosa)* is grown chiefly for its fruit, which has a sprightly flavor. It also has merit as an ornamental plant for hedges or as a filler in the shrub border. The leaves are small, dark green and glossy; the branches are dense and fairly upright. Like some other members of the tribe, it produces plentiful suckers. Now that easy ways of propagating it have been found, it will be possible to produce select nonsuckering Mongolian cherries which have acceptable cherries as well as ornamental value.

The Nanking cherry *(P. tomentosa)* has edible fruit and showy bloom. The leaves are rough, medium sized, and the tip growth is sometimes killed by drying winter winds. As there are superior *prunus* species and hybrids blooming about the same time as the Nanking, it is not considered seriously as an ornamental shrub, but select forms with either red or yellow fruits are desirable.

Japonica — The shrub that is sometimes called Japonica by English people is *Chaenomales japonica* and is not really suitable for prairie gardens. Several forms have been tried with the same results; the shoots above the snow line perish, and occasionally the whole plant kills to the ground. When snow cover is early and deep, the pink or brilliant scarlet flowers are freely produced on lower branches; sometimes there are fruits which are quinces with no edible value, except that they contain large amounts of pectin and can be used with other kinds of fruit to make jam.

Forsythia — The forsythias are greatly admired for their wealth of bright yellow blooms in spring, especially by those who have seen them growing in the mild climate of the west coast and elsewhere. The kinds that grow in milder parts are useless here, where even the hardiest Korean golden bell *(Forsythia ovata)* may be killed back severely. In favored parts of the prairies, the Korean golden bell makes a five-foot shrub if given shelter and occasionally puts on a show of pale yellow flowers in early May. At other times the young wood is desiccated by cold, drying winds and the bloom, if any, is borne on the low, ground-level branches. Many new sorts are available but are too tender to be of much use in a prairie garden as they seldom produce bloom.

Hawthorn — Prairie gardeners have become more aware of the value of the hawthorn as an ornamental tall shrub or small tree since the introduction of the hybrid Toba. This is an interspecies cross developed at Morden a number of years ago. It is hardy in most parts of the prairies if sheltered from northwest winds and planted in well-drained, neutral soil. One of its parents is the fleshy hawthorn *(Crataegus succulenta);* the other is a double-flowering red form of the English may *(C. oxyacantha).* It has inherited the hardiness and good foliage of the fleshy hawthorn and the double flowers of the English may, though the color is pale pink deepening to carmine with age. Toba makes a vigorous small tree that needs some restraining if planted in a small garden.

There are a number of species that are showy in flower and fruit, hardy and quite ornamental. Where space is not limited and where the gardener has interest in a collection of trees and shrubs, these should be considered. The native fireberry hawthorn *(C. chrysocarpa)* is not to be overlooked in favor of exotic species; it makes a neat, rounded shrub up to ten feet, with showy, creamy white blooms and loads of scarlet berries in late summer. The Arnold hawthorn *(C. arnoldiana)* makes a sturdy, small tree with white flowers and bright crimson fruit; it is considered to be one of the best. There are many more, some with red, some with black berries; some have prodigious thorns long and sharp and some have handsome, deeply lobed leaves. The small garden will not, however, have room for more than one or two; the choice had best be restricted to Toba and the Arnold hawthorn.

Hydrangea — The hydrangeas with massive heads of blue, pink or white flowers, admired by those who live on the prairies, can only be grown as house plants here. The hardy species are limited to two that can be grown with reasonable chances of success, though attempts have been made to grow the climbing hydrangea *(Hydrangea petiolaris)* and a few others.

The most popular of the hardy sorts is the Peegee *(H. paniculata grandiflora)* and, although it abhors the dry prairie conditions, it is possible with special care to grow this handsome plant quite well. The name of the genus suggests water and this is what it wants but, at the same time, it should not be in soggy soil or the leaves soon turn yellow. In milder parts it is grown as a standard, single-stemmed specimen; in prairie gardens it must be kept low and should be pruned back severely in the spring. The flowers, which are produced on the young wood, are dense panicles, opening a creamy white and aging a deep pink. To grow the Peegee hydrangea well, it should be in rich, well-drained soil, sheltered from drying winds and well supplied with water from the time the leaves unfold until they fall in October.

The other hardy hydrangea, called Hills of Snow *(H. arborescens),* makes a medium-sized shrub with large leaves and heads of white flowers that are tinged slightly with green. Like the Peegee, it needs rich soil and moisture as well as protection from wind. In full sun, where the soil may be dry, it will be a poor thing but, if given a sheltered, east-facing spot and properly cared for, it can be quite showy. A new free-flowering clone called Annabelle produces large, roundish heads and creamy white blooms over a long period. It requires the same hard pruning in late April as recommended for the other hardy hydrangeas.

Elderberry — A number of elders are hardy and attractive shrubs for the prairie garden; the most popular is the cut-leaf form of the European red elder *(Sambucus racemosa)* called Redman. The lacy leaves, panicles of creamy flowers and the clusters of red berries make this a handsome, hardy shrub. It will be at its best in well-drained soil that is not too rich nor too moist. If it reverts to the type plant, chances are the soil is too heavily charged with nitrogen. A golden-leaved form with deeply cut leaves, *S. racemosa plumosa aurea,* has some ornamental value but should be used sparingly if at all in small gardens.

Ninebark — The ninebark, a close relative of the spireas, is an interesting, tall though not showy shrub. The arching branches bear clusters of creamy flowers and later the reddish seed pods are attractive. A golden-leaved form *(Physocarpus opulifolius luteus)* has limited use as an accent shrub.

Sumac — The smooth sumac *(Rhus glabra)* grows wild on dry hills in the eastern parts of the prairies, where it is admired for its handsome leaves and dense heads of reddish fruits. It has a few bad habits — suckering, gawkiness and bare lower branches. There is no place for it except in a large garden, where it demands a place in the sun and poor, well-drained soil. The glory of its autumn leaves, blood red for a brief period, places it in the front rank with the Amur maple and other shrubs that are esteemed for brilliant autumn foliage. A purple form of the smooth sumac with deeply cut leaves has not grown well in southern Manitoba.

The staghorn sumac *(R. typhina)* is a taller but similar shrub, not so hardy or desirable as the smooth sumac, though the curious naked branches, clothed with fine hairs to resemble a stag's horns, command attention. Another native, commonly called skunkbush *(R. trilobata),* has little merit as a specimen shrub and will be of interest only to those who have a flair for the uncommon. The leaves are small, divided into three sections; the flowers are greenish and the red fruit clusters are sticky. Like the leaves, they give off a pungent smell when handled.

A closely related plant, remembered by older gardeners as the smoke tree and formerly known as *R. cotinus,* is now correctly *Cotinus coggygria.* It is not fully hardy but those who have admired it elsewhere may try to grow it here. In most seasons, they must content themselves with leaves but occasionally, when winter is not so harsh, it will produce the sterile flowers and peculiar hairs that create an illusion of purple gray smoke. Spring pruning will be a regular chore in spite of selecting the best possible site, which will face southeast.

Euonymous – The common names used for members of the genus are numerous, including spindle tree, burning bush, wahoo, bush bittersweet and strawberry bush. There are several choice shrubs among them, from two-foot specimens to twenty-foot trees. A number are evergreen and mostly tender in prairie gardens; a few of the deciduous ones have handsome fruits and brilliant leaves in September.

The dwarf euonymous or burning bush *(Euonymus nana)* has narrow, dark green leaves that are retained through the winter under the snow. It makes a sprawling, two-foot plant, useful in certain areas where the soil is poor and dry. The bright pink seed pods, hanging down on long stems, split open to reveal orange scarlet seeds in the manner of the bittersweet. A variety from Turkestan *(E. nana turkestanica)* makes a taller and neater plant that loses its topmost leaves; sometimes the tip growth is killed.

The winged euonymus *(E. alata)* makes a choice hedge or specimen shrub, with pale green leaves in summer changing to brilliant orange in September. A dwarf variety *(E. alata compacta),* three feet high, has brilliant orange red leaves in certain areas; in others, the color is not so good. It seems to do best where the soil is not too rich but well drained and calcareus. Both the type plant and the compact form have showy red fruit, quite small but produced freely on established plants in full sun. The twigs and small branches are curiously winged with corky appendages which are obvious when the leaves fall. A species called *maakii* makes a ten-foot shrub, has good foliage and a profusion of orange and red fruits. The European spindle tree and the improved forms such as *aldenhamensis* are not fully hardy and are subject to mildew in some areas.

Tamarisk – The Amur tamarisk *(Tamarix pentandra)* has graceful branches with scale-like leaves and pink or reddish plumes of billowy flowers in late summer. Although the Amur tamarisk is the hardiest of the genus, its tip shoots are damaged occasionally. The injury to the young wood makes little difference, as hard pruning is done in the spring in any case to encourage new shoots and showy bloom. It is tolerant of dry soil and heat, looks well when viewed at close range and makes a distinctive summer hedge. Several other species have been tried without success, though some are apparently root hardy.

Viburnum — The viburnums are a large group of shrubs, mostly deciduous and ranging from a few dwarf forms two or three feet high to twenty-foot spreading trees. The evergreen species are too tender for the prairies; the common lauristinus *(Viburnum tinus)*, a winter-flowering species, is esteemed in mild climates and is native to the Mediterranean regions.

A number of hardy viburnums are available; some have handsome flowers or fruits and some have attractive autumn color. The American highbush cranberry *(V. trilobum)* grows over a large area of the prairies, usually in moist, shady spots. Select dwarf forms make useful shrubs for the small garden, but usually the native plants grow six or seven feet high. The deeply lobed leaves are medium green, then reddish; the flowers are flat clusters of creamy white in June. The bunches of berries are bright crimson by September and hang on the bush through winter. The European highbush cranberry *(V. opulus)* is a similar but more compact plant. The leaves are usually attacked in June by aphids and the plants lack the brilliant autumn color of the American highbush cranberry.

The common snowball tree or guelder rose *(V. opulus rosea)* is a form with round heads of white flowers in June. The flowers are sterile, so no fruit is developed. The leaves are often disfigured by aphids, which curl the edges inwards. Early spraying before the aphids are safe in the curled leaves gives control. The wayfaring tree *(V. lantana)* makes a spreading shrub with handsome leaves and flat clusters of white flowers. The fruit is first green, then red and finally purple black; the leaves are not colorful in the fall. The nannyberry *(V. lentago)* makes an upright shrub over ten feet high with shiny leaves and large panicles of creamy white flowers in June. The flowers are followed by bunches of black berries; the leaves are red in the fall.

Some of the choice viburnums have been tried at the Morden Experimental Farm with little success. The Koreanspice *(V. carlesii),* for example, has flowered on the low branches occasionally but is considered much too tender for the prairies. Like the fragrant viburnum *(V. fragrans),* which is a tender species from China, the Koreanspice bears clusters of very sweet-scented flowers which appear before the leaves unfold. Several hybrids with the Koreanspice as one parent are available but are not hardy; only the knowledgeable gardener who is prepared to give them special care will be inclined to plant them.

The hardy viburnums require little pruning to keep them in shape. Old wood is removed when the flowers fade; occasionally, it may be necessary to hard prune the highbush cranberry in late April.

Weigela — The weigelas are popular shrubs in milder parts, where they are esteemed for their showy pink or red flowers. A hardy species from Manchuria bears the misleading name *Weigela florida venusta.* A selection from this species, introduced by Dr. Skinner and named Dropmore Pink, proved to be the only weigela of any value on the prairies until recently. For a number of years it has bloomed regularly in some areas, making a rounded shrub about four or five feet high. A new one called Centennial, raised at the Morden Experimental Farm, promises to extend the range of weigelas across the prairies. The Dropmore Pink or Manchurian weigela was used as the seed parent in the cross that produced Centennial, the pollen parent being Pink Profusion. The new hybrid has vigor and hardiness and a habit of dense growth. The flowers are freely produced, two or more in clusters along the stem, and the color may be described as an attractive shade of old rose.

The weigelas have no particular merit after the flowers have faded; the leaves are not attractive nor do they color in the fall. The varieties Bristol Ruby, Eva Rathke, Pink Profusion and others which are grown in milder parts are useless here. The Manchurian or Dropmore Pink and the new Centennial are hardy and reliable in a sheltered garden, planted on the east side of shelter and in moist soil.

False spirea — The false spirea is a common shrub with attractive compound leaves and creamy plumes in early July. It grows well in shade and prefers neutral or slightly acid soil. It spreads by suckers which are freely produced but not difficult to control. The seed pods ripen a rich brown and are not unattractive. In some areas it may be necessary to prune the branches low in the spring but, in most parts of the prairies, the false spirea is fully hardy and requires little spring pruning. The common false spirea *(Sorbaria sorbifolia)* is the one most frequently seen in prairie gardens; it sometimes reaches more than five feet when planted on the north side of buildings where the soil is moist. A species called the Kashmir false spirea *(S. aitchisoni)* has reddish stems and huge panicles of creamy flowers. It is not fully hardy, but survives in favored spots and sometimes puts on a show of bloom.

Snowberry — The western snowberry or buckbrush *(Symphoricarpos occidentalis)* is an abominable weed of the dry prairies. The snowberry *(S. albus)* and its variety *laevigatus* are sometimes cultivated and have merit in shaded areas. The leaves are dark green and dense; the flowers are inconspicuous but the soft white berries add late interest.

Flowering currant — The most handsome of the flowering currants, *Ribes speciosa,* with its brilliant red pendulant flowers, is not hardy on the prairies and there is no acceptable substitute. The hardy currants are represented by the golden currant *(R. aureum)*, the Alpine currant *(R. alpina)*, the clove currant *(R. odoratum)*, the Siberian currant *(R. diacanthum)* and a dwarf hybrid of the wild gooseberry called Dakota. The Alpine and Siberian currants are most useful as hedges or specimen shrubs in the foundation border. They are not showy in bloom or fruit but the bright green leaves are attractive as long as they are free of spider mites and leaf spot. The golden currant makes a five-foot bush with yellow flowers and black edible currants. It is found wild in some parts of the southern prairies and is said to be plentiful on the southern slopes of the Cypress Hills in Saskatchewan. The clove currant is a similar but superior plant, with yellow flowers bearing a rich spicy scent and large, sweet black currants. The hybrid gooseberry Dakota Dwarf *(R. missourienses hybrida)* makes a dense, four-foot bush with attractive dark glossy leaves that mature to a rich bronze.

Russian olive — The Russian olive makes a small tree or spreading shrub with narrow silvery leaves and sweet-scented yellow flowers in late June. It is not a long-lived tree and in some parts of the prairies it may not get to be more than a spreading, tall shrub. It must have well-drained soil, not too rich nor too wet. It is tolerant of dry alkaline soil and intense heat but may be injured by frost and drying winds. The hardiest strains make substantial trees in sheltered gardens and may be used to good effect as hedge plants.

Silverberry — The native silverberry or wolf willow *(Elaeagnus commutata)* is not often planted, and those who have dug it from the upland meadows have been disappointed more often than not. It has a deplorable suckering habit and a need for poor, dry soil that tends to be alkaline. It varies a good deal in height: some plants are three feet high; others grow to six feet or taller. The silvery leaves are most attractive; the yellow flowers, which are freely produced in clusters in the leaf axils, scent the air with a heady perfume. Like other native plants, the silverberry is difficult to establish in the home garden, but it is possible to grow it on sunny banks where the soil is lean and well drained.

Buffaloberry — The buffaloberry *(Shepherdia argentea)* found wild around sloughs and coulees is a thorny, tall shrub with gray leaves and red berries. It is sometimes planted as an ornamental tall shrub or windbreak but it has no place in the home garden. It is subject to leafhoppers that fly up when the branches are disturbed; suckers are another nuisance.

Seabuckthorn — The common seabuckthorn *(Hippophae rhamnoides)* or Russian sandthorn is not often planted in prairie gardens, though it is hardy and the bright orange fruits which are produced only on female plants are most attractive. Plants of both sexes are needed, so only in the large garden is it practical to grow them. The common seabuckthorn makes a tall shrub with narrow, gray green leaves. The fruit is produced in dense clusters and remains on the tree through the winter.

Nine

Hedges

When the early settlers first came to the prairies, they surrounded their homes with hedges for shelter and privacy. Caragana and lilac were used extensively, both hardy and well adapted as hedge plants. Since the early days there have been changes in the architectural styles of prairie homes and gardens and, while hedges of caragana and common lilac no longer mark the boundaries of home grounds as they once did, they do play an important part in landscape gardening.

Types and Uses of Hedges

There are many uses for a hedge; it can be a garden ornament, a thing of beauty in itself, or it may have utilitarian value as well. A hedge may be a live screen to hide an unsightly object; a tall hedge may provide shelter or a background of greenery for a flower border. The living-out area of the home garden, where comfortable seats are provided and facilities for cooking are available, can be enjoyed to the full in these days of more leisure; the shelter and privacy afforded by hedges add to that enjoyment. The three well-defined areas of the home garden can be separated by hedges; a medium-tall hedge may be used to screen the service and clothes-drying area from the outdoor living room or pleasure garden; a low hedge makes a tidy and attractive division between the flower garden and the vegetable patch beyond.

The design of modern homes and public buildings seems to lend itself to the use of hedges at their foundations: low-cut hedges accentuate the horizontal lines of some buildings; curved hedges and those which have been trimmed to a turreted top, which leaves regular sections of the hedge taller than the rest, can enhance the beauty of buildings with low horizontal lines.

The home gardener must decide for himself whether or not he needs a hedge, keeping in mind the space he has and also the cost of maintaining a hedge in good condition. Hedges are sometimes planted along driveways and, while a neat hedge looks well enough in such a spot, chances are it will trap snow, piling it in the driveway where it becomes a nuisance. Give serious thought to the kind of hedge for a particular place — is it for shelter and privacy. If so, it must be five or six feet high to be of much use. With the long prairie winter in mind you may decide on an evergreen hedge; a six-foot hedge of native or Colorado spruce will keep out the wind and give a comfortable feeling of warmth. You may feel a need of relief from the sombre green of evergreens and the bare whiteness of snow; if so, plant a hedge with colorful bark, a redstem willow or Siberian dogwood.

The cost of a hedge and the upkeep of it must be seriously considered too. Evergreen hedges, for example, are more costly to buy than deciduous ones, but they require far less trimming to keep them in good shape. A once-yearly pruning keeps most evergreen hedges tidy, whereas some deciduous hedges need to be trimmed three or four times a year. There is another important consideration in making the choice between deciduous or evergreen; when an evergreen hedge becomes old and decrepit, there is no way to rejuvenate it. It should be rooted out and replaced with young plants. A deciduous hedge, on the other hand, pruned back to the old wood, will start new shoots to make a new hedge.

Some consideration should be given to soil and site. Certain plants are healthy in alkaline soil; others not tolerant of it soon become sick. Saltbush, buffaloberry and Russian olive are examples of plants that grow well in alkaline soil to make good hedges. Pines, Amur maple, species of malus and pyrus and Japanese roses are examples of plants that thrive in neutral or slightly acid soil.

Hedges, like trees and shrubs, should be in proportion to their surroundings. A tall hedge along the front of the property will make the house appear to be closer to the sidewalk than it really is. Unless a front hedge is kept very dwarf, it will detract from the look of the property as a whole. Plants with coarse leaves, such as those of the Chinese lilac (Syringa villosa), have no place in a small home garden. On the other hand, fine-textured, small-leaved plants will tend to give the effect of spaciousness. In farm gardens, hedges can be more informal when used as windbreaks or to relieve the boundless open spaces of the prairies; hedges with larger and coarser leaves can be used and those with purple or golden foliage, whereas in the small garden such plants are out of place.

Some hedges are thorny or grow so densely they keep out animals. Hawthorn and barberry are useful for this purpose, as are the saltbush and pygmy caragana. The fireberry hawthorn *(Crataegus chrysocarpa)* and the fleshy hawthorn *(C. succulenta)* are native species useful as hedge plants. The saltbush *(Halimodendron halodendron)* and the pygmy caragana *(Caragana pygmaea)* make dense, spiny hedges. The multiflora rose *(Rosa multiflora),* widely advertised as a "living fence," grows into an impenetrable thicket of spiny branches in the milder parts of the continent but it is useless in prairie gardens. The roots are hardy enough but the top growth kills to the snow line or below. The Altai rose *(Rosa altaica)* and the Hensen's hedge rose are fully hardy and both will make satisfactory informal hedges.

Hedges with colorful bark – The following hedge plants can be used effectively to brighten up the winter landscape if the plants are coppiced, a form of pruning where last year's shoots are cut back to leave stubs two or three inches long. The new growth has the most colorful bark.

> Siberian dogwood *(Cornus alba sibirica)*
> golden willow *(Salix alba vitellina)*
> redstem willow *(Salix alba chermesina)*
> little-leaf linden *(Tilia cordata)*

Hedges that bloom – Some hedge plants have showy bloom; lilacs and a number of spireas are examples. When grown for this purpose, an entirely different pruning technique has to be followed, which is explained in detail on page (105).

Several spireas make good flowering hedges; the threelobe, the garland and the Vanhoutte have arching stems covered with clusters of white flowers in June. The garland spirea *(Spirea arguta)* and the Vanhoutte spirea *(S. vanhouttei)* are suitable for some parts of the prairies, though occasionally they suffer some winter injury. When this happens, they are cut down in April and the bloom is sacrificed for that year. The Oriental spirea *(S. media sericea)* and the Pikow spirea *(S. pikoviensis)* make good flowering hedges; both are hardier than the garland and the Vanhoutte. The Anthony Waterer and Froebel spireas are not so spreading and the pink flowers are borne later.

The common lilac is one of the best flowering hedges, although its prolific suckers can be a nuisance unless a regular once-a-year desuckering is done in October. The Altai rose makes a good flowering hedge with moderate suckering; the single cream flowers are borne in great profusion during late June. Though the flowers are fleeting, lasting only a few days should the weather be hot and dry, the glistening black fruits that follow are of long-season interest.

Hedges that grow quickly — The home gardener wants a hedge to grow quickly; at the same time, he doesn't want to spend too much time trimming it, and a fast-growing hedge will need trimming far more often than one that grows slowly. The Siberian elm *(Ulmus pumila)* is the fastest-growing hardy hedge plant. It is not unusual for young, vigorous plants to grow three feet in one season. The hardy Manchurian strain of *U. pumila,* which is sometimes called Dropmore, Harbin, Manchua or Chinkota elm, has slender twigs and small leaves. The bush honeysuckle *(Lonicera tatarica),* the Amur maple *(Acer ginnala)* and the Siberian peashrub *(Caragana arborescens)* also grow fairly rapidly but not so fast as the Siberian elm.

The Planting and Care of Hedges

Choosing the stock — When the decision to plant a hedge has been made and the most suitable kind chosen, the next step is to know the best-sized plants to set out. Young, vigorous stock will make the best deciduous hedges. Two- or three-year-old plants that have been once transplanted in the nursery are easy to grow, cheaper to buy and more satisfactory in every way than larger specimens. If you have a long stretch of hedge to plant, the cost of the plants may be a factor in determining what size to use. One-year-old seedlings may not have much fibrous root but you can buy them at half the cost of transplanted stock. With a little extra care in planting, they will come along satisfactorily to make a good hedge, though they will take a year longer.

A well-kept evergreen hedge is superior to a deciduous one but it will cost more to buy and will need extra care in transplanting. Young, foot-high plants are the best for making a hedge; older ones make a hedge faster but they cost a great deal more. Where cost is not a prime concern, two- to three-foot spruce trees, moved with a ball of soil on the roots and planted in a straight row, will give the appearance of a hedge immediately. You can do the same thing with the hardy pyramidal cedar *(Thuja occidentalis)*. Brandon is the hardiest form of pyramidal cedar thriving all across the prairies. Pines, on the other hand, must be planted while still young; three- or four-year-old seedlings with bare roots can be transplanted safely in early May. The pines do best in sandy, well-drained soil that is not too heavily charged with lime.

Preparing the soil for a hedge — In most parts of the prairie region the soil is fertile and deep, requiring no special preparation before planting a hedge. In any case, it should be dug over or rotovated a foot deep, removing all perennial weeds. If quack grass gets a footing in a newly planted hedge it will be hard to eradicate without disturbing the roots of the hedge plants. Besides this, weeds of any sort sap the soil moisture to debilitate the young plants. Where the soil is light and low in humus, dig in three or four inches of well-rotted barnyard manure. Do this in the autumn in readiness to set out the plants in the spring as soon as the soil is workable.

Spring planting is best for deciduous hedges; evergreens can be planted in mid-May, August or in early September. Autumn planting is much preferred for evergreens but only if the soil is moist or a satisfactory means of watering is available. The main disadvantages of setting out evergreen hedge plants in the spring is the danger of hot, dry weather striking the plants before they get a chance to become rooted in the new soil. Evergreens transpire moisture constantly, whereas the leaf buds of deciduous plants are dormant in the spring and the plants therefore in less danger of drying out.

Planting a hedge – For deciduous hedges of medium height, space the plants one and one-half feet apart in a single row. Low hedges which are used to line the front of properties may be spaced a foot apart; tall ones for windbreaks or informal barriers may be spaced two feet between each plant.

Years ago, when hedges were made by planting a double row of caragana or lilac, they soon became so wide that trimming was made difficult. A single row of plants will make the best kind of hedge; it can be kept at a reasonable width, whereas a double row of plants not only increases the cost of plants and planting, but makes more work when it comes to trimming.

The actual planting is simple enough. You need a garden line and a shovel or spade to dig the holes. Stretch the line tight where the hedge is to be planted; mark off the divisions at the proper spacing, then dig the holes. Make them large enough to hold the roots without crowding.

Make sure to keep the roots of the young plants in moistened sacking. Do not lay the plants out on the top of the soil where they are exposed to the air. Small plants may be carried conveniently in a pail partly filled with water. Set the plants a little deeper than they were when growing in the nursery row, placing them in the centre of the hole, then filling in with fine soil. Gently shake the plant to settle the soil around the roots, then make it very firm by tramping.

The importance of firm planting cannot be stressed too often; plants in loose soil, especially when the weather is warm with drying winds, will soon perish unless they are firmed and watered. When the planting is finished, leave a saucer-shaped depression around each plant; fill the depressions with water to give each plant a thorough soaking and let the water seep away before levelling the soil.

Pruning and shaping deciduous hedges — When one- or two-year-old deciduous plants are used for hedge making and set out in early May, cut them back to six or nine inches above ground level. This hard pruning will force new shoots to start from the base to lay the foundation of a dense hedge. Homeowners who are anxious to enjoy the shelter and privacy of a new hedge will be reluctant to carry out such drastic pruning, but the wise gardener will realize the need of hard pruning to give a thick hedge. When older plants are used, the pruning should not be so severe, cutting back about one-third of the top growth. The aim is to get a bushy hedge as quickly as possible; the best way to do it is to prune the plants properly at planting time to develop a hedge with many low branches and twiggy shoots. Unless the deciduous hedge plants are cut back when you plant them, they grow leggy and you never have a satisfactory hedge.

The hedge plant received from the nursery must be vigorously cut back at planting to encourage strong shoots to develop from the base.

The kind of hedge you get will depend to a large extent on the way the young plants are cared for. The most important phase of hedge making comes in the early stages of the plant's development. To build a dense, thick hedge, a good foundation must be laid by proper pruning and shaping while the plants are still young and before they have grown too large. The shape of your hedge may be a matter of preference; there are good shapes and bad shapes, but the practical gardener will realize that a rounded or pyramidal hedge is preferred in prairie gardens since flat-topped hedges are more liable to be broken down by the weight of snow. There is another important reason why a pyramidal hedge should be chosen. A hedge with a broad, flat top will shade the lower branches and, without the benefit of sunshine, the lower twigs will die to leave bare spaces. To keep the lower parts healthy, the hedge is trimmed to a shape that is wider at the bottom than it is at the top. To be in good proportion, a pyramidal hedge should be two and one-half feet wide at the ground and five feet high; the top should be slightly rounded and not more than a foot wide. Another advantage of a narrow pyramidal hedge is that there is no wide top to trim. When first shaping the hedge, use a garden line to keep the top level.

Some hedges that grow fast will need trimming more often than those that grow slowly. Some can be kept neat and tidy with an annual trim; others need several prunings to keep them in shape. There is a tendency to cut deciduous hedges too soon; it should be remembered that the plant needs its leaves to manufacture food. When most of the first crop of leaves is cut off, the plant's growth is seriously retarded. The proper time to give the deciduous hedges their first trim of the season is mid-June in most parts of the prairies and a week later in northern areas. The hedges that require more than one trimming should receive the last one not later than early September.

Pruning and shaping evergreen hedges — Evergreens such as spruce, juniper and cedar *(Arborvitae)* are not pruned in the same way as deciduous hedge plants. No pruning is done at planting time and practically none is needed for two or three years afterwards. A hedge of young spruce trees, planted in the spring two feet apart, should have the leader or tip shoot pinched out in July of the following year. At the same time, check the side branches to see that they are not out of line; if they are, snip them off.

GOOD HEDGE FORMS

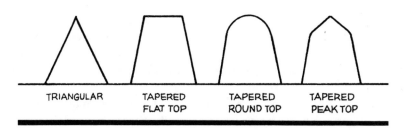

| TRIANGULAR | TAPERED FLAT TOP | TAPERED ROUND TOP | TAPERED PEAK TOP |

POOR HEDGE FORMS

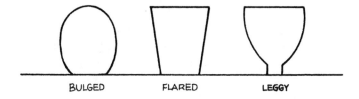

| BULGED | FLARED | LEGGY |

Coniferous evergreens will not recover when branches are cut off to the main trunk. Whatever pruning is needed should be done once a year, in early July, when the current year's growth is completed. Only a portion of the young, current year's growth should be cut and, while the hedge is young, a pruning knife or secateurs should be used. As the hedge becomes denser, pruning is more rapidly done with a pair of hedge shears.

PRUNING PINES

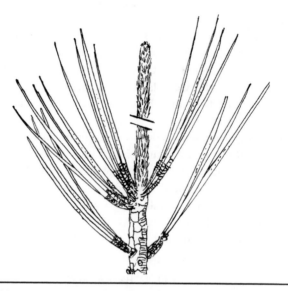

Cuts should only be made at a point half-way down the new candle or shoot — never back to the old wood.

Pine hedges, especially those of the long-needled species, always look more attractive when they are carefully trimmed with a knife or secateurs. When the long needles are mutilated with the hedge shears, the natural beauty of a pine hedge is lost.

Hedges of the eastern white cedar have a longer season of growth than those of spruce; a second trimming in early September will keep them neat and tidy. You can trim them closely, using a sharp pair of hedge shears.

Topiary — A type of hedge trimming popular in Victorian times known as topiary has long since fallen out of favor, though there are still to be found some examples in European gardens. Figures of birds, animals, even chessmen were shaped at the top of slow-growing plants such as yew and holly. This style of hedge trimming fitted in with the formal and geometric garden designs then in vogue. It took considerable time to keep the "birds" and "animals" in shape and required a good deal of skill. Occasionally one sees attempts at this sort of thing with the kind of hedges we grow in prairie gardens but, as a rule, the results are not worth the effort required.

Pruning flowering hedges – If hedges are planted to provide a show of bloom, they cannot be sheared in the summer or the wood that produces the bloom will be cut off. Common lilac, spireas and shrub rose hedges should be pruned every second or third year by cutting out the old wood to ground level and reducing the other shoots to keep the hedge in shape. The common lilac suckers badly; some kinds will produce a forest of suckers that spread rapidly to widen the hedge and sap moisture and nourishment needed by the main branches. To keep a lilac hedge within bounds and to build up the current year's shoots so that they bloom profusely the following year, ruthlessly destroy the suckers by chopping them out either in the spring or fall while the plants are bare of leaves.

Maintaining hedges with colorful bark – Willow hedges, either golden or redstem, must be cut back every year in April to produce the young wands that are colorful in the winter and early spring. The previous year's shoots are cut back, leaving two or three buds. These will develop into six-foot wands by the end of the season. The old branches of the Siberian dogwood should be cut out in the spring to encourage young shoots to start from the base. These, like the shoots of the willows, will light up the winter landscape with their highly colored bark. The three-year-old branches of the Siberian dogwood should be cut back to a foot from the ground in early spring so that new shoots will start from the base.

What to do with an old hedge – Old deciduous hedges that have become shabby and unthrifty may be restored to health and vigor by hard pruning. A tall caragana or lilac hedge, for example, can be rejuvenated in one year, starting in October by cutting down the main branches to a height of two feet. The side shoots are left until the following April, when they are cut off close to the remaining branches. The skeleton outline of the hard-pruned hedge should be in the same proportion of width to height as it was formerly. No further pruning is done until the following year, except to reduce the most vigorous shoots to half their length in July. Thereafter, the pattern of pruning will be the same as outlined for a young hedge.

Evergreen hedges that have lost their beauty through old age cannot be restored as deciduous ones can be; the plants will not grow new shoots from the old wood. Since there is no way of pruning an old evergreen hedge to rejuvenate it, dig it out in the fall, replacing it with young stock in the spring.

Old hedges of hawthorn, hardy pear or crabapple that have become shabby may be restored to their former health and vigor by a method of pruning called layering. This is done in April when the old wood is cut back to stubs one and one-half feet high. The young, thin shoots are then pulled down to a horizontal position and tied to the stubs with strong twine. New shoots soon appear from the horizontal branches to furnish the base of the hedge with new growth. By the end of the season, the wounds will have healed, the stubs covered with new shoots and the hedge will look as good as new.

Fertilizing hedges — In most parts of the prairies the soil is rich in plant nutrients. Hedges planted in rich soil often continue to grow late in the season as a result of too much nitrogen; when this happens, the soft shoots are liable to winter injury. On the other hand, hedge plants that have been growing for a number of years, producing young shoots only to have them pruned back several times each year, will exhaust the soil of nitrogen and phosphate. The leaves will pale and get smaller; the lower twigs will become unthrifty and die. When these signs are obvious, the soil needs to be built up with rotted barnyard manure and chemical fertilizer. Three or four inches of rotted barnyard manure should be spread along the base of the hedge to make a foot-wide strip on either side. Turn the manure into the soil by shallow digging to avoid disturbing the hedge roots. The summer rains will make soluble the nutrients in the manure, gradually releasing them to feed the roots.

Chemical fertilizers, applied at the rate of one pound to each ten feet of hedge, will give immediate response if made soluble by water or rain; dry fertilizer does no more good in the soil than it does in the bag. Old hedges should have the fertilizer distributed on each side at a point in line with the edge of the lowest branches. Rake it in or cover it with a mulch, then soak the whole area with water from the garden hose. Use either 27.14.0 or 11.48.0, applying the first dose in May, a second one in September.

Summer mulching — A layer of rotted manure, peat or garden compost will be beneficial as a summer mulch in keeping the soil cool and conserving moisture. A summer mulch works wonders in those parts of the prairies where weeks of drought are the rule rather than the exception. Besides the manure, peat and garden compost, straw and lawn clippings can be used effectively. A newly planted hedge can be helped greatly to withstand heat and drought by laying on a mulch in early July. A thin layer of peat, not more than one inch thick, will be just as effective as deeper layers of the other suggested materials.

Insects — Hedge plants, like all others, are subject to insects and diseases. Be on the lookout for the leaf-eating caterpillars in June. They come in a variety of colors and sizes and often do a lot of damage before the gardener is aware of their presence. Spray with stomach poison as soon as damage is observed.

Spider mites cause severe damage to some hedges; the deciduous ones — potentilla, pigmy caragana and honeysuckles — are most likely to be infested. Spider mites are hard to see with the naked eye but, if you let them build up large populations, the damage they do soon becomes obvious and the plants are seriously weakened. Evergreens, too, can be seriously damaged by spider mites; look for them on spruce and cedar *(Arborvitae)* hedges when the needles turn palish and the plants look unthrifty. By saturating the plants with Kethane or Aramite, following the instructions on the package, you can easily control spider mites. Both these chemicals are effective insecticides if mixed in the right proportions and applied to the foliage, directing the spray to the undersides of the leaves when spraying deciduous plants. During the hot, dry weather of July and August, spray your hedge with water under high pressure from the garden hose. If you do this occasionally, preferably in the cool evening, spider mites will find it difficult to get a footing.

Aphids or plant lice are fast-breeding insects; most species are shades of green, though some are black, gray or reddish brown. Sometimes enormous populations are built up on willow, American elm, hawthorn, spruce and other hedge plants. Being soft bodied, they are very susceptible to contact sprays of Malathion or Black Leaf 40 (nicotine sulphate). A teaspoonful mixed in a gallon of soapy water is enough to kill them.

Several species of scale insects attack certain hedge plants, the most common being scurfy scale and pine needle scale. Scurfy scale, a waxy, gray substance about an eighth of an inch long under which hide colonies of insects that suck the plant's juices, can do tremendous damage to cotoneaster, hawthorn, crabapple and hardy pear before the cause of the trouble is found. There is no scale on the leaves; the insects are confined to the branches and twigs, where they remain under a wax tent or scale for most of the year. In June, usually when the lilacs are in bloom, they emerge to wander around to start new colonies. When the infestation is heavy, the hedge soon becomes unthrifty; the leaves get smaller, paler and whole sections of the hedge will die out.

Pine needle scale, found on all species of pine, fir and spruce, is white, large enough to be seen with the naked eye and most likely to be found on hedges in sheltered gardens where the circulation of air is poor. The best remedy is to saturatte the plants in early June, or when the lilacs are in bloom, using four tablespoonfuls of Malathion (fifty percent emulsible concentrate) in a gallon of water, adding a tablespoonful of detergent if the water is hard. A second dose, applied in August, will take care of any females which may have escaped the first spray.

Diseases — Certain hedges, such as cotoneaster, wild pear, crabapple and Saskatoon or serviceberry, are subject to attacks of fireblight. This is a serious bacterial disease with devastating results to highly susceptible varieties. It is recognized by the scorched appearance of the young shoots and leaves turning brown; when it attacks the pear, the leaves turn black. The dead leaves cling to the shoots and cankers form at the base of the infected wood. In June, when the weather is hot and humid, fireblight is most likely to strike as the new shoots are lush and more easily infected. The disease spreads rapidly, being transmitted by bees and other insects. There is no satisfactory chemical control for fireblight, though treatment with streptomycin is said to give some measure of control. You can prevent the spread of fireblight by cutting the infected branches well below the point of infection as soon as the disease is seen. The pruning tools should be disinfected after each cut by dipping them in lysol and the prunings should be promptly burnt.

Some hedges are liable to be infected with mildew, an unsightly and debilitating disease that disfigures the leaves and tender shoots of alpine currant, common lilac and a number of other hedge plants. Powdery mildew is recognized by the masses of grayish white fungus growth on young leaves and stems. When the attack is severe, the leaves, young shoots and flower buds are greatly distorted. The fungus damages the plants by sending out growths that feed on the tender stems and foliage. Late in the season, tiny black spores can be seen in the masses of gray mildew; these are the resting spores that can winter over on fallen leaves. It may seem strange that mildew is a problem in areas of low rainfall but this is so, due to the dry air that ripens the spores and the high humidity at the surface of the young shoots at night. The disease usually makes an appearance late in the season, when cooler nights and heavy dews provide optimum conditions for the rapid propagation of the spores. A standard old-time remedy is flowers of sulphur dusted on the infected plants while the leaves are wet with dew. Karathane is a more modern chemical for the control of mildew; use it according to the directions on the container.

Leaf spot diseases can seriously disfigure the foliage of alpine currant, hawthorn, caragana and a number of other deciduous plants. Infection is most likely to be heavy in periods of damp, humid weather. Captan or some other fixed copper fungicide, applied at ten-day intervals, will keep leaf spot in check. When the chemical is washed off by rain, the plants are liable to be reinfected by new spores, airborne from adjacent diseased plants.

Whatever methods of insect or disease control are applied, none is effective unless the insects are contacted with the chemical, or the leaves poisoned and the disease-preventative chemical kept on the foliage for as long as the spores are present.

Deciduous Hedges for the Prairies

In deciding what to plant to make a suitable hedge, first consider how tall you want it — a dwarf hedge up to two feet high, a medium-low hedge between two and three feet, a medium-tall hedge four or five feet or one that is to be maintained at six feet or higher. There are plenty of good hedges in each of these height ranges; some are more expensive to buy than others and some take more looking after.

Dwarf hedges — First choice among the dwarf hedges are pygmy caragana *(C. pygmae),* Alpine currant *(Ribes alpina),* bush cinquefoil *(Potentilla fruticosa),* dwarf euonymus *(E. nana)* and the Pallas buckthorn *(Rhamnus pallasii).* All these, planted a foot to fifteen inches apart in a single row, will make splendid dwarf hedges which may be closely trimmed without harming the plants.

The pygmy caragana tends to broaden at the base unless you narrow it by cutting the low branches close while they are still dormant in the spring. The shoots, being very wiry, are hard to cut unless a well-sharpened pair of hedge shears are used. Unless spider mites are controlled, the pygmy caragana hedge will look rather rusty by the end of the summer.

The Alpine currant, one of the most popular low hedges, makes a dense, twiggy hedge with small, bright green leaves. Like the pygmy caragana, it tends to broaden at the base but may be kept narrow by occasionally pruning back the dormant low shoots in the spring. Leaf spot disease can mar the foliage causing premature leaf drop.

The bush cinquefoil makes a neat hedge or may be grown informally to preserve the bloom. The leaves are fine, medium green on some varieties and darker green on others; the starry, bright yellow flowers are freely produced from July until October. Regular spraying with water from the garden hose, especially in the evening hours following a hot day, will keep the spider mites in check; otherwise, they suck the juices from the leaves to give them a rusty look.

There are no broad-leaf evergreens hardy enough as hedge plants on the prairies, but one that comes close is the dwarf euonymus. It may correctly be called a semievergreen, for it holds its leaves when planted in a well-sheltered spot where it is likely to be under snow for most of the winter. It has narrow, dark green leaves, slender twigs, and may be kept down to a foot-high hedge for many years. It is well suited to a shady spot but does equally well in full sun. When exposed to the northwest winter winds and when the ground is bare, the leaves fall and there may be some winter injury to the young growth. When this occurs, a hard pruning in early May will restore it completely by season's end. The dwarf euonymus is highly recommended as a choice low hedge and one that stands close clipping remarkably well.

The Pallas buckthorn is not a common hedge plant, though it is fully hardy and is suitable for making a neat, low hedge. The twigs are slender, the leaves narrow, dense and dark green. It stands close clipping and needs several trimmings during June, July and August to keep it neat and tidy. It is not susceptible to leaf spot or insect damage and stands long periods of dry weather.

Medium-low hedges — The medium-low hedges in the height range of two to three feet are popular in small urban gardens, either along the front or to divide one section of the garden from another. There are a number of suitable ones — sweetberry honeysuckle *(Lonicera coerulea edulis)*, hedge cotoneaster *(C. lucida)*, threelobe spirea *(S. trilobata)*, Siberian currant *(Ribes diacanthum)*, winged euonymus *(E. alata)* and Turkestan euonymus *(E. nana turkestanica)*.

The sweetberry honeysuckle makes an ideal hedge with dense leaves, roundish, small and blue green. The main branches are quite rigid, the twigs slender; in the leaf axils are curiously superimposed buds. These buds are next year's shoots and are arranged one above the other in bundles of three or four. This honeysuckle is completely free of disease and highly resistant to insects, making it an attractive hedge all through the season.

Several cotoneasters make good hedges; hedge cotoneaster *(C. lucida)* is a popular choice though the Pekin cotoneaster *(C. acutifolia)*, an almost identical species, is just as good. The roundish leaves are small, dark green, and both species can be closely clipped to make a neat hedge. Fireblight and scurfy scale can be damaging, so control measures must be applied at the first sign of trouble.

The threelobe spirea makes a hardier and dwarfer hedge than either the garland or the Vanhoutte. It stands close clipping to make a formal hedge or it may be grown as a flowering hedge, pruning out the old wood every two or three years.

The Siberian currant is a fully hardy, well-adapted hedge plant with slender twigs and small, bright green leaves. It stands close clipping and its general appearance is much like the Alpine currant, except that it grows more upright.

The winged euonymus makes a sturdy, rigid hedge with twigs that are curiously winged with corky bark and densely clothed with pale green leaves. In the fall, the leaves are brilliant orange red for a brief period; later, when the leaves have fallen, tiny scarlet fruits are revealed. The winged euonymus is a first-class hedge, hardy, easy to maintain and tolerant of dry soil. The Turkestan euonymus, a hardier form of *E. nana,* is taller. It makes a good hedge in sun or shade, needing very little care beyond an annual trimming. The Turkestan euonymus stands heat and dry weather remarkably well and in mild winters it retains most of its leaves.

Medium-tall hedges — Hedges three to five feet high make useful screens and shelters to surround the living-out area or to make a division between one part of the garden and another. Hawthorns make splendid hedges in this medium-tall group, requiring minimum attention other than a once-a-year trim in June.

Two native species are useful in this group, the fleshy hawthorn *(Crataegus succulenta)* and the fireberry hawthorn *(C. chrysocarpa)*. Of the two, the fleshy hawthorn makes the best hedge. It can be kept alive and healthy for forty years or longer by controlling diseases such as cedar-apple rust *(Gymnosporangia),* scale and fireblight. Every ten years or so, when the old wood is cut back hard in April, fresh young growth makes a new hedge.

Some rosybloom crabapples make good medium-tall hedges. Strathmore, being upright and twiggy, is one of the best. Almey, on the other hand, is too spreading; the branches and twigs are thicker, making it unsuitable in a hedge.

The native highbush cranberry *(Viburnum trilobum)* makes a fine informal hedge which can be maintained with very little pruning at five feet or so. The leaves are large and handsome, turning a rich red in the fall. Trimming with the hedge shears is not recommended as it mutilates the leaves. Pruning is best done in the spring before the leaves open, cutting off stray twigs and branches to keep the plants in line. This kind of pruning preserves the showy panicles of creamy flowers, which are followed by bunches of cranberries, glistening red in September. When you clip a highbush cranberry hedge in June, you cut off the shoots that will bear the flowers. The fruit has a value in the kitchen or it may be left to hang on the bough until the winter birds seek it.

The buffaloberry *(Shepherdia argentea)* makes a thicket of dense, spiny twigs with small, gray green leaves. It stands close clipping, dry saline soil and can be kept shoulder-high for many years. A kind of leaf hopper sometimes infests the buffaloberry, flying in all directions when the leaves are disturbed. The damage done to the foliage is negligible but the leaf hopper nuisance would deter the homeowner from planting a buffaloberry hedge in the living-out or pleasure garden. In any case, gray-leaved plants tend to strike a dull note in small gardens and should be used sparingly.

A sharp contrast to the gray leaves of the buffaloberry is the purple of Shubert chokecherry *(Prunus virginiana Shubert)*. It starts out with green leaves in the spring, looking like a common chokecherry. By July the leaves are purplish and remain so for the rest of the growing season. Shubert chokecherry is fully hardy, tolerant of drought and suitable as a five-foot hedge. When grafted on common chokecherry it suckers wildly; on the European birdcherry *(P. padus),* it is not quite so vigorous but less prone to suckering.

A hardy pear tree makes a neat hedge with palish green leaves, glossy all through the summer and turning a brilliant orange red in the fall. Fireblight may be a problem in some areas and, when the soil is heavily charged with lime, the hardy Ussurian pear *(Pyrus ussuriensis)* will soon have sickly yellow leaves.

Tall hedges — Tall hedges are useful for screening unsightly objects, for privacy or to give shelter from wind. There is a long list of good ones: some grow fast; some take much longer to make a hedge but are more permanent.

The common lilac *(Syringa vulgaris)* and caragana *(C. arborescens)* make hardy, tall hedges. The caragana is esteemed as a windbreak hedge where more choice plants are not easily grown. It has ironclad hardiness, tremendous drought tolerance and no bad suckers. In the spring, when its fresh green, delicately patterned leaves unfold, it is quite unsurpassed. But the leaves dull with age and, when infected by leaf spot, fall prematurely to leave the plants completely defoliated before the summer is past. The common lilac has an abominable habit of producing a forest of suckers which, if not ruthlessly destroyed, broaden the base of the plants and debilitate the main portion of the hedge. On the credit side, it has thick, dark green leaves persistent until November and free of insect pests and disease. Clipped to make a formal hedge, the flower buds are destroyed. Grow the lilac naturally, keeping a check on suckers by chopping them out in the fall and pruning out-of-line branches when the flowers have faded, and it will remain a most attractive flowering hedge.

Other lilacs better adapted for hedge making are the Chinese lilac *(S. villosa)*, Hungarian lilac *(S. josikaea)* and the Amur lilac *(S. japonica amurensis)*. The Chinese lilac grows tall and has large, coarse leaves, dull green and not particularly attractive. The Hungarian lilac has more refinement; the leaves are dark green, glossy and smaller than those of the Chinese lilac. It does not sucker and may be maintained at five feet for many years. The Amur lilac grows tall, is fairly upright with fine branches densely clothed with large leaves, bright green above, grayish green beneath. Like both Chinese and Hungarian lilacs, the Amur is nonsuckering and makes a choice hedge, fully hardy and tolerant of dry soil. Much of the beauty of these large-leaved lilacs is destroyed when they are trimmed with hedging shears. It is well worth taking the extra time to prune them with secateurs or a pruning knife to avoid mutilating the leaves.

Tall hedges can also be made with native ash, elm and oak. They are not for small gardens but, where there is plenty of room, they deserve consideration. They stand close clipping very well but look best when pruned once a year with secateurs. The native green ash *(Fraxinus pennsylvanica subintegerrima)* should be used more often as a tall barrier. It has tremendous drought resistance, is slow growing and long lived. The compound leaves are late in coming and among the first to fall, but not before they turn bright yellow. Old ash hedges quickly recover when cut back to two-foot stubs in April. The American elm *(Ulmus americana)* makes a fine tall hedge with medium-sized leaves, dark green and handsome while they are free of aphids and the disfigurement of leaf galls. Old hedges can be rejuvenated in the same way as recommended for the ash. The native oak tree would hardly be considered as a hedge plant but it does make a hardy, dense windbreak when young plants are set out two feet apart. Occasionally, when late frosts have retarded the buds, an oak hedge may not be fully clothed with leaves until May is well along. To compensate for this, the leaves are slow to drop, becoming first a sombre brown; when branch and twig are bare of leaves, they reveal a peculiar corky bark to make interesting winter pictures when outlined against a blue sky.

The larches, though cone-bearing trees, drop their needles in the fall. Both the native tamarack *(Larix laricina)* and the Siberian larch *(L. sibirica)* will make good hedges. The native larch has bluish green needles and small cones. The Siberian has bright green needles, much larger cones and seems to be better adapted to close clipping. Both are most attractive when first the new needles appear, and again briefly when they turn a rich golden yellow in September.

Evergreen Hedges for the Prairies

Spruce — There is a fairly good choice of evergreens hardy enough for the prairies and suitable for hedges, the most common being the native spruce *(Picea glauca)* or the Colorado spruce *(P. pungens)*. Both stand close clipping but only the current year's growth should be pruned. The native spruce has fairly short needles, mostly dark green, though some have a bluish cast. The Colorado spruce has longer needles, more often bluish, and seems better adapted and longer lived than the native spruce.

Pine — Several hardy pines make good hedges; they look best when grown informally, pruned once a year with a pruning knife or secateurs. One of the best pine hedges is the Swiss stone pine *(Pinus cembra),* with dark green needles in bunches of five, indicating that it belongs to the white pine group. The plants are a good deal more expensive than other pines generally used for hedging, but the extra cost is warranted. The Swiss stone pine grows fairly slowly and may be kept as a medium hedge for many years. Pruning should be done once a year in July, snipping out the centres of the current year's growth with the secateurs, taking extra care so that the long needles are not cut.

The Scots pine *(P. sylvestris)* makes a natural evergreen barrier when the trees are planted two feet apart and allowed to grow with only enough pruning to keep the out-of-line shoots from spoiling the symmetry. The Scots pine can also be grown as an informal hedge, pruned in the same way as recommended for the Swiss stone pine.

The lodgepole pine *(P. contorta latifolia)* and the red pine *(P. resinosa)* are not good hedge plants in prairie gardens. Both have yellowish needles in the high-lime soil and the lodgepole pine often turns brown from drying winter winds. Swiss mountain pine *(P. mugho)* is a variable species growing to twenty feet or taller with many lateral branches that tend to broaden the base, making this species unsuitable as a hedge. The dwarf Swiss mountain pine *(P. mugho pumilio)* makes an excellent low evergreen hedge, however. Except to keep stray shoots in line, it requires no pruning.

Cedar – The so-called cedar *(Arborvitae)* is not often used as a hedge plant in prairie gardens. It is not because there are no hardy sorts but, rather, because the plants are costly and difficult to establish. Even the hardiest sorts need extra care, a spot selected for them where they are sheltered from the drying northwest winds. Dry soil and searing winter winds will turn parts of a cedar hedge brown and spoil its general appearance. It will recover from a slight browning but, when the damage is repeated for several winters, the hedge becomes unthrifty and parts of it may die outright.

Several hardy cedars make good hedges; the Brandon cedar, the St. John's Lake cedar and the Ware or Siberian cedar are recommended. The Brandon cedar, which has been propagated from cuttings taken from the original tree growing on the grounds of the Brandon Experimental Farm since 1890, is a narrow pyramid with dark green foliage and a high tolerance to drought. It may be grown as an informal barrier, setting the plants three feet apart, or as a close-clipped hedge, the trees planted two feet apart. Its natural shape is the best to follow to make a narrow pyramid, starting the year after the plants are set out by clipping the top and sides lightly. The St. John's cedar, a hardy strain from northern Quebec, has lighter foliage than the Brandon cedar and, as the plants are usually raised from seed, there is some variation in plant habit. It makes a good formal hedge but has a tendency to broaden at the base and, in dry weather, spider mites become a problem. The Ware or Siberian cedar has a somewhat spreading habit but can be trained into a shapely hedge. The foliage is dark green and suffers no winter browning unless it is exposed to harsh winter winds or neglected by allowing the plants to go into winter dry at the root.

Juniper – The Rockymountain juniper *(Juniperus scopulorum)* makes a fine hedge in some parts of the prairies. It stands heat and drought and can be close clipped to make a formal hedge. Where the soil is rich and moist, the Rockymountain juniper will not do and, where adjacent plants of hawthorn produce a source of infection for cedar-apple rust, the juniper provides the alternative host plant. Select specimens, silvery blue and shapely, are too expensive for hedges, but seedlings in shades of blue green and varying in stature and texture can be clipped to make a satisfactory hedge. The Rockymountain juniper in its native habitat is fully exposed to all winds and weather; to coddle it by providing shade and shelter or by enriching the soil with high-nitrogen fertilizer is to kill it with kindness.

Balsam — The balsam fir *(Abies balsamae)* is altogether different; it needs a neutral soil, shade and plenty of moisture. Where these conditions can be provided, it will make a rigid hedge with fine twigs densely clothed with dark green, flattish needles. It may be kept at five or six feet for a number of years when given an annual trim in July. Evergreen hedges are worth the extra care it takes to keep them shapely, free of insect damage and protected from the drying winds. They are particularly attractive in the wintertime when most other hedges are bare, giving the home garden a warm, cosy look.

Ten

Making a New Lawn

How much space should be devoted to a lawn? In the front garden the grass area is very important: it should not be cluttered up with flower beds, and the variety of grass should be chosen for its appearance rather than for its hard-wearing qualities. When you make a lawn in the back garden or living-out area, however, you may have to consider first the long-wearing quality of the grass you decide to use. If the back lawn is to be a playground for children, you will need the kind of grass that makes a tough sod: a mixture of creeping red fescue and Kentucky bluegrass is a good choice. If the traffic on the lawn is not going to be heavy, you may use a more refined variety of grass; in fact, a plot of grass may become a hobby with some gardeners who have the inclination and time to spend in keeping it well groomed.

Preparing the Seed Bed

It is false economy to lay a few inches of good soil over basement clay and sow grass seed on this, expecting to make a good lawn. It simply won't work. The appearance of the lawn is so important to the rest of the garden that time and money spent on the proper grading of the site and the adequate preparation of the soil will be well repaid in a first-class lawn.

It takes six inches of topsoil, well enriched with humus and with plenty of nitrogen, to make good turf. The subsoil should not be so heavy that excess water will not drain quickly away. It may be necessary to spread a layer of well-rotted manure and sand over the subsoil, working this in by digging or by rotovating before the topsoil is put on. With the subsoil loosened to ensure good drainage and the topsoil spread evenly over it, the surface can now be made firm and level by treading and raking. Small areas are best firmed by treading the soil; larger lawns may be rolled. Whatever method is used to prepare a good seed bed, the job should be well done; once the seed has been sown there is not much you can do about depressions and high spots, so keep raking until the surface is quite firm and even.

In some places, making a lawn by laying sods is practical but, in many areas, suitable turf is difficult to get. There is no merit in laying sod composed of coarse grasses and perennial weeds; the weeds may be killed by chemicals but the grass will remain as coarse as it ever was. The preparation of the soil for sod laying is the same as already outlined for sowing grass seed. The sods are usually cut by machine, ensuring turfs of even size and thickness. The ground is made level by raking; the turfs are then fitted together and the cracks covered with fine soil. The sods are firmed by rolling or by tamping them with the back of a spade. Afterwards, the new lawn is given a good watering. The sodding can be done at any time during the growing season (from April to October), but cutting and laying sod in the torrid heat of July will only be successful if you can keep the sods from drying out, keep plenty of water on hand and work swiftly.

Sowing Seed

The best time to sow grass seed on the prairies is late August or early in September, though in northern parts of the prairies September may be too late in some years. The chief advantages of sowing grass seed at that time of year are warm soil and less competition from weeds, which are usually much more troublesome in the spring. Perennial weeds, such as dandelions and quack grass, can be killed in the summer months either by digging or by the use of chemicals. Annual weeds will not be a problem in August if the area to be grassed down has been kept black by regular hoeing during the summer. The young grass plants will make better headway in the warm soil of August than they will in the spring, when the soil may be cold and starved of nitrogen.

The question of adequate moisture has to be considered: it is always risky to sow grass seed and have to rely on rains to keep the soil wet enough to start germination. Once the seed sprouts, the young plants grow freely if the soil is kept moist but, if you happen to run into a spell of warm, dry weather and you have no means of watering, the young plants may perish.

Grass seed is more evenly distributed by a mechanical seeder than it is by hand but, if hand sowing has to be done, divide the seed into two equal parts; sow one portion over the whole area as you walk north to south and the remainder as you walk from east to west. When the seeding is done, rake the area, lightly covering as much of the seed as you can. By finishing off with a light roller, most of the seed will be in contact with the soil and will start to grow in a week or so if the soil is kept moist.

Water is vital to start germination, but too much, applied too heavily, will wash out the seed and saturate the soil, making bad growing conditions for the young plants. Grass will not remain healthy for long in soil that is constantly wet and packed down so hard that the life-giving air is pushed out. A fine-nozzled sprinkler will make the best job of watering and, if the weather is hot, it is better to water during the evening hours than in the heat of the day.

Varieties of Grass Seed

General purpose — The best general-purpose lawn is made with sixty percent Kentucky bluegrass and forty percent creeping red fescue. Buy the seed in separate lots and mix it yourself. Ready-mixed seed can be bought and may be cheaper, but these mixtures may contain coarse grasses unsuitable for making a fine lawn. The cost of the seed, relative to the cost of fertilizer and the work of getting the soil in shape, is secondary, so buy the best from a reputable seedhouse.

Two select strains of Kentucky bluegrass, Merion and Park, have special merit. Merion has dark green, broad-bladed leaves and makes a deep, spongy sward, thick enough when well established to keep out dandelions and other perennial weeds. Merion grass is more difficult to germinate than ordinary Kentucky bluegrass and it will need higher doses of nitrogen to keep it thrifty. It costs more, too, but the extra cost is offset by lower seeding rates. Ordinary bluegrass seed is sown at the rate of four pounds per one thousand square feet; it is wasteful to sow more and false economy to sow less. If you skimp with the seed, you will have a patch job to do and this is never satisfactory. Merion, on the other hand, can be sown two pounds per one thousand square feet.

The other strain of Kentucky bluegrass, called Park, has bright green leaves that are narrower than those of Merion. It will germinate more quickly than Merion to make a dense sod the first season and it requires less fertilizer to maintain in good condition. It makes a finer but less durable lawn.

Special varieties — Annual bluegrass *(Poa annua)* is a weed grass that is prevalent in the shaded areas of some lawns. It thrives under trees where perennial grasses are difficult to grow because of tree roots and dry soil. Annual bluegrass makes a low plant with bright green leaves and seed stalks that usually escape the mower blade to ripen and scatter seed. The seed germinates freely in the fall, wintering over to make rapid growth in the spring. By midsummer, the weed grass will be dying out and the lawn will look shabby. Where it is unwanted, its growth can be checked by fertilizing and watering the permanent grasses to encourage vigorous growth.

If a tough turf is required in areas where soil is poor and moisture is low, Chewings fescue *(Festuca rubra commutata)* is recommended. It is capable of withstanding heavy traffic and is a good choice for the backyard, where children play. It makes a dense, uniform turf with narrow, blue green leaf blades.

Canada bluegrass *(Poa compressa)* is a coarse grass suitable for areas where the soil is low in fertility. It also thrives in heavy clay soil where the drainage may be less than ideal. It is inferior to Kentucky bluegrass but is a good substitute in areas where conditions for growing that grass are poor.

Perennial ryegrass *(Lolium perenne)* is sometimes used to make a temporary lawn or as a "nurse" grass in lawn mixtures. It has coarse leaves and tough seed stalks that are hard to cut. Perennial ryegrass has merit as a summer lawn where permanent grass is to be sown later on. It soon covers the ground to prevent weeds from starting.

Clover — Whether you add clover to your lawn grass seed is a matter of choice. It is true that the nitrogen which is fixed by the bacteria forming the nodules on the roots of clover is beneficial to grass, but there are several bad features of clover in a lawn. In periods of dry weather, when the clover suffers less than the grass, it spreads to make dark green patches which give the lawn an uneven appearance. It is not uncommon for these patches to kill out when snow cover is sparse, leaving bare spots which have to be reseeded in the spring. When White Dutch clover is added to a lawn grass mixture, it should not be more than five percent of the total.

The Care of New Lawns

Mowing a new lawn — When new grass is about three inches high, it should be cut with a sharp mower. A reel-type machine is preferred as it makes a clean cut, whereas a rotary mower is likely to bruise the leaves. Set the machine to cut at two inches; if you cut closer you may damage the young grass plants.

If you sow your lawn in August it may not need cutting until the following spring, depending upon the weather — a long, open fall will encourage the grass to keep growing and, if there is plenty of moisture in the soil, the grass will grow long. A new lawn will come through the winter in better condition when you leave it three inches high; if you shave it off just before freeze-up, the young grass plants may die. It is, however, unwise to let a thick thatch build up, as it may become matted by the weight of snow and the roots may rot.

Wintering a new lawn — In open areas, where the snow is likely to blow off a newly sown lawn, you must put up a snow fence or cover the exposed area with boughs or a layer of flax straw. If dry weather should persist into October, causing the ground to crack, scatter a light dressing of well-rotted manure or garden compost over the new lawn and give it a final watering before the ground freezes. Heavy doses of high nitrogen fertilizer are needed in the growing season to keep the grass green and lush. When the soil warms in April to start the lawn into new growth, apply ten pounds of 16.20.0 per thousand square feet; repeat the dose in mid-June and again in early September. Choose a time when the grass is dry, spreading the fertilizer evenly, then give the lawn a good soaking.

A new lawn may have a number of small depressions in spite of firm treading and thorough raking. These small hollows can be filled in by spreading a layer of rotted manure or compost over the lawn in October. This top dressing should be left rough to catch snow; it will break down to fine soil by spring with the action of frost and wind.

Weeds — Perennial weeds, once a big problem in lawns, are not difficult to kill with chemicals. The broad-leaved dandelions and plantains are sprayed when the plants are in lush growth and the weather is warm. Small-leaved weeds such as chickweed require heavier doses of herbicide to kill them. Use the amine form of 2-4-D, following the directions on the container. Take care not to spray if the weather is windy — you can damage plants in your own garden and maybe in your neighbor's garden, too.

Quack grass is most difficult to eradicate once it is entrenched in a lawn. The effort required to dig it out of an area where you intend to make a lawn will be well spent. No chemical is selective in killing quack grass already established in a lawn but you can kill it with one of several chemicals applied the year before you sow the grass seed.

Diseases — Diseases of grass are not serious in prairie gardens; the most prevalent is snowmould, which does a lot of damage in some seasons. It is easily recognized by the grayish cobwebs usually found in areas where the last of the snow is lingering. It is more likely to be found in the shady parts of the lawn where the snow piles deep in the winter. If it is allowed to go unchecked, it penetrates the grass roots to kill them. When this occurs, patches of dead grass remain an eyesore for many weeks unless these areas are reseeded or sodded.

When first you see the tell-tale patches of gray mould, sweep the area with the house broom; the idea is to speed up the drying of the grass to prevent mould from spreading to the grass roots. Chemical compounds sold under trade names are available and they give good control of snowmould; use them in October according to the manufacturer's instructions.

Mildew attacks some kinds of grass; Merion, for example, is susceptible when planted in shady areas. As a general rule, prairie lawns are not seriously affected by mildew but, where it is a problem, it can be controlled by using Karathane according to the directions on the package.

Eleven

Roses

The Romance of the Rose

Wherever man has made a garden, he has planted a rose. In all parts of the temperate zones, both north and south, in the subtropics and even in the far north, one finds roses of one kind or another.

The first settlers on the western plains brought roses from their old homesteads in Ontario, and those who came here from across the sea brought roses from France, England and other European countries.

The history of the cultivated rose goes back a long way, predating the Christian era by a thousand years or more. The Romans had rose gardens and Pliny describes methods of growing roses from seed. Prior to Elizabethan times, little was recorded about rose growing in England; shortly before the Stuarts came to the throne, however, Gerard published his herbal, in which he describes a few native species including the dogrose. Not long after, John Parkinson, in his *Paradisi in Sole,* described more than twenty kinds of roses. According to him, all were satisfactory when grown on their own roots. He proved his knowledge of taxonomy in refusing to accept the commonly held premise that roses grafted on the wild broom would produce yellow flowers. The broom is a legume; the Elizabethans, however, simply assumed that, since it bore yellow flowers, it would induce yellow roses.

Before the turn of the nineteenth century, cultivated roses were mostly varieties of the French rose *(Rosa gallica)* and, later, the damask, Bourbon, noisette and the hybrid perpetuals. The hybrid perpetual dominated other roses throughout most of the nineteenth century but gave way to the hybrid tea, largely because of the remontant or ever-blooming habit of the hybrid teas.

The hybrid tea or "tender" rose — The original hybrid teas were mainly shades of red and pink; there were not many whites and no yellows. Before the color range could be extended, new species had to be blended with the hybrid teas. Deep yellow roses were first introduced into the hybrid tea group when the French hybridist, Pernet-Ducher, managed to cross *R. foetida* with a hybrid tea rose to produce the celebrated variety Soleil d'Or, which was the first pure yellow hybrid tea.

The earliest yellow hybrid teas, or pernetianas as they were called, had many faults: they lacked fragrance; they were excessively thorny and were very susceptible to black spot. The modern hybrid teas have been developed by intercrossing existing varieties; in some instances, a continued program of inbreeding has resulted in weak plants. The best results have been obtained when distinct lines have been developed separately and then brought together. The super rose, Peace, is an example of heterosis or hybrid vigor. One parent of this famous rose was Johanna Hill, an American rose descended from Ophelia, another famous rose in its day. The other parent was a seedling of Charles P. Kilham crossed with Margaret McGredy; both these varieties were raised by the famous firm of McGredy in Portadown, Northern Ireland, and were developed by concentrated line breeding.

A number of polyantha roses came into prominence during the early years of the twentieth century; Mme. Norman Lavasseur and Orleans rose are two that contributed a good deal to the Poulsen hybrid polyanthas. These, in turn, were used with the hybrid teas and other roses to produce a group of showy roses loosely called the florabundas. The popularity of these useful bedding roses continues to increase as their capacity for continuous and showy bloom is appreciated by home gardeners and by those who have the responsibility for our public parks. However, while there is no denying the importance of the florabundas in bedding schemes, the strong appeal of the more shapely hybrid teas will still make them first choice with those who delight in producing a first-class specimen rose.

Still another class of roses have been developed by crossing the florabundas with the hybrid teas to produce the grandifloras (an unacceptable name in European countries, but commonly used in America and in Canada). The grandifloras are more perfect in form than the florabundas and some varieties are so much like the hybrid tea rose that it is difficult to distinguish between them.

With the object of increasing winter hardiness in the hybrid tea roses,

Brownell, an American rose breeder from Rhode Island, used the well-known climbing rose, Dr. Walter Van Fleet, with an old hybrid perpetual called General Jacqueminot. The progeny, crossed with Crimson Glory, produced a number of pink and red seedlings called the Brownell subzero roses.

Later on, Brownell used Condessa de Sastago, a popular hybrid tea, with the brilliant yellow Souv. de Claudius Pernet as one of its parents, to produce yellow and orange shades in his new roses. The subzero roses are not fully hardy in prairie gardens, though the plants seem to last longer than the ordinary hybrid teas. To be sure of them wintering in good shape, it is necessary to mound them in the same manner as prescribed for the hybrid teas.

Climbing and rambling roses — The climbing and rambling roses are not important in prairie gardens and only the dedicated rosarian will attempt to grow them. Rambling roses are hybrids of the climbing Memorial rose and other hardy species. All ramblers are climbers but, as a general rule, they are less hardy than climbers that are not ramblers.

The history of climbing roses in America goes back to the mid-nineteenth century, when Queen of the Prairies and Baltimore Belle were widely grown. Both varieties had the native prairie rose *(R. setigera)* as one parent, the other being *R. gallica* or one of the noisette roses. *R. setigera* is native to the eastern United States and parts of Ontario but is not fully hardy in prairie gardens.

The multiflora rose has been advertised all across the prairies as a suitable hedge rose and thousands of plants have been set out in good faith only to have them killed out the first year. It has been used to some extent as an understock but in prairie gardens it is not so well adapted as the dogrose *(R. canina)*. The multiflora rose crossed with the China and noisette roses produced a number of summer-flowering ramblers with large clusters of showy blooms. Later on, the well-known Crimson Rambler was introduced from Japan and paved the way for Tausendschon and other well-known ramblers.

With the introduction of the Memorial rose *(R. wichuraiana)*, which is the true rambling rose, with its glossy, disease-resistant leaves and long-flowering habit, better climbers soon were developed. Among the early ones were Dorothy Perkins and Excelsa, both originating in America.

At the same time, the French hybridists produced a number of excellent climbers by crossing the Memorial rose with some of the hybrid teas. One of the best is Albertine, with glossy leaves, pink flowers and a sweet scent. The American rose breeder, Van Fleet, used the Memorial rose to produce the well-known Dr. Walter Van Fleet and American Pillar. New Dawn is a sort of Dr. Van Fleet and, while it is not so vigorous as Van Fleet, it has the merit of blooming over a longer period. The Macartney rose *(R. bracteata)* crossed with a double yellow tea rose produced an outstanding climber called Mermaid. *R. gigantea* crossed with certain tea roses has produced a number of interesting climbers but, as would be expected, all are very tender. With the exception of New Dawn and Dr. Van Fleet, none of these climbers are of any use in prairie gardens.

Another group of climbing roses has evolved from the hybrid teas, most commonly through bud mutations but occasionally from cross pollinations. Some of the mutations have remained stable but many have reverted to the bush habit of the hybrid teas.

Shrub roses – The hardy shrub roses are either once-blooming natural species from Asia and North America, or hybrids which have been developed by crossing the species with other roses. The natural species have single, five-petalled flowers that are produced once a year in June or early July. Some have ornamental fruits, red or purple black; some have red leaves in the fall, while others have reddish bark which lightens the winter landscape. These hardy roses are most valuable in the shrub border where they can be maintained in good condition by giving them the same general care the lilacs and other shrubs receive.

Tender Roses in the Prairie Garden

Since the end of World War Two, there has been an enormous increase in the number of roses grown in prairie gardens; thousands of hybrid tea and other tender roses are planted every year. The plants are purchased from nurseries, department stores and garden centres and, while there are some failures, a good number survive the winter to bloom again the following year and perhaps excite a novice gardener to become a keen rosarian.

In the small garden there may be room only for a few plants but, even so, they should be planted together in one bed where the soil has been specially prepared. An odd rose planted in the perennial border or along the house wall will add nothing to the landscape plan or the perennial border, nor will the tender rose stand much chance of surviving the winter when it has to compete for soil moisture and nutrients with shrubs. Roses need plenty of sunlight to grow healthy leaves and strong canes. If the plants are surrounded by tall trees or in the shadow of buildings for the greater part of the day, they will never be strong and may soon become infected with disease. For the best results, the rose bed should be laid out on the east side of the house if possible, sheltered from northwest winds and exposed to the morning sun.

Understocks – Most of the tender roses grown in prairie gardens are budded on either multiflora or the dogrose *(R. canina)*. The dogrose, because of its deep, penetrating roots, is preferred; roses budded on this stock have lasted longer in prairie gardens than the same varieties on multiflora. The main drawback to the dogrose as an understock is its lack of fibrous roots, which makes transplanting rather more difficult. On the other hand, roses on dogrose understock tend to ripen their wood earlier than those on multiflora and, as a result of this earlier ripening, are able to survive the winter in better shape.

It is interesting to note that Captain Hayward, a once-popular hybrid perpetual, lasted for twenty years in one prairie garden when grafted onto dogrose understock and when the plants were given the usual protection of a mound of dry, well-pulverized soil and a deep covering of straw. When the plants were finally dug up and the roots of the understock examined, they were four feet long. The deep, penetrating roots of the dogrose had served the plant well in periods of drought and were still functional after twenty years. The main feeding roots, however, were above the joint of union between stock and scion, which would seem to indicate that the roots of the old variety, Captain Hayward, are just as hardy as those of canina or dogrose.

The red-leaved rose *(R. rubrifolia)* is an ornamental plant and a close relative of the dogrose. As an understock for tender roses it has been rejected because of difficulties in propagating; the seed is slow and uncertain in germinating and the cuttings are slow to take root. Besides these serious faults, roses budded to *rubrifolia* are frequently infected with an insidious virus called witches broom or rosette virus. The disease is manifest in a conglomerate of malformed leaves sometimes colored bronzy red. When the virus infects young plants, they remain dwarf and fail to produce blooms. It appears that rosette virus is transmitted from native roses by a certain kind of mite. The common two-spotted mite, found on a number of garden plants, is not a vector of rosette virus.

Preparing the soil for tender roses — When the novice gardener realizes how deeply the roots of hybrid tea roses penetrate the soil and the large amounts of plant food used up in a single season, he will see how important it is to prepare the soil properly for roses before planting. It pays to add large quantities of organic matter to hold soil moisture and supply nutrients. The best source of humus or organic matter is rotted barnyard manure; a good substitute, if barnyard manure is difficult to obtain, is granulated peat made rich with chemical fertilizer. A bale of granulated peat contains six cubic feet, which is enough for a rose bed nine feet by five feet and, while the peat contains very little in the way of plant food, it will greatly improve the texture of the soil. By mixing two pounds of 11.48.0 with a bale of peat before you dig it in, you can supply nutrients as well as improve the water-holding capacity of the soil.

In prairie gardens, where the soil is likely to be high in lime, the acid peat is of special benefit in neutralizing the soil to make it better suited for growing roses. Most of the roses, both hardy and tender sorts, do best in soil with a pH of 6.5 to 7. Above this level, some kinds will show signs of chlorosis, which is indicated by yellowish leaves with green veins.

October is the best time of year to prepare the soil, digging it deeply or trenching as directed in chapter four.

Planting tender roses — There is no question that spring is the best time to plant roses, although you may move a rose safely in the fall if the plant is young and vigorous and the wood is fully ripened. If you are planning to make changes in the rose garden, digging out old, worn-out plants and discarding them or moving a young plant from one spot to another, you can do it in October with a reasonable chance of success.

Tests have shown that roses on *canina,* planted in October, survived the winter in good shape while similar sorts on multiflora, planted at the same time, suffered severe damage. The reason for this is the earlier ripening of roses budded on *canina.* Roses budded on multiflora stocks have not the same early ripening habit, as the stock tends to keep growing until late in the fall.

When you remove dead roses or those that are beginning to die, dig out the soil two feet deep and two feet wide if you intend to replant roses in the same spot. This entails a lot of work but is worth the effort, as it has been demonstrated that new plants do much better in new soil. The old soil can be spread around in the vegetable garden, where new soil for the roses is obtained.

A lot of hybrid tea and other tender roses are set out in prairie gardens as a result of impulse buying. The plants in colorful packages are offered for sale in department stores, garden centres and other places of business and thousands are sold every year. Not all the plants purchased from these sources are satisfactory but, if you get them before the roots get dry and plant them properly and without delay, there is a good chance of success.

By ordering early from a reputable nurseryman, you can be assured of first-class stock arriving at the right time and in dormant condition. Everything should be in readiness when the plants arrive so that they can be set in their permanent quarters without delay. The bundle should be opened, the roots straightened and placed in a tub of water for an hour or two. If for some reason there has been a delay in transit and the canes appear to be very dry, leave the plants with the roots in water overnight. The next day, dig a shallow trench and bury the plants for a few days to plump up the wood. Unless the plants are completely dried out, they will recover but there may be live buds only at the base. In any case, the top growth has to be pruned back to healthy buds, or eyes, and, if some of the top growth is dead, it does not matter.

The actual planting is simple enough but it should be done carefully so that the plant gets away to a good start. Dig a hole broad enough to hold the roots without crowding and deep enough to allow them to be fully extended. The depth of planting may confuse the novice. He should be guided by the kind of soil he has and by the point where the scion joins the stock on a budded rose. The novice may have been told to keep the point of union three or four inches below the surface of the soil; others, just as emphatically, have told him that the union should be set not more than one inch deep. If you compromise at two inches you won't go far wrong but, if your soil is light and sandy, planting a bit deeper will not

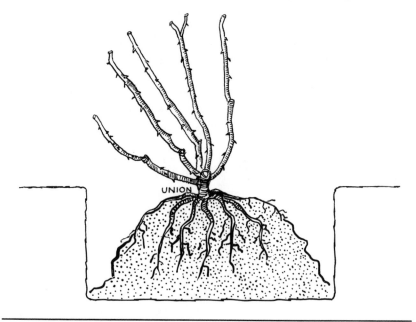

UNION

The young rose plants received from the nursery must be set in the soil with the union of scion and understock about two inches below the surface of the soil and the top growth reduced about two-thirds.

harm the plant. When the hole is dug and the subsoil loosened, place a shovelful of good soil in the bottom, setting the rose on this with the roots evenly spread out around it. Fill in with good soil, shaking the plant gently and pulling it up to the required position. The soil must be made very firm by treading to ensure that all the roots are in contact with the moist soil. Leave a shallow depression around each plant to facilitate watering. Give each plant half a pailful of water; let it seep in as you level the soil and mound it a few inches high around the canes. The mound of soil will protect the lower buds from frost or from drying out if the weather should be hot and windy.

Pruning tender roses — The hybrid tea and other tender roses are usually sold with part of the top growth cut off. Further pruning, however, is necessary and should be done when the plants are set out. First, remove all broken and weak stems; those that are less than pencil thickness will not produce good bloom. Shorten the remaining shoots to three or four buds, with the topmost one facing outwards.

Towards the end of May, the old, established plants are pruned by cutting out dead canes and those that are less than pencil thickness, for these will not produce good blooms. A well-grown rose will have four or five shoots of finger thickness. Each one is cut back to an out-facing bud,

leaving three or four dormant buds to grow and produce the first flowers. Use a sharp pruning knife or secateurs to make a clean cut close to the bud. Seal the wounds with tree paint to insulate the canes and keep out borers.

BUSH ROSE UNPRUNED

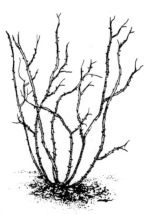

BUSH ROSE PRUNED

The darker shoots on the first figure indicate old wood which must be cut out to ground level. Tender roses only produce blooms on the current year's wood.

Summer care of tender roses — The care of newly planted roses will follow the routine for the maintenance of old, established plants. This means a regular supply of water and several doses of fertilizer, using 11.48.0 at the rate of two ounces to the square yard in mid-May. Repeat the dose when the flower buds form and again in July when the first flush of bloom is over. A regular program of spraying and dusting should begin in early June to control insects and diseases. In prairie gardens, where the hot sun and drying winds are hard on roses, it is most important to keep the plants well supplied with moisture and to keep the insects from sucking the juices from the stems and leaves. Plants that have to fight insects and disease through the summer will not stand much chance of surviving the winter. Prolonged feeding and watering, however, will keep the plants green and delay ripening of the canes; after the end of August, therefore, discontinue fertilizing and water only sparingly. It is not unusual to get a severe frost in September and, if the roses are green and lush, they suffer a lot of damage.

The pattern of blooming for the hybrid tea roses is a flare-up in July, followed by a few weeks when the blooms are not so freely produced nor so large and colorful as they were in the early part of the season. Later on, when the torrid heat of midsummer has passed, the quality and size of the blooms improves and may outdo those produced in July.

Insects — The most common insects found on hybrid tea and other roses are aphids, thrips and spider mites. Several others, such as the leaf-cutter bee, rose leafhopper and the rose curculio or snout beetle are seen occasionally. There are several species of aphids attacking roses, but the pale green rose aphid is most common. They multiply rapidly and are often seen in large numbers when the first flower buds are developing. The insects secrete a sticky substance called honeydew and are easy prey to the nymphs of the ladybug.

Thrips are brownish, elongated insects with rasping mouth parts, with which they damage the leaves and flowers by sucking the juice. They are most active in warm, dry weather and do serious damage to the rose petals, spoiling the blooms.

The leaf-cutter bees cut circular pieces from the leaves, storing them in the pith of rose stems as food for their young. They are not a serious pest in prairie gardens but, where they have been observed, it will pay to paint the pruning wounds with tree paint.

The rose leafhopper is a tiny, yellowish green insect that flits from leaf to leaf, sucking out the plant's juices and causing damage similar to that of the spider mites. The rose curculio or snout beetle is about one-quarter of an inch long, reddish with a black snout. It feeds on the flower buds of both wild and cultivated roses, eating out holes and spoiling the blooms. Eggs are laid in the rose hips or seed pods where they hatch and develop to fall to the ground and pupate. They winter over in the soil to emerge in the spring, ready to attack the flower buds.

Spider mites are tiny insects, reddish when mature, somewhat paler when young. They make rapid headway when the weather is hot and dry unless they are controlled with the proper insecticides. Enormous populations are built up in a matter of days, to suck the plant's juices and to leave it in a debilitated state. Damage by spider mites is recognized when the foliage takes on a grayish look. Close examination will likely reveal a heavy infestation on the undersides of the leaves. The spiders spin a web which can be seen plainly on plants that carry a heavy infestation.

To keep the roses clean and healthy, start a program of control as soon as the leaves unfold and keep it up all through the season.

Diseases — Black spot *(Diplocarpum rosae)* and powdery mildew are the most common diseases of roses in prairie gardens. Black spot is so widespread it scarcely needs description. The name itself describes the symptoms, which appear on the leaves as irregular brownish or black spots, frequently surrounded by a yellowish ring. The spots increase in size to cover the whole leaf, causing it to drop prematurely and consequently weakening the plant. The disease is most active in damp, humid weather and is spread by splashing water, which carries the spores. When the leaves are wet for several hours, the spores germinate to spread the disease. Black spot is most serious in areas with high rainfall but, even in the dry atmosphere of a prairie garden, it can be spread quickly by overhead irrigation. As water must be present on rose leaves for several hours before black spot infection can take place, keep the foliage dry as far as possible when you water your roses. All classes of roses are susceptible to black spot in greater or lesser degrees; those of Austrian briar ancestry, however, are especially prone to this disease.

The symptoms of powdery mildew *(Sphaerotheca pannosa rosae)* are characterized by the grayish white masses of spores on young shoots and flower buds. Heavy infestations cause swellings on the young shoots, stunt the plant's growth and distort the flower buds. Towards the end of the growing season, tiny black spores form in the patches of whitish mould. These are resting spores that can winter over on dead leaves and flower stems. Powdery mildew is not spread by splashing water; the spores are wind borne, so the disease can be severe in areas of low rainfall. The humidity at the surface of young leaves is high enough to germinate the spores and spread the infection. Powdery mildew can be rampant in September when the days may be warm and dry, the nights cool and damp.

In some areas rust is a destructive disease of roses but it is not serious in prairie gardens except when cool, humid weather persists for long periods in early summer. It is easily recognized by the small orange spore masses which occur on the leaves and leaf stalks as well as on flower buds. Spores are blown to other leaves where they start new infections. Black spores, formed late in the summer, winter over on fallen leaves and go through another phase of their life cycle before they infect the plants in the spring.

Several canker diseases attack roses but, while they are common enough in some parts, they are not considered serious in prairie gardens. Cankers first appear as reddish spots on the canes. They darken and increase in size, causing the bark to split and dry out. When the disease strikes the base of the cane, the leaves above the canker wilt and the cane dies. The danger of canker infection can be greatly reduced by making clean cuts when pruning and treating the wounds with tree paint.

Crown gall is a bacterial disease which usually occurs at ground level but may be found higher up on the stems. The bacteria does not kill the tissue; it stimulates abnormal growth to form galls. The galls are small at first, increasing in size to stunt the plant's growth. Control is largely a matter of preventing the spread of the disease by the prompt removal of infected plants and burning them. A similar gall caused by insects is sometimes confused with the galls caused by bacteria but, by cutting the galls open, either the insects or the cells in which they developed will be plain to see. Cut off the infected stems and burn them.

Wintering tender roses — In considering winter hardiness, the importance of conditioning the plants by properly hardening off the canes cannot be stressed too much. Early autumn frosts can do tremendous damage if the canes are still green and soft. In the prairie regions, the months of September and October are usually sunny with light frosts starting in mid-September, increasing in severity during October, followed by freeze-up in November. During this time the roses are being inured gradually to the colder weather by the action of sun, light frost and the reduction of soil moisture.

You can assist in the ripening process by cutting off the fertilizer and reducing the supply of water to a minimum. The wise gardener is guided by the weather and, if the fall months are extremely dry, he will continue to supply water in reasonable amounts and prepare to give the plants a final soaking just before they are mounded up for the winter. Plants in dry soil are more likely to suffer winter injury than those in soil that is well charged with moisture.

Before the plants are mounded for the winter, there are a few preliminary operations to be carried out. Clean up all dead leaves and debris; cut off all broken canes and dig out any suckers. Strong shoots growing from the base of the plant, sometimes more than a foot from the centre, are likely to be understock; if the leaves on these shoots have more than five leaflets, chances are they are the wild rose and must be cut out promptly. All the hybrid teas are best cut back in October, leaving stems about a foot and a half high, but the hybrid polyanthas and florabundas are best left unpruned until spring. Gather up all the prunings and dead leaves and burn them to destroy the spores of black spot and mildew. Some gardeners go to the trouble of picking off all the leaves, as a further precaution against disease.

The prairie climate varies a good deal but, even in the mildest parts, the hybrid tea roses need to be mounded up to survive the winter. The covering material used may be granulated peat, dry soil or dry sawdust. Tests carried out in Manitoba have shown that dry sawdust and granulated peat give better results than soil but, where soil is the only material available, it must be brought from another part of the garden and not gathered up from around the roses. The soil must be dry and well pulverized so that it can run down among the canes to insulate each one. For this reason, it is not recommended to tie the canes together before putting on the mound of soil; if the shoots are spreading near the ground, very loose tying is recommended. If the soil is wet and lumpy it will not be suitable for mounding, so drier and finer soil must be obtained or the roses will not winter well.

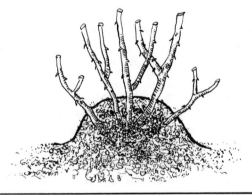

A foot-high mound of sawdust, peat moss or soil is placed on the tender roses in October after some pruning.

In the southern grassland areas, drift soil is obtainable and sometimes used for lawn dressing as well as for mounding roses. Drift soil is fine and powdery, easy to spread around the roses, but it has one fault; it is usually highly alkaline and, if used year after year, it will upset the chemical balance of neutral soil since some of the soil used for mounding is usually left around the plants in the spring.

The mounding should be done before the soil freezes. In the southern part of the prairies, the third week of October is the right time but, in northern areas, it is wise to get the first cover on the tender roses by the middle of the month. The material should be available in early October and ready to put on at short notice in case the weather suddenly turns bad.

The mounding is only the first phase of winter protection. A heavy layer of straw is put on about two weeks later, after some preparation has been made to forestall mice, which may do serious damage in the spring.

A few tablespoonfuls of poisoned grain placed in a tin can will take care of the mice. Gopher poison is used to contaminate the grain and the tins should be placed on their sides among the mounds of soil. Be sure to hide it from birds and be sure to destroy any leftover grain in the spring. The number of mice seems to vary from year to year and the amount of damage they can do depends upon the kind of winter we have. When the rose canes are girdled by mice, the top portion above the damage will die; if the girdling is low down on the plant, it may be killed outright.

By delaying the application of straw until the first week of November, or later if the weather is mild, the mice may find other places to spend the winter, but the straw must be put on before the plants are damaged by sudden subzero temperatures. There are several kinds of straw used to cover the roses: flax straw is preferred; it has the highest insulating value and does not blow around like cereal straw. If the flax straw is obtained in bales, it must be teased out before it is packed around and over the plants to a depth of two or three feet. In some areas, quantities of leaves are obtainable and, if used in a deep layer over the mounds of soil, they give good protection.

In spite of a generous cover of straw, the tender roses may winter badly if snow is sparse, the winter long and the cold intense. Snow is the best insulator — when it comes early and deep there is a good chance the roses will winter well.

There is often a temptation to remove the straw too early. It is not unusual to get a spell of mild weather in early April, only to have winter return a few weeks later. In the southern parts of the prairies the third week of April is about the right time to take off the straw, but it all depends on the weather; a week's delay will have no bad effect on the plants. It is better to keep them safe under the straw for a week longer than to run the risk of exposing the canes to hard frost. The mound of sawdust or soil is not taken off before the middle of May . . . even a bit later if the weather is bad.

It pays to keep some of the straw handy in case of a late spring frost. It is not unheard of to get twenty degrees of frost in May; when this occurs, it does tremendous damage to plants that have started into growth. If there is danger of a hard frost after the roses are uncovered, lay on a light cover of straw to protect the tender buds. When danger of hard frost is over, the pruning is done, after the same pattern outlined for the newly planted roses. The hybrid perpetual roses may have many more shoots than the hybrid teas and, being a bit hardier, they usually have more live wood in the spring. It is not necessary to cut back the shoots quite so hard as on the hybrid teas; in fact, six or seven buds can be left if they are green and plump.

Climbing and Rambling Roses in the Prairie Garden

In prairie gardens climbing roses are most uncertain, and only the keenest gardeners or those who have recently come to the prairies from the milder parts of Canada or from European countries, where these roses flourish, will be tempted to grow them. The only real chance of success is to plant the hardiest sorts against the house wall. Climbing roses on fences or pergolas will stand little chance of winter survival in prairie gardens, even if the plants are taken down and covered.

In tests carried out over a number of years with the hardiest known kinds, protecting the canes with several types of material, the tops invariably killed back to ground level and no blooms were produced. The tops must be kept alive if the plants are to bloom, as flowers are only produced on the last year's wood. There is nothing gained by covering the plants if only the roots remain alive. The varieties New Dawn, Blaze and Climbing American Beauty have been found the most satisfactory kinds to grow in prairie gardens and, if they are planted against the east or south wall of the house, there is a reasonable chance the plants will survive and bloom.

Starting climbing and rambling roses — Set the plants about two feet from the wall after making a wide hole two feet deep. Fill the hole with good soil, firming it around the roots, and support the canes on a trellis. In the fall, when the hybrid teas and other tender roses are mounded for the winter, the climbing roses are taken down from the trellis, the canes laid in a shallow trench and covered with dry sawdust or well-pulverized soil. The canes are best kept separate and not bundled together. Each one should be enclosed in the sawdust or soil and the material piled over them a foot or more deep. To keep the covering dry, lay on a few wide boards or a sheet of plastic and over this, a deep layer of flax straw.

If the snow comes early and deep and it can be kept on the plants all winter, there is a good chance the canes will be green when spring comes. There is a critical period when the canes are uncovered at the end of April. It is not unusual for green canes to shrivel and die when suddenly exposed to the drying winds and hot sun. By replacing a thin layer of the straw on the canes after the base covering has been taken off, you can inure them gradually to the hot sun and dry air. Sometimes the weather in May is reasonably warm, so the tops of the roses transpire moisture that cannot be replaced by roots still in frozen soil. When this occurs, the bark shrivels, the dormant buds dry up and all the work of protecting the plants through winter has been in vain.

Insects – If you succeed in getting the climbers through this critical period, there is a good chance of getting the plants to bloom. Special attention has to be paid to controlling insects, which are more of a problem on roses in the shadow of the house wall where the air is dry and favorable to the rapid increase of spider mites. Much of the trouble can be avoided if the canes are sprayed with water at high pressure in July and August. The spraying is best done in the evening hours, directing the water to the undersides of the leaves.

Summer care of climbing and rambling roses – Light doses of fertilizer such as 11.48.0 will be beneficial in June and July; a heaping handful to each plant is a maximum dose and it must be soaked in to do any good. During the summer, regular watering is important as plants near a house wall are often dry when plants elsewhere are in moist soil. Like the tender roses, however, climbers and ramblers can be severely damaged if the canes are still green when the first frost arrives; after the end of August, water and fertilizer should again be applied sparingly, to guard against prolonged growth.

Pruning climbing and rambling roses – The pruning of climbing and rambling roses differs a good deal from the hybrid teas; as the flowers of climbing roses are borne on canes that were made the previous year and not on the current year's wood, the old wood must be preserved. When the plants have done blooming in July, cut out to ground level all wood that is three years old or older. The ramblers are pruned in the same way as raspberries, since only one crop of bloom is produced on wood of the previous season's growth. After the canes have bloomed, they are of no further use and should be removed by cutting them down to the ground. Strong shoots from the base of the plant will supply next year's flowers if the shoots can be kept alive over winter.

Climbing American Beauty and Blaze will need to have part of the old wood removed in July when the plants have done blooming. New Dawn blooms on two-year-old wood as well as from the base of shoots made during the current year.

Shrub Roses in the Prairie Garden

There are a number of excellent shrub roses hardy enough for prairie gardens but some of them are rarely seen. A few of the best are *R. nitida, laxa, rubrifolia, spinosissima* and its variety *altaica,* and *hansa.*

R. nitida or the shining rose is found growing wild in Newfoundland and the eastern part of the continent. It has glossy leaves, dark green in summer and bronzy red in the fall. The tiny flowers are not freely produced nor are they showy, the color being soft rosy mauve. The season of bloom is soon over and the flowers are replaced by scarlet fruits. Later on, the leaves turn reddish to make a bright patch in the garden quite late in October. When the leaves finally fall, the red stems are revealed, to give interest in the winter and early spring. The shining rose will grow where other roses would fail; it manages to survive in places where the soil is lean and dry. It needs full sun and should be protected from harsh northwest winds in winter.

The Turkestan rose *(R. laxa)* is a fully hardy shrub rose from eastern Siberia with single white flowers followed by shapely orange scarlet fruits. It makes a five-foot bush and may be used as a background ornamental shrub.

The redleaf rose *(R. rubrifolia)* is grown for its reddish leaves. The flowers are small, rosy magenta and not very attractive, but the scarlet fruits are quite handsome over a long period.

The Scotch rose *(R. spinosissima)* has long been cultivated in European countries and has been used to develop many good shrub roses. It makes a low spreading bush about three feet high with attractive leaves and densely spined branches. It blooms in early July, bearing an abundance of white or pink flowers. The black fruits are carried on the plants through the winter.

The variety *altaica* from northwest Asia is one of the hardiest and most attractive roses for prairie gardens. It is taller and much more vigorous than the Scotch rose and well-grown plants are often six or seven feet high. The arching branches bear a profusion of single, creamy white flowers in late June, followed by roundish fruits, quite large and purple black. The altai rose is a good shrub for the back of the border or can be used to make a hedge, keeping it in line by cutting out stray shoots to ground level in July when the plants have done blooming. A hedge of altai rose in full bloom is a splendid sight and, if grown informally, it requires no special care.

The Persian yellow rose *(R. foetida persiana)* is an old variety that is frequently seen in prairie gardens, though it sometimes suffers some winter injury. In sheltered gardens the double, bright yellow blooms are freely produced in early July and are greatly admired. The leaves are handsome but highly susceptible to black spot, which is often responsible for a lot of the winter injury when the disease defoliates the plant in summer. A similar rose called Harrison's yellow is a hybrid between *R. foetida* and the Scotch rose *R. spinosissima.* It has been cultivated for a long time in prairie gardens and is esteemed for its soft yellow, semidouble blooms which are produced freely in late June and early July. It is not susceptible to black spot and for this reason is preferred to Persian yellow.

One of the best-known and most popular shrub roses is *hansa*. It was raised in Holland in 1905 and has been widely planted all across the prairies. The leaves are handsome and dark green if the plants are in neutral soil but, where the soil inclines to be alkaline, they turn a sickly yellow. The flowers are fully double, magenta red and are produced freely in July and sparingly through the season. It is not unusual to find good blooms on the bushes in October.

Several well-known shrub roses popular in the milder parts of Canada have been tested in prairie gardens. These include Dr. Hugo's rose *(R. hugonis)* and the handsome *moyesii*. The Dr. Hugo rose will survive in a well-sheltered garden where it will occasionally produce its pale yellow flowers in early June. More often than not, however, the stems dry out in winter and there is no bloom. *R. moyesii* has not survived in spite of wrapping the plant in straw.

Besides the hardy species roses and the Harrison's yellow, there are any number of hybrid shrub roses, many of them raised by plant breeders in western Canada. They are fully hardy without protection and can be used effectively in the landscape plans. Some of the best are Therese Bugnet, Betty Bland, Alysham, Wasagaming, Prairie Youth, Prairie Dawn, Metis and Cuthbert Grant.

Therese Bugnet is one of the best of all the shrub roses; it can be depended on to give a good account of itself all across the prairies. It is a complex hybrid of *R. acicularis, amblyotis, blanda* and *rugosa,* raised by Mr. Georges Bugnet of Legal, Alberta. It is one of the hardiest and most dependable of all the shrub roses. It makes a neat bush five or six feet high with large, double, rosy red blooms in July and later.

Betty Bland is a fine hardy rose developed by the late Dr. Frank L. Skinner of Dropmore, Manitoba, and has become one of the most popular prairie roses. It grows five feet high, bearing a profusion of bright pink flowers in July. The canes are reddish, giving it a long season of interest.

Alysham is a *hansa* – *nitida* hybrid raised by Mr. Percy Wright of Saskatoon. It has the attractive foliage of *nitida* with the double flowers of *hansa*. It grows three feet high and blooms freely in July.

Wasagaming is another good shrub rose raised by the late Dr. Frank L. Skinner of Dropmore, Manitoba. It has the *rugosa* rose as one parent and makes a spreading bush five feet high with dark green foliage. The bush is covered with double, sweet-scented, rosy pink blooms in July.

Prairie Youth was developed at the Morden Experimental Farm and has the altai rose and the sunshine rose *(R. sulfulta),* which is a prairie native, in its breeding. It makes a vigorous seven-foot shrub with arching branches bearing clusters of pure salmon pink flowers in July. The flowers are male sterile, so they produce no seed pods unless they happen to be fertilized with pollen from another rose. Prairie Youth is fully hardy in most of the prairie regions if sheltered from the northwest winds.

Prairie Dawn is a hardy repeat-blooming shrub rose raised at the Morden Experimental Farm. It blooms on the current year's wood in the manner of the hybrid teas, starting in July and continuing through the summer and early autumn. It makes an upright bush five to six feet high with dark green leaves and bright pink, semidouble flowers.

Métis is another hardy shrub rose raised at the Morden Experimental Farm by crossing Therese Bugnet with the shining rose *(R. nitida)*. It grows five feet high, making a finely branched shrub with small, glossy green leaves. Its lower stems have small thorns; the upper stems are thornless. The double flowers are a soft amaranth rose; the seed pods are bright red. The autumn foliage is bronzy red and the stems in winter are reddish. Métis has a long season of interest and is fully hardy all across the prairies.

Cuthbert Grant is a *R. sulfulta* hybrid raised by Mr. Henry Marshall of the Brandon Experimental Farm. It produces bright red flowers all through the summer on a three-foot bush. Some tip killing can be expected in winter but the plant quickly recovers and the new shoots soon make flower buds.

Twelve

Climbing and Trailing Plants

No plant gives the garden a more lived-in look than a climber, especially
the perennial or woody sorts. Climbing plants on fences give privacy and
shelter; when planted on the house wall they tie the house to its surroundings to make it part of the garden. In large gardens, pergolas and arbors
covered with live greenery will be cool retreats in the heat of the day.

The choice of suitable climbers is more restricted than in milder parts,
but there are a good many hardy woody climbers that are rare in prairie
gardens and there is no reason why this should be. Considering the charm
of climbers, it is difficult to understand why they are not seen more often.
They need support unless they are grown as ground covers; perhaps the
work of erecting a pergola or fence is what deters the average homeowner.
Those who would like to grow climbing plants will be well advised to start
with the hardiest sorts. Climbing roses are a poor bet: on fences or
pergolas they are useless; on house walls there is a reasonable chance of
success but the game is hardly worth the gamble, as it involves taking
down the canes in October, covering them for winter, uncovering them in
May and putting them back on the wall again.

The Planting and Care of Climbing and Trailing Plants

Building a pergola — A pergola is made with stout poles of oak or some other durable wood set in the ground two feet deep and extending seven feet above ground. Two rows of poles, ten feet apart with the poles spaced at the same distance in the row, make a basic frame. The poles are joined together by laying long poles on top of the uprights and securing them with spikes. Crosspieces are attached to form an arcade, over which vigorous plants will climb.

Climbers — Climbing plants should receive the same care and attention as the trees and shrubs. To grow vigorous, healthy climbers, the plants should be in good soil, should receive occasional doses of fertilizer when they show the first signs of unthriftiness and a good soaking of water when the soil gets dry. Spring planting is preferable, using young, vigorous plants, cutting them back to half their height and planting them firmly in good soil. The hardiest climbers can be transplanted safely in early October but only if the site is sheltered from harsh winter winds; if they are too exposed, the roots may dry out as the ground heaves in winter.

The Jackman clematis requires special care, but the procedure for planting it should serve as a pattern for other climbers. Most of the Jackman clematis are imported from Europe and sometimes have several inches of growth on them by the time they reach the home gardener. The new shoots must be protected from strong sunshine for a few days or they will be damaged. As soon as the plant is received it should be planted, watered, staked and tied, and shaded from sun if the new shoots are developing.

The time to plant is in early May, or as soon as you get the plant from the nurseryman. Dig a hole two feet deep and a foot and a half across. Loosen the subsoil and mix in a layer of rotted barnyard manure. Drainage is most important, so put a few inches of coarse gravel or old mortar rubble in the bottom of the hole. Fill it up with prepared soil — three parts fibrous loam, one part peat and one part sand. Firm the soil, then dig a hole large enough to hold the roots without crowding and set the plant with the crown just below the surface. Jackman clematis are susceptible to crown rot and this will be aggravated if the young plant is set too deep.

The flowers are borne on the current year's wood, so, when the top part of the vine is killed, it is not too serious. New shoots grow from the base and from the lower stems that have survived the winter, to flower in July. In October, the plant is taken down from the wall, cut back to leave stems about two feet high and covered with dry peat or sawdust. Over this put a cover of flax straw a foot deep and pile on snow through the winter.

With all climbers, pruning is a matter of cutting out dead branches in

April and thinning out overcrowded branches and shoots to keep the plant vigorous and within bounds.

Ground covers — Once you have established the ground covers, they need little attention except occasional hand weeding; those that flower should be sheared when the bloom is over. This does not apply to the lily of the valley, which is not showy in bloom but bears its flowers almost hidden among the leaves.

Climbing Plants for the Prairies

Grape — One of the most useful climbers is the riverbank grape *(Vitis riparia)*. It is fully hardy, with large attractive leaves and bunches of small, bluish grapes in September which are useful for jelly and for feeding the birds. The male and female flowers are borne on separate plants, so one of each is needed to ensure a crop of fruit. The pollen-bearing male flowers have a sweet scent not unlike that of wallflowers and, for this reason alone, the native grape is worth cultivating. It makes fairly rapid growth on a fence or pergola and may be trained on a trellis attached to the house wall. It must have well-drained soil and prefers a place in the sun.

The Virginia creeper *(Parthenocissus quinquefolia)*, sometimes called the false grape, is a native plant in the southeastern parts of the prairies and was used by the early settlers to cover fences and verandas. It has not found favor in modern landscape plans and this is a pity. One of the reasons for its lost popularity is its susceptibility to leaf hopper attack. These insects are a nuisance to both native grape and Virginia creeper, especially when the plants are near walks, where they are liable to be brushed. But the leaf hoppers should not deter more widespread cultivation of either climber; the insects can be controlled by spraying with Malathion and by wise planting.

The ordinary Virginia creeper is not able to cling to a wall or pergola, so it must be supported. A similar one with smaller leaves, the Englemann Virginia creeper *(P. quinquefolia englemanni),* has the necessary discs on the tendrils which enable it to cling to walls but it is not hardy in prairie gardens. The Virginia creeper is fully hardy, bears tiny bunches of blue black berries of no culinary value but makes up for this in its highly colored leaves in September.

Bittersweet — The American bittersweet *(Celastrus scandens),* found in southern Manitoba, is not cultivated to any extent in prairie gardens. This is a pity as it is useful for covering fences and pergolas. The bittersweet twines around trees in its native habitat or it may trail along the ground. The leaves are palish green, the flowers unattractive and mostly hidden among the foliage. The bittersweet comes into its own when the leaves turn yellow and fall in late September, revealing clusters of orange seed pods later to split open to show the scarlet seeds. Some plants have only male flowers, so there are no seeds. Nurserymen propagate selections that produce large clusters of seeds and these are the ones to plant. Bittersweet may not be showy in summer when only the leaves are visible, but there is no finer sight in the late autumn when leaves are gone than a plant of bittersweet climbing a tree or fence, festooned with bunches of bright orange and scarlet seeds.

Clematis — One of the largest groups of climbing plants is the clematis; while most clematis are not hardy enough for prairie gardens, there are a fairly large number of species and hybrids that do well. Some of these are native plants, rampant and adapted to most of the prairies. Others are not so vigorous and are more restricted in their range. As a general rule, all clematis like sun, well-drained soil and are tolerant of lime.

One of the hardiest and most vigorous is the western virgin's bower *(Clematis ligusticifolia)*. It stands the heat and dry soil remarkably well and grows twenty feet high in well-sheltered spots. For shading a veranda or covering an arbor or pergola, it is most attractive. The handsome leaves are dark green and, in July, the whole plant is covered with billowy panicles of white flowers. Its rampant habit can be curbed by cutting out some of the old wood every two or three years and shortening the young shoots by a third.

The Chinese clematis *(C. tangutica)* is equally hardy, though not so rampant nor so vigorous as the western virgin's bower. The bright green leaves are quite attractive all through the summer; the flowers, each on a slender stem, are nodding bells of golden yellow in July. The blooming season extends for a few weeks, then glistening, silvery seed pods are formed which fall to the ground in late September. Young plants are sometimes produced in unwanted places but this single fault should not deter one from planting a Chinese clematis. A Korean clematis called the hermitgold clematis *(C. serratifolia)* is similar, but flowers a bit later and makes a more vigorous plant. It is not so frequently planted as the Chinese clematis although it seems to grow well in most parts of the prairies. An interesting hybrid called Grace, raised by Dr. Skinner, is a hybrid between the western virgin's bower and *C. serratifolia.* It is a strong plant bearing masses of creamy flowers in July.

The Jackman clematis *(C. jackmannii)* includes a number of choice, large-flowered varieties which are not fully hardy in prairie gardens. In the past, the original one with purple flowers has grown very well in some areas. There is a good chance of success with the Jackman clematis if it is planted against the south or east wall of the house. On a fence or pergola with no shelter from winter winds and no warmth from the foundation wall, it is useless. Tests have shown that Jackman clematis die out repeatedly when planted away from a house wall, in spite of covering the vines with sawdust, peat or dry soil.

Honeysuckle — The honeysuckles include a number of climbing plants; a few are hardy enough for the prairies but many are much too tender. The woodbine or English honeysuckle *(Lonicera periclymenum),* a plant that brings back fond memories for some prairie dwellers who may remember hedgerows festooned with its sweet-smelling flowers, is not hardy here. The Dropmore scarlet trumpet honeysuckle, a hybrid between *L. hirsuta* and *sempervirens,* is a substitute for the woodbine but has no scent, nor does it grow so tall. The Dropmore honeysuckle blooms from mid-June until October and sometimes produces flowers opening in November. It makes a six-foot or taller plant on a trellis against the house, or it can be grown on a fence or pergola. Although it is hardy all across the prairies, it will make better growth and bloom over a longer period if protected from the northwest winds.

There are several native honeysuckles, both bush and climbing plants. The climbers could be used effectively in prairie gardens; the bush types cannot compete with improved bush forms. The twining honeysuckle *(L. glaucescens)* can be made to climb up to ten feet. The leaves are about three inches long in opposite pairs sometimes joined at the base. The pale yellow flowers appear in terminal clusters, followed by red berries.

The Japanese honeysuckle, which is admired in milder parts of the country, is much too tender for the prairies.

Moonseed — Canada moonseed *(Menispermum canadense)* is a native plant extending from the Atlantic to the eastern part of Manitoba, found chiefly in wooded areas and along the banks of streams. At the Morden Experimental Farm, it has persisted for thirty years against an east-facing wall but has never reached higher than a few feet. Its chief attraction is its dark green leaves, roundish at the base and lobed farther up the stems. The whitish flowers are not showy, nor are they produced freely. In moist soil and partial shade and where the plants can be protected from drying winds, the moonseed will make an interesting low climber.

Unthrifty climbers — The Chinese wisteria *(Wisteria sinensis),* which is greatly admired in gardens at the coast and in other mild areas, is not suitable for prairie gardens. It would be useless to attempt to grow this choice climber with its long chains of lavender mauve flowers and handsome leaves. The Japanese wisteria *(W. florabunda)* is said to be hardier, but both the Chinese and Japanese are much too tender for prairie gardens.

The actinidias are a group of climbing shrubs with handsome leaves, sometimes variegated. The hardiest species, *Actinidia kolomikta,* is not fully hardy in prairie gardens and may kill to ground level in severe winters.

Boston Ivy *(Parthenocissus tricuspidata),* one of the choicest species related to the Virginia creeper, is unfortunately much too tender for the prairies.

The climbing forms of evergreen such as *Euonymus fortunei vegetus,* commonly called the big-leaf wintercreeper, have been tried in Manitoba but killed to ground level. The hardy deciduous climbers can add a lot of interest to the garden and are worth cultivating, but plants that are only root hardy are useless.

Ground Covers for the Prairies

The usefulness of ground-covering plants has not been fully appreciated in prairie gardens but, as garden maintenance seems to become more of a time-consuming occupation, ground covers warrant more consideration. In most gardens there are problem areas, odd corners where it may be difficult to get anything to grow or sloping areas where grass has been difficult to maintain. Certain plants spread by underground shoots or stolons and, while a profusion of suckers may be deplored where they are in close contact with less adventurous plants, these rampant wanderers will fill those odd corners with greenery. Generally they grow well in poor soil and require a minimum of attention.

Ground covering plants – The variegated form of the goutweed *(Aego-podium podograria variegata)* is an abominable weed in some areas, spreading by underground shoots and penetrating deep in the soil. It grows in poor soil shaded from sun and is useful as a ground cover in areas where it cannot interfere with other plants. It has no merit as a border plant but it makes an acceptable ground cover with pale green, lobed leaves edged with silver.

The common bugleweed *(Ajuga reptans)* and its purple-leaved form have rosettes of roundish leaves, glossy bronzy green or purplish. It has survived for a number of years in some areas, spreading to make large mats. In full sun, the rosettes of greenery which are carried through the winter are sometimes browned unless the plants are covered in October with boughs or a thin layer of flax straw. In shaded areas, where the snow is likely to pile and remain through the winter, the bugleweed makes a reliable ground cover. Old plants should be divided and replanted every few years in the spring, the healthy portions being taken from around the edges and the worn-out centre portion discarded.

The bearberry *(Arctostaphylos urva-ursi)* is a prostrate woodland creeper forming large, dense mats of shiny, dark green leaves and bearing small red berries. It grows where the soil is acid and dry; in prairie gardens, where the soil is inclined to be alkaline, it is of no value.

Cotoneaster – The cotoneasters are known in prairie gardens as hedge plants and specimen shrubs. A small-leaved, low-growing species called adpressa has survived with occasional winter injury at Morden. It spreads with dense branches that hug the ground and shining dark green leaves that turn reddish in the fall. It occasionally produces a heavy crop of bright red berries and is only recommended for trial in favored areas where good snow cover and well-drained soil can be provided. The rock cotoneaster *(C. horizontalis),* admired for its glossy leaves, prolific quantities of orange red berries and the peculiar herringbone pattern of its winter branches, is much too tender for the prairies.

Euonymus — A hardy, low-growing form of deciduous euonymus, called the running euonymus or *E. obovata,* is used as a ground cover under trees and on shady banks in the eastern part of the country. In sheltered gardens, under good snow cover, it will survive and flourish reasonably well on the prairies.

Clematis — Some of the clematis may well be considered for ground covers on large sloping areas where the soil is dry. The Jouin clematis *(C. jouiniana),* which, on a pergola or fence, is likely to kill back to below the snow line, makes a good ground cover. It has handsome, dark green leaves; late in the season it produces an abundance of pale blue, tubular flowers that are showy and sweet scented. Several other hardy clematis can be used in the same way on sunny banks where the soil is well drained and not too rich.

Fleeceflower — The Japanese fleeceflower *(Polygonatum cuspidatum)* is new to prairie gardens but has been grown as a ground cover in some parts of the country for a number of years. It makes a tangled mass of roots that penetrates the soil deeply and spreads fairly rapidly to cover the ground. In southern Manitoba it grows about a foot high, with attractive roundish leaves that turn crimson in the fall. In late summer it produces small spikes of bright pink flowers in abundance. The leaves are browned by the first hard frost and the top growth is killed to the ground in the winter. The Japanese fleeceflower is a nuisance plant in the perennial border but it makes a first-class ground cover and seems to have no soil preferences. It grows well in full sun or half shade and should be cut down close to the ground every year in early May.

Periwinkle — The periwinkle *(Vinca minor)* is an old-fashioned plant with small, dark green leaves and blue flowers. It is not in general use in prairie gardens, though the herbaceous periwinkle *(V. herbacea)* is hardy in most areas and the common periwinkle may thrive in some parts. The herbaceous species, which is the best choice for prairie gardens, loses most of its leaves in winter and the trailing stems are sometimes damaged when snow cover is inadequate. It seems to do well where the soil is not too dry and in a sunny spot sheltered from the northwest winds. The common periwinkle has persisted at Morden for a number of years but has not made a dense ground cover nor bloomed very freely.

Gray-leaved plants — Gray-leaved plants do best in full sun where the soil is not too rich. One called snow-in-summer *(Cerastium tomentosum)* can be a nuisance plant in the rock garden where it may smother less vigorous plants but, on a sunny bank, it makes a good ground cover about six inches high with narrow, silvery gray leaves and a show of white flowers in June. After flowering, the plants should be trimmed back to keep them neat and within bounds.

Lily of the valley — The lily of the valley *(Convallaria majalis)* is common enough, yet its value as a ground cover plant is not fully appreciated in prairie gardens. It has been cultivated for a long time in old world gardens, where it is esteemed for its dainty, sweet-scented flowers. It grows well in shade — under trees, in the shadow of buildings or in the open. It spreads not too rapidly by underground stolons, making a dense carpet of greenery about six inches high. The leaves remain healthy and attractive all through the summer and should be left on the plants through the winter to hold a cover of snow. In the spring when the old top growth is pulled off, top-dress the plants with an inch or two of rich soil. New plants are best set out in August, digging the plants carefully and dividing them into pieces with two or three dormant shoots. Plant them six inches apart in well-prepared soil, watering them and covering the new planting with a layer of flax straw in October.

Ground ivy — *(Nepeta hederace)* is known by many common names and usually cursed as an abominable weed. It creeps along the ground in shady spots, sometimes venturing into the lawn to thrive there if the grass is poor. It makes a useful ground cover where it can run at will without interfering with other plants. The leaves are gray green and roundish with scalloped edges; the flowers, which are borne freely on plants in the sun, are violet blue. The moneywort or Creeping Jenny *(Lysimachia numularia)* is a more refined plant, though it too can become a nuisance in some places. It grows in sun or shade with small, bright green leaves and golden yellow flowers.

Pink — The maiden pink *(Dianthus deltoides)* is a fine edging plant used along the front of the perennial border or in the rock garden. It forms neat mats of dark green leaves and bears a profusion of pink or red flowers from June until August. It makes a useful ground cover for a sunny bank, requiring little attention beyond an annual shearing when the flowers fade.

Phlox — The moss phloxes provide masses of color in the rock garden or at the front of the perennial border in May. The value of these evergreen trailing plants has been overlooked to a large extent but there is no denying their usefulness as ground covers. The one called Arctic phlox *(Phlox borealis)* is by far the best as a ground cover; the leaves are bright green all the year round. Towards the end of May, the plants start to bloom and are covered entirely with tiny, bright pink flowers. The Arctic phlox should be in the sun where the soil is well drained; it needs to be covered with boughs in the fall if the plants are exposed to the northwest winds and bare of snow.

Stonecrop — The stonecrops *(Sedum)* are a large group of plants; some are herbaceous — the tops die in winter — and others hold their leaves all the year round. One of the best for covering the ground is a Siberian species called the evergreen stonecrop *(S. hybridum)*. It makes a low plant with glossy leaves and yellow flowers in June and July. The orange stonecrop *(S. kamschaticum)* is a taller plant growing a foot high in partial shade. A variegated form *(S. kamschaticum variegatum)* has green and yellow leaves, yellow flowers and reddish seed pods, giving it a long season of interest. A pink-flowered stonecrop called *S. ewersi* grows about six inches high with neat roundish leaves of blue green and pink flowers. *S. spurium* has evergreen foliage and pink flowers in July and August. Any of these stonecrops make good ground covers in full sun or partial shade, as long as the soil is well drained and the plants protected from sun in the early spring.

Thyme — The old-fashioned thyme, used in the kitchen and in sunny places on the rock garden, makes a fine ground cover. It can be used effectively between paving stones or it may be planted on a sunny bank. The soil for thyme should be gritty and not too rich in humus. There are several forms of mother of thyme *(Thymus serphyllum)*, with leaves smelling either of lemon or caraway, as well as the ordinary thyme that is used in the kitchen.

Thirteen

The Perennial Border

A border of herbaceous perennials, if properly planned and cared for, will be a source of pleasure from the first warm days of early spring until long after the most tender plants have been cut down by frost. Herbaceous plants make annual top growth that flowers, then dies down, storing the next year's growth buds underground. In prairie gardens, where spring is eagerly awaited, the perennial border gives the first signs of life; some hardy bulbs push their shoots through the ground while the last of the snow lingers in shady nooks. But some perennials are slow to waken; they show no signs of life until May is well advanced. It is not unusual to see the nodding bluebells of the Siberian squill *(Scilla sibirica)* opening in late April and the pure white chalices of the bloodroot *(Sanguinaria canadensis)* soon following. There is an excitement in watching for the return of the favorite perennials, recognizing them by their first pale green or pinkish shoots. If the border has been well planned, it will include some of the earliest bulbs as well as some of the later hardy chrysanthemums and asters, to give a long season of bloom and interest.

Designing the Perennial Border

The size and location of a perennial border will have to fit the property; choose a place in the sun away from encroaching tree roots or hedges. When it comes to deciding the size of the border, remember that it should not be less than six feet wide or it will be difficult to arrange the plants effectively.

Before you plant perennials, make a plan showing where each kind has to go. You should know the height, color and season of bloom to arrange the plants to the best advantage. As a general rule, the tall plants are placed at the back, the medium-tall ones in the centre, shorter ones towards the front with the lowest ones along the edge. To avoid a monotonous repetition, put a few tall plants here and there among the medium ones and a few medium ones towards the front.

The earliest flowers are bulbous plants; squills, grape hyacinths and many kinds of tulips will give patches of bright color before most of the other plants show signs of blooming. Bulbs are most effective when planted in groups of a dozen or more; a few scattered specimens will add nothing to the perennial border. Be bold when you plant spring-flowering bulbs. Choose brightly colored varieties and keep the colors separate; mixed plantings are pretty enough but not so effective as bold groups of single colors. Many of the hardy lilies which bloom in July have orange-colored flowers which are difficult to associate harmoniously with certain shades of pink. Keep these orange lilies away from the pink lythrums and other flowers of similar color. You can neutralize the harsh shades of orange with patches of white; shasta daisies and the sneezewort achillea are useful for this.

A mixture of colors is generally harmonious if a few basic rules are followed. Start at one end of your border with the soft shades of yellow, blue and pale pink, leading into the brighter colors towards the centre, where the bright scarlets, dark crimsons, purples and rich yellows will catch the eye in bold contrasts. Taper off with the medium and paler shades to the soft yellows, blues and pinks at the other end. No plan should be followed too rigidly, however; if the perennial border is only twenty feet or so in length, a random mixed planting will be more effective. Use plenty of white-flowered perennials among the reds and use rich yellows among the blues to accentuate these colors by contrast.

Most of the plants set out in the home garden perennial border are arranged in groups of three; in large borders, groups of five or more are used to make bold patches of color. The size of the mature plant is, however, the determining factor. The small perennial border may not have room for a group of three peonies, for example; one will be sufficient. Other vigorous or spreading plants such as bleedingheart, goldenglow, sea lavender and daylilies may be used singly, too. Each of them needs to be spaced three to three and one-half feet apart to look its best.

A PLAN FOR A PERENNIAL BORDER

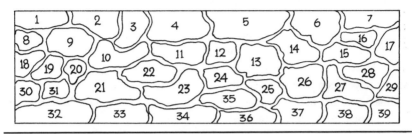

(1) monkshood; (2) larkspur; (3) aster, tall; (4) globethistle; (5) Oriental poppy; (6) sunflower; (7) scabious; (8) shasta daisy; (9) gasplant; (10) eryngo or sea holly; (11) lythrum; (12) goatsbeard; (13) peony; (14) campion or lychnis; (15) bleedingheart; (16) phlox, tall; (17) speedwell; (18) blanket-flower or gaillardia; (19) aster, dwarf; (20) *Anemone sylvestris;* (21) bearded iris; (22) hardy mums; (23) daylily; (24) sea lavender; (25) sneezeweed; (26) babysbreath; (27) balloonflower; (28) rosyveil gypsophila; (29) penstemon, dwarf; (30) stonecrop; (31) clustered bellflower; (32) Carpathian bellflower; (33) bugle flower; (34) maiden pink; (35) meadowrue; (36) alumroot or coral bells; (37) meadowsweet; (38) moss phlox; (39) thyme

In spite of good planting, the perennial border will never be completely satisfying and this is one of its fascinating features. There will be mistakes in arrangement not seen until the plants are well established and flowering; there will be winter losses from time to time, leaving gaps that may have to be filled with makeshift material in the spring. And, unless you curb them, some rampant sorts will crowd out the weaker ones.

It is a good plan to carry a few spares in the reserve garden; a row of perennials in the vegetable garden may be useful to fill gaps in the border and may also be a source of cut flowers. As a last resort, certain annuals may serve as emergency fillers; some kinds will not look out of place but others are not at all suitable. The most useful annuals for the purpose are the Marguerite carnations, gloriosa daisies, statice, annual chrysanthemums, tulip poppy, pansies and violas. The annuals to avoid using in the perennial border are marigolds, petunias and salvias.

The Planting and Care of the Perennial Border

Preparing the soil for the perennial border — Most of the perennials are planted in the spring, starting after the ground has thawed out and dried up so that working is pleasant. The planting season continues for as long as the plants remain dormant. When the top growth is six inches or more, successful transplanting is uncertain as the top growth wilts when exposed to drying winds and hot sun. Late-transplanted perennials will recover quickly, however, when the roots are set firmly in moist soil and the tops sprayed occasionally with water from the garden hose. Guard against too much water at the roots; in soggy soil, the young plants will have difficulty putting out new feeding roots.

Certain perennials should be planted in the fall — this is not to say spring planting is unsuccessful, but there is nothing to gain by cultivating some plants through the first summer. Peonies, for example, are offered for sale by some nurserymen and garden centres in the spring. These plants have been dug in the fall and stored in cold rooms for the winter. Unless they are planted early, before the eyes or dormant buds start to shoot, they make little headway the first year. Healthy portions with three to five eyes set out in mid-September will overtake the spring-planted stock in most instances. Peonies root deep into the subsoil, but the dormant buds should not be set deeper than two inches below the soil level or blooming will be delayed.

Hardy lilies are planted in September. A few trumpet lilies and others of borderline hardiness are available from dealers in the spring; these are planted in May. Different kinds of lilies are planted at different depths. Some, called stem rooters, have annual roots on their lower stems; these are planted deeper than those with basal roots only. The proper depth to plant the various lilies and other hardy bulbs will be found in chapter fourteen. Groups of hardy lilies look well among the perennials; plant them in threes or fives of one variety, setting the bulbs on a layer of coarse sand to ensure good drainage. Some will start to grow before spring frosts are over; Hanson, Martagon, and the hybrids of these two species, together with the Caucasian lily, are all early starters. A layer of flax straw, placed around the stems in October, will keep the soil frozen longer in the spring and retard growth, so take the straw off promptly when the new shoots come through the ground, always ready to replace it if frost threatens.

Summer care of the perennial border — A newly planted perennial border will need little attention the first year except for regular hoeing to keep down annual weeds and prevent the soil from baking. The perennial weeds will not be a problem if the ground has been prepared properly. If dandelions or quack grass have been allowed to invade the perennial border, they will soon penetrate the heart of peonies and other deep-rooted plants; when this occurs, it may be necessary to dig up the whole plant and pull it apart to get rid of the weeds. Chemical weed control is not practical in the perennial border; even spraying adjacent grass areas may be dangerous unless the amine form of 2-4-D is used carefully on a calm day.

The perennials vary in their requirements; deep-rooted peonies, for example, seldom need watering once they become well established. However, in periods of summer drought the leaves tend to wilt; when this happens, the plants should be soaked with water from a slow-running garden hose. The critical time in the seasonal growth of peonies occurs immediately after the blooms have faded, when the plant is initiating the next year's flower buds. If the soil is dry when these new buds are developing, next year's blooms will suffer. The shallow-rooted plants will need more frequent watering; the hardy chrysanthemums, for example, often suffer from drought, especially in the early part of the summer before the stolons or suckers which make the flowering shoots are well rooted. If watering is necessary, be sure to soak the soil thoroughly; frequent light sprinklings that wet the surface only will encourage surface roots, liable to injury, rather than penetrating, protected roots.

In early August, when the first flush of bloom is over, the perennial border is in the doldrums for a few weeks; the bearded irises, peonies, bleedinghearts, scarlet lightning, Oriental poppies and delphiniums have bloomed, leaving the border looking drab. It is often neglected at this time and more attention is given to the annual borders that are just coming into their own. The perennial border should be given a summer clean-up when the delphiniums have finished flowering; start by cutting off spent blooms before spreading a light dressing of fertilizer and watering it in. If delphiniums are cut down when the flowers fade, the plants fertilized and given plenty of water, a second crop of flowers will be produced in September. The stems will not be so tall nor so robust as those that produced flowers in July but they will add a bit of color to the border at a time when tall blue flowers are not plentiful.

Fertilizing perennials — If you have prepared the soil by deep digging, adding rotted barnyard manure, the new perennial border will need no additional nutrients for several years. When the plants show signs of unthriftiness — the leaves are smaller and paler, the flowers lose some color, the stems are shorter — give the whole border a dose of 11.48.0 at the rate of two ounces to each square yard. Scatter the fertilizer evenly around each plant; keep it off the leaves or you may burn them. Rake in the fertilizer before giving the whole border a good soaking.

In the fall, spread on a layer of rotted barnyard manure; two or three inches will be sufficient to give winter protection and release nutrients slowly when the covering is dug into the border in the spring. Certain perennial plants are not herbaceous, that is, the top growth does not die down in the fall but is carried through the winter in a green state. Some of the sedums are in this group; so are the perennial candytufts, the bergenia, heuchera and the thymes. Where these plants have been included in the perennial border, special care must be taken not to smother them with rotted manure.

Staking perennials — Tall plants usually need stakes or they are damaged by wind and beaten down by rain. Bamboo makes good supports but it is expensive; willow wands and pieces of twiggy branches are quite accept-able substitutes. The hollow stems of delphiniums are not strong enough to support their heavy flower spikes in summer storms of wind and rain. Too often, the stems are bundled together like sheaves of wheat, then tied to a stake; they should be separated, each one tied with soft string to a strong stake. A few pieces of twiggy branches will support the medium-tall perennials that tend to flop. Place three or four pieces around each plant before the shoots get too tall; by getting the supports in position while the plants are still young, the new shoots can grow up through the twigs. Good staking will give adequate support without being conspicuous, and it must be done before, not after the plants have been damaged. When plants are blown down or beaten into the ground by violent summer rains, no amount of staking will restore their former poise.

Wintering perennials — Not all the perennials found in prairie gardens are fully hardy; without the protection of snow, some die out when exposed to wind and extreme temperatures. Those with leafy tops are susceptible to damage from sunscald and desiccation. Snow gives the best protection; when it comes early and deep and remains until April, the perennial plants are usually safe from winter harm. Top growth will help to hold the snow and should not be cut off until spring if the border is exposed to the northwest winds. In sheltered gardens, where snow can be expected to pile and stay, the tops may be cut off to ground level in October. The only merit in this is that it gives the border a neat appearance. Even more effective than the old growth in holding snow and protecting perennials is a layer of flax straw or pieces of evergreen or deciduous branches. Flax straw is much preferred to the cereal straws because it doesn't pack down tightly or blow around.

Perennials may survive the winter only to die in the spring. The shallow-rooted chrysanthemums and the Michaelmas daisies can be smoth-ered by the excess water of melting snow, or the young shoots may dry up if the weather in May is hot and windy. It often happens that the old portion of a chrysanthemum plant kills out, leaving only the stolons or suckers alive. These stolons have few if any roots and, if the soil dries out before they are established, the whole plant dies. Watch such plants closely in the spring and recover them if they appear to be languishing.

The hardy chrysanthemums and perennial asters will benefit from a top-dressing of fine soil put on the plants in the spring. Work it around the base of the plants to a depth of an inch or so, but do not bury the young shoots. Most of the damage to the moss phloxes, the thymes, bugle flower and evergreen sedums is done in the early spring, when the snow melts to expose the plants to drying winds. When the straw is removed from these plants, shade them from unseasonable warm weather with a few boughs.

The Canterburybells, sweetwilliams, hollyhocks and pansies are usually treated as biennial plants, grown from seed one year to flower the next. They sometimes persist a second winter or even longer, but they are not considered permanent plants for the perennial border. Their winter survival is not certain and casualties run high when the plants are bare of snow in the late winter and early spring. When the leafy rosettes of Canterburybells are browned by dry winds, there is little or no bloom. When the tops of sweetwilliam die, the bloom is destroyed though the roots are still alive. The same holds true for pansies. Hollyhocks, too, are not reliable, though the single-flowered varieties come through the winter well enough where the soil is dry. Heavy layers of wet leaves will cause the tops of these leafy plants to rot off; only the lightest cover of flax straw or a layer of boughs is needed to keep the snow from blowing off and the ground from thawing out too soon in the spring.

Propagating Perennials

Some perennials may be grown from seed, and this provides a quick way to raise a patch of plants. Seed is the natural way of plant increase but there are some drawbacks to raising plants in this way. Plants from seed are usually a mixture of colors and plant types, many of them inferior to the mother plant. Seeds from named varieties of peonies, irises, pyrethrums, Oriental poppies or any other perennial which has been developed by hybridization will give seedlings that are generally inferior to the seed parent. On the other hand, seeds of the Maltese Cross *(Lychnis chalcedonica)*, gasplant *(Dictamnus fraxinella)* and other perennials considered to be true species will give seedling plants that are similar to the mother plant.

Because the named varieties of perennials cannot be reproduced true to type from seed, other methods are used. Plant division is the chief method of propagating named varieties, though stem cuttings are used for some. Grafting is rarely used as a method of increasing perennials but improved forms of babysbreath *(Gypsophila paniculata)* are sometimes grafted on seedling roots of the type plant. Cuttings, graftage and division are methods of vegetative propagation, sometimes referred to as asexual propagation, producing plants which are a part of and therefore identical to the parent. There is no difference in color, height or plant habit. All the Festiva Maxima peonies in the world and all the Peace roses came, originally, from one solitary plant. The commonest perennials which may be raised satisfactorily from seed are delphiniums, gasplant, blanket flower, lupins, Oriental poppy, pyrethrum, Missouri evening primrose, blazingstar, veronica and viola.

Perennials from seeds — There is no particular merit in sowing perennial seeds indoors and, unless one has a cool greenhouse, it is better to sow in the open ground or in a garden frame. Some perennials sown early indoors and later transplanted to the open ground will bloom the first year but, for all you get out of them, you may as well sow outdoors and wait for bloom the following year. Indoor sowing is done in February, using a sterilized mixture of two parts loam, one part peat and one part sand. Shallow boxes may be used but four-inch clay pots are better; a four-inch pot will hold all the seedlings needed for a home garden and plenty more to give away or discard.

Drainage is very important, so place an inch of coarse gravel in the pot; add an inch of the rough portions of the soil mixture left after it has been screened through a half-inch sieve. Fill the pot with fine soil, made firm by pressing with the lid of a suitable-sized can, leaving half an inch of space between the level of the soil and the rim of the pot. A fairly good job of sterilizing the filled pots is done by placing them in a 180-degree oven for forty-five minutes. When the pots are ready for seeding, stand them in a bowl of water until the surface and the whole soil mass is saturated, then let them drain before sowing the seed. If you make a good job of baking the soil and use boiled water, or water to which a drop of Panodrench has been added, damping-off fungus that causes so much damage to seedling plants can be avoided.

All the seeds should be sown just thick enough to give a stand of plants; in most instances, seed is sown much too thickly, with the result that the seedlings crowd one another, become weak and more susceptible to fungus diseases. The depth of sowing is governed by the size of the seed: lupins have large seeds and should be sown half an inch deep; Canterbury-bells, which have fine seeds that fail to germinate when covered too deeply, require only the lightest sprinkling of soil. Cover the pots with glass to prevent the rapid evaporation of moisture from the surface. Put paper over the glass to keep out the light.

Most perennial seeds germinate satisfactorily at room temperature, though some such as delphinium and Oriental poppy will germinate better where the temperature is ten to fifteen degrees cooler. There is a wide difference in the time of germination: some seeds sprout in a few days; others take a few weeks. Lupins, for example, will germinate in four or five days at seventy degrees, providing the hard seed coat has been nicked to allow moisture to penetrate. Delphinium seed may take three weeks — it may not grow at all if the seed has been stored at a high temperature. Delphinium seed, gathered from select plants in the home garden, should be kept in the refrigerator until the seed is sown; otherwise, it deteriorates quickly.

The seedlings are handled in the same manner as annuals, transplanting them into shallow boxes when the first true leaves are formed. The soil for transplanting is made by mixing three parts loam with one part peat and one part sand. Space the seedlings one to two inches apart, according to their size. Water them and shade them for a few days and transfer the boxes outdoors to a frame towards the middle of May. In June, the young plants are lined out in a sheltered part of the garden, set in rows a foot apart. By September, most of them will be ready for planting in the perennial border. Any that are too small should be left where they are until spring comes; cover them with dry leaves and a few twiggy boughs.

Outdoor seeding is practical either in the open ground or in a garden frame. If a garden frame is being used to raise annual plants, it can be used for sowing seeds of perennials when the annuals have been planted out. Open ground sowings should be made in a sheltered part of the garden where the soil has been prepared by digging in a liberal amount of peat and sand. The surface must be well pulverized to make a smooth, level seedbed, using a garden fork to dig the soil six inches deep. Firm the seedbed by treading, then rake off any lumps or stones. Sow the seed in rows four to six inches apart, using the wider rows for the sorts with the largest seeds. Scatter the seeds very thinly, covering them lightly with fine soil firmed by tamping with the back of the rake. After watering the seeds carefully with a fine-nozzled watering can, shade the seedbed from sun and wind with burlap or cotton. The covering must be taken off as soon as the seeds sprout, but the young plants should be shaded lightly until they make their first true leaves.

When the seedlings are an inch high, thin them out, leaving one plant every three inches in the row. The most vigorous plants usually develop flowers with poor, washed-out colors; discard these in favor of the smaller ones, which are more likely to be superior in color and plant habit.

Propagating perennials by plant division — Some perennials are divided and replanted in the spring, some in summer and others in the fall. In every case, the plants to be divided are dug carefully to preserve as much root as possible. It is important to do the dividing and replanting at the proper time; the late-flowering perennials are best done in the spring, around the first of May, the early flowering ones in the fall. There are some exceptions: the bearded irises, Oriental poppies and bleedinghearts transplant best in early August; mid-September is the best time to move peonies; lilies can be transplanted safely at the same time and up until the middle of October.

The perennials that are transplanted in the spring are mostly those with fibrous roots — daylilies, phlox, heliopsis, lychnis, thalictrum, rudbeckia and veronica. These pull apart quite easily into pieces with several shoots. It may be necessary to use a knife to cut the woody centres of phlox or similar plants, but the knife should only be used as a last resort.

Lythrums are the most difficult perennials to divide, especially when they get old. The roots are woody, very hard, and need an axe to split them. It is recommended that young plants be raised from cuttings rather than plant division.

The hardy chrysanthemums and perennial asters or Michaelmas daisies need more regular dividing than most perennials. The best plants are grown from single pieces carefully removed from the mother plants in early May. You can take them off two weeks earlier if you have a garden frame, lining them out in six-inch rows, spacing them three inches apart in the row. By early June, vigorous plants with masses of fibrous roots are ready for planting out. The old woody portions are of no use and may be discarded; only the basal shoots make satisfactory plants.

DIVIDING OLD CHRYSANTHEMUM

The old plant is discarded after the suckers have been removed with their roots attached.

The bearded irises require special treatment; start by lifting the old plants carefully in early August, after preparing the soil for the new planting by digging it over and adding a handful of 11.48.0 to the square yard. The roots, or rhizomes as they are rightly called, are easily separated by pulling them downwards. Make new plants with one or two fans of leaves attached to a portion of rhizome with plenty of fibrous roots. The old, dark-colored rhizome is of no use to the young plant and may be cut off. Trim back the leaves to six inches above the root, shaping them to form an inverted V. Treat the young plant divisions with Captan before you replant them. If you can't plant them in a spot where bearded irises have not previously been grown, the next best thing is to replace the soil where the old plants were growing with soil taken from another part of the garden. There is a tendency to plant bearded irises too deep; the fleshy portion of the roots should barely be covered with soil but the fibrous roots must go straight down. The easiest way is to dig a hole deep enough to hold the fibrous roots without doubling them up. Place a low mound of soil in the centre of the hole, setting the fleshy portion of the plant on the mound. Fill in with finely pulverized soil; tramp firmly, leaving the rhizome just below the surface and a saucer-shaped depression around each plant for water. Unless the ground was bone dry when the young plants were set out, no further watering will be needed after the first soaking.

Some lilies do so well in prairie gardens that, periodically, the bulbs have to be dug up, separated and replanted, and the surplus bulbs given away or discarded. The tiger lily *(Lilium tigrinum)* and the candlestick lily *(L. croceum)* are in this group. Both increase by natural bulb division, the bulbs getting ultimately smaller and the flowers less attractive. When this occurs, a new planting should be made, changing the site if this can be done. Dig the soil deeply for lilies, adding peat or leaf mould and sand. Rotted manure, unless it is completely decomposed, is not recommended; in any case, it is best to keep it in the bottom layer of soil away from the roots of the bulbs. There is scarcely a reference made to lily planting without emphasis put upon the importance of soil drainage. Lilies simply will not tolerate soggy soil, so choose a site where water from melting snow is not likely to lie in the spring. Dig the bulbs carefully, preserving all the roots. Lily bulbs are actually modified stems; that is, the scales are the leaves, so they should never be dried off in the same manner as tulips. The bulbs are replanted singly, spacing them a foot apart, six inches deep on a layer of sand. The propagation, planting and general culture of hardy lilies is dealt with in detail in chapter fourteen.

Peonies last longer when undisturbed than most perennials; twenty-year-old plants are not unheard of nor are they necessarily worn out, but there comes a time when old plants may be debilitated seriously by encroaching tree roots that sap the soil nutrients and moisture. The shade from hedges and shrubs will also weaken the plants, as full sun for most of the day is needed for healthy growth and profuse bloom. When the job of rejuvenation cannot be postponed longer, choose a new site and make a new planting. In a small garden it is not easy to find an alternative site for peonies; the plants take considerable room and they may have to be replanted in the same spot. If this is so, the soil must be changed. Dig holes two feet deep and two feet across, taking the soil away to the vegetable garden. Fill the holes with new soil — the vegetable garden soil will do — then tramp it firmly before digging holes for the young plants.

Dividing and replanting peonies is a major operation, requiring hard labor to get the old plants out of the ground without chopping the roots to pieces and consummate skill to break the plant up in suitable-sized pieces with sufficient root and healthy eyes or growing shoots to ensure its survival. The best time to operate is in September, choosing a sunny day to make the work pleasant and to allow the sun to soften the fleshy roots. Peony roots, being thick and turgid when first dug out, are liable to be broken easily. A lot of root damage can be avoided when the plants are exposed to the sun for several hours before the cutting-up begins. When the roots have been softened, the old plants can be pried apart by thrusting two garden forks, set back-to-back with the tines close together, down through the heart of the plant. Using the fork handles as levers, the old plant can be split in two quite easily. The halves can now be divided again to make four pieces, using the forks in the same manner as before. Further dividing can be done by pulling the roots apart, using a knife where necessary. Pieces with three to five eyes are best for transplanting;

DIVIDING A PEONY

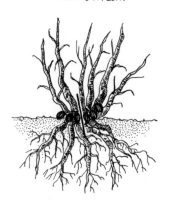

larger ones are more difficult to reestablish. Single-eyed pieces take a year or so longer to reach flowering-sized plants; otherwise, they are quite satisfactory. Peonies take several years to become well established in new ground and typical flowers should not be looked for until the third year. Flowering buds produced sooner will not be up to the standard of a particular variety, so pick them off and wait another year for first-class blooms.

Propagating perennials from stem and root cuttings – Some perennials with woody stems, such as lythrum, are difficult to divide; young plants may be raised from cuttings of new shoots taken in May. Make the cuttings about four inches long, trimming off the lower pair of leaves before dipping the ends in rooting powder (Hormodin is effective) and inserting them one inch deep in pots of sand. Two dozen cuttings planted in a five-inch pot will root in two weeks or so, ready to be transplanted to a garden frame or to the open ground. While the cuttings are rooting, careful attention to watering is needed and, for the first week, they should be shaded from bright sunshine. The young plants make good headway the first summer, but they should not be transplanted to the perennial border or wherever else you plan to use them until the following spring.

Root cuttings are not used to any extent to increase perennials, though some species respond to this means of propagation — anchusa, Oriental poppy and statice *(Limonium)* will grow from two-inch portions of root about pencil thickness or slightly thicker. The root portions are taken from the plants in the fall, making a diagonal cut at the bottom, a horizontal cut at the top. Plant the roots in a garden frame, spacing them an inch apart in six-inch rows. Make the trenches three inches deep with an inch of sand on the bottom. Push the root pieces into the sand, then cover them with fine soil. Fill the frame with dry leaves covered with plastic sheeting or boards to keep out snow. Remove the covering in early May before the new shoots start from the root cuttings. The young plants make rapid growth through the summer and, by September, are large enough to plant in the perennial border.

Perennials for the Prairies

The following list of herbaceous perennials has been compiled after extensive tests in prairie gardens. The perennials are listed in alphabetical order by common name, giving botanical name, plant height, season of bloom, color and hardiness rating. Except where otherwise marked, all are fully hardy in the general prairie region. In the northern areas, where the soil is not so heavily charged with lime and where snow usually comes early and deep, perennials that prefer a neutral or acid soil do much better than in the grassland areas, where the soil is high in lime. In some parts, where chinook winds bare the ground of snow in midwinter and strong, dry winds desiccate green leaves, the moss phlox, perennial candytuft, Canterburybells, sweetwilliam and similar plants survive without injury only when given protection. It is most important for plants that have to carry a rosette of leaves over winter to be protected from sudden temperature changes in early spring with a cover of boughs or flax straw.

Adonis *(Adonis)* — The adonis is a pretty, May-flowering plant with single yellow flowers and ferny leaves. Both the spring adonis *(A. vernalis)* and the Amur adonis *(A. amurensis)* are recommended for the front of the border; the latter has somewhat coarser leaves and larger flowers. Both species make fine rock garden plants, flowering about the same time and complementing the squills.

Alumroot *(Heuchera)* — The heucheras, sometimes called coral bells, have rosettes of dark green, scalloped leaves and wiry stems of elegant flowers in shades of pink or dark red. The varieties of *H. sanguinea* are not fully hardy but a new race of hybrids developed at the Brandon Experimental Farm are fully hardy, attractive perennials. The variety Brandon Pink is a foot and a half high with dense foliage and elegant sprays of bright pink flowers in July. The flower stems remain attractive as the seed pods develop.

Anemone *(Anemone)* — The native prairie anemone *(A. patens)*, often erroneously called crocus, is sometimes cultivated but, under perennial border conditions, it does not thrive. In the rock garden, where the soil is not too rich in nitrogen and where it gets full sun, it will survive and open its lavender gray flowers in the early spring. The snowdrop anemone *(A. sylvestris)* makes a spreading plant a foot and a half high with dark green leaves and nodding flowers, pure white and scented. It grows well in a moist, shady spot but flowers more freely in the sun.

The Chinese anemone *(A. hupehensis)* is not fully hardy all across the prairies unless under a heavy snow cover. It is similar to the Japanese anemone, which is quite tender in prairie gardens. The Chinese or Hupeh anemone has attractive leaves and lilac pink flowers on wiry stems a foot and a half high. The flowers open in late August and continue to bloom through September when most other perennials have finished blooming.

Astilbe *(Astilbe)* — The astilbes have finely divided leaves and feathery plumes, either white, pink or red, on stems about two feet high. They do not like the usually dry summer of prairie gardens. The roots are hardy but, unless the soil is kept moist and well enriched with humus, the plants soon become unthrifty. The most dependable varieties are Moerheim, Magnifica and Ceres. Moerheim has white flowers; the others are shades of pink. They all need plenty of water at the root and frequent top syringes of water in periods of drought; otherwise, spider mites may become a serious problem.

Avens *(Geum)* — The Siberian avens *(G. urbanum sibiricum)* is fully hardy in prairie gardens, whereas the better known varieties of *G. chiloense*, Mrs. Bradshaw and Lady Stratheden, are not. The Siberian species is only a foot high, blooming in May and June with orange-colored flowers.

Babysbreath or chalk plant *(Gypsophila)* — The gypsophilas include a number of interesting plants for the perennial border, from one-foot specimens to the common babysbreath that grows two and a half feet high. The prairie soils, being well charged with lime, suit the plants well.

In some areas, the babysbreath *(G. paniculata)* has escaped from cultivation to become a well-established wild plant. The double-flowered babysbreath *(G. paniculata florepleno)* can be grown from seed, but only a portion of the seedlings will be double. Bristol Fairy, an improved form of *G. paniculata*, is sterile; plants are increased by grafting and by cuttings. The common babysbreath and its improved forms bloom in July.

Rosyveil, a variety of *G. repens*, is a double-flowered pink a foot high, fully hardy, blooming in July and August. Bodgeri, another form of the creeping gypsophila *(G. repens)*, has double white flowers in July.

Gypsophila pacifica makes a spreading, three-foot plant with graceful panicles of carmine pink flowers.

All the gypsophilas require well-drained soil and full sun. The roots of *G. paniculata* and varieties are thick and penetrate the soil deeply, so that old plants cannot be successfully divided and replanted. Young plants raised from seed or cuttings should be used.

Balloonflower *(Platycodon)* — The balloonflowers are related to the bellflowers and need the same general care. The flower buds swell up before opening, hence the common name. As the plants are late in starting, there is danger of hoeing them off as they emerge, so the location of the plants should be marked when last year's tops are cut off. The soil for balloonflowers needs no special preparation; a sunny location where the soil is well drained is best.

The common balloonflower *(P. grandiflora)* is blue; an improved form called Mariesi has dark purple flowers. *P. grandiflora roseum* has pinkish flowers with darker veins.

Beebalm *(Monarda)* — Cambridge Scarlet, a variety of the Oswego beebalm *(M. didyma),* has been tried without success on the prairies; in milder parts, it is a common border plant esteemed for its heads of scarlet flowers and sweet-scented leaves.

The Wildbergamot beebalm *(M. fistulosa)* is scattered over a wide area of the prairies in upland meadows. A white form called Minnedosa, found by Mr. Henry Marshall of Brandon, makes a good plant for the perennial border; the type plants are usually shades of mauve. Mr. Marshall has also introduced a hybrid monarda called Souris, two feet high with scented leaves and pink flowers.

Croftway Pink and Sunset are two other hardy hybrid monardas: Sunset is rose pink; Croftway is paler. Both have survived at Morden for many years.

The beebalms need well-drained soil, full sun and good air circulation. Plants in half shade near buildings where the air is stagnant are liable to be infected with mildew.

Bellflower *(Campanula)* — The bellflowers are a large group; most of them are perennial though there are a few annual bellflowers and a few that are rampant weeds. All need well-drained soil and most do best in full sun. They range in height from a foot for the Carpathian bellflower *(C. carpatica)* to almost three feet for the peachleaf bellflower *(C. persicifolia).* The Carpathian bellflowers, either white, pale mauve or deep violet blue, make useful edging plants. They flower from early summer until September on fine, wiry stems. The peachleaf bellflower needs rich, moist soil and seems to do best when shaded from midday sun. There are white, pale blue and deep purple varieties. Some have double flowers and all make a dense rosette of basal leaves which must be preserved over winter to protect the crown of the plant from desiccation. The peachleaf bellflower does better in the northern areas than it does in the south, where the torrid heat of midsummer and the frequent lack of good snow cover in winter debilitate the plants.

The clustered bellflower *(C. glomerata)* and its various forms are among the hardiest and best. The Dahurian clustered bellflower has two-foot stems topped with a dense cluster of purple flowers in July. The low-cluster bellflower *(C. glomerata dahurica acaulis)* is a dwarf about six inches high with flowers of much the same color as the Dahurian. The clustered bellflowers spread fairly rapidly by underground stolons to make dense mats of foliage. Every three or four years, they should be divided and replanted or they encroach on less vigorous plants.

The bluebell campanula *(C. rotundifolia)* is the harebell or bluebell of Scotland. It grows wild in sunny uplands on the prairies as well as in Europe and Siberia. It is not often found in the perennial border, though there are improved forms offered for sale by some nurserymen and these are well worth growing. It grows a foot or so high with slender stems of nodding bells from July until September.

The spotted bellflower *(C. punctata)* is rather coarse with large, hairy leaves and two-foot stems of lilac mauve flowers.

The Canterburybells *(C. medium)* are not long-lived plants. They are treated as biennials and usually die out after blooming. When raised from seed sown in June, they flower in July of the following year. The seedlings, when two inches high, are transplanted to frames and spaced six inches apart in one-foot rows. In mid-September, the young plants can be planted in the perennial border. Lift them with plenty of soil on the roots or they suffer a setback from the disturbance. As the soil in the perennial border may be very dry in September, several waterings may be necessary to get the plants established. Cover with a thin layer of dry leaves, flax straw or evergreens in October. These biennial bellflowers are useful for filling gaps in the perennial border when winter damage is severe; a few plants left to winter over in a frame can be used for this purpose. The colors include delicate pinks and blues as well as pure whites and deep purples. The cup and saucer varieties of *C. medium* are preferred to the singles.

Bergenia or giant rockfoil *(Bergenia)* — Formerly called megasea, a division of the saxifraga family, bergenias are distinctive border plants. The leaves are large and handsome, turning a reddish bronze in the fall. The dense heads of bloom, produced in early May, often get nipped by a late spring frost.

The heartleaf bergenia *(B. cordifolia),* with broad, roundish leaves and rosy purple flower trusses, is one of the best. The strapleaf bergenia *(B.

ligulata) has narrower leaves; the blooms are similar.

The bergenias require well-drained soil, either in sun or partial shade, and a cover of twiggy branches or flax straw to protect the crowns from winter injury by holding the snow. Under a deep cover of snow, the leaves survive the winter in good shape. In areas where sunlight is restricted and where tree roots tend to sap the soil moisture, the bergenias tolerate these conditions and make handsome ground-cover plants.

Blanketflower *(Gaillardia)* — The blanketflowers bloom throughout the summer, requiring little attention except to remove the spent blooms. The flowers are attractive shades of yellow and red with maroon centres. They prefer a hot, dry location in full sun where the soil is sandy. Heavy soil, excess moisture and shade will cause the plants to rot at the crown but, in light soil and full sun, the gaillardias remain vigorous for several years. New plants are easily raised from seed; named varieties can be purchased from nurserymen. The Portola hybrids are yellow and red; Burgundy is deep reddish maroon; Goblin is a dwarf, compact variety.

Bleedingheart *(Dicentra)* — The most common bleedingheart *(D. specta-bilis)* is an early flowering, hardy plant with graceful stems of pendulant, heart-shaped flowers. The roots penetrate the soil deeply; the bushy plant has a three- or four-foot spread and is three feet high when established. The tendency to precocious growth enhances the danger of frost damage in the spring; plants on the south side of buildings will suffer most, unless growth is retarded by mulching with straw in October. Dividing and transplanting old plants is best done in August. Dormant plants which have been stored over winter can be transplanted in the spring. Other species suited to the prairies are the fringed bleedingheart *(D. eximia),* the Pacific bleedingheart *(D. formosa)* and an improved form of the former called Bountiful. These bloom in June; they average one foot in height but are not as showy as *D. spectabilis.*

Bloodroot *(Sanguinaria)* — The bloodroot is a choice, early flowering, native plant with bluish green, scalloped leaves and cup-shaped, pure white flowers in May. A double-flowered form is available but is not more attractive than the type plant. The bloodroot does best with plenty of humus in the soil and in a spot where it is shaded for most of the day. The flowers are borne singly on slender stems about six inches high.

Bluebell *(Mertensia)* — The Virginia bluebell *(M. virginica)* is one of the earliest perennials, opening its nodding bells in May. By the middle of the summer the foliage has died, leaving a gap in the border; it is therefore best planted near a spreading, later-blooming plant. It does best in moist soil and partial shade.

Boltonia *(Boltonia)* — Sometimes called the false chamomile, these tall, aster-like perennials are not fully hardy in prairie gardens. The white boltonia *(B. asteroides)* and the violet boltonia *(B. latisquama)* have occasionally bloomed well in September with graceful, five-foot stems of white and pale blue daisies. The boltonias are of borderline hardiness but they will survive in well-sheltered gardens if they are replanted every two or three years and given the protection of a layer of flax straw in October.

Brunnera *(Brunnera)* — Brunnera was once known as the forget-me-not-flowered anchusa, now as *B. macrophylla*. The leaves are broad, dark green and dense; the panicles of blue flowers are not unlike forget-me-nots. The plants are about a foot high with dense foliage and the flowers are borne freely in July. The best chance of winter survival is in well-drained soil, facing east, with a deep snow cover.

Bugbane *(Cimififuga)* — These tall, upright plants need rich, moist soil. The leaves are deeply lobed, dark bronzy green and handsome all through the growing season. The flowers are creamy racemes, borne on slender stems carried well above the leaves.

The cordate bugbane *(C. cordifolia)* is three or four feet high and flowers in July and August. Black snakeroot or the Cohosh bugbane *(C. racemosa)* is taller, sometimes over six feet, with two-foot flower spikes.

Bugle *(Ajuga)* — The bugle is a fine perennial ground cover. The Geneva bugle *(A. genevensis)* has dark green leaves and blue flowers in June. The carpet bugle *(A. reptans)* has dark, bronzy green leaves and bluish flowers in June. *A. genevensis* is six inches high, *A. reptans* not much more than three. Both cover the ground fairly rapidly in either sun or shade; in sun, however, there is danger of scalding in early spring unless the plants are covered in October with twiggy branches.

Bugloss *(Anchusa)* — The Italian bugloss *(A. azurea)* is not long-lived in prairie gardens. The leaves are dark green, coarse and hairy; the intense blue flowers are borne on four-foot stems. When the top is cut off in the fall, water accumulates in the hollow stub to rot the crown of the plant. The heavy roots penetrate the subsoil deeply to stay alive when the crown of the plant rots off. By placing a mound of soil over the anchusas in October, you increase their chances of winter survival. Pieces of roots may be used as cuttings.

Buttercup *(Ranunculus)* — The tall buttercup *(R. acris florepleno)* grows about two feet high, has deeply lobed leaves and small, double buttercups all through the summer and early fall. The plants thrive in ordinary soil, either in sun or partial shade.

Candytuft *(Iberis)* — This is a one-foot evergreen plant used in rock gardens and towards the front of perennial borders. It needs well-drained soil, full sun and some protection from drying winter winds. The dense clusters of white flowers open in early June; the leaves are narrow, dark green and attractive all through the season. Varieties of the evergreen candytuft *(I. sempervirens),* Snowflake and Purity, have thrived in full sun and in partial shade.

Carnations and pinks *(Dianthus)* — The pinks and carnations are a large family of plants useful for the perennial border or rock garden. Some are almost prostrate; others are two feet high.

The sweetwilliam *(D. barbatus),* though not long lived and generally treated as a biennial, is a useful stopgap in the perennial border. Seed sown in June will provide plants for next year's bloom. The plants are easy to grow in either a garden frame or a sheltered spot; treat them in the same way as outlined for the Canterburybells. The dense rosettes of foliage must be preserved over winter by covering the plants with brush to keep the snow from blowing away.

The maiden pink *(D. deltoides)* makes dark green mats covered with bright rose red flowers in June and July. After flowering, cut off the flower stems to make the green mats more attractive.

The Carthusian carnation *(D. carthusianorum)* has dense heads of crimson flowers on two-foot stems. The leaves are dark green and rather sparsely produced. Unless the plants are assured of being dry in the spring in soil that is not too rich but has plenty of sand, there will be danger of winter killing.

The shadow valley carnation *(D. caryophyllus)* of unknown origin is a hardy, red-flowered border plant that seems to do much better in some parts of the prairies than others. In some gardens, the plants have been attacked repeatedly by a fungal disease. Healthy plants flower in July and continue until fall, retaining their leaves through the winter if covered with snow. There are two forms of shadow valley carnation, similar in every way except that one is only nine inches high while the other grows to a foot and a half.

Grass pinks *(D. plumarius),* in white and shades of pink, do well in sunny borders where the soil is gritty. Some have double flowers and some are single: all need snow cover to save the tops from the searing winter winds.

A number of hybrid pinks, including the well-known Mrs. Sinkins, have been tested on the prairies; none are fully hardy, though the Allwood pink *(D. allwoodii)* survived several winters in southern Manitoba.

Centaurea *(Centaurea)* — The globe centaurea *(C. macrocephala)* is a coarse, four-foot plant with large heads of yellow, thistle-like flowers in July. It is not particularly attractive in a perennial border of small proportions, being better suited as a background plant in an odd corner.

The mountainbluet centaurea *(C. montana)* is sometimes called the perennial cornflower. The flowers are similar to the annual cornflower or bachelor buttons. The plants are a foot and a half high; the flowers, usually purple though there is a white form, are produced all through the summer. Both the globe and mountainbluet centaureas grow in ordinary soil in full sun or partial shade.

Cephalaria *(Cephalaria)* – The Tartarian cephalaria *(C. tatarica)* is a six-foot spreading plant with pale yellow, scabious-like flowers in July and August. The flowers have long, wiry stems and last well in water. The plant is a useful background for a wide perennial border but in small gardens it has no proper place.

Cerastium *(Cerastium)* – The snow-in-summer *(C. tomentosum)* is a common, gray-leaved, creeping plant about six inches high, used as an edging for borders, as a ground cover and sometimes as a rock garden plant. The flowers are white and the leaves become silvery as summer progresses. Severe pruning after the flowers fade will keep a check on its rampant spread. It survives in poor soil but needs full sun to flower profusely.

Chamomile *(Anthemis)* – The two forms of the golden chamomile *(A. tinctoria,* Kelwayi and Moonlight, are good border plants thriving in hot, dry soil. The leaves are ferny, dark green; the flowers are yellow daisies. Moonlight is pale lemon yellow; Kelwayi is golden yellow. Both are about one and one-half feet high and bloom in July.

Chrysanthemum *(Chrysanthemum)* – The group of chrysanthemums includes a number of interesting and useful perennials besides those known as the hardy "mums."

The florist's pyrethrum *(C. coccineum)* has large daisies, either single or double, in shades of pink to deepest red as well as pure white. The flowers, borne on slender stems in June, last for a long time in water. Named varieties, mostly of English origin, are available from some nurserymen; otherwise, select seedlings can be used. The florist's pyrethrum, which is also known as the painted daisy, grows two feet high with finely cut foliage of dark green and bright daisies in June and July. The named varieties are increased by dividing the old plants in August, or new plants can be raised from seed sown in May.

The oxeye daisy *(C. leucanthemum),* condemned as a weed in Manitoba, is a useful border plant with white, yellow-centred daisies in June and July. A double form called Sedgewick is not so robust as the species, nor will it keep its doubleness if planted in rich soil. The oxeye daisy grows a foot and a half to two feet high, producing an abundance of showy daisies that soon scatter their seed unless the spent blooms are cut off. The seed germinates readily and the young plants can be a nuisance in the perennial border.

The Pyrenees daisy *(C. maximum),* often erroneously called the shasta daisy, is not fully hardy except where early and deep snow covers the plant. The varieties Esther Read and Wirral Supreme are choice, double-flowered forms of the so-called shasta daisy. They rarely survive a prairie winter and should be lifted in the fall, boxed up or potted and wintered in a cool, well-lit basement.

The Mediterranean chrysanthemum *(C. corymbosum)* makes a bushy, two-foot plant with ferny, dark green leaves and composite heads of white daisies in July. Old plants tend to weaken and die but new ones from volunteer or self-sown seedlings soon take their place.

The giant autumn daisy *(C. uliginosum)* flowers on five-foot stems in October. The leaves are deeply lobed, dark green and not unattractive; the daisies are of medium size with white petals and greenish yellow discs. The giant autumn daisy makes a good background plant for the border or odd corner where other plants, more demanding of soil, moisture and nutrients, fail to thrive. It deserves to be better known in prairie gardens; it stands considerable abuse, although it pays to give the plants a good soaking in periods of dry weather. Through the summer months they are often neglected and in October, when the daisies open, they are small and emaciated from the effects of drought.

Varieties of hardy garden "mums" which have been developed by plant breeders in western Canada are useful perennials. They flower at a time when most annuals are dead and most perennials, except asters and one or two others, have finished blooming. They need regular dividing or they soon die. Every second year, pull off the rooted stolons (basal shoots) in early May, replanting them in good soil.

Clematis *(Clematis)* — Besides the better-known woody plants, there are several herbaceous clematis that make excellent border plants. The narrow-leaf clematis *(C. angustifolia)* is a bushy plant about two feet high with panicles of sweet-scented, white flowers. A similar plant, sometimes called the bush or ground clematis *(C. recta),* makes an upright, four-foot plant with a profusion of white flowers followed by feathery seeds. The bush clematis starts to bloom in June and continues through July.

The solitary clematis *(C. integrifolia)* has blue nodding bells in July on three-foot plants: all three are sprawling plants unless staked with twiggy branches. Prairie soils generally suit these herbaceous clematis if good drainage and a sunny spot are provided.

Columbine *(Aquilegia)* — These useful border plants have decorative leaves and graceful flowers. Most are not long lived in prairie gardens unless protected from the columbine borer. The hybrid longspurred columbines are most popular and easily raised from seed. The Colorado columbine *(A. coerulea)* grows one foot high with blue and white flowers and glaucous leaves. The Alpine columbine *(A. alpina)* is about the same height with deep blue flowers and dark green leaves. The common American columbine *(A. canadensis)* has nodding flowers of red and yellow on stems two feet high. Most of the columbines flower in early summer but the leaves are attractive until late autumn. Plant them in well-drained moist soil in partial shade or in full sun.

Coneflower *(Rudbeckia)* — The coneflowers include a number of herbaceous plants, some fully hardy and long lasting, others that seem to die after a year or two. One of the most common is the goldenglow coneflower *(R. laciniata florepleno),* a five-foot spreading plant with attractive, double yellow flowers in August and September.

The blackeyed Susan *(R. hirta)* is popular as an annual plant known as the gloriosa daisy. It survives the winter in well-drained soil that is not too rich in nutrients. The flowers are four inches or more across in shades of yellow and brownish red.

The showy coneflower *(R. speciosa),* the sweet coneflower *(R. subtomentosa)* and the orange coneflower *(R. fulgida)* are not fully hardy but are worth a try in poor, well-drained soil where the snow lies deep in winter. The showy coneflower has yellow florets surrounding a cone-shaped black disc. The plants are two feet high, blooming in July and August. The sweet coneflower makes a four-foot plant bearing soft yellow and brown flowers in August and September. The orange coneflower is a foot and a half high; the flowers are yellow with a brown disc.

Corydalis *(Corydalis)* — The Siberian corydalis *(C. nobilis)* is an interesting, early flowering perennial with ferny leaves and dense heads of yellow, brown-tipped flowers in May. It should be planted adjacent to a spreading plant such as clematis so that the dying foliage of the corydalis, which is unsightly, can be hidden from view. The Siberian corydalis, starting early in spring, is liable to frost injury unless growth is retarded with a mulch of flax straw put on the plants in October.

Cranesbill *(Geranium)* — The true geraniums are hardy, herbaceous plants. The plant most commonly called by this name is of another genus — *pelargonium.* The hardy geraniums are the easiest to grow, surviving in nooks and crannies where the soil is thin and moisture scarce. They have deeply lobed leaves, dark green in summer, orange red in fall. The flowers are mostly shades of violet red, lilac pink or mauve, opening in June and continuing for a month or more.

The lilac cranesbill *(G. grandiflora)* makes a bushy plant up to two feet high with lavender blue flowers in July. The Caucasian cranesbill *(G. ibericum)* grows about a foot and a half high with violet blue flowers in the early summer.

Dames rocket *(Hesperis matronalis)* — Dames rocket is an old-fashioned, tall biennial border plant with mauve or white sweet-scented flowers in early June. The dames rocket or sweet rocket seeds freely to produce plants for the next year's bloom. It is partial to shade but grows well in full sun.

Daylily *(Hemerocallis)* — The old-fashioned daylilies have either yellow, orange or tawny flowers; new sorts are pink, apricot and reddish brown, some with attractive throat markings. The new ones are not as robust as the old varieties, nor are they quite as hardy. Daylilies require no special soil; they thrive in full sun or partial shade and have no problems with insects or disease. The leaves are strap-shaped and bright green; the flowers are clustered on tall stems set well above the foliage. The individual flowers are rather fleeting — they last but a few days; the buds, however, continue to open over a long period. Moreover, some varieties bloom early, some late and, by growing a collection of different varieties, you can have bloom from June until September. A few of the best of the older sorts are Gaiety, Gracilis, Ajax (all yellows), Wondergold, Linda, Apricot (orange apricot shades) and Black Prince, Minnie and Burma (dark maroon shades).

Dragonhead *(Dracocephalum)* — The best of the dragonheads is one formerly called Nepeter Souvenir de Andre Chaudron, now correctly identified as a variety of *D. sibiricum*. It grows two feet high with pungent, gray green leaves and spikes of blue flowers from July until September. It does well in light, sandy soil and full sun, spreading fairly rapidly by its underground shoots.

The bigflower dragonhead *(D. grandiflora)* is one foot high with large spikes of blue flowers in July.

Echinacea *(Echinacea)* — Purple coneflower *(E. purpurea)*, sometimes called a rudbeckia, is not fully hardy. Occasionally a plant survives the winter to open its crimson purple flowers in August. The native narrow-leaf coneflower *(E. angustifolia)* is not often cultivated; it thrives in sunny locations and seems tolerant of alkaline soil. It makes an erect plant up to two feet high with purplish flowers on stiff stems. It is found in the dryland areas all across the prairies.

Eryngo or sea holly *(Eryngium)* — The sea holly is a sturdy, deep-rooted, drought-resistant plant with roundish heads of steel blue flowers in July. The bluetop sea holly *(E. alpinum)* is three feet high, the amethyst sea holly *(E. amethystinum)* about half that height. The dried flower heads make attractive winter bouquets.

Fleabane *(Erigeron)* — A number of fleabanes have been tried in prairie gardens but few are reliably hardy. The most satisfactory ones are the Oregon fleabane *(E. speciosus)* and its varieties, Merstham Glory and Quakeress. The Oregon fleabane has small, lavender blue daisies on two-foot stems. Merstham Glory has larger flowers with mauve petals and golden stamens. Quakeress is similar, with lilac pink daisies. The flowers open in July and last for almost a month.

Foxglove *(Digitalis)* — The common foxglove *(D. purpurea),* not fully hardy in prairie gardens, is treated as a biennial. There are improved forms and new colors but they stand little chance of winter survival.

The perennial yellow foxglove *(D. ambigua)* is hardier and grows to two feet, with yellow, brown-spotted flowers. An annual variety, resembling the common foxglove, will flower the first year when the seed is sown early in a greenhouse.

Gasplant *(Dictamnus)* — The gasplant is a hardy, rugged, long-lived perennial growing about three feet high with dark green, compound leaves, richly pungent when handled. The flowers are airy panicles of pink or white in June, giving off a volatile gas. The seed pods are bronzy green and ornamental. Gasplants do best when left undisturbed for long periods; some twenty-year-old specimens are healthy and vigorous.

Gayfeather *(Liatris)* — The gayfeather or blazingstar includes a few native plants found in sunny uplands where the soil is usually dry and lean. The tall gayfeather *(L. scariosa)* makes a three-foot spike of purple flowers that spring from rosettes of narrow leaves. The spike gayfeather *(L. spicata)* is only half as tall. The flowers are dense spikes of rosy purple in July. The gayfeathers have the peculiarity of opening their flowers from the tip of the spike, the bottom flowers opening last.

Gentian *(Gentiana)* — The gentians are usually considered rock garden plants and quite difficult to grow, but some are suitable for the border and require no special care. The native Andrews or bottle gentian *(G. andrewsi),* also called the closed gentian, makes a two-foot plant with handsome, dark leaves and violet blue flowers in July. It needs moist soil and partial shade. The seven-lobed gentian *(G. septemfida)* is less than one foot high, spreading along the ground and bearing clusters of clear blue flowers in July and August.

Globeflower *(Trollius)* — The most reliable of this group is the Ledebour globeflower *(T. ledebouri).* The leaves are deeply lobed and dark green, the flower stems about two feet high with double yellow flowers like buttercups.

The common globeflower *(T. europaeus)* has survived for several winters when under deep snow. The plants do best in moist soil and partial shade.

Globethistle *(Echinops)* — The blue gray, thistle-like heads of the small globethistle *(E. ritro)* are attractive in the perennial border as well as being useful dried decorations. It makes an upright, three-foot plant densely clothed with spiny leaves. The Ruthenian globethistle *(E. ruthenica)* is a foot taller; otherwise, it is much the same. Both thrive in sun or partial shade in odd corners where the soil is dry and poor.

Goatsbeard *(Aruncus)* — Formerly called *Spiraea aruncus,* the goatsbeard *(A. sylvester)* is one of the most handsome perennials. It grows best in moist soil that is rich in humus, making a handsome plant four to five feet high. The large compound leaves are attractive all summer, turning a rich bronzy green in September. The panicles of creamy white flowers turn to bronze seed pods useful as decoration in the border or in flower arrangements.

Goldenrod *(Solidago)* — A form of the Canada goldenrod *(S. canadensis)* .called Golden Wings makes a five-foot plant with graceful panicles of yellow flowers. The Missouri goldenrod *(S. missouriensis)* is about three feet tall with deep yellow flowers; both sorts flower in September. The goldenrods have no special soil requirements and tolerate some shade. Blooming late in the season, the goldenrods complement the blue Michaelmas daisies.

Grapehyacinth *(Muscari)* — The common grapehyacinth is a tiny, bulbous plant six inches high with stems of closely clustered, deep blue bells. A white form is available though less attractive. The plants bloom in May and early June; the bulbs are planted in September or early October in light soil and full sun. The flower spikes are cut off before seed forms to exhaust the plants; the top growth, though unsightly, must be allowed to dry off naturally or the bulbs deteriorate.

Groundcherry or Chinese lantern plant *(Physalis)* — The strawberry groundcherry or Chinese lantern plant *(P. alkekengi,* formerly *P. franchettii),* is grown chiefly for its ornamental seed pods. The flowers are small, white, and buried among the coarse leaves. The plants increase by underground stolons but are not too rampant. When the seed pods color orange red in September, the stems are stripped of leaves and dried for use as winter bouquets.

Heliopsis *(Heliopsis)* — The rough heliopsis *(H. scabra)* has coarse leaves and yellow flowers on three-foot stems in July and August. Several improved forms are available. One of the best is Incomparabilis, four feet high with bright yellow flowers in July.

Hollyhock *(Althaea)* — Single hollyhocks are fully hardy in the southern prairies; double ones occasionally survive in sheltered borders but are best treated as biennials, sowing the seed outdoors in June for flowering in July and August of the next year. Store the seedling plants over winter in a cool basement and plant them out in early May.

Incarvillea *(Incarvillea)* — The Delavay incarvillea *(I. delavayi)* has occasionally survived under a deep snow cover but it is not recommended for prairie gardens. The plants are two feet high; the compound leaves are dark green; the trumpet-shaped, rosy purple flowers are produced in July.

The Olga incarvillea *(I. olgae)* is taller and hardier but not so showy. The flower stems are three feet high; the blooms are pink and open in July.

Iris *(Iris)* – The irises form a large group of herbaceous and bulbous plants, many being fully hardy in prairie gardens. Some need full sun and well-drained soil; the bearded irises and the dwarf or Crimean irises are in this group. A number of species are handsome plants with ornamental seed pods and foliage of season-long interest. The named varieties of the hybrids produced from *I. sibirica* and *I. orientalis* are among the finest border plants; their colors range from pure white through shades of blue to deepest purple. These so-called beardless irises need no special soil, but thrive best in a deep loam with plenty of humus to hold moisture.

The bearded or flag irises are a complex group of hybrids involving a number of species. The bearded irises provide delicate shades of blue, pink and yellow as well as subtle shades of reddish brown, apricot and buff. Some are up to three feet high but most are about two feet. A race of very low-growing iris sometimes called the Crimean flag irises are only a foot high in shades of yellow, blue and deepest purple, besides a pure white sort. Both the bearded irises and the Crimean flags should be planted in full sun where the soil is well drained. If soggy soil conditions persist for long, the fleshy roots rot; the same thing is liable to happen when these sun-loving perennials are planted in the shade.

The season of iris bloom is brief but the handsome, sword-shaped leaves are attractive until late in the fall. The lime-charged prairie soil is usually well suited, though not all bearded irises are fully hardy; some of the new introductions, especially those with pink flowers, have not been long lived in prairie gardens. The novice grower will be well advised to plant varieties listed in local catalogues. The iris fancier may go farther afield in search of novelties.

Some of the best of the Siberian hybrids are Blue Oriole, Butterfly and Blue King, in blue shades; Mantane, White Dove and Snow Crest in whites; Caesar, Perry's Blue and True Blue in deep violet blue colors and Pembina, purple and white. The species irises are widely different in stature and season of bloom; some flower in May, others in June and July. The first to bloom is the Rockymountain iris *(I. missouriensis),* opening its small, lavender mauve flowers in May. The yellowflag *(I. psuedacorus)* does remarkably well in dry soil, although in its native home it thrives in moist places. The stems are three feet high; the heavy leaves are bright green and the flowers open in June. The seashore iris *(I. spuria)* is about a foot high with yellow and lilac blooms in June.

The Japanese irises *(I. kaempferi)* are not hardy in prairie gardens. Attempts to grow them near a pool where soil moisture was adequate have failed. The Manchurian form *(I. kaempferi mandschurica),* however, has survived and flowered well in deep, moist soil. The dark purple flowers, which resemble the Japanese iris, open in July and continue to bloom for a month.

Jacobsladder *(Polemonium)* — The polemoniums are hardy border plants with attractive, pinnate leaves; usually, they bear blue flowers. The Greek-valerian polemonium *(P. caeruleum)* or Jacobsladder is two feet high with dense, compact leaves and pale blue flowers in June and July. The skunkleaf polemonium *(P. pulcherrimum)* grows only a foot high but is otherwise similar to *P. caeruleum.* The polemoniums need no special care but prefer moist soil and partial shade.

Knotweed *(Polygonum)* — The knotweeds include a number of useful plants, largely herbaceous though some are rampant climbers. The fleece-flower knotweed *(P. cuspidatum)* is two feet high with roundish leaves and pinkish flowers in August. The tops are tender to frost both in the spring and in the fall. The roots are fully hardy and spread rapidly to make a good ground cover.

Ladybell *(Adenophora)* — Like the campanulas, the adenophoras need an open, sunny position where the soil is well drained. The early ladybell *(A. stylosa)* is one of the best: the nodding bells are pale blue on two-foot stems; the leaves are gray green.

Larkspur *(Delphinium)* — The tall, perennial larkspurs are the ones seen most often in perennial borders. The dwarf Chinese or Siberian larkspur *(D. grandiflorum)* has finely cut leaves and elegant sprays of blue or white flowers. The plants are compact, about two feet high, and need well-drained soil in full sun. The tall delphiniums, which are fine for grouping towards the back of the border, need deep, rich soil, plenty of water as the flowers open and support for the fragile stems.

Named varieties are not used to any extent in prairie gardens; most are raised from seed of the Pacific giants or some other notable strain. Seed may be sown indoors in February, then transplanted, first in boxes like annuals and finally to the open ground in June. The following spring the young plants may be moved to a permanent place in the border. This should be done as soon as the ground thaws and becomes dry enough to work. If you delay, the plants soon grow too big to move without a severe setback.

Select plants can be increased by dividing them in the spring. Softwood cuttings, taken when the shoots are about four inches high, also provide a means of propagation.

A new delphinium called Pink Sensation survives in the southern prairies. It grows to three feet with fine leaves and soft pink flowers in July; sometimes it flowers again later. Pink Sensation is an interspecific hybrid with *D. nudicaule* as one parent. It is completely sterile and, though it occasionally produces a few seed pods, they contain no seed.

Lily *(Lilium)* — Lilies are among the choicest hardy plants and are now available in a wide variety of forms and colors. Canadian plant breeders have developed scores of new varieties in the past twenty years, including white trumpet lilies, as well as a number of excellent yellows, dark reds and unique shades of pink and apricot. Most hardy lilies do well in prairie gardens as long as they are planted in well-drained soil.

In the perennial border, groups of up to a dozen bulbs should be planted rather than one or two. A collection of lilies shows better and is easier to look after if given a separate border and sheltered from hot sun; some species, such as *L. henryi*, tend to bleach if exposed to bright sunshine.

Some of the species can easily be raised from seed; the Korean lily *(L. amabile)*, the morningstar lily *(L. concolor)*, the nodding lily *(L. cernuum)* and the coral lily *(L. pumilum)* are examples. Named varieties are grown from bulbs planted, usually, in September or early October. Certain lilies of borderline hardiness will flower satisfactorily from dormant bulbs set out in May after being stored over winter in a root cellar. Golden Clarion, Green Dragon and a number of others are in this group. By mounding a few inches of granulated peat and a foot or two of flax straw over the plants in October, it is possible to bring the bulbs safely through the winter and have them in bloom again in July. Some hardy lilies start into new growth before danger of spring frost has passed; cover these early starting sorts in October with a layer of flax straw to retard spring growth. Hanson's lily *(L. hansoni)*, the Martagon hybrids and the early flowering Caucasian lily *(L. monadelphum)* are in this group.

The following select dozen have been chosen from 150 varieties and species tested for success in prairie gardens: the varieties Lemon Queen, White Princess, Edith Cecilia, Bright Cloud, Muriel Conde, Burnished Rose, Brocade, Nubian, Dunkirk, and the species *L. amabilis, L. martagon* and *L. henryi.*

Lily of the valley *(Convallaria)* — The well-known lily of the valley *(C. majalis)* makes a fine ground cover, either in shade or half sun. The delicate white bells are esteemed for sweet scent in May and June. Overgrown roots are divided and replanted in rich soil in August or early September. Top growth is cleaned off in spring before a light top-dressing of enriched soil is spread over the crowns.

Lionsheart *(Physostegia)* — The lionsheart, more commonly known as false dragonhead or obedient plant *(P. virginiana)*, is a valuable, late-blooming perennial. The plants are two feet high with dark green leaves and dense spikes of tubular flowers either pink or white. A variety called Vivid with reddish flowers is superior, but it is not fully hardy on the prairies.

Lungwort *(Pulmonaria)* — The lungworts are old-fashioned plants thought by the early apothecaries to be of value in treating lung diseases. Some have handsome leaves heavily blotched with silver.

The cowslip lungwort *(P. angustifolia)* is about one foot tall, has dark green leaves and blue flowers in June.

The Bethlehem lungwort *(P. saccharata)* is a foot high with leaves spotted silver and violet blue flowers.

Lupine *(Lupinus)* — The perennial hybrid lupines have been developed from the Washington lupine *(L. polyphyllus)* and the tree lupine *(L. arboreus)*. The Russell strain is the most popular, embracing a wide range of bright colors. Where the soil is neutral or slightly acid, the plants thrive for several years but, where the soil is high in lime, the plants soon sicken and die. Lupines do not transplant readily; the best chance of success is with year-old seedlings set out in the spring. The flowers are dense spikes opening in June; the leaves on healthy plants are dark green and remain in good condition until late in the fall.

Lythrum or loosestrife *(Lythrum)* — The lythrum or loosestrife has gained popularity in recent years due in large measure to the introduction of Morden Pink, which arose as a bud sport of *L. virgatum,* the wand lythrum. It grows four feet high, bearing slender spikes of pink flowers in July and August; its leaves are narrow medium green. In their natural state, lythrums are found in low-lying spots; when cultivated, however, they seem tolerant of dry soil, either in full sun or partial shade. The plants are best set out in the spring; fall planting is sometimes risky. Some of the best sorts are Morden Pink, Morden Gleam, Morden Rose, Dropmore Purple and Mr. Robert.

Meadowrue *(Thalictrum)* — This group of plants is generally hardy, with attractive leaves and graceful stems. A meadowrue grows in full sun or partial shade and is not particular about soil. The columbine meadowrue *(T. aquilegifolium)* has leaves that resemble the columbine and fluffy heads of mauve flowers in June; a purple variant of the same plant has dark foliage and violet purple flowers. Both plants grow to three or four feet.

The low meadowrue *(T. minus)* and the maidenhair meadowrue, a variety of *T. minus,* are a foot or so high with yellow flowers and rounded leaves that resemble the foliage of the maidenhair fern.

The Yunnan meadowrue *(T. dipterocarpum)* is not fully hardy in prairie gardens; it has died out even under deep snow cover. The Yunnan meadowrue is four feet tall with tiny leaves of medium green; the flowers are elegant sprays of lavender and pale yellow.

Meadowsweet *(Filipendula)* — The meadowsweets are a group of plants widely differing in stature, leaf shape and flower color, some known formerly as spireas, ulmarias and by the common names dropwort and Queen of the Prairie. The meadowsweets prefer a deep, moist soil but are fairly tolerant of drought, though the broad-leaved species often are infested with spider mites when the weather is dry for long periods. The pink-flowered sorts seem to prefer partial shade to full sunlight.

The dropwort meadowsweet *(F. hexapetala)* has large rosettes of dark green, ferny leaves that remain attractive all summer. The slender one and one-half-foot flower stems rise from the centre of the rosettes to bear panicles of creamy white flowers in July. There are both single and double forms. The Siberian meadowsweet *(F. palmata)* is taller; the plumed flowers are an attractive shade of pink on four-foot stems.

F. rubra, sometimes listed as *Spirea venusta,* is commonly called Queen of the Prairies. In moist soil it grows five feet high, bearing elegant pink plumes in July.

The European meadowsweet, sometimes called Queen of the Meadow *(F. ulmaria),* is a tall plant with broad leaves and rather dense panicles of creamy flowers. There are both double and single forms.

Monkshood *(Aconitum)* — The monkshoods are tall, late-blooming plants with dark green, glossy leaves; most have blue flowers. They prefer a deep, moist soil and some shade. Aconite monkshood *(A. napellus)* blooms in July with hooded purple florets on four-foot stems. A blue and white variety called Bicolor is popular. The monkshoods seem to do better in the northern parts of the prairies than they do in the south. In southern Manitoba, for example, there are serious problems with root rot diseases.

The late-flowering azure monkshood *(A. fischeri)* and Wilson's monkshood *(A. wilsonii)* are five feet high, blooming in September and October with spikes of deep blue flowers.

Nepeta or catmint *(Nepeta)* — The Ukraine nepeta *(N. ucranica)* is a bushy, one-foot plant with gray green leaves and purple flowers in July. A hybrid variety called Dropmore is a superior plant a foot and a half high with a profusion of light purple flowers from July until September.

Onion *(Allium)* — Several ornamental onions are useful plants in the perennial border; the rose-flowered nodding onion *(A. cernuum),* the yellow-flowered *A. flavum* and the blue-flowered *A. caeruleum* are among the best. The nodding onion grows to one foot and a half, the yellow one only a foot high and the blue one about two feet. All need a place in the sun where the soil is well drained.

Peavine *(Lathyrus)* — The perennial peavine *(L. latifolius)* climbs to about six feet bearing clusters of rosy purple flowers in July and August. The white form is not as vigorous as the colored: otherwise, it is similar. The perennial peavines or everlasting sweet peas need well-drained soil; the roots may be shaded but, to bloom profusely, the tops should be in full sun.

Penstemon or beardstongue *(Penstemon)* — This group of plants has been much improved recently by prairie plant breeders. They do best in warm, sunny locations where the soil is well drained. Many of them are native to North America.

The smooth beardstongue or sawsepal penstemon *(P. glaber)* is an attractive border plant with blue green leaves and dense spikes of tubular flowers in shades of blue or pink. The plants are about one and a half feet high; the flowers start to bloom in July and continue until September. The shell-leaf penstemon *(P. grandiflora)* has blue gray leaves and large, soft lavender blue flowers on three-foot stems. It thrives in rather lean soil in full sun and sets enormous quantities of seed unless the flower stems are removed.

The Torrey penstemon *(P. torreyi),* formerly known as a variety of *P. barbatus,* has narrow green leaves and scarlet flowers in July and August. Two hybrid penstemons from the horticultural field station in Nebraska, Flathead Lake and Prairie Dusk, are excellent border plants. Flathead Lake has scarlet flowers; Prairie Dusk is smoky purple. Both are two feet high and fully hardy if grown in full sun and well-drained soil.

Peony *(Paeonia)* – Peonies are the hardiest, showiest and longest lived perennials in prairie gardens. The leaves are dark green, deeply lobed and handsome all through the season, some coloring well in the fall. They need no special care once the plants are established in good soil, except to cut off the spent blooms, apply a dose or two of fertilizer and plenty of water in periods of drought. They prefer open, sunny positions; plants in the shade of trees or buildings will soon weaken. Each plant needs not less than a square yard of border space; those with weak stems need support. A dozen of the best are listed and described below.

Festiva Maxima white with prominent crimson flecks on some of the centre petals; blooms early, large, fragrant, but stems are rather weak.

Enchanteresse white with lemon tints and occasional crimson edging on the outer petals; blooms are large, well formed and faintly scented.

Alesia white, large, well-formed blooms of creamy white without blemish.

Sarah Bernhardt deep rose pink, suffused silvery pink; late, fragrant; produces a high percentage of good quality blooms.

Livingstone old rose pink with crimson markings; late, fragrant.

Edulus Superba bright pink with lighter guard petals; very early and reliable, sweet scented and good for cutting.

Katherine Havemeyer rose pink, outer petals paler; mild rose fragrance.

Mons. Jules Elie light rose pink; early, fragrant; blooms large, shapely and freely produced.

Tourangelle creamy white, suffused flesh pink; blooms large, fragrant and late.

Karl Rosenfield bright crimson, tinged magenta; blooms regularly with well-shaped, fully double blooms.

Felix Crousse brilliant crimson; large, early flowering; one of the best reds for cutting.

Mary Brand clear crimson; large, early blooms, fragrant and reliable.

Periwinkle *(Vinca)* — The common periwinkle *(V. minor)* is not hardy in prairie gardens but the herbaceous periwinkle *(V. herbacea)* makes a good ground cover. The leaves tend to brown when exposed to drying winter winds, so twiggy branches are placed on the plants in October to hold the snow. The herbaceous periwinkle has dark green, glossy leaves on trailing stems and single, violet blue flowers in July. It grows in light or heavy soil, preferably in partial shade.

Phlox *(Phlox)* — The summer phloxes *(P. paniculata),* the most showy of all the phloxes, are not fully hardy in prairie gardens. Of thirty-odd varieties tested, only a few have lasted more than one or two years. The most reliable are Bridesmaid, a white with pink eyes, Carillon, a carmine pink and Viking, a deep purple. The summer phloxes require a deep cover of snow in winter and deep, rich soil with plenty of moisture in July and August. Long periods of drought and hot weather will bring on heavy infestations of spider mites to weaken the plants and lessen their chances of winter survival.

Another group, similar to the summer phloxes but much hardier and flowering a month earlier, are called the Carolina phloxes *(P. suffruticosa).* The well-known Ada Blackjack, Moosejaw and White Pyramid are in this group. These varieties are fully hardy in prairie gardens and do best in deep, moist soil that drains well in the spring.

The moss phlox *(P. subulata)* is a green mat covered with flowers in May. Some are white and some are shades of pink; others are lavender blue or rosy red. The moss phloxes are fine edging plants for the perennial border, ideal for the rock garden and may be used effectively as ground covers. There has been some hybridization with other species — the lilac phlox, of which the lavender-colored G. F. Wilson is the best-known variety, is such a hybrid. The Arctic phlox *(P. borealis)* and Hoods phlox *(P. hoodi)* are similar to moss phlox. The Arctic phlox has bright, rose pink flowers and a green mat that holds its lively color all through the season, whereas the moss phlox turns a bronzy green in the fall. Some of the best varieties in this whole group of low phloxes are Fairy, G. F. Wilson, Arctic, Rosea, Temmiskaming, Sunningdale Red and the species *P. hoodi.*

A few less well-known phloxes, *P. amoena, P. arendsii* and the sweet-william phlox *(P. divaricata),* grow about a foot high, flowering in May and early June. They are not vigorous and soon deteriorate if they are overcrowded.

Plantainlily *(Hosta)* — The plantainlilies prefer shade and moist soil, but seem to adapt to full sun and drier soil remarkably well. The leaves are handsome, blue green or edged with yellow. Over a dozen sorts have been tested in prairie gardens but not all have survived. The most reliable are the blue plantainlily *(H. caerulea)*, with blue green leaves and slender, foot-long stems of soft blue flowers in July, and fortune's plantainlily *(H. fortunei)*, with dense, bluish leaves and lilac mauve flowers. They make attractive foliage plants through the summer months and, like the rest of the hostas, should not be frequently transplanted.

Plumepoppy *(Macleya)* — The plumepoppy, formerly known as *Bocconia,* is a tall, rank-growing plant with broad, scalloped leaves of gray green. The flower stems are six or seven feet high; the flowers are creamy pink, followed by tawny seed pods. The plumepoppy does best in deep, moist soil and, as the new shoots start early, they must be protected from spring frost. Two species are available: *M. cordata,* with large, heart-shaped leaves, grows up to seven feet; *M. microphylla,* which is slightly taller, has smaller flowers.

Poppy *(Papaver)* — The Oriental and Iceland poppies are fairly common in prairie gardens. The Oriental has deep roots and is more permanent than the Iceland poppy. The flowers are mostly scarlet, about two feet high, opening in June and soon shedding their petals. The plants become shabby as the flower stems and lower leaves die. To avoid this unsightliness, plant poppies near later flowering, spreading plants such as medium-tall perennial asters. Some Oriental poppies are white, some an old rose or deep maroon.

The modern Iceland poppy is a dainty plant with slender stems of elegant poppies in many unusual shades. It does best in northern areas, where cool nights simulate the growing conditions found in its natural home. The Oriental poppies are best transplanted in August; seed or seedling plants of the Iceland poppy may be planted in the spring in the spot where the plants are required to bloom.

Primrose *(Primula)* — The primulas do best in moist, cool soil; the hardiest sort is the auricula *(P. auricula),* sometimes called the dusty miller because of the farina on the leaves. It grows not more than one foot high with flowers in shades of red and yellow. The flowers open in early July and continue for a month. Seed is freely produced unless the flower stems are cut off after the plants have done blooming. The plants can be divided after they have bloomed or young plants can be raised from seed.

The Cortusa primrose *(P. cortusoides)* makes a compact, nine-inch plant with dark green leaves and pink flowers in May. The Siberian primrose *(P. sibirica)* is a dwarf, six-inch plant with lilac pink blooms in May.

Rockcress *(Arabis)* — This dwarf, early flowering plant is suitable for edging the perennial border or for use in the rock garden. The wall rockcress *(A. albida)* has white flowers, either single or double; the Alpine rockcress *(A. alpina)* has pink as well as white flowers. Both are almost prostrate and, unless they are protected by a blanket of snow, they tend to winter kill.

Sage *(Salvia)* — The salvias do best in full sun where the soil is rich and well drained. The meadow sage *(S. pratensis)* is the most reliable in prairie gardens, where it sets seed freely to produce volunteer plants in abundance. The leaves are dark green and coarse; the flowers, on two-foot stems, are either blue or white and open in June. The azure sage *(S. azurea)*, the sticky sage *(S. glutinosa)* and the violet sage *(S. nemorosa)* have been tested in prairie gardens and found to be much too tender.

St. Brunolily *(Paradisea)* — The St. Brunolily *(P. liliastrum)* is often included with *Anthericum*, a genus containing a similar plant, the St. Bernardslily *(A. liliago)*. The St. Brunolily has narrow leaves and open racemes of white flowers. It thrives in ordinary soil either in sun or in shade. The St. Bernardslily is similar but blooms a bit later. Another similar perennial, *A. ramosum*, is a graceful, two-foot plant with narrow leaves and slender stems of tiny white flowers in July; later on, the green seed pods are ornamental.

Scabious *(Scabiosa)* — Several hardy scabiosa are useful border plants, the most popular being the Caucasian scabious *(S. caucasica)*. They do best in well-drained soil that is reasonably moist and fertile. The Caucasian scabious has dark green, deeply cut leaves and graceful flowers on two-foot stems in July, August and September. The colors are cream and pale lavender to deepest purple. The named sorts do not come true from seed but may be increased by dividing the old plant in the spring. The seedlings take two years to bloom.

Fischer's scabious *(S. fischeri)* has smaller flowers and finer leaves. The flowers are purple and open in July.

The dove scabious *(S. columbaria)* and its rose-flowered form have gray green leaves and roundish mauve or rosy flowers from July until September.

Sea lavender *(Limonium)* — The big-leaf or wide-leaf sea lavender *(L. latifolium)* has dark green, leathery leaves and deep, penetrating roots. The flowers are billowy sprays of lavender blue in July and August and may be used for making winter bouquets. The plants are two feet high, attractive all through the season and, once established, can be left undisturbed for ten years or longer. They are easily raised from seed but named varieties must be increased by division or by root cuttings.

Siberian wallflower *(Erysimum)* — The Siberian wallflower, formerly called *Cheiranthus allioni*, is now officially *E. asperum*. It is not long lived, generally dying out after blooming. Plants are easy to raise from seed sown in the summer to bloom the following year. They are a foot high, bushy and covered from June until September with bright orange, sweet-scented flowers. The best chance of success with the Siberian wallflowers is to set out young plants in well-drained, gritty soil that is not too heavily charged with nitrogen, exposing the plants to full sun.

Sneezeweed *(Helenium)* — These late-blooming plants are not fully hardy in prairie gardens unless they are under a deep blanket of snow. Several named varieties of the common sneezeweed *(H. autumnale)* have been tested; a few of the best are Chipperfield Orange, Pelegrina, with bronze flowers, *H. rubrum,* with red flowers, and Riverton Beauty, a true yellow. All are four feet high and need deep, moist soil. The heleniums bloom in September, making heads of daisy-like flowers to furnish the perennial border with warm autumn colors just before the hardy chrysanthemums and asters come into full bloom. For this reason they are valuable and should be given special care by watering in periods of drought and by laying on a light cover of flax straw in October.

Soapwort *(Saponaria)* — The rock soapwort *(S. ocymoides)* is more useful in the rock garden than in the perennial border; the plants are about six inches high with pink flowers in June. The double form of the bouncing-bet soapwort *(S. officinalis florepleno)* is two feet high with light pink flowers that darken with age. The bouncingbet has two bad faults; it spreads rapidly to choke out less vigorous plants and has a tendency to revert to the single form after a year or two in the border.

Solomonseal *(Polygonatum)* — The Eurasian solomonseal *(P. multiflorum)* is a fine plant for the perennial border, tolerating shade or full sun and having no special soil requirements. The roots wander a bit but are not too obtrusive. The two-foot stems are well clothed with dark green leaves; the flowers are pendulant white bells edged with green. Solomonseal will grow in odd, shady corners, providing an attractive patch of greenery as well as some useful stems for cutting.

Speedwell *(Veronica)* — The herbaceous speedwells are a large group of plants ranging from creeping mats to tall border plants three or four feet high. The woolly speedwell *(V. incana)* grows a foot high with silver gray leaves in neat clusters and spikes of violet blue flowers. A white-flowered form, *V. incana alba,* is less attractive; a pink one, *V. incana rosea,* is not as vigorous as the type. The woolly speedwell is useful for rock gardens as well as for the front of the border and does best in lean soil and full sun.

The taller speedwells, spike speedwell *(V. spicata)* and the bastard speedwell *(V. spuria),* are both excellent border plants. The spike speed-well has either blue, pink or white flowers on three-foot stems; the bastard speedwell is about two feet high with slender spikes of deep blue or pink flowers.

The clump speedwell *(V. maritima subsessilis),* sometimes listed as *V.*

longifolia, is not fully hardy; the plants are three feet high with dark green leaves and large spikes of dark blue flowers.

The speedwells are easy to grow in sun or partial shade. The plants are increased by division, as seedlings give a variety of plant types and flower colors.

Squill *(Scilla)* — The Siberian squill *(S. sibirica)* is one of the first plants to bloom, often opening its blue bells while the last of the snow lingers in shady nooks. The tiny bulbs should be planted in colonies where they can remain without disturbance, to spread by bulb increase and seedlings to form a blue carpet. The scillas do best in the shadow of medium shrubs, being assured of sunlight for at least part of the day.

Starwort or Michaelmas daisy *(Aster)* — Most are fully hardy, though some of the English hybrid Michaelmas daisies flower too late to be of much use in prairie gardens.

The Rhone aster *(A. acris)* has fine leaves and small, starry flowers in dense panicles of lavender blue. The plant is two feet high; the flowers open in September and continue for a month. A new dwarf form of the Rhone aster *(A. acris nana)* is available. It resembles the original species in every way except that it grows only a foot high.

The Alpine aster *(A. alpinus)* is a six-inch dwarf with solitary stems of lavender blue daisies in July.

The various forms of the Italian aster *(A. amellus)* are all good border plants: Beauty of Ronsdorf is pink; King George is a rich violet blue and Perry's Favorite is lilac pink. All are about two feet high, flowering in August and September, and have gray green leaves. They do best in a sunny location where the soil is well drained. When snow cover is adequate, they survive the winter in good condition, but drought and the depredations of the tarnished plant bug can be responsible for failures.

The heartleaf aster *(A. cordifolius)* and the heath asters *(A. ericoides)* are not fully hardy in prairie gardens. Under deep snow they survive the winter but often bloom too late to make a show. The roundish leaves of the heartleaf aster and the slender, fine leaves of the heath aster are attractive in the border.

The largest group, the Michaelmas daisies *(A. novibelgii),* includes the finest in size and color; all are fully hardy providing snow cover is early and adequate, but many flower too late. They need transplanting about every two years and some tall varieties need stakes to support the flower stems. The most dependable sorts are Plenty, a strong variety three feet high with large, lavender mauve, yellow-eyed daisies, Pacific Amaranth, two feet high with magenta flowers, and Morden Lavender, a foot and a half high, making a mound of lavender blue in September. Blandie, a newer variety, has white daisies on three-foot stems.

A hybrid group of dwarf asters with the bushy aster *(A. dumosus)* as one parent includes two hybrids, Morden Fay and Morden Cupid. Both are only six inches high; Fay is lilac mauve and Cupid is white. Other dwarf asters recommended for the front of the border are Victor (lavender blue), Marjorie (mauve) and Niobe (white). These are compact plants growing a foot high to make a mound of color in late September. The season of bloom for these dwarf asters as well as for the regular Michaelmas daisies will vary as much as ten days. The reason is obscure; it is thought, however, that drought and excessive heat tends to retard the blooming season. When they bloom late they are apt to be damaged by frost, though a few degrees will do no harm.

The New England asters *(A. novae-angliae)* are tall, with coarse leaves and woody stems. The compact roots need less attention than the Michaelmas daisies. The flowers are dense heads, mostly rosy red or purple, and open in late September. Some of the best are Lil Fardell (four feet, rose pink), Morden Crimson, (five feet, rosy red) and Morden Purple, a sister plant with violet purple flowers. Harrington's Pink is a choice salmon pink variety but it is not early enough for the prairies. Tests with Harrington's Pink and several other named varieties of New England asters, including two called Adorable and Shakespeare, show them to be root hardy but much too late in blooming to be of any use in prairie gardens.

Asters grow in ordinary garden soil, needing no special attention except an occasional watering when the soil gets dry. The Michaelmas daisy group requires biennial transplanting; the others can remain undisturbed for up to five years.

Stonecress *(Aethionema)* – Two species, *A. pulchellum* and *A. stylosum,* do well in open, sunny spots where the soil is light. Both bloom in June and July. The flowers are pink and rose, resembling a miniature candytuft with fine, blue gray leaves. Seed is produced abundantly unless you cut off the spent flower heads promptly.

Stonecrop *(Sedum)* – A great number of stonecrops are available but not all are fully hardy in prairie gardens. Most of them are more suitable for the rock garden than the perennial border and all should have full sun and well-drained soil. One of the most common is the orange stonecrop *(S. kamschaticum);* it makes mats of light green leaves and masses of yellow flowers on six-inch stems in July.

Ewers stonecrop *(S. ewersii)* has bluish leaves and heads of pink flowers. The plants grow up to a foot high and bloom in July. The evergreen stonecrop *(S. hybridum)* is a foot-high plant with glossy leaves and yellow flowers in July; the Siebold stonecrop *(S. sieboldii)* is about a foot high with blue gray leaves and soft pink flowers in July.

The showy stonecrop *(S. spectabile)* is a more compact plant with upright stems and flat heads of flowers in August and September, either pink, white or red. The leaves are light glaucous green or variegated gold.

The two-row stonecrop *(S. spurium)* is a creeping plant less than six inches high with roundish leaves and pink or red flowers in July.

The flower stems of all the creeping stonecrops should be cut off as the flowers fade; the green mats will continue to be attractive until the snow comes.

Sundrop or evening primrose *(Oenothera)* — Several species have been tested but none has proved as hardy or as satisfactory as the Missouri sundrop *(O. missouriensis)*. The common sundrop *(O. fruticosa)* and its improved form, *youngii,* have survived under deep snow cover; the showy sundrop *(O. speciosa)* is slightly hardier but not fully reliable. The Missouri sundrop or evening primrose has large glossy leaves, cup-shaped, pale yellow flowers on slender stems and interesting winged seed pods. The plants are leafy, about a foot and a half high and in bloom from July until late autumn. They prefer a sunny spot where the soil is not too rich nor too heavy.

Sunflower *(Helianthus)* — The perennial sunflowers are mostly tall, spreading plants that are useful for the back of the border. The willowleaf sunflower *(H. salicifolius)* grows five feet high with stems densely clothed with pendulant leaves. The small yellow flowers open in late September and, if the weather is mild, continue for a month. The plant is not fully hardy unless under a deep snow cover.

The Miss Mellish sunflower, a variety of *H. rigidus,* has coarse leaves, rampant roots and large, golden yellow flowers in September. The plants are fully hardy but need restraining or they crowd out less vigorous plants.

Tansy *(Tanacetum)* — The common tansy *(T. vulgare)* is sometimes culti- vated as a border plant, though it is a naturalized European weed in some parts. The fern-like, dark green leaves are handsome and aromatic, but the dense clusters of yellow flowers borne on three-foot plants are not particularly attractive. The plants spread rapidly by underground stolons to crowd out less vigorous plants. Tansy will grow in dry corners where other plants are unthrifty.

Thermopsis *(Thermopsis)* — The Caroline thermopsis *(T. caroliniana)* makes a four-foot plant with spikes of yellow flowers resembling lupines. It is fully hardy, making a good perennial for the back of the border, and requires no special care.

Thyme *(Thymus)* — The thymes are prostrate plants suitable for rock gardens or the edge of perennial borders. The soil must be well drained and not too heavily charged with nitrogen; the plants do best in full sun. The mother-of-thyme *(T. serpyllum)* varies with white, pink or reddish flowers. All have tiny leaves and spread to make mats, green throughout the whole season except when covered with blooms. Some have lemon- scented leaves and some smell of caraway, while others have the usual pungency commonly associated with the plant. The woolly thyme is similar to the mother-of-thyme except that the leaves are gray.

Toadflax *(Linaria)* – The common toadflax or butter-and-eggs toadflax *(L. vulgaris)* has become naturalized in some parts. It is sometimes cultivated though often condemned as a noxious weed. The Macedonian toadflax *(L. macedonica)* is a spreading, two-foot plant with narrow, gray green leaves and spikes of yellow flowers in July resembling miniature snapdragons. It revels in hot, sandy soil and makes a good border plant in spite of its rampant habit.

Violet *(Viola)* – The violets or perennial pansies include a number of showy border plants as well as some more suitable for the rock garden. The bedding violas, hybrids and forms of the horned violet *(V. cornuta)* are sometimes grown as annuals as they are not fully hardy in prairie gardens.

The Greek violet *(V. gracilis)* has dainty flowers, either yellow or violet blue, on slender stems a foot high.

The Canada violet *(V. canadensis)* is sometimes cultivated; the plants are a foot high, compact, with broad leaves and white, yellow-centred flowers in June. The violas do best in moist soil and all except the bedding types prefer partial shade.

Wildindigo *(Baptisia)* – Where lupins will not grow, the blue wildindigo *(B. australis)* may be substituted. The leaves and flower spikes are similar to lupins but the color is restricted to deep blue. The flowers open in July on four-foot stems; the black, ornamental seed pods soon follow.

Wormwood *(Artemisia)* – Wormwood is grown for its ornamental, sometimes aromatic leaves, either green or silver gray. The Russian wormwood *(A. sacrorum)* has woody four-foot stems and fern-like leaves, dark green and attractive. Hard pruning in the spring to remove dead tip growth will keep it compact and healthy.

The beach wormwood *(A. stelleriana)* has silver gray, deeply lobed leaves on stems about a foot high. A variety called Silver Mound with finely divided, silky foliage of silver gray makes a fine plant for a hot, sunny spot. Both need hard pruning in April to induce young, vigorous growth. All the wormwoods do best in poor soil that is low in humus and nitrogen, well drained and in full sun.

Yarrow *(Achillea)* – Some have gray leaves; all need well-drained soil and prefer a sunny location. Common yarrow *(A. millefolium)* is not often cultivated, but the red-flowered Cerise Queen makes a good border plant two feet high. It blooms freely in July and later. The leaves are dark green and finely divided.

The double-flowered varieties of sneezewort yarrow *(A. ptarmica)*, Boule de Neige and Perry's White, make excellent border plants flowering in July. Both are about two feet high with narrow, dark green leaves and heads of double white flowers. The plants spread rapidly by stolons and therefore require replanting in spring every three or four years.

Silvery yarrow *(A. ageratifolia)* is fine for the front of the border or rock garden. It needs a hot, dry soil to intensify the silvery, finely cut leaves. The grayish white flower heads are not particularly attractive.

Yucca *(Yucca)* – The small soapwood yucca *(Y. glauca)*, native of the badlands areas of the Great Plains, is sometimes cultivated. Fully hardy, it can be used effectively in the perennial border. The plants are perennial but not herbaceous; the leaves are sword shaped and remain green all winter. The plants must have full sun and well-drained soil low in humus; in moist soil, the plants soon rot off. The handsome spikes of creamy white flowers open in July; seed is not usually formed without the aid of a certain species of moth. Another yucca species, the Adams needle *(Y. filamentosa)*, has been tested and found to be too tender for prairie gardens.

Fourteen

Bulbs and Plants
with Fleshy Roots

A number of plants have swollen roots of one kind or another. Not all are true bulbs but they are grouped together and loosely called bulbous plants. Tulips, narcissi, hyacinths, crocus, amaryllis, gloxinias, certain begonias, gladioli, dahlias, lilies and many other plants not so well known are in this group.

Tulips and lilies are both true bulbs though they differ a good deal in appearance. The tulip, like the onion, has a basal plate to which is attached the embryo plant, surrounded by layers of tissue which are modified underground leaves that sustain the young plant until it has made new roots and top growth. Lily bulbs are more loosely constructed. The basal plate is surrounded by fleshy scales, each attached to the main stem but separate from the others. By developing new growth buds on the basal plate, new bulbs are formed.

The gladioli, crocus and similar plants have roots that form a solid mass of storage tissue with a basal plate, from which grow the roots and one or more growth buds on the upper side. When the corm, as it is rightly called, has served its function in supplying nutrients to the plant as it emerges from dormancy, it dies and a new one is superimposed on the old.

A tuber is something different again; like the corm, it has a solid mass of storage tissue but no basal plate. The shoots appear from eyes or growing points; the potato is a good example. Tuberous begonias and dahlias have tuberous roots but they differ from potatoes; the new shoots on tuberous begonias develop on the top side only and only on the neck portion of dahlias are there dormant buds. There is another difference, too: dahlias make new tuberous roots every year; tuberous begonias simply increase in size.

The large family of irises has members with all sorts of root systems. Some have fibrous roots; others have rhizomes or fleshy roots, while still others are true bulbs. The true bulbous irises, native to the Mediterranean and Near East regions, are not hardy in prairie gardens. The well-known bearded or flag irises and certain other species have rhizomes; these are solid underground stems with growth shoots on the top and roots on the undersides.

Plants with swollen roots, whether they are classed as bulbs, tubers, corms or rhizomes, must have good drainage. If hardy bulbs are planted in low spots, where the water from melting snow is liable to linger for weeks in the spring, chances are the bulbs will die. Sandy loam is good for bulbs if it is enriched with humus and plant food. Heavy soil can be improved by adding generous quantities of granulated peat, well-rotted barnyard manure or garden compost. To ensure good drainage around lilies, tulips

CORRECT DEPTH TO PLANT BULBS

and other hardy bulbs, set the bulbs on an inch of coarse sand. In prairie gardens we are blessed with a deep, fertile soil in most areas but, even so, the hardy bulbs will give better response if you dig in two ounces of 11.48.0 per square yard at planting time and supplement this with a side dressing of 27.14.0 when the plants are a foot high.

Bulbs in the Prairie Garden

Tulips — Of all the hardy bulbs grown in prairie gardens, tulips and lilies are the most important. The tulips outnumber the lilies in the number of bulbs planted but, as a general rule, they are not so long lived. The chief reason for the tulip's short life in prairie gardens is a general lack of knowledge of its basic requirements. The most useful and reliable sorts are the Darwins and the Cottage tulips. With the best care, these bulbs can be expected to increase year after year, producing flowers just as attractive as those from the original bulbs; on the other hand, if they are neglected, the flowers soon decrease in size and finally the bulbs die.

Planting tulips — A regular program of tulip culture should start when new bulbs are planted. Prepare a place for them in the spring, digging deep and adding humus according to the needs of the soil. If you grow annuals where the tulips are to be planted in October, choose the tender kinds that are blackened by the first frost so that you can root them out with no pangs of remorse and get the ground ready in time for tulips. Fork over the ground in readiness for planting the tulips in October. The depth of planting is governed by the kind of soil. Eight inches is not too deep if the soil is sandy but, where it is heavy, five or six inches deep will do. Set the bulbs six inches apart, keeping the varieties separate for the best effect. A bed of mixed tulips can be gay and attractive but it is not as striking as bold patches of separate colors, either blending harmoniously or contrasting sharply.

There are many spots in the home garden where tulips can be fitted in without disturbing the permanent plantings. Separate beds of tulips will spotlight the garden in May and early June. Patches of Darwin and Cottage tulips will give early color in the perennial border; groups of tulips in front of shrub borders give bright patches of color against a background of greenery and certain species tulips add early interest in the rock garden.

Summer care of tulips — If your tulip beds are to be planted with annuals, you will have to decide to do one of two things — either lift the tulip plants intact as soon as the petals fall, or simply leave them where they are, cutting off the flowering stems. If you decide to lift the plants in June, dig them out carefully with soil on the roots; transplant them to a trench in the shade of a hedge, making it deep enough to hold the roots and the white portion of the stems. Cover the roots with fine soil made firm around the stems by treading, then let the garden hose trickle water to soak the soil thoroughly. In a month or so, when the leaves have turned brown, the bulbs can be dug up. Pull off the tops and old roots before you lay the bulbs in shallow boxes, storing them in a warm, dry place to finish ripening. When they are quite dry, store them in a cool basement until the time comes to plant them again. Meanwhile, the bulbs are sorted into sizes; those of walnut size or larger will be planted back in the flower beds in October for next year's bloom. The smaller bulbs should not be discarded even though they will not bloom the following spring; they should be lined out in the vegetable garden to grow for a year. Plant them in a trench four inches deep where the soil is rich and well drained and where the young plants will be in full sun for most of the day.

If you decide to leave your tulip bulbs undisturbed for two or three years, cut off the flowering stems as soon as the petals fall; otherwise, seed pods soon form to exhaust the plant for no good purpose. All the leaves must be left on to manufacture food for the new, developing bulbs. Not only must the leaves be left on the plant; they must be allowed to mature and die naturally. When the flower stems have been cut off, clear the bed of weeds and loosen the soil between the bulbs in readiness for the annuals. Certain fast-growing annuals such as marigolds or petunias, interplanted among the tulips, will soon hide the unsightliness of the dying foliage. By the early part of July, the tops of the tulips are usually brown and should be removed by twisting the stem and giving it a gentle pull. Carry away the tops and burn them to destroy the spores of botrytis, a disease that sometimes attacks tulips. Competition for soil moisture and the encroaching roots of vigorous perennials will hinder the natural increase of tulips, so dig the bulbs up every two years and replant them.

Tulips for the prairies — Besides the Darwin and Cottage tulips, there are other distinctive types, all useful and equally hardy. The single early tulips, a separate species, are best for indoor culture in pots and pans; outdoors, they tend to bloom too early and are often spoiled by bad weather. There are doubles of the same type but they are not so shapely as the singles. Following the early tulips in season of bloom are the Mendels and Triumphs; these are hybrids between the early flowering tulips and the Darwins. They have a full range of colors; the flowers are large and the stems taller than the early flowering tulips, but not so tall as the Darwins. Other later flowering varieties include Rembrandt, Bizarre, Breeder, lily-flowered, Parrot and peony-flowered tulips.

The Rembrandt and Bizarre tulips have flowers with stripes and feathered petals, giving the blooms an ornamental look. Use them sparingly with the brighter colored Darwins and Cottage tulips. As cut flowers they are esteemed for unique blendings of unusual colors. The Breeder tulips bloom about the same time as the Darwins; the colors are mostly dark coppery red, orange bronze and deep purple. To show off the Breeder tulips to the best advantage, plant them among the lighter and brighter colored Darwins. The lily-flowered tulips have elegant flowers on slender stems; the petals are reflexed and the colors are attractive shades of yellow and red. Parrot tulips have blooms with deeply fringed and waved petals. The older sorts have weak stems, not strong enough to support the heavy flowers; newer varieties are stronger, though they are sometimes beaten down in bad weather. The colors range from pure white through shades of yellow and red to the darkest maroon and orange shades. The Parrot tulips are worthy of a place in the garden but are not the best choice for formal beds. The peony-flowered tulips have huge double flowers on sturdy stems; some are over two feet high. The blooms open about the same time as the Darwins and there is a wide choice of colors.

An interesting group of tulips with branching stems are distinct from the usual single-stemmed varieties. These are called multiflowered tulips and some produce up to six good-sized flowers from a single bulb.

The numerous species tulips are hardy and useful rock garden plants and some can be naturalized in the shadow of certain shrubs. Too much root interference will restrict the natural increase of the bulbs but, when the soil is light and well drained and the roots of the sheltering shrubs not too aggressive, these species tulips will give a good account of themselves.

The waterlily tulip *(T. kaufmanniana)* is a species from Turkestan with variable flowers on short stems and broad leaves. A number of attractive hybrids are available; all are less than a foot high, blooming early in a fascinating array of colors that are mostly blends of cream and yellow, pink and red. Alfred Cortot has bright red petals, each with a black base and with leaves peculiarly marked with purplish stripes. Caesar Frank has rich yellow petals shaded carmine on the outside and edged with yellow. Another called Fritz Kreisler has large, salmon pink flowers.

Another tulip from Turkestan called Tarda does well in prairie gardens; the pale yellow, star-shaped flowers have cream-tipped petals suffused with yellow at the base. The bulbs increase fairly rapidly in light, well-drained soil. The species tulip *fosteriana* and its variety, Red Emperor, bloom too early to be of much use in prairie gardens. The huge, brilliant red flowers, opening in April when the bulbs are planted on the south side of the house, often are damaged by bad weather. One of the most beautiful species tulips is *T. greigii,* with vivid orange scarlet flowers; the base of each petal is zoned with black. The plants are about nine inches high and the leaves are mottled with brown spots. *T. clusiana,* the lady tulip, has dainty flowers on stems not more than a foot high; the petals are cream, washed with carmine on the outside.

Lilies – Not so long ago, practically the only lilies we saw in prairie gardens were rows of tiger lilies, a few patches of candlestick lily and perhaps a plant or two of coral lily. Nowadays there are scores of new lilies, mostly hybrids, a good many of which have been produced by Canadian plant breeders. The hardy lilies fill a gap in the perennial border that occurs when the June-flowering irises, peonies and Oriental poppies are over. The lily enthusiast will reserve separate space for his collection, planting five or six bulbs of only the most vigorous sorts in separate groups and in specially prepared soil.

Preparing the soil for lilies – It has been said time and time again that lilies must have good drainage and this cannot be overemphasized. Lily bulbs in soggy soil will not last long, so take pains to select a spot where the spring run-off water will not linger. The soil must be properly prepared as the bulbs should remain undisturbed for a number of years, producing strong stems and flowers as long as sufficient plant nutrients are available. Dig the soil deeply, loosening the subsoil and working in a few inches of well-rotted manure, garden compost or granulated peat. If your soil is heavy, it will pay to trench the soil as directed in chapter four, a foot and a half deep. The topsoil will be improved by mixing it with peat and sand; manure should not be mixed with the topsoil unless the manure is completely decomposed. Garden compost and the ashes of a bonfire can also be used to lighten the topsoil, though wood ash can upset the soil balance if too much is used.

Planting lilies – If you intend to plant groups of lilies in the perennial border, dig holes a foot and a half deep, loosen the subsoil and mix peat and sand with the topsoil, adding a handful of 11.48.0. September is the best time to plant lilies; the sooner the job is completed after the middle of the month, the better. Late planting, followed by hard frost before the ground has been insulated by snow, is often the cause of failures. To guard against early, deep-penetrating frosts, lay on a six-inch cover of flax straw as soon as the bulbs are planted. Some lilies of borderline hardiness are offered for sale in the spring. The bulbs are dug in the fall, packaged in plastic bags and stored over winter in a cool cellar. The bulbs are large, mostly stem-rooting sorts and should be planted in May not less than six inches deep; in sandy soil, nine inches will not be too deep as long as the drainage is adequate. Set each bulb on an inch of sand to protect the basal plate from rotting, spacing them a foot apart and, in October, mound them with a foot of dry sawdust or peat.

Lilies for the prairies – In recent times, prairie plant breeders have developed a number of hardy hybrid lilies using *Lilium cernuum, willmottiae, tigrinum* and a few other species. As a result of this work we have a large group of hybrid lilies in a wide range of heights and colors, including many subtle shades not previously seen in lilies. Some of the new sorts are excellent as cut flowers, although some restraint must be used when cutting lily stems or the bulbs will be weakened. Never remove more than a third of the top growth and never let seed pods form unless you intend to use the seed.

The true species are of special interest to the collector as they include some of the most graceful of all lilies. The hardiest ones will do well in

STEM-ROOTING LILY

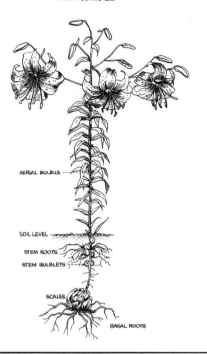

AERIAL BULBILS

SOIL LEVEL

STEM ROOTS

STEM BULBLETS

SCALES

BASAL ROOTS

Stem roots are produced below the soil level. The bulblets and the bulbils (if removed from the stem and planted) will grow into large, flowering bulbs.

prairie gardens; some demand a certain amount of shade while others do best in slightly acid soil. The following species have been tested over a long period in prairie gardens.

The Korean lily *(L. amabile)* and its yellow-flowered form thrive in full sun or partial shade. The flowers are orange red on slender two-foot stems in early July. The yellow amabile is identical except that the flowers are bright yellow. Both are easy to grow either from seed or natural bulb increase. The bulbil lily *(L. bulbiferum)* has orange-colored flowers on two-foot stems in late June. It has little to recommend it except earliness and the peculiar habit of producing quantities of bulbils in the leaf axils. The morningstar lily *(L. concolor)* has orange red blooms with pointed petals that give the flowers a starry look. The plants are not more than two feet high and seem to revel in full sun. There are several forms of the Dahurian or candlestick lily *(L. dauricum)* ranging in color from yellow to deep orange. They are easy to grow in full sun or partial shade. *L. duchartrei* is an unusual lily; it grows three or four feet tall but the bulbs are thumbnail size or smaller. The flowers are creamy white, each petal recurved and overlaid with purple spots. If it finds a happy home it becomes naturalized, increasing by stolons and seed. The best place for this lily is in the shadow of shrubs where the soil is deep and well charged with humus, and where the bulbs can be left alone. In suitable soil and surroundings, it will display its elegant, sweet-scented flowers profusely in July.

The Hanson lily *(L. hansoni)* is hardy enough but rather difficult to manage. It starts too soon in the spring and may get damaged by frost. It grows about three feet high with heavy, dark green leaves arranged in whorls. The flowers have thick, orange yellow petals overlaid with brown spots. The Hanson lily is one of the parents of a race of hardy lilies with strong stems up to five feet high and flowers in subtle shades of apricot yellow and shaded pink. Brocade and Sutton Court are two of the best.

L. martagon, sometimes erroneously called the Turkscap lily, is the other parent of Brocade and Sutton Court. It is native to a wide area of Europe extending to Siberia and is one of the oldest lilies in cultivation. Martagon lilies are not so well known in prairie gardens in spite of their hardiness and general adaptability. They grow about four feet high and, like the Hanson lily, the leaves are arranged in whorls. The original species has purplish flowers, heavily spotted and not particularly attractive. A pure white martagon with unspotted petals and paler green leaves is a choice lily. Another martagon called Cattaniae has dark, burgundy red flowers. The martagon lilies are not stem rooters, so plant the bulbs not more than six inches deep in well-drained soil, preferably in a spot where the flowers will be shaded from the hot sun for part of the day.

L. henryi is another hardy species which has been neglected by prairie gardeners. It is best planted on an east-facing border, shaded from hot sun and protected from westerly winds. The bright orange yellow flowers are not sunworthy and, if the plants face southwest, the blooms are usually blanched and unattractive. Although the stems of henryi push through the ground quite early, it is the last of the hardy lilies to bloom, often carrying the odd flower into September. The bronze green stems are thick at the base but become slender as they grow tall. As the flower buds form, sometimes thirty or more on a stem, the stems bend over and may need support. Lilies should only be staked as a last resort; the grace and charm of henryi will be lessened when the stems are supported, even when the staking is inconspicuous. The best stakes are made from willow wands of finger thickness, with the butt end thrust into the ground close to the stem and tied in several places with soft twine or raffia. The huge, purple bulbs of henryi should be planted not less than eight inches deep – in sandy soil, an inch or two deeper. The underground stems produce bulblets which can be removed in September and planted four to six inches deep in a garden frame to increase the stock.

The Caucasian lily *(L. monadelphum)* is another relatively unknown lily in spite of its ironclad hardiness and tolerance of high-lime soil. It is one of the earliest lilies to bloom, sharing the spotlight with bulbiferum. In most years it is in full bloom by the twentieth of June; this means it has to get away to an early start so, like the martagons, it is vulnerable to late spring frosts. To lessen the chances of spring frost damage, retard the growth by laying on a six-inch cover of flax straw in October, removing it as soon as the shoots push through the soil. Be ready to replace a light covering of straw if frost threatens. Spring frosts are particularly debilitating as they damage the plant's food-manufacturing leaves. The stems are about four feet high, well clothed with bright green leaves and pendulous, sweet-scented, bell-shaped flowers of rich yellow. The tips of the petals are recurved; some are spotted, while others are plain. Monadelphum will ripen enormous quantities of seed unless the faded flowers are removed, but to raise flowering-sized bulbs from seed takes about five years. The seed will develop tiny bulbs but no top growth is made the first year.

The coral lily *(L. pumilum)* is native to Siberia and western China and is one of the easiest lilies to grow, though the bulbs are not long lived. Plants raised from seed will flower in two years and this is the best way of maintaining a stock. The flowers are orange red on slender stems about two feet high; the leaves are quite narrow and produced rather sparsely. Plant the bulbs about four inches deep, preferably in a sunny spot where the soil is sandy.

The tiger lily *(L. tigrinum)* is a common plant in old gardens where the bulbs thrive with a minimum of attention. The stems are up to three feet high and well clothed with dark green leaves. The nodding flowers are orange vermilion heavily overlaid with black spots. Although the tiger lily stands considerable abuse, there is no reason to relegate it to an odd corner and neglect it. Well-grown plants can hold their own with the best of the hardy species, and prolong the lily display to August when most of the other lilies are over. A double-flowered tiger lily and one with yellow flowers are available.

The Willmott lily *(L. davidii willmottiae)* makes a vigorous six-foot plant with as many as forty blooms on a stem. The flowers are of medium size, bright orange red suffused with dark spots. The petals are thick and attractively reflexed. The Willmott lily has been used extensively by Canadian plant breeders to produce a large number of choice hybrid lilies.

The regal lily *(L. regale)* has been planted extensively in prairie gardens and, in some areas where the soil is light and deep snow insulates against penetrating frost, it survives year after year. Elsewhere on the prairies it may not be long lived, the basal plate rotting in a year or two. When this happens, new bulbs often start from the healthy scales to produce flowering bulbs in about two years. It is not unusual for regal lilies to disappear for a year, reappearing the following year with a few emaciated stems bearing only a single bloom or none at all. Healthy plants grow three feet or higher with large trumpets of pure white petals suffused with golden yellow in the throat. Some may have a tinge of rosy purple on the outside of the petals and all carry a heavy scent. They are easily raised from seed sown in a garden frame and, with proper care, the young plants will develop one or two flower buds the second or third year.

The madonna lily *(L. candidum),* long esteemed for its purity and delicate fragrance, is not fully hardy in prairie gardens, although some success has been reported with a hardier strain from the mountains of Salonika. It differs from most lilies in requiring a lime soil and in making a rosette of basal leaves in the late summer. The leaves are extensions of the bulb scales; for this reason, the bulbs should not be planted too deeply. The best chance of success is with bulbs planted in August, three inches deep in well-drained soil on an east- or north-facing border. To protect the basal leaves, cover them in October with a foot of dry sawdust or granulated peat; over this lay a few branches and some dry leaves. Snow is the best insulator, so pile it on the madonna lilies and chances are the rosettes will be healthy and green when the snow melts. The madonna lily is deserving of all the winter comfort you can provide; although you may not be able to produce the vigorous stems each with a dozen or more blooms that you may have seen only in pictures, a solitary, sweet-scented chalice is reward enough.

Other hardy bulbs — A number of minor bulbs are available and, though they are not all fully hardy, the keen gardener will try to grow as many as he can. Two of the hardiest and most satisfactory are the Siberian squill *(Scilla sibirica)* and the grape hyacinth *(Muscari botryoides).*

The scillas are the first to bloom, sometimes flaunting their nodding blue bells amid the snow. If they are undisturbed in well-drained soil, a colony is soon established by seed and bulb increase. A similar plant called Pushkinia has nodding, gray blue flowers, each petal lined with darker blue.

The grape hyacinths are fully hardy, easy to grow and attractive in May and early June with dense spikes of nodding blue flowers. The plants have glossy, dark green leaves and flower stems about six inches high. Like the scillas, they do best in sandy soil. Under ideal conditions the bulbs make rapid increase and the plants become overcrowded; when this occurs, dig them up in July and replant them in new soil.

Another hardy bulb rare in prairie gardens is the ixiolirion. It flowers in June on slender stems a foot or so high, each with several flowers having recurved petals of soft lavender blue. The plants do best in sandy soil that is well drained and fully exposed to the sun.

The true crocus *(Crocus vernus),* the snowdrop *(Galanthus nivalis),* a similar plant called snowflake *(Leucojum vernum)* and another spring-flowering plant called glory of the snow *(Chionodoxa luciliae)* are not fully hardy in prairie gardens, but in sheltered spots, near the warmth of basement walls, for example, the enthusiast with nostalgic memories of these old-world harbingers of spring will persevere with them. By laying on a deep cover of straw in October to prevent the early, deep penetration of frost and to retard growth in the spring, it is possible to winter the bulbs reasonably well, but they are usually not very long lived.

Several species of *Fritillaria,* a genus closely allied to the true lilies, are hardy and some are most attractive. The smallest one, the yellow fritillary *(F. pudica),* has yellow, nodding flowers in May and early June. A taller one called *F. pallidiflora* is a more vigorous plant with soft yellow flowers and blue green leaves. Both species will do well in light soil, reproducing plants from seed and natural bulb increase. A curious, dark-flowered fritillary *(F. ruthenica)* from the Caucasian mountains grows about two feet high; the flowers are dull, brownish red.

Hyacinths, daffodils and various narcissi are not hardy in prairie gardens, though it is possible to bring them through the winter in sheltered spots under deep snow. By and large, these half-hardy bulbs are a poor investment in prairie gardens and the wise gardener will grow the bulbs indoors. Varieties suitable for indoor cultivation are described later in this chapter.

Tubers in the Prairie Garden

Dahlias — Dahlias have been popular in prairie gardens since the early settlers brought in the old-fashioned red dahlia from Ontario around the turn of the century. For a while, the huge decorative and cactus sorts seemed to be most popular but, nowadays, the trend is to the smaller-flowered and longer-stemmed varieties, which are more useful as cut flowers. The prairie summer climate suits them well enough except for periods of torrid heat. The soil must be deep, well drained and well charged with nutrients, and plenty of moisture is required when the plants are in full growth.

Preparing the soil for dahlias — Dahlias are heavy feeders and the best plants are grown when the soil is dug deeply in the fall, adding rotted manure or garden compost generously; a three-inch layer will put the ground in good condition by spring. Before the tubers are planted, rake in a high-phosphorous fertilizer such as 11.48.0 at the rate of two ounces to the square yard. Later on, when the plants are growing freely, give them a second dose of fertilizer.

Planting dormant tubers — Dahlias must have a piece of the stem attached to the tuber or there will be no shoots. Though the tubers appear to have eyes like the potato, the growth buds are only initiated from the base of the stem. The time to plant dahlias from dormant tubers is when the wild plum blooms, which is May fifteenth or thereabouts. It is best to postpone planting should the weather at that time be cold and damp. Earlier bloom can be had by starting the roots in shallow boxes of light, sandy soil about the tenth of April. Place the box in a sunny window, watering the soil to

DIVIDING DAHLIAS

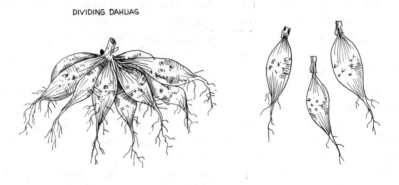

A portion of the old stem, from which the growth buds will be initiated, must be retained on each tuber.

keep it moist but not wet. The box can be set indoors around the middle of May if the weather is congenial, but be alert to the danger of night frosts and ready to bring the plants indoors if necessary.

When outdoor planting is to begin, dig a hole six inches deep and loosen the bottom soil with a fork. Set the tuber with the shoot pointing upward and cover it with two or three inches of fine soil. Space the tubers two feet apart and the rows four feet apart; mark the spot with a six-inch stick so that you can put in a permanent stake later without damaging the tuber. The hole is gradually filled with soil as the plant grows but a

TREES AND SHRUBS

Top Left: The November beauty of the native birch; the nearby common lilac is still in full leaf.

Top Centre: Almey, the choice rosybloom introduced at Morden that initiates flower buds on very young trees; note the patch of moss phlox, blooming as early as the crabapple.

Top Right: The white flowers of the Siberian crabapple and its tiny red fruits contrast well with the pink rosyblooms.

Lower Left: The glowing pink blossoms of the single form of *Prunus triloba*, less common but more attractive than the double-flowered plum.

Lower Centre: The bronzy foliage and the large quantities of fruit borne by some rosyblooms extend their season of interest deep into the fall.

Lower Right: Muckle plum, a nonsuckering, nonfruiting prunus hybrid that flowers in early May.

shallow depression is left to facilitate watering. When the plants are a foot or so high, the tall varieties should be staked. Strong stakes made of one-by two-inch lumber are thrust into the ground at the spot where the marker stick was put in. Tie the main stem to the stake at intervals of a foot or so, using old nylons, soft twine or raffia.

Pruning dahlias – Dahlias grown for exhibition are pruned to a single stem; side shoots and unwanted flower buds are pinched out as they appear. For garden decoration, remove the side shoots from the lowest pair of leaves, leaving the next pair and the two higher up the stem. This will give a more bushy plant with four lateral stems and a terminal shoot. At the end of each branch, a cluster of flower buds will develop. Select the centre one of these and pinch out the others. Each plant produces five large blooms when you prune the stems in this manner; if you need more, but smaller flowers, allow all the shoots to develop naturally.

The small-flowered dahlias used for cutting are best grown naturally and so are the bedding-type dahlias. It is important to keep the spent blooms picked from the single and semidouble bedding dahlias or the plants waste energy making useless seed.

Summer care of dahlias – When the plants reach full growth and the flowers open, plenty of water is needed. Weekly applications of the equivalent of an inch of rain will be needed in July and August if the weather is dry. The best way to put it on is to let the garden hose trickle water around each plant to soak the soil to a depth of one foot. Frequent light sprinklings will not reach the roots, so water the plants once a week as long as the weather in July and August is hot and dry.

Mulching the soil in early July with a two-inch layer of peat will be beneficial in conserving moisture and reducing the soil temperature, as well as preventing weeds from growing. If mulching cannot be done, the next best thing is to keep the soil stirred, using the push hoe to keep the surface tilled to maintain a layer of dust.

Dahlias are fair game for tarnished plant bugs, aphids, thrips and spider

---

EVERGREENS

Left: The distinctive upright cones of the alpine fir.

Top Centre: A dwarf form of the mountain pine, most widely planted of the pines grown in prairie gardens.

Top Right: The variety of evergreen shapes and textures is accentuated in a winter landscape; note the pines in the foreground and the spruce trees in the back.

Lower Centre: The golden form of the common juniper thrives in well-sheltered prairie gardens.

Lower Right: A dwarf form of the Colorado spruce, suitable for foundation plantings.

mites, which are particularly troublesome in hot, dry weather. Control measures for all these insects are found in chapter four. Several viruses attack dahlias and are easily recognized in mottled leaves and stunted plants. Root out all suspects and burn them.

Lifting and storing dahlias — After the stems are blackened by early, light frost, cut them off about three inches above the ground. You can dig the roots a week or two later but you must get them out of the ground before hard frost comes. The roots are easily damaged by careless digging, so they must be handled carefully. From the neck portion of the root, the next year's growth buds will be initiated; if this portion of the plant is ruptured, the adjoining root is useless. Use a fork to ease the plants out of the ground gently, pricking out the soil from between the roots if this is necessary. In sandy soil, the roots will be clean; in heavy soil you may have to remove soil with a sharp stick.

Set the newly dug plants in the sun for a few hours before you take them to the basement to finish drying; there, set them on the basement floor for a week or so before you pack them away for the winter. The roots store best in boxes of dry sawdust, peat moss or perloam. If you divide them before you put them away for the winter, the single root divisions can be placed in plastic bags after dusting them with sulphur or Captan. Pack the plastic bags in boxes with dry sawdust between each layer of bags. Periodic inspections are made to check humidity, dampening the sawdust if the roots appear to be shrivelling. The best storage temperature is about forty-five degrees and the air should not be too dry.

Tuberous begonias — Tuberous begonias do well in prairie gardens when you give them the special care they require. They are effective as mass plantings in a half-shaded bed or border; they make handsome plants for a window box or planter and certain kinds make fine hanging plants. They are tender to frost and fragile, so shelter from wind is necessary as well as protection from frost. The modern tuberous begonia was developed from a number of species native to the foothills of the Andes in South America, where the air is moist, the temperature even and where the plants are shaded from hot sun. Tuberous begonias are sensitive to light. Too much will burn the leaves; too little will make the plants grow spindly and may cause the blooms to drop prematurely. A north-facing border will suit them, providing the early morning and late evening sun is not obscured by buildings or tall trees.

The most popular and the easiest way to grow tuberous begonias is to start them indoors from tubers bought from a reliable seedsman. You can increase your stock by dividing tubers that have more than one shoot or you can root cuttings. Raising tuberous begonias from seed can be accomplished in the home if you pay regular and close attention to details of culture. Neglect for even a day can result in failure.

Starting tuberous begonias — Mix three parts granulated peat moss with one part sharp sand and fill a shallow box almost to the rim with the moistened mixture. Press the tubers into the mixture, making sure you have the concave or hollow side of the tuber uppermost. A temperature of not less than sixty-five degrees is needed and the atmosphere should be

NEW SHOOTS

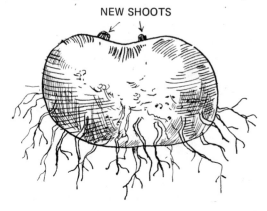

BEGONIA TUBER

The growth shoots, which may be difficult to distinguish among the root masses, emerge only from the concave or hollow side of the tuber; they must be planted facing upwards.

moist to promote good growth. Early March is the best time to make a start with tuberous begonias but you can delay planting a week or two if necessary.

Watering must be regularly tended to, dampening the peat mixture between the tubers but taking care not to maintain a soggy condition or the tubers may rot. When the young plants are about three inches high, pot them singly into five-inch pots. The soil must be spongy and rich in nutrients. A mixture containing two parts fibrous loam, one part rotted manure, one part granulated peat and one part sand, adding a cupful of 11.48.0 to each pailful, is recommended. The pots should be drained by placing a flat piece of crockery in the bottom, overlaid with an inch of rough peat. Begonias should not be potted too firmly; gentle pressure with the fingers will settle the soil around the roots. Watering must be sufficient and regular, taking care not to keep the soil in a constant state of saturation. When the first flower buds show color, feed the plants weekly with soluble fertilizer. A tablespoonful of 10.52.17 in a gallon of water can be beneficial to healthy plants; each one should get a cupful. Water the plants before you apply liquid fertilizer, or you may injure them when you apply it to dry soil.

If begonias are to be used for bedding, all the flower buds are allowed to open. Larger flowers are obtainable when you pinch out the two side buds in each natural three-flowered stem. The side buds, usually female blooms, have a single row of petals and a triangular seed pod; the centre bloom will increase in size when the side buds are removed.

Planting tuberous begonias — In most parts of the prairies, you can transplant tuberous begonias to the open ground in early June; even at this date it is not always safe, so be alert to the danger of a late frost and be ready to protect the plants with a sheet of plastic. When you set the plants out, point the leaves to the front and the blooms will be seen to the best advantage. Well-grown plants need not less than fifteen inches on all sides. The stems are soft and easily damaged by wind, so stake and tie them, using willow wands or similar stakes that are strong but not too noticeable.

Summer care of tuberous begonias — Tuberous begonias sometimes become infected with powdery mildew, a fungus which forms whitish patches on the leaves. (See chapter four for control of powdery mildew.) Bud drop can be a problem if proper growing conditions are not maintained; poor drainage, overwatering or extreme dryness and too much shade are the chief causes of both mildew and bud drop.

When frost threatens in September, you can dig the plants with soil on the roots and transplant them to pots of suitable size or to boxes. They will continue to bloom for several weeks in a sun porch or window. When the plants begin to look shabby, give them less water to induce the normal resting period; allow the plants to become quite dry between waterings, then stop watering when the leaves turn yellow. To ensure the proper ripening of the tubers and successful winter storage, give the plants the regular care you gave them when starting them into growth. When the ripening process is complete, the stems will easily separate from the tuber when you bend them over. The tubers are removed from the soil, packed in dry peat and stored at forty degrees. Examine them once or twice through the winter, dampening the peat if the tubers tend to shrivel.

Tuberous begonias from cuttings and tuber division — Extra good sorts can be increased from cuttings or tuber division. Large tubers with more than one shoot can be cut with a knife after they start to sprout. Dust the cut surfaces with Captan. Cuttings can be taken from started plants when they are three inches high, using the surplus basal shoots or side shoots when the plants are half grown.

The cuttings will root best in pots of moist peat and sand, using three parts peat to one part of sand. Shade the cuttings from bright sunshine by covering them with newspaper. Transplant the rooted cuttings to four-inch pots, which will be large enough the first year. The best chance of success with tuberous begonia cuttings is to take them as early as possible so that they get the full benefit of a long growing season. Give the young plants the same general care as recommended for plants started from tubers.

Tuberous begonias from seed — The enthusiastic house-plant grower may attempt to grow tuberous begonias from seed and will stand a good chance of success if he pays close attention to cultural details. Start with fresh seed from a specialist grower and be ready to sow in early March in a temperature of seventy degrees. Use a mixture of one part fibrous loam, one part peat and one part sharp sand screened through a quarter-inch sieve. Sterilize the soil mixture by baking it in an oven for half an hour at two hundred degrees; save the rough portions of the soil mixture for drainage. Use a five-inch clay pot scrubbed clean and placed in boiling water for a few minutes. Half fill the pot with broken crockery or coarse gravel, over which an inch layer of the rough soil mixture is placed. Fill the pot with the fine soil, gently pressing it down to leave a space of one-half inch between the soil level and the rim of the pot. Make the surface smooth and level with the lid of a tin. Stand the pot in a bowl of water long enough to saturate the soil; drain for half an hour before you sow the seed. Tuberous begonia seed is as fine as dust, so mix a teaspoonful of dry, white sand with it to facilitate even distribution. While the seed pot drains, prepare a seven-inch pot by scrubbing it and lining the bottom with several layers of wet newspaper. The seed pot is placed in the seven-inch pot to ensure insulation from dry air. Cover the pot with a piece of glass, over which a sheet of paper is placed.

Inspect the seed pot daily, turning the glass after wiping off condensation moisture. In about a week's time from the date of sowing the seed, the first signs of germination will be seen; the seed coats will split open to expose the white embryo plant. Prop up the glass with a matchstick to ventilate the seed pot and create a buoyant atmosphere for the young plants. Increase the ventilation as the plants grow, removing the glass altogether when the seedlings are large enough to transplant.

Careful attention must be given to watering at all times; in the early stages of growth it is best to stand the seed pot in a bowl of tepid water, allowing it to remain there until the surface of the soil is wet. The seedlings need plenty of light but must be shaded from direct sunlight. Transplant the seedlings into jiffy pots, using two parts fibrous loam, one part peat and one part sand. When the young plants are well established in jiffy pots, transfer them to five-inch clay pots or plastic pots, treating them in the same way as those raised from tubers.

Corms in the Prairie Garden

Gladioli — The gladiolus is the most popular summer-flowering bulb, or corm, as it is more correctly called. It has only limited use as a decorative plant in the garden but is unexcelled as a cut flower. For this reason it is best planted in the reserve garden or in the vegetable plot. Choose a sunny spot where the soil is deep, rich in nutrients and friable. Shelter from wind is necessary or vigorous sorts may have to be staked.

Preparing the soil for gladioli — In most parts of the prairies the soil is well suited to growing gladioli but, where it tends to be too heavy, you must dig in plenty of organic material. Rotted barnyard manure, granulated peat and garden compost are all suitable, adding sand where necessary to improve drainage. Prepare the soil by digging it deeply in the fall, leaving it rough over winter to mellow by spring from the action of frost. As soon as the ground dries in the spring, fork it over and rake it level in readiness for planting. Several applications of fertilizer will produce vigorous plants if the corms are healthy and if they get adequate water. Rake in the first dose of 11.48.0 before planting, after spreading it evenly at two ounces to the square yard. Another method of applying fertilizer is to dig a trench six inches deep, spreading the fertilizer in the bottom, then covering it with two inches of soil before setting the corms. A pound of 11.48.0 will be sufficient for one hundred feet of row.

Planting gladioli — In most parts of the prairies, gladioli can safely be planted around May tenth. The wise gardener, however, will wait a few days should the weather be too cold and damp. In the meantime, the corms should be brought from the cellar to a warm room. Corms are either large, medium or small. The large ones measure over one and one-quarter inches across, the mediums from three-quarters to one and one-quarter inches, the small ones, less than three-quarters of an inch. As a general rule, the large corms produce the best blooms and flower a few days earlier than identical varieties a size smaller. For general purposes, the medium-sized corms are a good investment, as they produce spikes of excellent quality with ordinary care.

The depth of planting varies a bit, depending on the size of the corm and the texture of the soil. In sandy soil, large corms are covered with five inches of well-pulverized soil; medium corms need four inches of soil over them and small ones about three inches. In heavier soils, slightly shallower planting is recommended. Planting distances can be single rows, spacing the corms four to six inches apart and the rows not less than two feet. You can make a double row, planting the corms six inches apart each way; the distance between the double rows should be three feet. To grow exhibition blooms, space the corms about a foot apart in the row and the rows at three feet. Keep in mind the gladioli need a lot of summer care — cultivating, fertilizing, watering and digging the corms is facilitated if you have sufficient room between the rows to work comfortably.

Summer care of gladioli — Gladioli use enormous quantities of water when the plants are in full leaf but, in the early stages of growth, excess soil moisture may cause the leaves to turn yellow and become diseased. During July and August, when the plants are well established and the weather is particularly dry, the general rule for other plants on the prairies — that is, weekly soakings the equivalent of an inch of rain — applies.

When the young plants are above ground, the surface soil is stirred with a Dutch hoe to kill seedling weeds and to prevent a hard crust from forming. The cultivating is continued as often as required and weeds growing between the plants in the row are pulled by hand where necessary.

Mulching is especially beneficial where the soil is sandy and in periods of dry weather. It conserves moisture by preventing the soil from cracking to increase the rate of evaporation. It is not beneficial when the soil has dried out, so soak the soil and destroy weeds by hoeing, then put on the mulch. The best time to put it on is when the plants are about a foot high, using granulated peat as first choice and flax straw or chive, sawdust or lawn clippings as substitutes. Mulching may do more harm than good if the soil is heavy and rains are frequent, since the base of the plant will be constantly moist and more likely to be infected by disease.

The most common insects attacking gladioli are thrips, aphids and two-spotted mites. The white grubs, larvae of the June beetle, are sometimes troublesome and, in new soil recently in sod, wireworms may tunnel into the corms and the young shoots. Control measures for these and other insects can be found in chapter four.

Cutting gladioli — As most gladioli are used as cut flowers, it is important not to damage the plants when the flowers are cut. With practice you can learn to cut the stems, at the same time leaving enough foliage to sustain the plant so that it can make new corms. The following method is recommended. Pierce the stem at a point about a foot from the base of the plant, using a thin-bladed knife. Make a diagonal cut through the flower stem, preserving the leaves, and pull the flower stem through the foliage. While it will have some leaves attached, there will be enough left behind to ensure good corm reproduction. It is best to cut the stems early in the day, choosing those with the lowest placed, fully open floret. They can be stored for a week at thirty-five degrees before they are used in the living room or on the show bench.

When gladioli are grown as decorative plants, the spikes should be cut off when most of the blooms have faded; otherwise, they look untidy and may produce seed to rob the plant of nutrients that are needed for making the new corms.

Harvesting and storing gladioli corms — In most parts of the prairies, it is safe to leave the corms in the ground until the first week of October. After this date there may be a risk, especially in northern areas where hard frost may interfere with the digging. Before you dig, go through the patch in search of diseased plants; those with yellow leaves may be infected with neck rot or virus. Root out all suspects and burn them. Choose a sunny day with plenty of air movement so that the corms will dry rapidly. Ease the plants out of the ground with a garden fork, laying them with tops on to dry in the sun. Some gardeners may prefer to cut off the tops before the plants are dug but the corms will dry quicker when they are left on. It is not recommended to leave the corms out overnight; even though the days are warm, the night temperature may drop below freezing to injure the corms seriously.

The after-ripening or curing of the corms is an important phase of gladioli culture; successful storage will depend to some extent on how well the corms are dried and cured. Cut off the tops before you spread out each variety in a shallow box to dry. In the daytime, the corms can be set out in the sun as long as the weather is warm. To complete the drying process, a warm, well-ventilated room where the temperature is eighty degrees or a bit higher is needed. The drying and curing is complete when the old corm parts from the new one with gentle prying from an old spoon. Only the loose skins should be removed; it is not recommended that the corms be peeled bare. After the corms have been cleaned, a few

GLADIOLUS CORM AND ROOTS

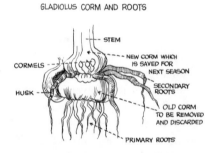

The secondary roots act as anchors for the new corm, always maintaining the plant at the proper depth in the soil.

more days at eighty degrees will seal over the base where the new corm joined the old one; this will lessen the chances of disease organisms entering.Dust the corms with a mixture of Captan. Only a fine film of dust is needed; a teaspoonful in a paper bag containing one hundred corms will be sufficient. Store the corms at forty degrees in a medium-dry atmosphere. Too much moisture may cause mould to form but, if the air is too dry, the corms shrivel.

Growing Bulbs Indoors

In the prairie regions, where winter comes early and sometimes lingers for six months, spring is eagerly awaited, especially by gardeners who are anxious to see the renewal of life in the garden. By growing a collection of Dutch bulbs indoors, you can be reminded of the coming of spring even though it may still be a long way off. A pot of daffodils can bring cheer through the stormy days of January and February and there is nothing complicated about the culture of potted bulbs. Failures are generally due to neglect or to a poor understanding of the basic requirements of potted bulbs, rather than to poor quality bulbs.

To grow potted bulbs you will need first-grade bulbs fresh from the seedsman, a variety of suitable containers, soil or special bulb fibre and a cool place to store the pots while the bulbs make root.

Bulbs for potting — Buy the best bulbs from a good seedhouse; the so-called bargain lots offered for sale at the end of the season, when they have been in warm storage for several weeks, are usually a poor investment at any price. These bulbs have likely been exposed to warm, dry air for long periods and have deteriorated as a consequence. First-grade bulbs will always produce larger blooms and more of them per bulb than smaller sizes, all other things being equal. There are many kinds available; the most popular varieties are the daffodils and various sorts of narcissi, hyacinths and tulips, both singles and doubles in the early-flowering class. Most of the bulbs come from Holland where bulb growing is a major industry. Large quantities are imported every year for forcing in greenhouses and for growing in the home in pots, as well as for planting outdoors to bloom at a season of the year when there are few other flowers in the garden.

Daffodils, various kinds of narcissi, hyacinths and tulips are available in the seed stores and other outlets in late September or early October. In selecting Dutch bulbs for forcing, choose those that are firm and free of blemishes. Some may have a soft rot starting at the base. You get the best choice when you buy early and you stand the best chance of success with early planted bulbs.

Tulips for potting — The early single- and double-flowered tulips can be forced into bloom in February by planting the bulbs in early October; the Darwins and Cottage tulips are not so easily forced unless cool conditions can be maintained for three months or longer. When tulips are introduced into a warm room too early, the flower buds abort.

Choice early single-flowered varieties for potting are Ibis (pink), White Hawk, Montressor (an older, brilliant yellow variety), Prince of Austria (brilliant orange red and very sweet scented) and Van der Neer (rosy violet, very easy to grow). Among the doubles, Scarlet Cardinal displays a black patch in the centre of each tulip when the flowers are fully open. Schoonard, another suitable double, is white; Murillo is white and pink and Mr. Van der Hoef is a deep yellow.

Hyacinths for potting — Hyacinths are obtainable in various shades of pink and blue as well as deep reds and purples. Pure white sorts are available as well as new shades of yellow and orange. These bulbs each produce one large spike and are most popular for forcing.

The Roman hyacinths, once used extensively for early forcing, are not grown to any extent today though the bulbs are still offered for sale by some seedsmen. The Roman hyacinth belongs to a distinct species, each bulb producing several slender stems of tiny bells. Multiflora hyacinths are similar to the Roman hyacinths in that they produce six or more stems to a bulb. The spikes of blooms are graceful and the stems slender; the color range is wider than the Roman hyacinths and includes pinks, whites, yellows and blues.

Daffodils and narcissi for potting — All daffodils are forms of narcissi but all the narcissi are not necessarily daffodils. The novice gardener may find it confusing to separate daffodils from narcissi but, by studying the classification system introduced by the Royal Horticultural Society, he will have a better idea. Every one of them is recommended for growing indoors.

There are eleven divisions. The first is made up of the trumpet daffodils, such as Golden Harvest and King Alfred in the all-yellow varieties, Mount Hood and Beersheba in the all-whites and Queen of the Bicolors and Mrs. E. H. Krelage in the bicolors. Division II is large-cupped narcissi with one flower per stem; Division III is small-cupped narcissi, also with one flower per stem. In division IV are the double-flowered narcissi. Division V contains the triandus narcissi with narrow leaves and several blooms per stem. Division VI contains the various cyclamineus narcissi with solitary nodding flowers. Division VII is reserved for the jonquils, the miniature daffodils with rush-like foliage and tiny, sweet-scented flowers. Division VIII contains the tazetta narcissi, which include the well-known paper white, the Chinese sacred lily, and the poetaz narcissi such as Laurens Koster. In division IX are the poeticus narcissi with pure white perianths and flat centres, usually yellow edged with orange or scarlet; the well-known Pheasants Eye is in this group. Division X contains the species narcissi and all forms not of garden origin. The final division is XI and it is given over to miscellaneous narcissi that cannot properly be fitted into the other groups.

Soil for potted bulbs — The soil for potted bulbs needs no special preparation; it must be porous to allow free drainage, so heavy clay soil had best be lightened by adding granulated peat and sand. Garden soil of medium texture can be used without mixing with peat and sand but, if these materials are on hand, use them. Soil previously used for growing potted bulbs should not be used again without being sterilized. Some bulbs, such as the paper white narcissi, can be grown in water; the bulbs are set on pebbles and the water level maintained up to the base of the bulbs, or just below it once roots have developed. Fibre for growing bulbs can be bought from the seed stores and may be used in place of soil. It is cleaner and usually free of disease organisms; otherwise, it is no better than soil.

Containers for potting — The earthenware flower pots in suitable sizes are standard containers for bulbs. Plastic pots and fancy porcelain dishes can also be used. A well-grown pot of bulbs will have a good show of bloom surrounded by healthy leaves. Whether the container is an earthenware flower pot or a fancy vbowl, it is most important that it be in proportion to the size of the plant and not so ornate as to detract from the bulbs.

Containers must be scrubbed clean if they have to be used for potting and must be rinsed thoroughly if detergents are used in the scrub water. Tests have shown that detergents are extremely toxic to the roots of bulbs, especially hyacinths. New clay pots must be soaked in water for several hours; if used as they are, they draw moisture from the soil and the bulbs may suffer.

The size of the container is important. Small-flowered hyacinths such as the yellow variety, City of Haarlem, look well in a four-inch clay pot. Top-sized (or largest) bulbs of more vigorous sorts need a five-inch pot. Three hyacinths in a six-inch pan will make a fine table decoration. Early flowering tulips, both single and double sorts, are attractive when six bulbs are planted in a five-inch pot. The daffodils and various narcissi are best planted in seven-inch azalea pots. These pots are not so tall as regular flower pots and are preferred for tall-growing bulbs which may look gawky in regular pots.

Potting bulbs — Some bulbs are potted deeper than others. Tulips, for example, should be covered with an inch of soil. Hyacinths are set with the tip of the bulb at soil level. Daffodils and narcissi should have the nose of the bulb just above the soil. To have the most showy pots of flowering bulbs, set the bulbs as close as you can in the pot without letting them touch. If the bulbs are touching, they push up the whole soil mass when the roots emerge; when this happens, you must repot them or they cannot be watered properly.

Clay pots have drainage holes in the bottom; cover the hole with a piece of broken crockery; over this, put an inch of roughage obtained by screening the soil through a half-inch sieve. Half fill the pot with fine soil, spacing the bulbs evenly and closely. Fill in with fine soil, pressing it around the bulbs with the fingers but not pounding it firmly. Leave room for water, allowing half an inch between the soil and rim of the pot for the small sizes, proportionately more for the larger ones. Label each pot with the name of variety and date of planting and give each pot a good soaking.

Tulips and hyacinths have clean bulbs with no roots attached; daffodils and narcissi may have old roots on the bulbs. It is best to remove these old dead roots before potting by twisting them off, as they take up room and absorb water.

Storing potted bulbs — The most convenient place to store potted bulbs is in a basement, if you can keep the temperature at approximately forty to forty-five degrees. An area partitioned off for vegetable storage will be a good place for potted bulbs. Cover the pots to keep out light and set traps for mice should this be necessary. Mice have a fondness for the tender shoots of tulips and hyacinths; daffodils and narcissi are less attractive to them. Potted bulbs are soon ruined in a warm basement, the top growth developing before the bulbs have made sufficient root to support it. When this happens, the flower buds abort and all the gardener's efforts are wasted.

Potted bulbs can be rooted outdoors by plunging them in a garden frame or against the south wall of the house. Cover the pots six inches deep with soil or granulated peat, making sure you have watered them thoroughly. If snow comes early and deep, the pots are safe until early December; after that, they should be removed to the coolest part of the basement at the first opportunity.

There are no hard and fast rules on the length of time the pots should be kept in the basement but they must be allowed to remain there until they are filled with roots and the tops are an inch or two high. The rooting time will vary according to the variety of bulb and the temperature of the basement. If you keep them at forty degrees or a few degrees lower, bulbs take longer to root than at forty-five degrees.

Another factor governing the rooting period is the condition of the bulbs. Wet weather in the bulb fields retards the drying and ripening process, resulting in green bulbs that take longer to root and produce flowers. Specially prepared hyacinths are available for early planting and may be had in bloom by Christmas. Bulbs potted in early October, such as hyacinths, early daffodils and narcissi as well as the early flowering tulips, should be ready for warmer temperatures by the middle of January, but be sure to examine the roots by removing the plant from the pot. Do this by placing your hand, with fingers spread out, over the top of the pot; turn it upside down and tap the rim gently on a firm surface, then lift off the pot. If the roots are coiled in a mass, chiefly at the base, and the top growth is two inches high, you can be reasonably sure that the plant is ready for forcing. If there is any doubt, leave it a week or so longer.

There are more failures due to bringing the plants from the basement too soon than to any other error. Shade the young shoots with paper for a few days when you first bring up the potted bulbs. Afterwards, keep them near a sunny window, increasing the supply of water as the tops grow. When the flower buds show, the plants need plenty of water. Well-grown plants will need watering daily and it may be best to stand the pot in a bowl of water to saturate the soil.

You can prolong the display of potted bulbs by bringing one or two pots from the basement each week. What to do with the plants after they have done blooming may be puzzling to the novice and, while the enthusiastic plant grower may succeed in flowering the bulbs another year, the game is hardly worth the gamble. Tulips can be dried off gradually when the flowers are faded and the pots stored in the basement until September, when the bulbs can be planted in the open ground. Since the other bulbs are not fully hardy in prairie gardens and there is little chance of getting them to bloom again in pots, they must be discarded.

Fifteen

Annuals

True annual plants put all their energies into one season's growth, starting as seed, flowering and returning to seed again, all in a matter of weeks. Not all the plants generally grouped as annuals fall into this class; some are tender perennials which are used as annuals by starting the seeds early in a greenhouse or on a sunny window sill. For the most part, true annuals are sun-loving plants with bright flowers which, on some sorts, are produced in great profusion. Some stand a few degrees of frost but salvias, marigolds and zinnias, for example, are blackened by the slightest touch of frost. Stocks, snapdragons, pansies and petunias are able to ward off several degrees.

There are many uses for annuals in gardens large and small. Beds and borders may be planted entirely with them. Shrub borders can be brightened up with patches of annuals planted along the front. They may also be used sparingly in the perennial border; when this is done, the wise gardener will be discriminating in his choice of varieties. Some kinds fit in very well and occasionally serve a practical purpose as fillers, but many others are out of place. The petunias, marigolds and zinnias seem to strike a wrong note in the perennial border; the daisy-like flowers of annual chrysanthemums, coneflower *(Rudbeckia)*, cornflower *(Centaurea)*, dusty miller *(Centaurea cineraria maritima)* and cupflower *(Nierembergia)*, on the other hand, will combine harmoniously with perennials. Where casu-

A PLAN FOR AN ANNUAL BORDER

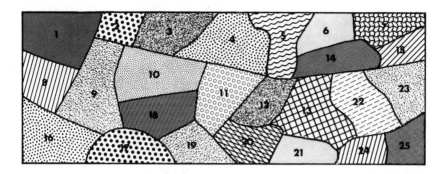

(1) snapdragon, tall yellow; (2) spiderflower, pink; (3) cosmos, red; (4) gloriosa daisy, yellow shades; (5) marigold, tall orange; (6) zinnia, white; (7) snapdragon, tall crimson; (8) cockscomb or celosia, tall crimson; (9) ten-week stocks, white; (10) marigold, tall yellow; (11) pot marigold or calendula, orange; (12) sage, scarlet; (13) petunia, white; (14) ten-week stocks, blue; (15) chrysanthemum, yellow shades; (16) marigold, dwarf yellow; (17) fossflower or ageratum, blue; (18) petunia, red; (19) centaurea or dusty miller; (20) verbena, pink; (21) snapdragon, dwarf yellow; (22) balsam, mixed colors; (23) petunia, rose pink; (24) purslane or portulaca, mixed colors; (25) marigold, dwarf orange

alties have occurred towards the back of a perennial border, a few seeds of castor bean or sweet peas will fill the gaps. The castor bean grows rapidly, the sweet peas more slowly and, unless the soil is rich and water available in periods of drought, sweet peas in a perennial border will not amount to much.

While waiting for permanent plantings of trees and shrubs to become established, annuals will add color and interest to a part of the garden that otherwise would be dull. Besides this, there are other special uses for annual flowers. Some are fine for cutting and some are grown for their fragrance; others have attractive foliage and still others have everlasting flowers useful for winter bouquets. Then there are certain kinds for window boxes, a few that will not look out of place in the rock garden and some that make attractive summer hedges.

While most annual plants do best in full sun, a few are tolerant of shade, where they will grow well enough but do not flower so profusely as in full sunshine. Annuals that tolerate some shade include *Browallia speciosa*, spiderflower *(Cleome spinosa)*, four o'clock *(Mirabilis jalapa)*, tobacco plant *(Nicotiana alata)*, mignonette *(Reseda odorata)* and violas. Soil is not so important, although some annuals prefer a light sandy loam with the sun beating on it all day long.

The Planting and Care of Annuals

Preparing the soil for annuals — Most annuals do not require rich soil; when rotted manure or heavy doses of chemical fertilizer are applied to a soil that is already quite heavily charged with nitrogen, the plants make luscious leaves but not many flowers. Quite a number of annuals grow naturally in impoverished soil in regions where the rain is adequate while the plants are growing but cuts off when they ripen their seed. Where the soil is heavy and high in nitrogen, add a layer of acid peat before you dig the annual bed. This will improve the soil texture without increasing its fertility to any extent.

Annuals for cutting — Instead of robbing beds and borders in search of cut flowers, the wise gardener will reserve a few rows in the vegetable garden for annuals grown especially for cutting. There is no end of suitable varieties which, when lined out in a sunny spot in the vegetable or reserve garden in June, will provide a long-time source of cut flowers without spoiling the formal beds. Snapdragons are among the best, choosing the tall, branching sorts; asters and cosmos, gloriosa daisy, larkspur, calendula, stocks, sweet peas and zinnias are also choice selections for cutting.

Sowing annuals outdoors — Most of the annual plants grown in prairie gardens are started in the greenhouse, transplanted into boxes and set out in June, but there are quite a number of annuals which may be sown outdoors in May where the plants are to bloom. Some seeds are so tiny that outdoor sowing is rather uncertain but, if the ground has been well prepared and worked to a fine tilth, there is a good chance of satisfactory germination. The chief causes of failure are due to covering the seed too deeply or allowing it to become dry while the seeds are germinating. The weather in early May is often dry and windy, so regular sprinklings of water are needed or the soil will dry out. Patches of open-sown seed in the annual border may be kept from drying out by laying on sheets of wet newspaper, holding them down at the corners with soil. When the seed is sown in patches, scatter it sparsely over the surface, then cover it with finely sifted soil. Only the lightest covering is needed; the tiny seeds of Shirley poppy will smother if buried too deep. The large seeds of annual lupins, castor bean and sweet peas should be covered with an inch or so of fine soil.

When annuals are sown in rows, make the rows a foot apart except for larkspurs, four o'clocks, zinnias and other tall varieties, which should be planted in rows a foot and a half or two feet apart.

Thinning annuals sown in the open ground — To realize their full potential, these outdoor-sown seedlings must be given sufficient room to develop. Overcrowding will result in stunted plants as they compete for soil, moisture and light; such plants bloom prematurely, set seed and soon completely exhaust the plant. Thinning is therefore one of the most important operations in growing annuals from seed sown outdoors. It must be started while the plants are still very small by carefully pulling out the surplus seedlings to leave the remaining ones an inch apart. When the seedlings have grown larger, further thinning will be needed. If the thinning can be done in periods of cloudy weather, so much the better and, if the soil is dry, water the seedlings before you thin them out.

Thinning is made easier when the soil is moistened; the shock to the remaining plants will be lessened, too. Two or three weeks after the first thinning, or when the young plants touch one another, a second thinning is done, giving each plant room enough to expand fully so that, when full grown, it barely touches its neighbor.

As a guide to the proper distance between each plant, consider the height of each variety at maturity. The candytuft, California poppy and quite a few others are less than a foot high, so six to nine inches between each plant is enough. The calendula, some of the larkspurs, cape marigold and some others grow a little taller and need more room; a foot and a half is ideal. Some tall larkspurs and zinnias are three feet high; these should be two feet apart. Castor beans, growing six feet or taller, should be three feet apart to show off their handsome leaves. The novice gardener is reluctant to pull up seedlings and destroy them but he must be ruthless if the survivors are to develop into vigorous plants.

Sowing annuals indoors — Most of the annual flowers that are set out in beds are started in a greenhouse or on a sunny window sill. Heated frames can also be used, as well as basement areas where special lighting and heating fixtures have been installed. Starting the seeds indoors involves certain risks which only the plant enthusiast will be ready to take. The failures are mostly due to starting the seeds too soon (by planting-out time they will be tall and spindly), to using soil that is contaminated with the spores of damping-off fungus and to buying poor-quality seed. The indoor-sowing dates recommended for prairie gardens are March seventh for the long-season sorts, April fifteenth for those that grow faster but still need indoor sowing in order to be in full bloom with the rest of the annuals.

The following varieties all do best when sown indoors; those marked with an asterisk are sown March seventh, the remainder on April fifteenth or shorty afterwards.

Common Name	Botanical Name
aster	*Callistephus*
balsam	*Impatiens*
bartonia	*Mentzelia*
bellflower	*Campanula*
blue-eyed African daisy	*Arctotis*

blue laceflower	*Trachymene*
bugloss	*Anchusa*
butterflyflower	*Schizanthus*
* carnation (Enfante de Nice, Marguerite)	*Dianthus*
* Chinese pink	*Dianthus chinensis*
* cockscomb	*Celosia*
* coneflower, gloriosa daisy	*Rudbeckia*
corn marigold	*Chrysanthemum*
cup and saucer vine, cathedral bells	*Cobaea scandens*
dusty miller	*Centaurea*
feverfew	*Chrysanthemum*
* flossflower	*Ageratum*
globe amaranth	*Gomphrena*
heliotrope, cherry pie	*Heliotrophium*
hollyhock	*Althaea*
hyacinth bean	*Dolichos*
jewel of the veldt	*Ursinia*
marigold	*Tagetes*
* pansy	*Viola*
petunia	*Petunia*
phlox	*Phlox drummondii*
pincushion flower	*Scabiosa*
* scarlet sage	*Salvia splendens*
* snapdragon	*Antirrhinum*
spiderwort	*Cleome*
star of the veldt	*Dimorphotheca*
statice	*Limonium*
strawflower	*Helichrysum*
summer cypress	*Kochia*
sweet sultan	*Centaurea*
sweet scabious	*Scabiosa*
sweet wivelsfield	*Dianthus*
ten-week stock	*Matthiola*
tobacco	*Nicotiana*
* verbena	*Verbena*

The soil mixture must be clean, porous and not too rich in plant nutrients. Two parts fibrous loam, one part granulated peat and one part sand is a basic mixture, providing good water-holding capacity and porous enough to allow free drainage of water. To lessen the chances of damping off, a fungal disease which can cause heavy loss to seedlings, treat the soil with one of the commercial soil sterilants, using it strictly according to the manufacturer's instructions. Reasonably good protection can be had by setting the seed pots in a bowl of boiling water for half an hour or by using a solution of formaldehyde. The solution is made by adding two tablespoonfuls of formaldehyde to a quart of water and thoroughly moistening the soil mixture with it before sealing the soil in a plastic bag. Two days later, spread the treated soil on the basement floor to air. In a week or ten days it can safely be used for sowing seed.

Besides the soil, the drainage material and the water used on the seedlings must be clean. Treat the drainage material, which may be pieces of broken clay pots or coarse gravel, in the same manner as the soil. The water, especially if taken from a cistern or dugout, should be boiled before using it on seedlings.

The home gardener will find a four-inch clay pot most suitable for sowing annuals indoors. Plastic pots may be used, though there is a greater chance of overwatering seedlings in plastic pots than in clay pots. Old pots should be scrubbed clean and rinsed thoroughly in clear water if detergent has been used in the wash water. One or two pieces of broken crockery are placed over the drainage hole; over this, lay an inch of smaller pieces of crockery or gravel. By sifting the soil mixture through a quarter-inch sieve, there will be sufficient roughage to place a layer over the broken crockery. The fine soil is now used to fill the pot, pressed down gently and made level with the lid of a tin. The levelled soil should be a quarter of an inch from the rim of the pot for the tiny seeds of petunia, snapdragons and other small seeds, half an inch for the larger seeds of pansy, ten-weeks stock and some others.

Before sowing the seed, stand each pot in a bowl of clean water deep enough to reach the rim, allowing it to remain long enough for the water to percolate to the surface of the soil. When the pots have been drained, they are ready for sowing. Petunia seeds are not only small, they are costly; take care not to lose them. By mixing a teaspoonful of dry, sifted sand with each package of seed, a more even distribution is possible. Put the dry sand in the seed package, shake it up and sow directly from the package. It is not necessary to cover these tiny seeds with the soil mixture, but a piece of glass and a sheet of newspaper must be put over the seed pots and must remain until the seeds sprout. During the period of germination, the glass is removed each morning to clear it of condensation and to check the soil moisture. Should the surface appear to be dry, water the pots immediately, using the same method as when the seeds were sown.

Transplanting seedling annuals — Transplanting should not be attempted before the seedlings have developed a pair of true leaves, nor should it be delayed too long or the seedlings become overcrowded and weak. When the seedlings first emerge, they are sustained by the cotyledons, or seed leaves, before the true leaves develop.

A suitable soil for transplanting is made by mixing three parts fibrous loam with one part granulated peat and one part sand. Boxes of convenient size are filled with the mixture after it has been screened through a half-inch sieve. Plant boxes, or flats as the gardener calls them, should not be too large nor too deep; a standard size is twenty inches long, fourteen inches wide and three inches deep. An inch layer of the rough portions of the soil is put in the bottom of the box as drainage, then the fine soil is filled in. Firm the soil and make it level with a piece of two- by four-foot lumber, leaving the surface half an inch below the rim of the box. The soil should be just moist enough to hold together when squeezed in the hand. If it is too wet, the job of transplanting will be made difficult; furthermore, seedlings will not make new roots in soil that is soggy.

A pointed stick of finger thickness, three inches long, is used for making the holes. Space the large seedlings two inches apart, the smaller ones an inch apart, firming the soil around the roots with the pointed stick. Water the seedlings before shading them with newspaper for a few days. When they recover from the mild shock of transplanting, keep them in a sunny window, turning the boxes every few days to ensure even growth.

Hardening off annuals – The shock of transplanting annuals which have been grown in a box and sheltered from wind and sudden temperature changes to the open ground, where the weather may be harsh, can be minimized if the plants are gradually inured to outside conditions by the process known to gardeners as hardening off. The process starts by transferring the boxes from the window sill to a heated garden frame. In the southern prairies this can be done safely by the middle of April, in northern parts, two weeks later. By the first week of May, the heat in the frame can be turned off, the frame sash removed in the daytime and, finally, a week or so before setting out the plants, it can be left off day and night.

Annual plants are set out in early June in most parts of the prairies but the wise gardener will be governed by the prevailing weather and not by the day of the month only. Pansies and snapdragons are tolerant of a few degrees of frost if they have been hardened, but even these plants can be severely injured by the sudden change from a warm greenhouse to freezing temperatures. The tender salvias, marigolds and zinnias are blackened by the lightest frost. In southeastern Manitoba, planting may begin around the last week of May; in northern parts, it is not safe to plant tender annuals until the middle of June unless they are protected with hotcaps or similar protectors. Some gardeners, most anxious to get an early show of bloom, will be tempted to set out the plants in May if the weather appears to be settled. But, in the long run, it has been found best to postpone planting until the first week of June.

Planting annuals — The actual planting is best done with a garden trowel, making a hole large enough and deep enough to hold the roots without crowding. The soil must be made very firm about the roots by treading. Loose planting is one cause of failure and poor watering another. Some gardeners make holes, fill them with water and puddle the plants in while the water is still in the hole. This is not recommended; leave the watering until the plant has been set and firmed in the soil. Choose a cloudy day if possible and, if you are transplanting annuals from boxes, water them well the day before you set them out. Each plant must have moist soil around it but the whole bed or border should not be soaked at planting time.

Summer care of annuals — The early summer care of annuals simply involves keeping the weeds down by regularly hoeing between the plants. As the plants grow to shade the ground, weeds will no longer be a problem. In periods of drought, water the beds thoroughly once a week. Daily light sprinklings not only waste water; the roots tend to come to the surface instead of penetrating the soil deeply in search of moisture and nutrients. Fading flowers should be cut off before seed pods develop to rob the plants of vigor and shorten the blooming season.

There is no merit in saving seed from annual plants since the resultant seedlings will likely be a mixture of nondescript plants mostly inferior to the parents. Some kinds of annuals are first generation or F_1 hybrids, which can be reproduced only by crossing the pure-line parents. By self-pollinating for several generations, certain strains of petunias, snapdragons and some other annuals are developed into pure-line strains. When these pure-line strains are crossed, the plants from this seed will produce what is called an F_1 cross or first generation. These plants are more uniform and, as a general rule, they are superior to open-pollinated strains. Open-pollinated seed from these plants will produce a variety of widely different plants that are totally unsuited for bedding out.

Insects and diseases of annuals — Annual flowers are not prone to attacks of insects or disease and only occasionally will it be necessary to control aphids, spider mites and leaf eaters. In June, aphids may attack certain plants. When this occurs, spray them with Malathion or nicotine sulphate, using a teaspoonful in a gallon of soapy water. When the weather gets hot and dry, spider mites appear on salvias and some other plants; for these tiny sucking insects it is best to spray with Kelthane, using two teaspoonfuls in a gallon of water. Cutworms are sometimes troublesome when they nip off the young plants soon after they have been set out. Chemicals such as Aldrin, Dieldrin and Heptochlor will prevent damage if used according to the manufacturer's instructions.

Zinnias and pansies are liable to be infected with mildew, a disfiguring disease that is manifest in masses of grayish spores on leaves and tip growths. Infected plants are coated with a gray powdery substance in which is contained the spores or seed; the fungus penetrates the surface of the leaves and soft stems. Plants set out in shady places where the air circulation is poor will likely be attacked. Pansies, for instance, are usually infected towards the end of the season, when dry weather helps the spores to multiply rapidly and cool nights create conditions that favor good germination. Leaf spot diseases are not a serious problem as a general rule but long periods of warm, damp weather may start the spores germinating on such plants as zinnias and salvias. Captan is a standard control for leaf spot disease and Karathane for mildew. Both are used as sprays, mixed according to the directions on the container.

For the small home garden, it is better to buy all-purpose dusts or sprays which will give control of all common pests and diseases than to buy individual remedies for each insect or plant ailment.

Annuals as climbing plants – Climbing plants have a charm all their own. In prairie gardens we are not blessed with too many woody climbers, so we should make full use of the annual climbing plants to hide unsightly objects, cover fences and even bare walls. Sweet peas are annual climbing plants, but they are not suitable for covering walls and do much better when cultivated intensively to produce long-stemmed flowers. Their culture will be dealt with extensively in the following section. A few of the best annual climbers for prairie gardens are the morning-glory *(Ipomoea purpurea)*, the hyacinth bean *(Dolichos lablab)*, the cup and saucer vine *(Cobaea scandens)*, the ornamental gourd *(Cucurbita)* and the nasturtium *(Tropaeolum)*. The ornamental gourds and nasturtiums may be raised from seed sown in the open ground; the others should be sown indoors and transplanted to the open ground in early June.

Morning-glories sown outdoors are too late in flowering; being tender, the plants are often struck down by early frost just when the blooms are opening. A surer way is to plant two seeds in a jiffy pot, using a mixture of light soil, peat and sand. Sow the seeds the first of May, placing the pots on a warm window sill or in a warm greenhouse. Morning-glories look their best on the east side of the house or garage where they get the sun for part of the day. There is some difficulty in germinating the seeds unless they are steeped in tepid water overnight to soften the hard seed coat.

The hyacinth bean has handsome dark green leaves and rosy purple, pea-shaped flowers followed by purplish red seed pods. There is no chance of getting much out of the hyacinth bean unless you start the seed indoors. Sturdy plants from three-inch jiffy pots, set out in June when all danger of frost is past, will grow six feet or more in warm, moist soil.

When planted against a wall, the young plants must be supported on a trellis or wire netting.

The cup and saucer vine, or cathedral bells, is a tender perennial vine propagated from seed sown in early March in a warm greenhouse, using light soil with plenty of peat and sand added. The leaflets are produced in pairs on a stout stem terminating in a tendril by which the plant climbs. The bell-shaped flowers are violet or purple. A white-flowered form and one with variegated leaves are rarer plants.

Climbing nasturtiums may be grown from seed sown in the open ground in May. The large, roundish leaves have a peppery flavor and are sometimes used in salads. The flower buds, too, are used in seasoning; the green seeds are pickled. The climbing nasturtiums are not so popular as the dwarf types but they should not be overlooked as rapid-growing, showy climbers. They produce many more flowers when planted in lean soil; where the gound is rich in humus and plant food, nasturtiums produce enormous leaves but few flowers. While the plants tolerate some shade, they do best in full sun. They are fine for covering fences or may be allowed to ramble over an old stump or other unsightly objects.

The ornamental gourds are trailing plants which may be trained on fences or pergolas. The supports must be strong enough to hold the plant with a full crop of fruit. The seeds are sown in the open ground about May tenth, unless facilities are available for starting them in the greenhouse or on a sunny window sill. The young plants grow rapidly in warm, moist soil but, like the cucumbers, melons and other cucurbits, they are extremely tender to frost. The fruits ripen in September, varying in shape and color — green, orange, or combinations of both. Some have smooth skins; others are warted. When used for decoration, they are sometimes waxed or varnished.

Sweet peas — The sweet peas are the best known of all the annual climbers esteemed for fragrance and for their usefulness as cut flowers. The modern varieties include several dwarf types — Bijou, American and Knee-hi. The Bijou sweet peas make bushy, foot-high plants carrying a profusion of flowers in the usual range of sweet pea colors. The American and the Knee-hi sweet peas grow about a foot and a half, needing some support to keep the plants from sprawling over the ground.

The newer kinds of tall sweet peas are said to tolerate heat much better than the older Spencer varieties. The Cuthbertson, Galaxy and early multiflora belong in this group and will produce an abundance of long-stemmed flowers. The sweet pea fancier and those who would win prizes at the shows incline to the named varieties of Spencer sweet peas, however, which will produce the finest specimens when properly grown.

To grow first-class flowers, the soil must be well prepared, with rotted manure, peat or old garden compost added. The time to start is in the fall, digging a foot-wide trench, a foot and a half or two feet deep. The good soil, which is nearest the top, is placed on one side of the trench, the next layer on the other side. The loose soil is then shovelled out before the bottom is forked up, mixing in a layer of compost or the remains of a garden bonfire. Old manure is mixed with the second layer of soil before it is replaced in the trench and made firm. The topsoil will need no additional nutrient except a dressing of 11.48.0 at the rate of two ounces to each yard of row.

Tests have shown that fall seeding is hazardous and poor stands of seedlings have resulted when mice have eaten the seeds or when excess spring moisture has rotted them. Spring sowing should be done just as soon as the soil is workable; the best row of sweet peas I ever saw in a prairie garden was sown the first week of April. It is seldom possible to get in the garden in early April but, as soon as the ground has dried, no time should be lost in sowing sweet peas; the seed is slow in starting and the young plants will tolerate light frost.

Where sweet peas have occupied the same ground for several years, there will likely occur a build-up of various harmful soil fungi which will infect the roots. A reasonably good job of soil sterilization can be made with commercial formaldehyde, using one pint in fifteen gallons of water, applying the solution at the rate of one gallon to each square foot of surface to be sterilized. To get the best effect, the sterilized soil is covered for two days with wet burlap. After removing the burlap, stir the soil, letting it air for a week before sowing the seed, treating it first with Arasan, Semesan or some other disinfectant. The ridge of soil marking the trench is raked level and the seeds spaced about an inch apart in a trench made two inches deep. When the seedlings are a few inches high, support them with pieces of twiggy sticks; later on, taller sticks or wire netting will be necessary.

Intensive culture of sweet peas — The sweet pea fancier will devote extra time and regular care to grow the kind of specimens that win prizes at the show. For the best results, the plants should be grown single-stemmed, or on the cordon system, as it is called. Sweet peas grown this way produce long-stemmed, substantial flowers.

The soil is prepared in the same way as already outlined, except that the trench is made wider to allow for two rows of plants fifteen inches apart. Two feet of width and two feet of depth will provide ample root run for the plants. If the soil has been well enriched with rotted barnyard manure, vigorous growth can be maintained with little added nutrient. The seeds are set three to a station, nine or ten inches apart. When the young plants are two inches high, select one at each station, removing the others. Later on, when the selected plant has six leaves, pinch out the tip growth to induce strong shoots to break, or start from the base. The most vigorous of these basal shoots is retained (once again, the weaker shoots are pinched out); all the plant's energies will now be confined to this single stem.

The plant must be supported before it can be damaged by wind. Six-foot bamboo canes or heavy wires may be used, fastening them top and bottom to wires attached to posts at either end of the row. The plant, which by mid-June will have all its growth concentrated in one single stem, will grow rapidly, requiring almost daily care — tying, removing tendrils no longer needed for support and removing side shoots. The first one or two flower stalks should be picked off in the early bud stage, as they will not be of first-class quality. Weekly doses of a mild stimulant may be given when the vines have reached the tops of the stakes; use 10.52.17 fertilizer at the rate of a level teaspoonful in a gallon of water, giving each plant a cupful. Make sure the plants are not dry at the root when applying fertilizer, or too heavy a concentration will be taken up by the roots and the plants will be damaged. The topsoil is sometimes deceptive; it may be moist but the subsoil, where the roots are foraging for food, may be dry. On the other hand, a dry surface soil may be overlying a wet subsoil.

When the plants have reached the tops of the stakes, the ties should be loosened carefully, the vines removed from their supports and laid along the row. To keep the wind from blowing them out of line, tie them loosely to the bottom wire. The tip growth is started up the most conveniently located stake and the cultural procedure of disbudding the side shoots and removing the tendrils is repeated. Young plants, grown from seed sown indoors in March and set out in the open ground in late May or early June, will grow ten feet or more by the end of the season.

Annuals for the Prairies

The following selective list of annuals has been compiled from a series of tests in prairie gardens over a period of thirty years. Both botanical and common names are given; the arrangement is alphabetical by common name, to be of greatest use to the nonprofessional gardener. Sowing dates are given for all varieties that need to be started in a greenhouse or on a sunny window sill. Where no seeding date is given, the seeds can be sown in the open ground during the first week of May.

Amaranth *(Amaranthus)* — Some of the species of amaranths are esteemed for their reddish leaves and showy flowers. All must have well-drained soil; if set out in a cold, wet soil, you can expect trouble with root rots. Species plants average one and one-half to two and one-half feet. Love-lies-bleeding *(A. caudatus)* is a tall (five-foot), rather ungainly plant with dark leaves and reddish purple flowers that hang like ropes. Sow the seed

March 20 – April 1. Prince's feather *(A. hybridus hypochondriacus)*, a three-foot amaranth, has slender panicles of dark reddish brown flowers amid red leaves. Sow the seed March 20 – April 1. The leaves of Joseph's coat *(A. tricolor)* are brilliant scarlet crimson, strikingly marked with yellow and bronze green. Sow the seed March 20 – April 1. The height of the plants varies from one and one-half to two feet.

Baby blue-eyes *(Nemophila menziesii insignis)* – Baby blue-eyes makes a low, trailing plant with fine leaves and attractive flowers, either blue, or blue and white. It does best in cool soil, shaded from hot sun; excessive heat and dry soil soon make the plants shabby. Sow the seeds May 10 where the plants are to bloom.

Babysbreath *(Gypsophila elegans)* – Babysbreath is an easily grown, white-flowered plant used extensively in bouquets. The individual flowers are much larger than the perennial babysbreath but the inflorescence, or arrangement of the flowers on the stems, is not so graceful nor so suitable for use as dried flowers. Well-grown plants are a foot or two feet high; a pink-flowered sort is not so vigorous.

Bellflower *(Campanula)* – Most of the bellflowers are perennials, meant either for the rock garden or the perennial border, but the Anatolian bellflower *(C. macrostyla)* is an interesting annual species with large, open bells and prominent stigmas. The colors are lilac mauve, veined and pencilled with darker shades. The plants, which grow to a foot and a half high, do best in a sunny spot where the soil is well drained.

Bells of Ireland *(Moluccella laevis)* – Bells of Ireland is an old plant which has gained some notice from flower arrangers. It is of little decorative value in the garden, as the tiny white flowers are almost enclosed by greenish bracts. The stems of well-grown plants are up to three feet high. Sow the seed March 25 – April 1.

Blanketflower *(Gaillardia pulchella picta)* – The annual gaillardias have flowers that are similar to the better-known perennial gaillardias. The plants do best in well-drained soil on a sunny border where they will continue to produce their colorful daisies up until hard frost. Both single and double-flowered strains are obtainable in pale yellow shades through pink to red. The plants grow to two feet from seed started March 20 – April 1.

Blue-eyed African daisy *(Arctotis stoechadifolia grandis)* – The plant bears pale daisies with attractive dark blue centres; the leaves are grayish green and the plants showy from July until frost. The blue-eyed African daisy deserves to be better known. It does well in a sunny spot where the soil is well drained but not too rich in nutrients. The daisies, which are freely produced on slender stems, are fine for cutting. Sow the seed April 10 – 20. The plants grow bushy to one and one-half feet high.

Blue laceflower *(Trachymene caerulea, Didiscus caerulea)* – This useful annual plant has umbels of attractive blue flowers which are useful for cutting. It is tolerant of partial shade and, in moist soil, the plants reach two feet high and continue to bloom from July until hard frost.

Blue woodruff *(Asperula orientalis)* — The blue woodruff has fine foliage and dainty, pale blue flowers, mildly scented. The plants grow about a foot high.

Browallia *(Browallia speciosa)* — Browallia is a good blue-flowered annual for a shady spot; it continues to bloom all through the summer. Since the plants do well in pots, you can remove a few and take them indoors when frost threatens. Sow the seed March 15 — April 1. Plant height is one and one-half to two feet.

Butterflyflower, poor man's orchid *(Schizanthus)* — In those parts of the garden which are shaded from the hot sun and where the soil is not too high in lime, it is possible to grow this charming plant fairly well. Excessive heat, alkaline soil and drought will not be tolerated but, where soil and site are suitable and where parched plants can be given a soaking of water, the butterflyflower will respond with masses of beautifully ruffled flowers. The colors range from white to shades of apricot, pink, carmine, mauve and purple, some with plain petals, others with contrasting markings on the throat. The plants are about two feet high with bright green, fern-like leaves. Sow the seeds April 15 — 20.

California poppy *(Eschscholtzia californica)* — The California poppy is a sun-loving plant with deep roots and finely divided leaves of bluish green. The flowers are mostly orange or yellow but new varieties include cream, pink and cherry reds in both singles and doubles. If the seedlings are thinned so that each has a space of not less than six inches, the plants will develop lateral shoots and will continue to bloom until they are injured by hard frost. It is not unusual to see California poppies blooming in October. Well-grown plants are a foot high.

Candytuft *(Iberis amara, Iberis umbellata)* — The candytuft is a short-lived annual with dark leaves and flowers in varicolored umbels. By mid-August, the plants have usually done blooming and ripe seeds have fallen to the ground to germinate if the soil is moist. The candytuft is not recommended for a mixed annual border as the plants look shabby long before frost comes. Dwarf strains six inches high are obtainable, as well as taller sorts that grow a foot to a foot and a half.

Cape bugloss *(Anchusa capensis)* — Cape bugloss is an attractive biennial that blooms the first year from seed. The leaves are rough and dark green, the flowers intense blue; the plant grows to a height of about one foot. Sow the seed April 1 — 10.

Cape marigold, star of the veldt *(Dimorphotheca aurantiaca)* — Cape marigolds make bushy plants about a foot high, with dark leaves and daisy-like flowers in profusion from July until hard frost comes. New hybrids have flowers in delicate shades of yellow and apricot as well as deep orange and pure white.

Carnations and pinks *(Dianthus)* — Several perennial dianthus will flower the first year from early sown seed. The Enfant de Nice and the Chaubaud are two examples, both with double, sweet-scented flowers in a variety of colors on plants with gray leaves. Unless the seed is sown early to raise sturdy plants by setting-out time, there is not much chance of bloom before hard frost comes. It is possible to lift and pot the plants in late September, setting them on a sunny window sill where they will continue to bloom for several weeks.

Sow the seeds of Enfant de Nice and Chaubaud carnations in early February, transplanting the seedlings into three-inch jiffy pots when the young plants are about two inches high. Seeds of the Chinese pink are best sown March 20 – 25. The plants are about a foot high; the carnations grow to one and one-half feet. The heavy blooms tend to weigh down the stems, so they should be supported with stout pieces of brush. By removing all but the terminal flower bud on each stem, larger blooms will develop.

The Chinese or Indian pink *(D. chinensis)* and the variety *heddewigii* are treated as annuals, though the plants survive the winter occasionally. There are both single and double forms in a variety of colors, some with white petals that are blotched with sharply contrasting red.

Castor bean *(Ricinus communis)* — The castor bean is a bold plant with handsome leaves, bronze green or reddish, and nondescript flowers. Plants are started from seeds sown in jiffy pots or from open-ground sowing in May. The plants are not suited to small gardens but, where a six-foot plant is needed to give a tropical look to summer bedding-out schemes, the castor bean is recommended. The seeds contain a poisonous substance called ricinin, so guard against the danger of children eating them by picking off the inflorescence in the bud stage.

Centaurea *(Centaurea)* — Dusty miller *(C. cineraria)* is a tender perennial plant grown for its silvery leaves, useful for edging formal beds. It does best in full sun; in shade the leaves will lose some of their silvery sheen. The plants are leafy, about a foot high, and may be raised from seed sown March 20 – 25. *C. gymnocarpa* is a strong-growing perennial with silver gray leaves. Plants from early sown seed reach one and one-half feet and are useful as a foil in formal bedding. Sow the seed March 20 – 25.

The cornflower or bachelor's button *(C. cyanus)* is an easily grown plant persisting each year by volunteer seedlings. The flowers are mostly blue, but pinks and whites are available. Well-grown plants are three feet high and provide long-stemmed flowers for cutting.

The flowers of sweet sultan *(C. moschata)* are like refined thistles in shades of mauve and yellow; some are white. They are sweet-scented and useful for cutting. The plants reach two feet high and bloom from July until September.

China aster *(Callistephus chinensis)* — An old-fashioned and once popular plant, China aster is subject to a serious virus commonly called aster yellows and a root disease that causes the plants to wilt. The virus is transmitted by leaf hoppers and certain aphids, so it pays to keep the plants free of these insects. Where the site for asters can be changed every year and when wilt-resistant seed is used, there is a good chance of success, especially if the infected plants are rooted out and burned as soon as disease is suspected. Sow the seed April 10 – 20. The plants grow to a height of one or two feet.

Chrysanthemum *(Chrysanthemum)* — The annual chrysanthemums are not at all like the hardy perennial sorts but they are first-class plants, useful for garden decoration or as cut flowers. There are yellow, orange and maroon colors, some with contrasting zones. Some are rich crimson; others are white with bands of red and yellow. The plants are quite leafy and grow about two feet high. The species from which the annual chrysanthemums have been developed are *C. carinatum, C. coronarium* and *C. segetum.* Common names for these plants are annual chrys-anthemum, corn marigold and crowndaisy.

Cockscomb *(Celosia argentea)* — *C. argentea cristata* is a curious plant with an inflorescence resembling a cockscomb. The dense flower heads are not particularly attractive; the colors are maroon red surrounded by reddish leaves. The plants are a foot or so high. Sow the seed April 10 – 20.

The feather cockscomb *(C. argentea* var. *plumosa)* is a more attractive plant. The flowers are feathery plumes of scarlet, cerise, orange or yellow; the plants are one to three feet high with either green or reddish bronze leaves. The celosias are very tender to frost but, if well-grown plants are set out in June, they will make a striking show through July and until the first frost comes.

Corn poppy *(Papaver rhoeas)* — The Shirley poppies, esteemed for garden decoration and for cutting, are derived from this species. There are both single and double forms, in shades of pink and red with elegant flowers on wiry stems. The seeds are very tiny and, as the plants are difficult to transplant, it is best to sow the seeds in May where the plants are to bloom, covering them with a thin layer of fine soil. If the spent flowers are removed before they form seed pods, the poppies will bloom over a long period and grow to two feet.

Cosmos *(Cosmos)* — The cosmos makes a tall, branching plant with finely divided leaves and large, daisy-like flowers. The common cosmos has white, pink or crimson flowers on plants that are up to five feet high. The flowers, which are quite tolerant of frost, sometimes continue to bloom well into October. The yellow cosmos does not grow so tall; the flowers are smaller but are semidouble; some deepen to orange red. Sow the seed March 25 — April 1.

Cupflower *(Nierembergia caerulea)* — The cupflower is a dainty, blue-flowered perennial which can be flowered the first year from seed. The plants have dark green, narrow leaves on stems about six inches high. The cup-shaped flowers cover the plants from July until hard frost comes. Sow the seeds March 25 — April 1.

Dahlia *(Dahlia)* — Named dahlias are increased by tuber division and by cuttings, but certain early flowering bedding sorts can be flowered the first year from early sown seed. The bedding kinds are mostly single or semidouble on bushy plants. To get the best results, the soil must be rich and moist; the plants must be sturdy and well hardened when planted out and given plenty of room. Several good strains are available from the seedsmen and, by sowing individual seeds in jiffy pots April 20, strong plants are ready for outdoor planting in June. Selected seedlings may be dug up in the fall, storing the tubers in the usual way. There is no special merit in this, however, as the plants are so easily raised from seed. The Coltness Gem and Unwin hybrids are recommended as bedding plants, growing about two feet high. Pompon and cactus dahlias are also obtainable as seed; each will give up to fifty percent double flowers.

Farewell-to-spring godetia *(Godetia amoena)* — This species and *G. grandiflora* have been used to produce the modern improved forms, with elegant sprays of salmon pink, rose or red flowers. Some are more than two feet tall and provide excellent cut flowers; others are only a foot or so high and may be more useful as bedding plants. The petals have a satiny sheen that makes the flowers particularly attractive. Godetias do best when the seed is planted outdoors in May, but earlier bloom may be obtained from seed sown in jiffy pots April 15 - 20.

Feverfew *(Chrysanthemum parthenium)* — Feverfew is useful as an edging plant six to nine inches high, with yellowish green leaves. It is used also in carpet bedding. The flowers are dingy daisies which ary best pinched out to keep the plants neat. Sow the seed April 1 - 10.

Fossflower *(Ageratum houstonianum)* — Sometimes called *Ageratum mexicanum,* the fossflower is a dwarf, compact plant between four and twelve inches high used extensively for edging. The roundish leaves are dark green; the flower heads are fluffy in various shades of blue. Sow the seed March 15 - 20. The ageratums are quite susceptible to frost, so it is wise to delay planting them outdoors until all danger of frost is past.

Four o'clock, marvel of Peru *(Mirabilis jalapa)* — This fast-growing, tender perennial plant was much esteemed in old gardens, where it made sheltering three-foot hedges of shining, dark green leaves covered with flowers in shades of pink and red, yellow and white. The four o'clocks, a name given in reference to the plant's habit of opening its flowers in the late afternoon, have tuberous roots which may be stored like dahlias, but the simplest way to grow the plants is with seed sown in the open ground May 10 - 15.

Gloriosa daisy *(Rudbeckia hirta)* — The improved forms of the Black-eyed Susan, now called gloriosa daisy, are first-class plants for prairie gardens. They are easily raised from seed to flower the first year and occasionally the plants survive the winters. The huge daisies, in shades of yellow, mahogany red and dark maroon, are freely produced on three-foot plants. A double-flowered form has fully double, yellow flowers and some semi-doubles in shades of yellow and brown. Sow the seeds March 15 - 20.

Grecian or night-scented stock *(Matthiola bicornis)* — Grecian stock has been long esteemed for its sweet-scented flowers which perfume the evening air. During the day, the simple lilac pink flowers are closed and the whole plant unattractive, but the night-scented stocks deserve a place, if only for their scent. Sow the seeds outdoors in early May. The plants are about six to nine inches high.

Another well-known plant of the same genus, *M. incana annua,* is the common or ten-week stock. There are several strains, all with gray green leaves and spikes of flowers in a wide range of colors. The early flowering sorts are best in prairie gardens; the later ones sometimes fail to bloom. As double-flowered stocks are much preferred to the singles, which soon exhaust the plants by making useless seed, only the best strains having a high percentage of doubles should be sown. New, all-double varieties are obtainable, producing seedlings that can be segregated while the plants are still in the seed pods. Those with light green leaves are the doubles; the darker ones are single-flowered. Ten-week stocks are highly susceptible to root rot diseases, so plant them in well-drained soil that has not been enriched recently with barnyard manure. The high-lime soils found throughout most of the prairies are well suited to these old-fashioned and sweet-scented plants. Some kinds grow a foot high with dense spikes; others are over two feet tall, making them more suitable for cutting. Sow the seed in sterilized soil March 25 — April 1.

Herb treemallow *(Lavatera trimestris)* — The herb treemallow is a fast-growing, bushy plant with dark green, roundish leaves and single flowers of pink or white. It makes an attractive summer hedge or background for low-growing annuals. Plant the seeds outdoors in early May, thinning the seedlings to give each plant not less than a foot and a half of space. If given plenty of room, the plants are almost three feet high.

Hollyhock *(Althaea rosea)* — The annual hollyhocks are not so tall nor so double as the common biennial sorts but they are useful for the back of the border, where they provide a variety of color on stately plants five feet high. Sow the seed March 15 - 20.

Hyacinth bean *(Dolichos lablab)* — The hyacinth bean is an interesting annual climber with handsome dark green leaves and rosy purple flowers. Seeds are best sown in three-inch jiffy pots May 1, transplanting them to the open ground in June. The soil should be deep and well enriched with barnyard manure; plenty of moisture is required to ensure, vigorous growth. The hyacinth bean does well on an east-facing wall, often reaching ten feet when growing conditions are ideal.

Jewel of the veldt *(Ursinia anethoides)* — The jewel of the veldt is one of a number of composites or daisy flowers from South Africa with bright orange flowers, each zoned with purple. Well-grown plants are more than a foot high; the leaves are finely cut and the flower stems wiry, making this a useful cut flower. Sow the seeds March 10 - 20.

Larkspur *(Delphinium)* — The annual larkspurs, though not as well known as the perennial delphiniums, are fine plants for the border. Some grow three feet tall or even higher when planted in rich, moist soil. The colors include exquisite shades of salmon pink, rose, sky blue, lavender and deepest purple, as well as pure white. The rocket larkspur *(Delphinium ajacis)* and the stock-flowered larkspur are the species involved in the various strains obtainable at the present time. Another species called grandiflora or chinensis makes a bushy plant about a foot or so high with finely divided, dark green leaves and intensely blue flowers. Although it is perennial, it will flower from seed the first year. Outdoor sowing is best for the annual larkspurs but the seed must be sown while the soil is still cool. Volunteer plants from seed which has lain in the ground over winter are usually superior to those produced from spring-sown seed. This being so, autumn-sown seed should be considered, but only in places that are high and dry in the spring.

Lobelia *(Lobelia erinus)* — Lobelia is a well-known edging plant often alternated with the white sweet alyssum to make a blue and white border. There are white-flowered sorts and some newer crimson ones; the most popular variety has compact plants with dark green leaves and dark blue flowers. There are also trailing varieties which are useful in window boxes or planters. The seed is very tiny and rather difficult to start, so the home

---

HEDGES

Three hedges that are as varied in purpose as they are distinctive in appearance.

Top: The colorful bark of the redstem willow brightens a sombre winter landscape of evergreens and snow.

Centre: When planting a flowering hedge, the gardener must consider the season of bloom; this select, nonsuckering form of the Russian almond, although less commonly planted as a flowering hedge than spireas or lilacs, is the earliest pink-blooming shrub.

Bottom: The *Euonymus alata* makes a dense medium tall hedge.

gardener will be well advised to buy his plants from the florist. Seed is sown February 15 - 20, transplanting three or four seedlings together when they are half an inch high.

Love-in-a-mist *(Nigella damascena)* — This is an old-fashioned annual with finely cut leaves surrounding soft blue flowers, which are followed by ornamental seed pods. A white-flowered form is not so attractive. Sow the seeds in the open ground during the first week of May. Well-grown plants will reach a foot and a half by the end of the season.

Lupine *(Lupinus)* — The annual lupins are not so well known as the perennial ones but they are worthy of a place in any garden and, where perennial lupins are difficult to grow, the annual varieties should be substituted. The South American lupine *(L. mutabilis)* and the Hartweg lupine *(L. hartwegi)* are easy to grow from seed sown where the plants are to bloom. While the spikes are thin in comparison with the perennial lupins, the bright colors and easy culture make these annual lupins worthy of a place in the border, where they will grow to two feet or taller.

Madagascar periwinkle *(Vinca rosea)* — By starting the seeds early, these plants will bloom the first year. They grow about a foot high, bearing single flowers of pure white, rosy red or white with a carmine eye; the leaves are dark green and glossy. The plants should be in full sun where they will bloom profusely until hard frost strikes. Sow the seeds the same time as the pansies, February 10 - 20.

Marigold *(Tagetes)* — The marigold is a very popular annual in various shades of yellow and orange. Some are less than a foot high; others range from one to three feet. The low-growing sorts have been developed from *T. tenuifolia,* the striped marigold; the French marigolds have been developed from *T. patula* and the Aztec or African marigolds from *T. erecta.* These have been intercrossed to produce the present-day varieties. The single-flowered sorts are not so popular as the doubles, although there are several splendid ones with bright yellow flowers or mahogany red petals edged with gold. The leaves are dark green and finely divided, making a

---

ROSES

Top Left: Mrs. John Laing, one of the hardy hybrid perpetuals, is esteemed for its sweet scent.

Top Centre: Prairie Dawn, a hardy, repeat-blooming shrub rose of mixed ancestry that was bred at Morden.

Lower Left: Ena Harkness, a shapely and fragrant rose which produces good flowers through the summer and late into September.

Lower Centre: A seedling rose developed at Morden illustrates the beauty of a single, five-petalled rose.

Right: Rosa gallica, which is hardy in sheltered gardens, has been used to develop new bush roses at Morden.

splendid foil for the flowers, which are freely borne on some varieties from July until the first frost. Most varieties have a pungent odor which is disagreeable to some people; consequently, their use as cut flowers is restricted.

Mignonette *(Reseda odorata)* — The mignonette is a modest plant esteemed for its sweet scent. The flowers are dense spikes of greenish brown, not unattractive but neither are they showy. The plants do not transplant well, so the seed should be sown in the open ground in early May, making the soil very firm. Early thinning to allow each plant a space of six inches ensures sturdy plants with large spikes of bloom on plants a foot high. Bees are attracted to the flowers, which are produced over a long period.

Morning-glory *(Impomoea purpurea)* — This popular climbing plant has spectacular, widely flared trumpets of intense blue, crimson or white. To get the most from morning-glories, soak the seeds in water for several hours before sowing them singly in three-inch jiffy pots. Well-grown plants may reach ten feet and will bloom profusely if the soil is not too rich. Seed may be sown in the open ground when the soil has warmed but, quite often, the plants barely reach maturity before the frost comes to destroy them. By sowing the seed indoors around the end of April, well-rooted plants are ready for transplanting to the open ground in June.

Nasturtium *(Tropaeolum majus)* — Nasturtiums are well-known tender annuals with showy flowers and handsome round leaves. Some have trailing shoots six feet long; others are compact plants less than a foot high. The colors are usually shades of yellow, orange and red; new hybrids include cerise, apricot and dark mahogany shades. There are double as well as single strains: the doubles have a high percentage of fully double flowers; the rest are usually semidouble. Besides its use as a showy annual plant, the nasturtium has several culinary uses; the leaves are used for seasoning and the seeds are pickled. To get the best show of bloom, the plants should be in full sun and the soil well drained and not too rich in nutrients. Nasturtiums in soil that is heavily charged with nitrogen will grow enormous leaves but flowers will be few. Sow the seeds in jiffy pots May 1 or in the open ground May 20.

Nemesia *(Nemesia strumosa)* — Nemesia is a very showy plant that does well in those parts of the prairies where the nights are cool. In the foothills country, in northern areas and in gardens adjacent to large bodies of water, it will bloom profusely from July until September. It grows about a foot high, with light green leaves and a profusion of many-colored flowers. Nemesia prefers a neutral soil; too much lime tends to yellow the leaves and make the plants sick. Sow the seed March 10 - 20.

Ornamental gourds *(Cucurbita pepo overifa)* — Ornamental gourds are trailing plants which are used to cover trellises and fences. The leaves are large; the flowers are not showy but the fruits are ornamental. Some have smooth skins; others are warted. They range in color from yellow to deep orange. In the short season of the northern prairies, sow the seeds singly in jiffy pots May 1.

Painted tongue, velvet flower *(Salpiglossis sinuata)* — The salpiglossis makes a fine plant for the annual border and is useful for cutting. The flowers are broad trumpets of heavy-textured petals, beautifully marked at the base in contrasting color. The flowers are subtle blends of old gold, bronze, violet and dark red, besides attractive shades of yellow and cream. The foliage is rather sparse, so set the plants not more than a foot apart. In good soil, adequately supplied with moisture, a well-grown plant reaches to three feet. Sow the seeds March 15 - 20.

Petunia *(Petunia hybrida)* — The petunia is one of the most popular and showy annuals blooming over a long period. Young plants set out in the open ground in June start to bloom almost immediately and continue through the heat of midsummer, right up until hard frost destroys them. For the best results, they should have a place in the sun in moderately fertile soil that is well drained and not too heavy. Established plants can go for long periods without water; in fact, overwatering encourages leafy plants that are more susceptible to root rot diseases than those grown in drier soil.

There are three general types — the doubles, which are used effectively in window boxes and planters, and the grandifloras and multifloras, both single-flowered F_1 hybrids. Besides these most popular sorts, there are single bedding petunias in a wide choice of colors, and several strains of open-pollinated varieties, including the giants of California, which bear enormous single flowers with waved petals. Seed of double petunias, grandiflora and multiflora hybrids is not only very costly; it is difficult to grow without the facilities of a greenhouse or supplementary light in the home. The home gardener will be well advised to buy his plants from a florist or garden centre, where he will find a good selection of separate colors. Most varieties grow about a foot and a half high when planted in full sun where the soil is not too heavily charged with nitrogen and where the plants are not given too much water. For those who wish to raise their own plants from seed, March 15 - 20 is about the best time to start.

Phacelia *(Phacelia campanularia)* — This low, blue-flowered annual blooms freely in full sun or partial shade. The plants are about six inches high and are best raised from seed sown in early May where the plants are to bloom.

Phlox *(Phlox drummondi)* — This group of showy plants is easy to grow and contains many bright colors. Some are only six inches high, making compact plants useful for edging or for patches at the front of the border; others grow to a foot and a half and are useful as cut flowers. The plants do best in deep, moist soil that is well drained and exposed to full sun. Plants in shade will not bloom so freely nor will the colors be so bright. Sow the seeds about April 1.

Pot marigold *(Calendula officianalis)* — Pot marigold is one of the easiest plants to grow, either from seed sown April 15 indoors or in the open ground the first week of May. The leaves are light green, the flowers yellow or orange. The plants stand considerable frost and will bloom until late in the fall. Aster yellows, a virus that attacks many plants, is sometimes troublesome on calendulas. Infected plants should be pulled out and burned. The height of the plants is about two feet.

Purslane *(Portulaca grandiflora)* — Purslane is a sun-loving annual with thick leaves and a profusion of bright flowers. There are both single and double forms easily raised from seed sown in the open ground when the soil warms up. The plants spread over the ground to make a six-inch carpet through the summer months. The first frost destroys them but the seed pods burst, scattering seeds far and wide to provide next year's plants. Open-ground sowing is quite satisfactory, although young plants can be set out in June from seed sown indoors April 15 - 20.

Rose clarkia *(Clarkia elegans)* — The rose clarkia bears graceful sprays of attractive flowers in salmon pink, rose and crimson as well as white. When the plants are given enough room, they grow up to three feet high.

Sage *(Salvia)* — There are several species cultivated for their showy flowers; the most popular one is *S. splendens,* the scarlet sage. There are many varieties, some early, some late, either tall or dwarf. For prairie gardens only the earliest sorts are recommended, choosing the dwarf plants that grow about a foot high. New shades of old rose and lavender have been introduced, but these will never take the place of the scarlet sage. The plants have dark green leaves and spikes of flowers with colorful bracts. In periods of dry weather, spider mites may disfigure the foliage and debilitate the plants but, when these insects are controlled and the plants are in rich, moist soil, they make a brilliant show of bloom from July until the first frost strikes them down. It pays to sow the seeds early to have sturdy plants ready for planting out in June. March 15 - 20 is considered soon enough where night temperatures of sixty degrees can be maintained.

The mealycup salvia *(S. farinacea)* is an entirely different species, with slender spikes of blue or purple flowers not unlike those of the common lavender, though lacking the fragrance of that old-fashioned plant. The foliage is dense, grayish green, and the flower stems are white with farina, a flour-like substance. The species, a native of Texas, is much hardier than the scarlet sage, which is a Brazilian species. The mealycup salvia prefers a place in the sun and well-drained soil. The full-grown plant is almost three feet high; it is not unusual for it to bloom into October. Sow the seeds at the same time as *S. splendens* but give the young plants much more room; a foot and a half for each is not too much.

Scarlet flax *(Linum grandiflorum)* — The bright red flowers of scarlet flax are borne freely on foot-high plants from July until September. It is a useful plant for edging or for making bright patches of color towards the front of the annual border. Outdoor sowing is preferred, as the young plants do not transplant readily.

Scarlet tithonia *(Tithonia rotundifolia speciosa)* — Scarlet tithonia is a Mexican plant that does well in prairie gardens. The bright, orange scarlet flowers resemble single dahlias and are fine for cutting. Well-grown plants are three feet high, continuing to bloom from July until September. Sow the seeds March 10 - 20.

Siberian wallflower *(Erysimum asperum,* formerly *Cheiranthus allionii)* — In the northern areas, where deep snow cover can be depended upon, the Siberian wallflower often survives the winter. It is not long lived anywhere, so it is best raised from seed sown March 1 - 10. The plants are bushy, about a foot high, with bright orange or yellow, sweet-scented flowers.

Snapdragon *(Antirrhinum)* — Snapdragons are perennial plants not hardy enough to survive the winter in prairie gardens, but they will flower the first year from seed. There are dwarf, intermediate and tall varieties in a wide variety of bright colors. The latest sorts are F_1 hybrids, which are more uniform and true to color than the open-pollinated varieties. Sow the seeds March 7 - 15. The height of the plants ranges from six inches for the Floral Carpet series to three feet for the Rocket F_1 hybrids.

Snapweed, garden balsam *(Impatiens balsamina)* — The garden balsam makes sturdy plants with thick, succulent stems studded with flowers in the leaf axils. Improved strains have the blooms well displayed above the leaves, whereas the flowers of older varieties were mostly hidden by the foliage. The flowers are white, pink or red; some have mottled petals in contrasting shades. The plants are quite bushy, about a foot high and, if planted in rich, moist soil, they bloom for a long time. Sow the seed April 1 - 10.

Snow-on-the-mountain *(Euphorbia marginata)* — The snow-on-the-mountain is a fast-growing annual spurge (a group of plants characterized by their milky juice) with light green leaves margined with white during the late summer. It does best in a sunny border in soil that is not too rich in nitrogen. The plants are about two feet high and quite bushy; they set seed readily to produce quantities of volunteer plants.

Spiderflower *(Cleome spinosa)* — The spiderflower is a tall, branching plant with large leaves and heads of attractive flowers either pink or white. It makes a useful background and is tolerant of some shade. When the plants are given sufficient room in moist soil, they continue to bloom from July until September. Sow the seed March 25 — April 1. Healthy plants will grow four to five feet high.

Statice, sea lavender *(Limonium)* — Several species of statice are grown as annuals; two of the most common, *L. sinuatum* and *L. bonduelli,* provide blue-, white- and rose-colored flowers as well as yellow. New strains include subtle shades of apricot, lavender and cream as well as deep rose and dark purple. The flowers are esteemed for winter bouquets, holding their colors well if cut and dried when full blooming. Sow the seed March 15 - 20. Statice does best in light soil and full sun, reaching about two feet by the end of the season. Another species, *L. suworowi,* sometimes called Russian statice, has pendulant spikes of rose pink flowers on plants about a foot high. Sow the seeds March 20 — April 1.

Strawflower *(Helichrysum bracteatum)* — The strawflowers, commonly dried and used for decoration indoors, are not particularly attractive as plants; for this reason they should be in the reserve garden, where they will produce their peculiar flowers with strawy bracts. The flowers are dried for winter use by cutting them before they open to reveal their centres and hanging them heads-down in a dry, cool basement. Wires are used as substitute stems; sometimes the flowers are dyed. The natural colors are white, cream, pink and reddish brown. Well-grown plants are three feet high. Sow the seeds March 1 - 10.

Summer cypress, firebush, belvedere *(Kochia)* — Summer cypress makes a neat, compact plant with dense, narrow foliage, bright green in summer and reddish in the fall. The flowers are of little interest and the numerous, self-sown seedlings are sometimes a nuisance. As a summer hedge, it requires no trimming and is tolerant of extreme heat and drought.

Sunflower *(Helianthus annuus)* — The annual sunflowers provide bold plants for the back of the border or for hiding unsightly objects. Some have composite heads of bloom more than a foot across on stems ten feet high. These can be used as summer windbreaks in the vegetable garden; the bare stalks also help to trap snow. Some sunflowers are only half as tall and some are not much more than three feet. These have handsome heads of bloom in many shades of orange, maroon, and reddish brown, with dark centres and petals banded in contrasting colors. Certain birds, being fond of the seed, are attracted to the plants in September. If there is any left after the birds have feasted, it should be harvested for winter bird food.

Sweet alyssum *(Alyssum maritimum)* — Sweet alyssum is a popular edging plant, six inches tall, usually with white flowers though shades of violet purple are available. The plants can be rejuvenated by shearing off the flower heads in August and will continue to bloom well into October. Sow the seed April 20 — May 1. Sweet alyssum, being tolerant of light frost, continues to bloom well into September.

Sweet scabious *(Scabiosa atropurpurea)* — Sweet scabious is an easily grown plant, sometimes called the pincushion flower, with rounded heads of flowers in a wide variety of colors. The flower stems are slender and poised well above the leaves, making useful, long-lasting cut flowers. The plants are two and one-half to three feet high, upright in habit, and bloom over a long period if the spent blooms are removed before the seed is formed. Sow the seeds March 25 — April 1.

Tickseed *(Coreopsis, calliopsis)* — Several species are commonly found in gardens, most having yellow, daisy-like flowers with purple brown centres. They range in height from one to two feet and bloom over a long period if seed pods are prevented from exhausting the plants and the soil is not allowed to dry out. *C. tinctoria,* sometimes called *Calliopsis marmorata,* has finely cut foliage and starry flowers in shades of yellow and brown. *C. stillmanii,* known to some gardeners as leptosyne, makes a foot-high plant which is covered for most of the summer with a profusion of tiny, bright yellow flowers.

Toadflax *(Linaria maroccana)* — Toadflax is not a popular plant in prairie gardens, though it is well adapted and easy to grow. The spikes of bloom resemble miniature snapdragons of various colors — pink, yellow, purple and white. The plants have narrow leaves and grow to about one foot. Sow the seeds April 1 - 10.

Tobacco plant or nicotine *(Nicotiana alata, Nicotiana affinis)* — The old-fashioned tobacco plant was grown chiefly for its heavy scent, which is most noticeable during the evening hours when the flowers are open. At other times, the plants look droopy; for this reason, the plants were often relegated to a position at the back of the border where they were overshadowed by more showy plants. Nowadays there are new kinds, Crimson Bedder, for example, with red flowers that stay open in the daytime but lack the scent of the old-fashioned nicotine. The Sensation strain has a wide range of colors, including lime green; the flowers do not close during the day nor do they have much scent. A dwarf white nicotine is only fifteen inches high, making it a useful bedding plant. Another called Miniature White has pure white, sweetly-scented flowers on two-foot-high plants. Sow the seeds in sterilized soil April 1 - 10. The young plants make good headway in a minimum temperature of sixty-five degrees.

Verbena *(Verbena hortensis)* — Verbena makes a one-foot spreading plant with dark green leaves and umbels of sweet-scented flowers in a wide range of bright colors. The plants do best in full sun, in soil that is well drained and rich in humus. Plants set out in June start to bloom in July and continue through September. Another species, *venosa,* is not as well known as it deserves to be; the plants are about a foot high bearing violet purple flowers. Verbenas are tolerant of dry soil and, if the spent flowers are removed before seed is formed, the plants continue to put on a show of bloom until hard frost comes. Sow the seeds March 10 - 20.

Viola, tufted pansy *(Viola tricolor* var. *hortensis)* — The violas are more compact than the pansies; the flowers are smaller and mostly unmarked. In those parts of the prairies where snow comes early and lies deep through the winter, the plants may survive for several years; elsewhere, they tend to die out sooner. It is best to start seed the same time as pansies, setting the plants out at the same time. There are splendid colors, including ruby red, deep apricot, yellow, white and many shades of blue. New, improved forms of the old-fashioned johnny-jump-up violas include a dark purple variety and one with lavender and yellow flowers, making dense, low-growing plants covered with tiny violas until the snow comes.

The pansy *(Viola tricolor)* may be treated as a biennial, flowering from seed sown outdoors in summer and transplanted in September. In some parts of the prairies the plants persist for several years, but the best results are obtained from seedlings set out in late May. Both pansies and violas should be started from seed sown February 10 - 20. Both pansies and violas are tolerant of partial shade but, in areas where nights are cool, the plants are best in the sun. Pansies and violas planted in shaded places where the circulation of air is poor usually become infected with mildew by the end of the summer.

Virginia stock *(Malcomia maritima)* — Virginia stock is a well-known, old-fashioned annual with tiny flowers in a variety of colors all through the summer and early autumn. The plants are less than a foot high and may be grown from seed planted directly in the ground.

Viscaria, campion *(Lychnis viscaria)* — These dwarf plants are useful edgings or fillers in the rock garden. They are variant shades of blue, pink, crimson, scarlet or white. Sow the seeds April 1 - 10.

Wild cucumber *(Echinocystis lobata)* — Sometimes the wild cucumber becomes a nuisance plant, as volunteer seedlings spring up in unwanted numbers. It is useful for covering unsightly objects during the summer months. The leaves are palish green; the flowers are creamy, followed by small spiny fruits.

Zinnia *(Zinnia elegans)* — Modern strains of the popular annual have been developed from this species. There are many different classes, varying in plant height and in the size of the flowers. Some have broad petals; some are quilled to resemble cactus dahlias. The small-flowered pompons or lilliput zinnias and some of the other varieties with finer stems are preferred for cutting. The huge blooms of the giant and dahlia-flowered zinnias make bold patches of color in the border. The narrow-leaf zinnia *(Zinnia linearis)* makes a fine edging plant a foot high with masses of single, bright orange flowers zoned with maroon. Zinnias do best in full sun, in rich soil with plenty of moisture; dry soil and poor air circulation invite attacks of spider mites and mildew. In the short frost-free season of the prairies, zinnia seed is best sown indoors May 1. Outdoor sowings in mid-May are sometimes quite successful but well-grown plants in jiffy pots will start to bloom earlier to make a better show.

Annuals for Special Use

Suitable annuals for edging flower beds —

dusty miller	*(Centaurea cineraria)*
dwarf marigold	*(Tagetes hybridum)*
fossflower	*(Ageratum houstonianum)*
lobelia	*(Lobelia erinus)*
purslane	*(Portulaca grandiflora)*
sweet alyssum	*(Alyssum maritimum)*

Annual climbing plants —

canary creeper	*(Tropaeolum canariensis)*
cup and saucer vine	*(Cobaea scandens)*
gourds	*(Cucurbita species)*
hyacinth bean	*(Dolichos lablab)*
morning-glory	*(Ipomoea purpurea)*
nasturtium	*(Tropaeolum majus)*
sweet pea	*(Lathyrus odoratus)*

Best cut-flower Annuals —

blue laceflower	*(Didiscus coerulea)*
butterflyflower	*(Schizanthus hybrids)*
carnation	*(Dianthus hybridus)*
China aster	*(Callistephus chinensis)*
gloriosa daisy	*(Rudbeckia hirta hybrids)*
larkspur	*(Delphinium ajacis hybrids)*
marigold	*(Tagetes hybrids)*
painted tongue	*(Salpiglossis sinuata)*
pot marigold	*(Calendula officianalis)*
snapdragon	*(Antirrhinum majus)*
sweet scabious	*(Scabious atropurpurea)*
sweet sultan	*(Centaurea moschata)*
zinnia	*(Zinnia elegans)*

Annuals for a summer hedge —

castor bean	*(Ricinus communis)*
four o'clock	*(Mirabilis jalapa)*
summer cypress	*(Kochia trichophila)*
sunflower	*(Helianthus annua)*
treemallow	*(Lavatera trimestris)*

Annuals that tolerate some shade —

baby blue-eyes	*(Nemophila insignis)*
blue woodruff	*(Asperula orientalis)*
four o'clock	*(Mirabilis jalapa)*
mignonette	*(Reseda odorata)*
pansies	*(Viola tricolor)*
spiderflower	*(Cleome spinosa)*
tobacco plant	*(Nicotiana affinis)*
Virginia stock	*(Malcomia maritima)*

Sixteen

The Vegetable Garden

The day of the large vegetable plot, where potatoes, carrots, turnips and other root crops as well as cabbage were grown for winter food, is past. Nowadays, the vegetable plot may only be large enough to grow the summer requirements of salad plants, some peas and beans and perhaps a row or two of carrots and beets. But home-grown vegetables are still superior to commercial produce, especially the kinds that lose flavor quickly once they have been harvested. Sweet corn and peas are good examples, and young carrots pulled from the garden have a delicate flavor not found in mature roots.

There have been changes in the vegetable garden just as remarkable as those affecting ornamental plants. Plant breeders have developed earlier and better-adapted strains for prairie gardens. Sweet corn and tomatoes can now be grown in northern parts where these crops were unreliable not so long ago. Some attention has been paid to dwarf strains of peas, corn and cabbage. Compact, dwarf tomatoes are available and bush-type marrows and squash. There is no reason why the backyard gardener, with limited space, cannot enjoy fresh vegetables in season by carefully planning his vegetable plot so that he makes the best possible use of the available space.

Home-owners will often spend a good deal of time and money planning the front garden and the living-out area to the exclusion of the vegetable garden, which is left to be planted in a haphazard manner. Time and money are thereby wasted, since a poorly arranged vegetable garden will disrupt the harmony of the entire landscape plan. A well-planned vegetable plot is both attractive and functional; the most efficient and productive arrangement of plants tends also to be most pleasing to the eye.

Tall plants are best kept together at one end of the plot. Sweet corn, for instance, is better in a block of plants than in a long row, the reason being that corn is a wind-pollinated plant and pollination is improved when such plants are set out in a block. Although tall plants will overshadow dwarf varieties, shutting out sunlight, the fast-growing radishes, leaf lettuce and peas are not threatened, since they may be harvested before the tall vegetables get too high. A row of radish, for example, will occupy the ground for only five or six weeks and the leaf lettuce not much longer; early peas, sown in April, will be ready for use by the first week of July. There is, therefore, no reason why rows of these vegetables cannot be planted fairly close to sweet corn and other tall plants.

Perennial Vegetables in the Prairie Garden

Perennial vegetables have been given short shrift by prairie gardeners. Rhubarb is something the neighbor grows and is glad to give away; asparagus is generally considered a long-term project — the three year wait from planting until the first shoots are harvested is apparently considered too long. The backyard garden may not have room for many of the perennial vegetables, which must be planted all together at one end of the vegetable plot where they will not interfere with the culture of the annual crops, but even the smallest garden can accommodate a plant or two of rhubarb and a patch of asparagus; a few clumps of chives take very little room along the walk or in some odd corner. Highly nutritious when picked fresh, refreshing in the spring when appetites are jaded from a steady diet of root crops, the perennial vegetables deserve more consideration in prairie gardens.

Asparagus — Asparagus is esteemed by most people for its succulent stems, produced over a six-week period in the spring. Sometimes a bird-sown seed produces a plant in the perennial border or in some odd corner, where it is allowed to grow for the sake of its ornamental foliage. A few odd plants will provide enough tender stems for a small family so, if you are tempted to uproot a volunteer asparagus plant, consider leaving it to provide greenery as well as a few stems for cutting.

The preferred soil for cultivated asparagus is a deep, medium loam that is rich in humus and well drained. A place in the sun is needed, where the soil will warm up quickly in the spring, but there must be no chance of melted snow lying around the crown of the plants or the roots may rot. It was once considered necessary to go to a lot of trouble in preparing the soil for asparagus, but there really is no need. It should be remembered, however, that asparagus is a perennial crop, occupying the ground for twenty years or longer, so deep digging, adding a thick layer of rotted barnyard manure, is recommended.

To make an asparagus bed, prepare the soil in the fall and let it lie rough over winter. As soon as it is dry in the spring, rake it level and set out the plants. One-year-old roots, grown from seed sown in your own backyard or purchased from a nurseryman, make the best planting stock. If you raise the plants from seed, make a sowing as soon as the ground is dry enough to work in the spring. Drop the seeds an inch apart in a trench two inches deep. Cover them with an inch of fine soil. If you plant several rows, space them a foot apart and sow a few radish seeds in with the asparagus to mark the rows; the asparagus is slow to germinate and the first shoots are fine and easily overlooked in hoeing.

A year later, the young plants are moved to their permanent quarters; plant them in rows four feet apart, setting the single crowns about a foot and a half apart in the row. Cover the crowns with two inches of fine soil made firm around the roots. No watering will be needed unless the ground becomes very dry but a dressing of ammonium phosphate, at the rate of one ounce to the square yard, will be beneficial if applied in June and watered in. Weeds must be kept down or they can be a serious problem. Dandelions, plantains and other broad-leaved weeds can be killed by spraying with low volatile 2-4-D.

If the young plants are properly cared for, growth will be rapid and vigorous plants will be produced after two full years' growth. A few shoots can be gathered the third year but overcutting will exhaust the plant and do permanent damage. One or two shoots from each plant will not be missed; select the crowns with the strongest shoots. Established patches of asparagus will supply shoots every other day from early May until the middle of June, when no more stalks should be cut. When the last stalks are harvested, clean the patch of weeds and fertilize the bed with 11.48.0, spread evenly at two ounces to the square yard. A thin layer of rotted manure spread over the bed when the cutting is finished will conserve moisture and slowly release plant food when rain comes.

Rhubarb — Rhubarb is one of the hardiest and most abused plants in the garden. It comes from the dry parts of Siberia and its roots are perfectly hardy to frost. The cultivated plant is often relegated to some odd corner where the soil is poor and where the roots are entangled with quack grass . . . it deserves better treatment. When planted in rich soil, it will respond with succulent stems from vigorous crowns. The tangy acid flavor is justly relished in the spring as a sauce or in pies. Some varieties have green stems but the popular kinds are red fleshed.

The young plants are set out in the spring, spacing them not less than three feet apart. If more than one row is required, four feet should be allowed between the rows. Each plant should have one or two eyes or growth shoots and they should be set about two inches below the surface.

It takes three years for the young plant to get established and during this time no stalks should be pulled. Seed stems, which are produced freely on some varieties, should be cut out near the base of the plant as soon as they appear; otherwise, they rob the plant of nourishment needed to produce thick stalks. A few plants supply the needs of the average family but there is a limit to the number of stalks that should be pulled from a plant. Thick stalks are usually ready on three-year-old plants by the first week of June. Not more than one-third should be pulled at any one time and, after the middle of August, no more stalks should be gathered.

In large gardens, where rhubarb may be plentiful and where a corner of the basement can be darkened, it is practical to force a plant or two. Strong crowns are dug up in the fall, left to freeze on top of the ground until the early part of December, then boxed up in soil and taken to the basement. The plants are kept in the dark, the soil moistened occasionally and, by Christmas, the tender, delicately flavored stalks can be gathered. The forced stalks are a delicacy in the winter, one plant yielding weekly servings for the average family over a period of several months. In the spring, the old crowns are best discarded as they take several years to recover from the forcing.

Chive — Chives are perennial herbaceous plants used fresh in the spring to season soups and to give salads a mild onion flavor. The plant is a native of Britain and will grow freely in ordinary garden soil with little attention. The grassy leaves are cut as required to maintain a continuous supply of young shoots. Every three or four years the clumps are lifted, divided and replanted in new ground. To prolong the season of chives, a plant may be potted up in the fall and grown on the kitchen window sill.

Horseradish — This well known condiment, used with roast beef, belongs to the cabbage and turnip family and is found in waste places growing wild. It is not often cultivated and only those who are aware of its digestive properties would bother to give it a place in the perennial vegetable garden. It grows in ordinary soil either in sun or in shade and may be started from root cuttings. The shoots should be about pencil thickness, four or five inches long, with the tops cut horizontal, the bottoms slanted. Plant the cuttings in the spring, covering them with two inches of soil. The roots are perfectly hardy but, when required for winter use, the plants should be dug and stored like carrots.

Cool Weather Vegetables in the Prairie Garden

Endive — Endive will be grown only by those who have a flare for novelty vegetables and an appreciation of its distinct flavor in a salad. It is closely related to chicory and needs the same general culture. The broad-leaved endive is not so popular as the curled varieties for use either as cooked vegetables or as salad plants. The plants do best in a light soil. The seed should be sown in May; make the rows a foot apart and cover the seed half an inch deep. Thin the seedlings to stand about nine inches apart. In the fall, surplus plants can be boxed up and taken to the basement where they are kept in the dark to blanch the leaves. In the garden, a few plants can be tied up in July like cos lettuce if blanched endive is required in the summer.

Lettuce – Lettuce is the most important part of a salad; both loose leaf and head lettuce can be grown well in prairie gardens. The cos lettuce, esteemed for its delicate flavor in European countries, is not grown to any extent on the prairies. Lettuce does best in a medium loam soil enriched with humus and plant food.

Usable leaf lettuce can be produced in a few weeks by sowing the seed outdoors as soon as the soil warms in the spring. In a small garden, the rows should be a foot apart and the seeds sown thinly, about half an inch deep. When the young plants are an inch high; thin them so that each is spaced about two inches. Later on, every other plant can be pulled and used for salad. By choosing a variety that stands hot weather without bolting to seed (once a plant puts out seeds, it becomes very bitter), by thinning the plants before they become overcrowded and by keeping the ground moist, it is possible to pick tender leaves over a long period.

To grow crisp heads of lettuce, rich soil, cool weather and plenty of water are needed. In some parts of the country, young plants started from seed sown in a greenhouse or garden frame are planted out in the same manner as cabbage. In most prairie gardens, the seed is sown where the plants are to remain and it is possible to produce first-class heads in this way if a few simple directions are followed. Prepare the seedbed by raking the soil level and breaking up the lumps. The rows should be fifteen to eighteen inches apart, and seed sown half an inch deep. The importance of firming the soil over the seed rows cannot be overstressed. The novice may be reluctant to tramp on the rows of planted seed but this is necessary; it firms the soil around the seed to ensure even germination. It is not uncommon for the top inch of soil to be dry in the spring and it may be necessary to pull back the dry soil before making a shallow trench where the soil is moist; poor stands of plants can often be attributed to seed lying in dry soil. It is most important to thin the young plants while they are still small; overcrowding is probably the chief cause of failure in growing head lettuce. The young plants can be used when they are a few inches high. The final thinning will leave the plants not less than nine inches apart for the compact varieties and one foot for larger sorts.

Aster yellows, a virus disease, is likely to attack both leaf and head lettuce when they go to seed. It is good gardening to pull up and destroy lettuce when the plants show the first signs of bolting; otherwise, the virus can be carried by leafhoppers to other susceptible vegetables such as carrots and celery.

Radish — Radishes are not relished by everyone but they form an important part of a salad, adding bright color and piquant flavour. Radishes are easy to grow on any well-drained, light soil that has been worked to a fine tilth. The plants are often poorly grown because the seeds are sown too thickly in lumpy soil. The result is tough or hollow roots with a hot, pungent flavor.

Radishes must be grown quickly to produce small, highly colored, good-quality roots. The first sowings, which can be made as soon as the ground dries up in the spring, may be destroyed by frost but the loss will not be serious if this should happen. In most areas it is considered safe to sow radish around the tenth of May, making the rows a foot apart, covering the seed an inch deep. It pays to drop the seeds singly an inch apart, thinning out every other plant when they have developed their first true leaves.

When the weather is warm and dry, flea beetles can be troublesome, attacking the seedlings as they push through the ground to puncture small holes through the cotyledons or seed leaves. Flea beetles often destroy the seedlings before the unwary gardener realizes what is happening. The insects are shiny black, tiny and quick in their movements. By dusting the seedlings as they emerge with Derris, good control can be obtained. (Derris dust, which is nonpoisonous to humans, is preferred to D.D.T.)

Celery — The self-blanching varieties of celery are the most popular, though they lack the flavor of the white and pink varieties which have to be blanched by mounding soil around the stalks or by putting boards on either side of the rows. Celery can be used before the plants are fully grown; in salads and soups, leaves and stalks can be used to give a distinctive flavor.

The home gardener may not bother with growing celery; if he does, he will likely buy a few plants from the nursery or garden center rather than go to the trouble of growing them from seed. As the plants require a long season, the seed must be sown indoors around the middle of March. The seeds germinate slowly, so cover the seed pots with glass and paper to keep the soil from drying out rapidly. There must be no check in growth by allowing the young plants to remain dry or the temperature to fall below forty degrees when the seedlings are transplanted to a garden frame or hotbed.

Young, well-hardened plants can be set out in the open ground by the first of June on good land, well enriched with rotted manure. Regular watering in periods of drought is necessary to obtain stalks of good quality. When the young plants are a foot high, a two-inch mulch of granulated peat will be beneficial. Before hard frost comes, celery plants still in the garden should be lifted with soil attached to the roots and replanted in boxes of soil. The plants are watered well and the boxes stored in the basement where the temperature should be about fifty degrees. By careful management, which means picking off bad leaves and keeping the soil moist, it is possible to have fresh celery until Christmas.

Onion — Onions, in one form or another, are enjoyed by most people either cooked or raw. In the early summer, fresh green onions are relished in salads, the young plants being produced from sets (immature bulbs) or from seed. The sets are obtained from seed stores or markets and planted a few inches apart in well-worked soil as soon as the ground dries up in the spring. You can produce sets quite easily by sowing seed thickly in ground that is not too rich, allowing the plants to grow without thinning and without attention except to keep them free of weeds. In August the bulblets are harvested, dried and stored in the same way as large onions, selecting those that are about the size of a wax bean for planting the next year. Larger bulbs can be used in soups or as boiled onions.

Onion sets will produce large bulbs if planted outdoors in the spring and given the same treatment as transplanted seedlings, but most of the sets planted are pulled for green onions. To grow large onions from seed requires a long season so transplanted seedlings are therefore preferred to open ground sowings. The seed is sown indoors March first, earlier if heated frames are available to grow the seedlings when they are transplanted from the seed pot. The roots of onions are long and easily broken, and careless handling sets the young plants back. The mistakes commonly made in transplanting onions to the open ground are setting the young plants too deep, doubling up the roots instead of allowing them to go straight down and not making the soil firm enough. The young plants should be spaced about six inches apart in the row, with the bulb portion of the plant set just below the soil level. Regular attention to weeding, fertilizing and watering the plants in periods of drought will produce large bulbs. By the third week of August, the plant's growth should be arrested (to allow the bulbs to harden off) by carefully bending over the tops. Careless trampling will bruise the tops and may cause the neck portion to rot. The bulbs must be lifted and dried before frost comes. Spread them in the sun, covering them if night frost threatens, then finish the drying process in a cool, well-ventilated room. The bulbs can be hung in ropes or stored in slatted boxes; the storage place should be dry and the temperature about forty degrees.

Fair-sized bulbs can be grown from seed sown in the open ground in early May. Sow the seed thinly in rows a foot apart after making the seedbed very firm and raking it to a fine tilth. The seedlings must be thinned when a few inches high, and those first young plants used in salads and soups. The final thinning will leave the plants three or four inches apart. Because the roots penetrate the soil deeply to take a firm hold, the thinning is best done following a rain; otherwise, the tops break off, leaving the roots to grow again. The mature bulbs are harvested and stored in the same way as those raised from transplants.

The multiplier onion is used to produce green onions, one from each of its divisions, in the same manner as sets, by planting dormant bulbs in the spring. The bulbs that are not used as green onions are left in the ground to ripen and may be harvested and stored for winter use. They will keep better than onions, the bulbs remaining firm and useable until the first green onions are ready in the spring.

The cabbage family — The cabbages and related plants form an interesting group of vegetables. The leaves of some are eaten raw, cooked or pickled; the flower buds of others, either in single or multiple heads, provide highly nutritious food when cooked, pickled or preserved by freezing. Another member of the tribe produces vegetative shoots in the leaf axils that develop into miniature cabbages or sprouts. Still another produces swollen stems and is a substitute for turnips. The cabbage, which is most important, is grown in large quantities in market gardens, and most home gardens have room for a few early sorts to provide tender heads for salads and for boiling.

Satisfactory heads can be grown from seed sown in the open ground the first week of May; young plants, from a sowing made earlier in a greenhouse or garden frame, can safely be planted out towards the end of May if they are first hardened off. To produce good cabbages from open-ground sowing, the seeds should be dropped three or four together at six-inch intervals and covered with half an inch of fine soil made firm by treading. The seedlings must be protected against the ravages of flea beetles and thinned to leave only one plant at each station. When the leaves grow large enough to touch one another, every other plant can be pulled up and used. The remainder will make large, firm heads.

The young cabbage plants of an early sort, transplanted in late May, will be ready for use in late July. When cutting the early heads, leave a few leaves on the stump; second growth from these early cabbages develops usable small heads in September. Cabbage tends to split when the heads reach full size, especially when heavy rains follow a period of drought. By loosening the roots, then firming the soil around them, you may prevent the heads from splitting.

Late cabbage, used to make sauerkraut or stored for use during the winter in salads or as a boiled vegetable, is not grown in such large quantities now as it was years ago. Surplus heads should not be discarded when the vegetable garden is cleaned off in the fall. Solid heads can be stored in perforated plastic bags in a cold basement room; if the temperature can be kept at about thirty-five degrees, the cabbage will remain in good condition until Christmas or longer.

Red cabbage, grown mostly for pickling and occasionally used in salads, is not popular in prairie gardens. The culture is the same as outlined for the green-leaved varieties. It is palatable as a cooked vegetable and may be stored for long periods in a cold basement.

Cauliflower – The cauliflower is somewhat more exacting in its requirements than cabbage. It is less hardy, thrives best in very rich soil and must be grown rapidly to ensure high-quality heads. Cool weather, moist soil and plenty of water will produce the finest cauliflower. Crop failures result when poor plants are set out too late and hot, dry weather sets in before they become well established; when this occurs, the young plants start heading before they have reached normal size, yielding a small curd of poor quality. The curd, or flowering head, should be dense and pure white. When it first becomes visible, the outer leaves should be tied together to shut out strong light; if the curds are exposed to the sun, they become yellow and bitter to the taste.

Young plants which have been grown from seeds sown in the greenhouse or a garden frame are set out in the open ground when all danger of frost is past, usually not before June first in most parts of the prairies. The rows should be not less than two feet apart, with the plants spaced about a foot and a half in the row. It is important to grow the young plants without a check, so well-hardened plants should be set out in firm soil, kept free of weeds and given plenty of water when the soil becomes dry.

A purple-headed cauliflower, which becomes green when cooked, is something of a novelty. It requires the same culture as the ordinary varieties and is recommended for freezing.

Broccoli – There are two kinds of broccoli, a plant that is similar to but hardier than cauliflower. The heading types are not grown in prairie gardens but the sprouting broccoli, both green and purple sorts, are valuable greens either fresh-boiled or frozen. Seed may be sown outdoors in early May; transplants are set out June first. The tender shoots are gathered before the flower buds open and, where the plants are in rich soil and well supplied with water, sprouting broccoli will give a supply of greens for six weeks or longer.

In the milder parts of the country, the heading types of broccoli can be grown; the young plants are set out in the spring and the heads are ready for cutting in the fall. Some hardy sorts are able to stand mild winters to head up in the spring, but only in the Pacific coastal area and in the mildest parts of eastern Canada is it possible to grow these winter broccoli.

Brussels sprouts – In the prairie provinces, Brussels sprouts are not grown so well or so extensively as they are in other parts of the country. They are not relished by everyone, but have long been regarded as one of the finest green vegetables. The most reliable sorts for prairie gardens are the F_1 hybrids, which produce a heavy crop on good land where ample supplies of water can be given in periods of drought.

The plants should be set out early, about the third week of May, as they need a long season of growth to produce firm sprouts. The soil should be rich, deeply dug and well firmed for Brussels sprouts; any attempt to grow them in poor, loose soil will end in failure. The plants are set out in rows not less than two feet apart, spacing them about a foot and a half in the row. The sprouts are formed in the axils of the leaves developing from the base of the stem, and harvesting begins when the first sprouts are about walnut size. During the summer, regular hoeing to keep weeds down is necessary; occasionally, aphids will attack the plants and must be controlled by spraying with Malathion.

Savoy cabbage – The Savoy cabbage is closely related to the Brussels sprout, though it is more like the cabbage in appearance. It is not grown to any extent in prairie gardens though fairly good heads are occasionally seen at the local shows. The heads are dark green, surrounded by large rugose leaves, handsome and attractive. The Savoy cabbage requires the same general culture as ordinary cabbage and will be tried by those who have come from European countries where the Savoy is esteemed as a hardy, late-season cabbage.

Root Crops in the Prairie Garden

Kohlrabi – The kohlrabi, which belongs to the cabbage family, resembles a turnip more than a cabbage. It is not grown extensively in prairie gardens although good roots can be produced quite easily. The swollen stems which develop just above ground level taste like turnips and, where those vegetables are difficult to grow, make a good substitute. The kohlrabi is better adapted to light soil than turnips and appears to stand heat and drought without getting bitter.

The seed is sown outdoors in mid-May in drills drawn a foot apart and half an inch deep. Early thinning to leave the seedlings three inches apart and a final thinning to six inches will give the young plants sufficient room for full development. Kohlrabi is fit for use when the swollen stems are about the size of a tennis ball; surplus roots may be stored like turnips. The seedlings should receive the same protection from the depredations of the flea beetles as the other members of the cabbage family.

Turnip – The summer turnip must be grown quickly in deep, sandy loam to obtain tender, delicately flavored roots. Dry weather, excessive heat and poor cultivation results in tough roots with a bitter taste. The seed is sown in early May, scattering it very thinly in rows drawn a foot apart; the seeds are covered with soil to a depth of half an inch. Thin the young plants so that, by July, when they have reached maturity, they have a full six inches. Be on the watch for flea beetles.

Swedes — The swede turnip, or rutabaga, is a hardy turnip that stores well to provide wholesome winter fare. In northern areas of the prairies it does much better than in other parts but, generally speaking, good quality roots can be produced over a wide area. It requires the same culture as the summer turnip except that the seed is sown later, around the tenth of June in most seasons. Cool, moist weather is favorable; heat, drought and highly alkaline soil tend to destroy the sweet flavor of swedes and, where these conditions are severe, the roots are quite unpalatable. The plants should have more room than summer turnips; two feet between rows is not too much and, by maturity, the seedlings should be thinned to stand not less than six inches in the row. The swedes are the last of the vegetable crops to be harvested, sometimes as late as the third week of October. A few light frosts will not injure the roots; in fact, the flavor will be improved.

Beets — The garden beet is esteemed as a valuable root vegetable and for its leaves, which may be cooked in the same manner as spinach. The young roots may be boiled and served as a vegetable or preserved in pickles. Beets do best in deep loam, rich in nutrients and humus but not rank with fresh manure; when fresh manure has been dug into land to be used for beets or other roots, it will produce coarse plants with rough, ugly roots. The globe or turnip-rooted varieties are preferred to the long beets, which are not grown to any extent in prairie gardens.

Early crops can be harvested from a sowing made in mid-May, or earlier if one is prepared to take a chance on frost. Sow the seeds very thinly, as each one contains several germs capable of making plants. The first thinnings should be done when the young plants are two inches high. The tops by now are ready for use as a boiled vegetable. The produce of later thinnings can be used to make small pickles or may be boiled and served fresh. When the first frost comes, the mature roots which still remain in the ground are carefully lifted and their leaves twisted off. If the leaves are cut close to the crown rather than twisted off, the roots bleed and lose much of their flavor. Beets can be stored in a cool cellar, packed in dry sawdust or peat.

Swiss chard — The Swiss chard or sea kale beet, which is a close relative of the well-known beet root, is a nutritious, easily grown vegetable. The leaves are cooked like spinach; the succulent leaf stalks are cooked separately and served like asparagus. A short row of chard will provide a supply of summer greens from July until hard frost comes in October. The plants will yield abundant quantities of leaves if only the outside ones are gathered, leaving the centre leaves to grow to full size. Chard is easy to grow from seed sown around the middle of May. The seedlings are thinned to stand a foot apart, the rows spaced not less than two feet to produce the finest specimens. A variety with red stalks and veins has some ornamental value.

Spinach — Spinach is a wholesome and health-giving vegetable not relished by everyone; in fact, there are some who find it most unpalatable. The dark green leaves are glossy and heavily wrinkled. To be of most value, spinach should be ready for picking as early in the summer as possible. When other vegetables are in good supply, spinach will be overlooked but, left to grow until the middle of the summer, spinach plants will tend to bolt. Premature seed making can be delayed, however, if the young plants are in rich soil and given plenty of room for their full development. Sow the seed in early May, spacing the rows a foot and a half apart; thin the seedlings to stand a foot apart before they become crowded. Gather the outside leaves as soon as they are large enough and pull out plants that show signs of bolting.

Carrot — Next to the potato, the carrot is the most popular root crop in prairie gardens. It is highly nutritious, with a sweet, delicate flavor most appreciated when the roots are young and tender. It is served raw in salads or as a cooked vegetable. Young roots are preserved as a canned product and mature carrots will keep well in a cool cellar.

In most parts of the prairies, good samples can be produced with very little trouble by sowing the seed in early May. Make the rows not less than a foot apart, drilling in the seeds about half an inch deep. The soil should be deep, rich in plant food but not recently charged with fresh manure or the roots will be fanged. Sow the seeds thinly and cover them with fine soil. When the seedlings are about two inches high, thin them out to stand an inch apart. Later on, when the roots are of finger thickness, every other one can be pulled for use. Roots with green tops can be avoided if a thin layer of soil is mounded up around the plants after the final thinning. Where the soil is not deeply dug or where it is naturally rather shallow, the stump-rooted sorts will give a better return than the intermediate or long carrots.

The roots for storage are harvested in early October; they should not be long exposed to sun or dry air. It is best to choose a cloudy day for digging, cutting off the tops close to the crown and discarding roots which may be blemished or injured mechanically. Carrots can be washed and dried before they are placed in plastic bags for winter storage or, in larger quantities, they can be packed in dry sawdust or peat. Carrots are more likely to go bad than beets or swedes, so extra care is needed in maintaining clean storage conditions.

Parsnip — The parsnip, a long-season root, is not relished by everyone but, when properly cooked, it is a nourishing, substantial food. It requires a deep soil that is not especially rich. The ground for parsnips should be dug deeply in the fall, left rough over winter and forked over lightly in the spring just as soon as it becomes dry enough to walk on. The hollow crown and other long-rooted varieties are difficult to dig from dry, hard ground; Guernsey and other short-rooted kinds should be used where difficulty in digging has been experienced.

Early sowing of fresh seed is important, as parsnip seed soon loses its vitality. As soon as the ground is dry, make the drills an inch deep and a foot and a half apart. Because the seed is light and papery, sowing is tedious if there is much air movement; choose a calm day, therefore, dropping a few seeds every three or four inches along the row. A few seeds of radish, sown at the same time, will germinate in a few days and serve as markers so that hoeing may begin before the parsnip seedlings emerge.

Parsnips improve in flavor after the October frosts and may be dug for storage or left in the ground all winter. There is no merit in allowing the roots to stay in the ground since they are useless as long as the ground remains frozen and must be dug early in the spring before the tops start to grow and spoil them. They are harvested and stored in the same way as carrots but, unless the humidity of the storage area is kept fairly high, parsnip roots will shrivel.

Legumes in the Prairie Garden

The legumes best suited to cultivation on the prairies are beans and peas, esteemed in the summer as wholesome fare fresh from the garden. There are many types, tall as well as dwarf kinds, and most can be preserved for winter use either canned or frozen.

Beans – The bush beans, which are also known as French beans or snap beans, are the most widely grown varieties. There are two main groups; of the two, the wax or yellow-podded varieties are not so popular as the green. Both kinds are extremely tender to frost, so planting is usually delayed until the last week of May or later still in northern parts. Earlier sowing can be made if the seed is planted in hills and the young plants covered with hot caps.

Normal sowings are made in rows not less than a foot and a half apart, making the drills a full two inches deep and covering the seed with fine soil made firm by treading. There is no merit in sowing the beans too thickly; dropping a single seed every two or three inches will give a stand of plants which may be thinned to leave one plant every six inches. The soil should be rich, well drained and not too heavy. If the soil has been dug deeply to allow the free penetration of roots and if the plants have been given water copiously in periods of drought, they bear enormous crops of succulent beans over a long period.

The success of the crop is dependent on good culture, on keeping the plants healthy and free of insects and on regular harvesting of the beans while they are still young. Several virus diseases are known to infect bush beans, so a careful watch and the prompt destruction of diseased plants should be an important part of bean culture. It is not advisable to work among bean plants when the leaves are wet or you may spread leaf diseases.

Pole and runner beans — Pole beans can be grown quite well in prairie gardens and, with proper care, will yield heavy crops of large, high-quality beans. Not many gardeners will go to the trouble of putting up the required supports for a row of pole beans but consideration should be given to stringing a row of plants along the side of a building or growing a few plants along a fence. The vines grow six feet or higher; the beans are dark green and roundish, remaining in good condition longer than the bush types. They have a rich flavor when either boiled freshly picked or used as a frozen product.

The scarlet runner bean has been used as an ornamental climber since the early settlers came to the prairies. Few gardeners appreciate the quality of the green, immature pods or know how to produce a heavy crop. The ground should be dug deeply in the fall, adding a generous amount of rotted barnyard manure. The time of sowing and the spacing is the same for bush, pole and runner beans. A single row will provide all the beans needed for an average family; the seeds should be sown singly three inches apart and two inches deep at the same time the bush beans are planted. Thin the plants until they are about nine inches apart, and provide six-foot poles to support the vines.

To ensure a set of beans, spray the flowers during the evening with water from the garden hose; otherwise, the flowers tend to fall off before they are pollinated, especially in dry weather. Runner beans are fit for use when the pods are full grown but still tender. They are used in the same way as the bush beans and seem to be preferred by those who enjoyed them in England.

Broad Bean — The broad bean is the only frost-hardy bean grown in prairie gardens, yet it is not grown to any large extent. It is largely old-country gardeners, appreciative of its unique flavor, who will be inclined to plant a row of broad beans. There are two classes of broad beans, the longpod and Windsor; both can be grown quite well in most parts of the prairies, the longpod yielding heavy crops of acceptable quality. The Windsor, however, is considered to be of superior flavor and most attractive.

The best chance of success comes when the beans are planted as soon as the ground dries up in the spring. Double rows nine inches apart are the most satisfactory way to sow the seed, spacing each seed three inches apart, then thinning the crop so that each plant is spaced at six inches.

The soil should be heavy loam, dug deeply in the fall and enriched with rotted manure.

Cool, moist weather ensures a good set of beans. In hot weather, the flowers should be lightly sprayed with water to assist in setting the beans; when the first beans are visible, nip out the tip growth and, if necessary, spray the plants to control aphids. The shelled beans are used before they are fully sized; if allowed to ripen, they are useless as food.

Lima bean – The lima bean has great economic value in the warm, long-season parts of the continent but it is not recommended for prairie gardens. Tests of the earliest sorts carried out in the warmest parts of the prairies have not been satisfactory.

Pea – No other vegetable is so eagerly awaited as the first dish of fresh garden peas and no other vegetable is more nutritious. Since fresh peas are rich in phosphates and vitamins, as well as being rapid-growing plants, it is understandable that they quickly exhaust the soil of plant food. The soil for peas should be rich with rotted barnyard manure and dug deeply to give the roots room to spread and penetrate the soil for food. The work of preparing the soil is best done in the fall, leaving the soil rough to get the full benefit of the sweetening effects of frost.

There are two main classes of peas, the round-seeded and the wrinkle-seeded. There is a third class of edible podded peas but they are not grown to any extent in prairie gardens. The earliest crop is gathered from a sowing of a round-seeded variety made as soon as the ground dries in the spring. The round-seeded sorts such as Alaska will germinate in cold soil and the young plants will stand several degrees of frost without harm. It is sometimes possible to make a sowing towards the end of April and to pick the first peas before the month of June is out.

The main crop will be from a sowing of the wrinkle-seeded varieties made during the first week of May or shortly afterwards. Make a trench about six inches wide and about two inches deep, scattering the seeds thinly and covering them with fine soil made firm by treading. The shallow, six-inch trench is preferred to a narrower and deeper trench, which tends to overcrowd the young plants. Two inches should be allowed between each plant for proper development and, where the seedlings are thicker, they should be pulled out when the first true leaves unfold.

Most of the varieties grown in prairie gardens are dwarf, between one and two feet high. The tall sorts, which produce large, handsome pods if given good cultivation, are not grown to any extent. In most instances, the plants are left to grow without support but it pays to keep the vines off the ground by stringing binder twine along the rows or by using pieces of brushwood. There are no particular problems with insects or disease if the plants are well grown. Hot weather shortens the cropping season unless the plants are given soakings of water and mulched with peat or something similar to conserve moisture and to keep the soil cool. Aphids are sometimes found on peas and, towards the end of the season, mildew may make an appearance. The aphids are controlled by spraying with Malathion; the mildew seldom appears before the crop has been harvested, so there is no point in using a fungicide. It is wiser to pull up the vines when the last peas have been gathered, make a pile in a vacant spot and set fire to them.

It is sometimes difficult to get good germination when peas are sown in June for late crops. If the weather turns hot and dry, poor germination will result unless special precautions are taken. The seed for these late sowings should be soaked in water until it swells up, then sown in trenches made after the top few inches of dry soil have been raked to one side. The trench should be six inches wide and two inches deep, the same as already outlined for the earlier sowings. It may be necessary to water the trench if the soil is very dry; if so, do this before sowing the seed.

The home gardener who is interested in novelties may be inclined to try the edible-podded or sugar peas. They require the same general culture as ordinary peas but are cooked in the pod in the same manner as the green beans.

Solanaceous Vegetables in the Prairie Garden

Potato – The potato has been a staple food of western nations for well over two hundred years. It made its most rapid advance and greatest economic impact in Ireland, where it was cultivated on a large scale by the middle of the eighteenth century. The peasants produced enormous crops and were completely dependent on the potato as their most important food. The folly of being so dependent on a single crop was demonstrated in 1848, when a million people died of hunger and disease as a result of a crop failure due to blight. In a few years, another million left the country, driven away by poverty and starvation.

Today the potato is still an important food plant, highly economical and nutritious. It is a valuable source of carbohydrates, vitamins and minerals, containing small quantities of vitamin C and the B complex as well as iron and large quantities of starch. Potatoes can be served in so many ways that a daily serving rarely becomes tiresome, nor does the flavor pall. The young, new potatoes are a delicacy awaited and esteemed like the first green peas and sweet corn.

Potatoes do well in most parts of the prairies, though the ideal climate has a temperature range of sixty-five to seventy-five degrees during the growing season and fairly moist air. A satisfactory crop can be produced on a wide variety of soils but the best samples are grown on deep, fertile loam that is well drained. The land for potatoes is dug deeply in the fall; well-rotted manure is added and the soil allowed to winter over in a rough state. To enjoy new potatoes in early July, sprout a few tubers by setting them in a shallow box placed in a warm, well-lighted room. If the tubers are set out early in April, strong purplish sprouts about half an inch long will develop by the first week of May. The tubers are best planted whole, taking care not to rub off the sprouts by rough handling. The started tubers are set out towards the end of May in a sheltered spot in full sun; cover the emerging shoots with hot caps or draw a little soil over them should frost threaten. The dormant tubers that are planted for the main crop should be cut in two or four pieces, according to their size. The pieces selected for planting should weigh about two ounces and have at least one strong eye. Whole potatoes of suitable size can be used as single sets but, where a large patch is to be planted, it is more economical to cut the tubers. The cutting is best done just before planting, treating the wounds with a disinfectant to ward off soil-borne diseases. Preparations for treating the tubers, obtainable through seed houses, should be used as directed on the container and are especially recommended where disease has been a problem.

There is a tendency to plant potatoes too deep, which, especially in heavy soil, may cause the tubers to rot. The sets are planted about a foot apart, in rows spaced at two feet in a small garden; where there is plenty of room, three feet of space is recommended. Make the holes deep enough to allow a light dusting of fertilizer to be placed below the tubers; cover the fertilizer with an inch of soil and the tuber with not more than three inches. The soil should be kept stirred to keep the weeds in check and to maintain a fine tilth. As the plants grow, the soil should be drawn up around them to prevent the tubers that form near the surface from greening. Potatoes that are exposed to strong light soon become green and the green pigment is poisonous.

Several pests and diseases are common on potatoes. Colorado potato beetles lay clusters of orange-colored eggs on the undersides of the leaves; the eggs soon hatch and the voracious larvae devour the leaves rapidly. The young beetles are easily controlled by dusting the infested plants with one of the commercial all-purpose dusts. Leaf hoppers and aphids should be controlled or they carry virus to healthy plants; Malathion is recommended for leaf hoppers and for aphids. Heavy infestations of leaf hoppers cause the leaves to curl and then dry up, a condition known as hopperburn.

Common diseases of potatoes are virus, bacterial ring rot, early and late blight, blackleg, scab and rhizoctonia. The all-purpose dusts contain suitable chemicals for the control of all such diseases and, if used regularly, will keep the plants healthy. The spray program should begin when the plants are nicely through the ground, repeating the dose at ten-day intervals throughout the growing season. Some varieties of potatoes take scab more than others and, in gardens where the soil is highly alkaline, scab will always be a problem once the soil becomes infected with the disease. It is wise to move the potato patch to a new site each year and to obtain certified seed stocks every second year to ensure freedom from virus and other diseases.

In the small garden, the potato patch may only be large enough to supply summer needs, with none for storage. Where potatoes are grown in sufficient quantity for winter storage they should be harvested about the middle of September, choosing a sunny day so that the tubers will dry off quickly. Mature tubers, carefully dug and properly dried, have a higher dry matter and starch content than those which were dug too soon. Immature tubers have a higher water content; the skins are soft and bruise easily and the flesh can be discolored. In most home basements, the temperature is too high to store potatoes for very long before sprouts develop. The ideal storage temperature is forty degrees, with a free circulation of air. Light must be kept out or the tubers turn green. Small quantities can be stored in slatted boxes, each holding half a bushel; the winter supply for a large family will need to be stored in a bin.

Tomato — In most parts of the prairies; it is possible to ripen tomatoes on plants set out in the open ground the first week of June. New varieties being developed by prairie plant breeders are extending the range of tomato growing to northern areas where, previously, tomato plants rarely produced ripe fruit. The improved quality of tomatoes ripened on the plant induces most home gardeners to set out a dozen or more plants either purchased from the nurseryman or home grown.

The plants must be started from seed sown indoors the first week of April in pots of light, well-drained soil. The pots are filled to within half an inch of the rim with sifted soil, then saturated with boiling water. When the soil has drained and cooled, the seeds are planted half an inch apart and lightly covered with fine soil. By spacing the seeds, sturdier plants can be grown; if they are sown too thickly, the young plants become weak and spindly. The seeded pots are placed in a warm room where the night temperature is not lower than sixty degrees. Cover the pots with pieces of glass and paper to keep out light and reduce evaporation; the seedlings emerge in about six days and the paper and glass can be removed. A place in the sun will get the young plants away to a good start if regular attention is given to watering, keeping the soil well moistened but never soggy wet.

When the seedlings are about an inch and a half high, transplant them into boxes of light soil, spacing them two inches apart. The boxes should be of a convenient size to fit on a window sill unless the home-owner has a greenhouse. Some gardeners will prefer to use three-inch jiffy pots instead of boxes of soil. The jiffy pots are packed in shallow boxes and the plants grown in the same way as seedlings transplanted in boxes of soil. The extra room provided by the jiffy pots and the advantage of setting out the plant without disturbing its roots is well worth the added cost of the pots.

Before the plants are set out in the open ground, they must be inured to outdoor conditions, or hardened off. The process needs to be done gradually. First, take the boxes to a heated frame which has a well-fitted sash and extra covers in case of frost. A two hundred-watt light bulb in a well-constructed frame three feet by six feet will keep out twenty degrees of frost if the sash is covered with a blanket at night. By removing the sash in the daytime when the weather is favorable and finally removing it altogether, the young plants are made ready for planting in the open ground. Planting in early June is reasonably safe in the southern prairies but elsewhere, hot caps or some other protectors can advance the season of ripe fruit by ten days or two weeks. The protectors cover the plants as they are set out; as the weather warms to seventy degrees or more, the protectors are ventilated by making a two-inch hole on the south side. As the plant grows to fill the protector, the ventilating hole is enlarged to make room for the whole plant to emerge.

The hotcap is first ventilated on the south side and the opening gradually enlarged as the plant grows to fill the protector.

It is most important to grow the plants without a check, as a sudden change in the soil moisture is one of the causes of blossom-end rot. Blossom-end rot starts as a physiological disturbance, manifest as a spot at the blossom end of the fruit. As the spot increases in size, the base of the tomato becomes rotten and useless. It is most likely to occur when plants that are in lush growth are suddenly subjected to drought. When the situation is reversed and a period of drought is followed by heavy rains, the fruits tend to crack and split open.

There are two types of plants, the determinate or bush tomatoes and the indeterminate or staking tomatoes. The bush tomatoes find favor with most prairie gardeners; the staking varieties are grown by those who are prepared to devote more time to their culture for the sake of better-quality fruit. The staking tomato, if allowed to grow naturally, makes a large, spreading plant with an abundance of leaves and fruit that is very late in ripening or may not ripen at all. Staking tomatoes will ripen the lower trusses of fruit in most parts of the prairies if strong plants are put out in June and grown on a single stem. They should be set two feet apart in rows three to four feet apart; strong, four-foot stakes are placed in the ground with each plant at the time of planting. The pruning starts when the first side shoots appear in the leaf axils. These growths are pinched out while they are still small so that all the plant's energy is directed into the main stem. During the latter part of June and through most of July, the pruning will have to be done every few days and the main stem tied to the stake as required. Soft string, raffia or twistems can be used as ties to secure the plant to the stake loosely, so as not to interfere with the expansion of the stem. The flower truss develops at a point on the main stem about half-way between the leaves. This simplifies the pruning

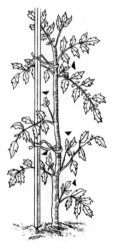

The shoots growing in the leaf axils are removed to concentrate energy in the main stem. Flower trusses are never produced in the leaf axils, but emerge on the main stem at a point midway between the leaf axils.

operation, as only vegetative shoots develop in the leaf axils. Tomatoes are self-pollinating; the anthers dehisce to drop pollen on the developing stigmas. When the flowers are opening, it may help the set of fruit to tap the stakes to distribute the pollen.

It is not necessary or desirous to remove the lower leaves of bush or staking tomatoes to speed up the ripening process; plants which have had the lower leaves removed expose the fruits to strong sunlight that bleaches the skins and downgrades the quality of fruit. Tomatoes need heat to ripen their fruit; light is important for the proper functioning of the leaves. Mature, green fruit can be ripened in a dark, warm cupboard. It is not recommended to store them in the basement; cool, damp storage provides ideal conditions for the rapid propagation of disease organisms.

Husk tomato — Two or three species of husk tomatoes or ground cherries have a limited value as preserves. The fruits have a papery covering and are either yellow or black. The yellow-fruited physalis ripens its fruit quite early and is much larger than the black. The plants are easy to grow; in the warm, longer season areas, the seed can be planted outdoors; elsewhere, it is given the same treatment as the tomatoes. The plants spread widely, needing about two feet each way for their full development and a place in the sun where the soil is well drained.

Pepper — Peppers vary in shape and size, in color and in flavor. The sweet green peppers are the type grown chiefly in prairie gardens. The fruits ripen yellow or red and are used in salads, pickles and as stuffed peppers. The hot cayenne peppers with long, tapering fruits are used for seasoning and are not so important as the sweet peppers.

The plants are started from seed sown indoors towards the end of March; they are transplanted to frames and then outdoors when danger of frost is past. The general culture is similar to that of tomatoes, but the plants should be spaced a foot apart in two-foot rows. Peppers will do best in full sun where the soil is not too heavy, but well drained and rich in plant nutrients.

Eggplant — The eggplant is not an important crop in prairie gardens although, in the warmer parts, it can be grown successfully. The fruits are large, usually black or purplish black, and each plant produces only one or two. The plants, which are extremely tender, should be started from seed sown in mid-March, gradually inured to outdoor conditions and set out in the open ground not before the end of the first week of June. The spacing should be the same as that recommended for the peppers; the soil should be light and friable, rich in nutrients and well-drained.

Cucurbit Vegetables in the Prairie Garden

The cucurbits include the cucumbers, melons, marrows, pumpkins and squash. They are tender plants, mostly trailing, though some are bush types. The cucumbers are most popular in prairie gardens; a few plants will provide sufficient fruits for salads and pickles. All members of the cucurbit family are extremely tender to frost, so seeding must be postponed until the ground has warmed and danger of frost has passed. The last week of May is reasonably safe in the southern prairies but sowings made at this time in other areas may be destroyed by frost unless plant protectors cover the young plants.

Cucumber — Cucumbers can be grown in hills or in a continuous row.

Seedlings from a sowing made in hills can be protected from a light frost by placing hot caps in position when the seed is sown; a few hills protected in this way will provide enough early cucumbers for an average family. The hills are spaced four feet apart on all sides and four or five seeds are planted to each. The seedlings are thinned to three plants to a hill by the time they reach the four-leaf stage.

The main crop for pickling may be planted in a continuous row. Half a dozen seeds are dropped at six-inch spacings in rows four to six feet apart. The seed is covered with an inch of fine soil which should be moist and warm for quick germination. The young plants are later thinned to stand singly at a foot apart.

Cucumbers do best in full sun where the soil is rich in humus and well drained. Light doses of high nitrogen fertilizer applied in June will stimulate rapid growth. A side dressing of 16.20.0, raked and watered in along the row, will be most beneficial when the first flower buds open.

Plant breeders have developed cucumber plants that produce a female flower at every leaf joint. These gynaeceous or all-female plants need a pollinating variety to ensure a crop of fruit. Some have a percentage of a pollinating variety mixed with the seed, but a good set of fruit is assured if ordinary varieties are planted near the all-female plants. It is important to keep the fruits picked off while they are in the immature stage. If you allow them to ripen on the vine, they quickly exhaust the plant and reduce its productivity.

Melon – Muskmelons and watermelons are not important crops in the home garden, though ripe melons can be produced in most seasons on the southern prairies. To obtain the best results, seed should be sown under hot caps around the third week of May. Choose a site sheltered from the northwest and open to the full sun; the soil must warm up rapidly to get the plants away to a good start. Success in producing ripe melons will depend on choosing an early variety, planting the seeds as early as it is safe and the number of frost-free days. Every so often, we get a long growing

---

PERENNIALS

From Top Left:
Lupins, in flower briefly in June.
Bristol Fairy, an improved form of the double-flowered babysbreath.
The Oriental poppy gives early and brilliant red flowers that soon drop their petals.
Morden Pink lythrum blooms profusely over a long period.
The gaillardia or blanketflower, an improved native plant that blooms all through the summer and into the fall.
Peonies have ironclad hardiness with showy flowers in July.
The hardy, award-winning Morden Cameo chrysanthemum, flowering in September.
The gasplant blooms freely in July; later on, the seed pods are attractive.

season with high temperatures both day and night during July and August and no killing frost until September is well advanced. When this occurs, both muskmelons and watermelons will produce high quality, fully ripe fruit. Melons demand abundant heat; cool, damp weather retards growth and delays the set of fruits.

Melons are a practical crop in gardens where room is not restricted and where the soil is suitable. It is useless to attempt to grow melons on heavy, cold soils. Muskmelons need plenty of room; two or three plants in hills four feet apart will cover the ground. If the seed is planted in rows, thin the plants to stand a foot apart when they have made four leaves. In the farm garden there may be room for several rows; if so, space them four or five feet apart.

Watermelons take more room than muskmelons; only in areas where the soil is light and the number of frost-free days adequate to ripen the fruit is it possible to grow them with any success. The Mennonite farmers of southern Manitoba brought seed of early watermelons from their homeland in Russia and, in most seasons, they managed to produce ripe fruit. Watermelons are produced on large acreages in Georgia and other southern states in America. Modern transportation usually makes it more worthwhile to ship these melons to prairie cities and towns than to spend time and energy cultivating them.

Vegetable marrow – The vegetable marrow is not an important crop in prairie gardens, although people from England consider the young, tender fruits a delicacy. The bush types are preferred for their compact habit of growth but the trailing or vine types may be trained on supports if space is limited, or they can be used to cover a pile of manure or a compost heap.

Like the rest of the tribe of cucurbits, marrows are tender to frost and outdoor sowing must be delayed until the end of May. Sow three seeds to a hill, spacing the hills four or five feet apart for the bush marrow. Thin the seedlings to a single plant when they have three or four leaves. Well-drained, fertile soil and a place in the sun is required, as well as plenty of water when the plants are growing freely. Overfeeding with high nitrogen fertilizers will produce more leaves than fruits; lighter stimulants

---

BULBS

From Top:

The monadelphum or Caucasian lily, June-flowering and heavily scented.

The florets of the daylily, which is not a true lily, fade quickly, but a selection of varieties gives bloom over a long period.

The centifolium lily is hardier, taller and more reliable than the better-known regal lily.

Tulipa tarda, a May flowering species suited to the rock garden.

will ensure a regular supply of young marrows from August until frost comes.

Marrows must be picked while they are still young; fruits that have reached a length of eight to ten inches are fit for use and should be harvested without delay. If marrows are allowed to ripen on the vine, the plants soon become exhausted. The hybrid marrow zucchini, known as squash, is gaining in popularity in prairie gardens. The culture is similar to that of the bush marrows except that it is even more important to cut the fruits while they are still quite small.

Pumpkin — Large pumpkins are grown for fun; enormous fruits are usually on display at the local shows, where they arouse considerable interest and comment. The varieties with smaller fruits and finer-grained flesh are preferred for culinary use. The pumpkin is a trailing plant which may be allowed to run rampant to cover a large area or trained on a sturdy fence. Seed is sown about May twentieth in hills two feet apart, and covered with an inch of soil. As a general rule, pumpkins are slow to set fruit, the plants producing a tremendous amount of growth before the first fruits set. The growth should be allowed to develop freely but, after the first fruits have set, a limited amount of pruning can be done. Nip back the tip growths to a point three or four leaves beyond the fruit and allow only one fruit to set on each shoot.

A bush-type pumpkin with small fruit of good quality has been developed by the horticultural field station at Cheyenne, Wyoming. It is particularly valuable for the small garden and should be given the same general culture as the bush marrow. Pumpkins must be mature and ripe before they are harvested; the rind should be hard, whereas the rind of the marrow should be soft and easily pierced with the thumbnail. Pumpkins will keep for months when the fruits are fully ripe and harvested without bruising. A week or ten days in a warm room finishes the ripening process; the fruits are then placed on a shelf where the temperature is forty degrees and the air quite dry. In cool, damp storage the fruits soon go bad, especially if they have been bruised to allow the entry of disease spores.

Squash — The squashes are a mixture of several species. Some are used while the fruits are small and immature; others are grown to full size, for use in the late summer and fall or for winter storage. There are many different kinds in varying shapes and sizes. The bush types are most practical for the small garden; those with long vines take up too much room. The buttercup, patty pan and acorn squashes, all bush types, are unique. Some varieties are green, some golden orange; others are creamy white or bluish gray. The texture of the skin varies from smooth to rough or warted. The various forms of hubbard squash are favored for winter use; the flesh is fine grained, bright orange and makes a pie filling similar to pumpkin.

The culture of squashes is the same as that outlined for marrows. They are all extremely tender to frost, so seeding outdoors should be delayed until late in May. Earlier sowings, covered with hot caps, are practical in southern areas.

Sweet Corn in the Prairie Garden

Sweet corn is one of the delicacies of the prairie garden, relished by most people when the cobs are picked at the peak of quality and cooked without delay. In most parts of the prairies, there is a wide range of varieties and in most seasons they can be depended upon to produce good quality cobs. In northern areas, however, where frost-free days are more limited, only the earliest sorts should be planted.

Sweet corn is a warm weather crop requiring a deep, fertile soil with plenty of nitrogen and moisture. Since the corn plant is wind-pollinated, sow the seed in a block rather than in a single row. May tenth to twentieth is corn planting time in the southern prairies; begin about a week later in other parts. It is not uncommon for the tip growth to be frozen as the plants emerge but they will usually recover and go on to produce a crop. Space the seeds four to six inches apart in the row and cover them with not more than two inches of well-pulverized soil. Thin the seedlings to single plants spaced at one foot and keep the topsoil stirred regularly to keep down weeds and to assist the young plants to grow rapidly. Where space is not limited, drop five or six seeds in hills spaced three or four feet apart on all sides. Reduce the seedlings to not more than three strong plants per hill and use a mechanical cultivator to work the soil both ways. In northern areas, where sweet corn may be a bit uncertain, cover the seeded hills with hot caps; always, of course, try to choose the warmest and most sheltered part of the garden for planting.

Any number of hybrid sweet corn varieties are on the market; most of them make tall, vigorous plants with large cobs. For uniform maturity and high tolerance of disease as well as heavy yields of large cobs, the hybrids are well recommended; on the other hand, there are those who still look to the open-pollinated Golden Bantam for high-quality sweet corn.

The popcorn is more or less a novelty plant that includes a few ornamental varieties as well as some that are used for popping. The ornamental sorts, Rainbow and Strawberry, make colorful table decorations for Thanksgiving and Halloween. The Japanese hulless and some others are best for making popcorn. The kernels must be ripe and thoroughly dry for popping; a two-year-old sample will likely pop better than fresh kernels. The culture of popcorn is the same as outlined for sweet corn.

Herbs in the Prairie Garden

Herbs are aromatic plants either annual or perennial; most of them grow well and take up little room in the garden. Some of the perennial herbs are hardy — mint, chives and thyme are examples, though mint may die out unless the plants are kept vigorous by regular transplanting. Some of the annual herbs require a long season, so they are sown indoors, transplanted to boxes and then to the open ground in June. Most of them, however, will make usable plants from seed sown in the open ground during the early part of May.

Anise *(Pimpenella anisum)* — The green leaves of anise are sometimes used in salads; the seeds flavor cakes and bread as well as soups and stews. Sow the seeds in May in warm soil; thin the plants to stand a foot apart.

Basil *(Ocymum basilicum)* — Sweet basil is a tender annual native to India and other parts of tropical Asia. It is used to flavor poultry, various meat dishes and fish. The plants require a long season, so the seed is best sown indoors in March, transplanting the young seedlings to boxes and then to the open ground in June. The flower stems are cut before the seed forms and tied in bundles to dry for winter use.

Borage *(Borago officinalis)* — Borage thrives best in a poor soil, preferably in full sun. The flowers, which are attractive to bees, are used for flavoring drinks; the leaves when young and tender may be used in salads. The plants grow up to two feet tall and need to be thinned to stand a foot and a half apart. Sow the seed in early May in soil that is deep and fertile.

Florence fennel *(Foeniculum dulce)* — Fennel is a sweet-tasting herb popular with some Europeans; it may be eaten raw or boiled. Sow the seed in May; thin the plants to about six inches and, when the bases of the stems begin to swell, the plants should be earthed up.

Hoarhound *(Marrubium vulgare)* — Hoarhound is a medicinal plant from which is extracted a substance used to relieve irritating coughs. Sow the seed outdoors in May and thin the plants to stand about a foot apart.

Marigold *(Calendula officinalis)* — The pot marigold is grown chiefly for garden decoration and for cut flowers. The seeds often produce volunteer plants in the garden and the young plants are tolerant of light frost. For culinary purposes, the flowers are dried to color drinks and flavor soups.

Marjoram *(Origanum marjoranum)* — The sweet knotted marjoram is used as a tonic as well as a flavoring for meat dishes, soups and salads. It should be gathered and dried for winter use just before the flowers open. Sow the seed in well-prepared ground in May, thinning the young plants to stand nine inches to a foot apart.

Mint *(Mentha viridis)* — Mint is not a long-lived plant in prairie gardens and, unless it is grown in a well-sheltered spot and transplanted every two or three years, it soon dies. It requires a well-drained soil and needs the protection of a deep cover of snow or the plants kill out in the winter. The shallow roots can also be injured when the plants are under water from melting snow in the spring.

Parsley *(Petroselinum crispum)* — Parsley is one of the most useful as well as one of the hardiest herbs in the garden. It will grow in poor soil but, to produce large, handsome specimens, a well-tilled heavy loam is best. Sow the seed as soon as the ground dries in the spring, scattering a few radish seeds along the row to facilitate early hoeing. Parsley seed is usually sown so thickly that the young plants start out crowded in the row; too often, they are allowed to stay that way. Early thinning is important, leaving the young plants three inches apart; later on, they are thinned to stand not less than six inches apart. By thinning the plants early, giving them sufficient room for their full development, and by gathering the outside leaves from the plant through the summer months, there will be less chance of the plants going to seed. Once the plant pushes up a flower stem it is of no further use. The leaves of parsley can be dried for winter use; at the same time the leaves are harvested, select a plant or two with well-curled leaves and transplant them to six-inch pots in October. In a cool, sunny window, they will continue to provide parsley through the winter.

The turnip-rooted parsley *(Petroselinum radicosum)* is rarely seen in prairie gardens, though it is easy to grow in ordinary soil. The leaves are not curled like the common parsley and are not so useful for flavoring. The roots thicken like parsnips and are used in soups and stews.

Purslane *(Portulaca oleracea)* — The succulent shoots of purslane are relished by some either as a cooked vegetable or served raw in a salad. It grows well in sandy soil and most prairie gardeners rightly consider it an abominable weed.

Sage *(Salvia officinalis)* — The well-known poultry-dressing herb is a perennial plant, usually cultivated here as an annual since it is too tender to stand the prairie winter. Young plants may be set out in June from seedlings started indoors in March, or seed may be sown in the open ground in early May. The plants should be six inches apart in well-drained soil, preferably in full sun, to develop a full, pungent flavor. The leaves are used either fresh or dried in meat dishes, soups and chowders.

Thyme *(Thymus vulgaris)* — The well-known aromatic thyme can be grown from seed sown indoors in March or in the open ground in early May. The tiny seeds need careful handling; the soil should be well pulverized and porous. Several thyme species are hardy, low-growing edging plants with colorful flowers. Some can be used as substitutes for the common thyme while others, such as the caraway-scented thyme *(Thymus herba barona)* and the lemon-scented thyme *(Thymus serphyllum citriodorum),* have special culinary uses.

Seventeen

Growing Fruit in the Home Garden

The early settlers soon found that many kinds of fruit grew wild all across the prairies. In sheltered areas, strawberries, raspberries, gooseberries and currants could be gathered in season to be preserved for food. In some parts there were blueberries or Saskatoons as well as chokecherries, highbush cranberries, plums and pincherries. It was not long before those who came from eastern Canada or European countries tried to grow apples and pears. One of the first to grow apples successfully in Manitoba was A. P. Stevenson, who made the first attempt in 1876. His earliest plantings were killed out but later ones, which included a number of hardy Russian sorts, did so well that a commercial apple and plum orchard was started, which by 1921 produced an annual crop of three hundred barrels. He is commemorated by the Stevenson Memorial Medal, awarded every three or four years to one who has made an outstanding contribution to horticulture on the prairies.

The Planting and Care of Fruit Trees

Shelter and moisture — Because of the work of pioneers in all three prairie provinces, suitable apples and plums, cherries and apricots can be grown and enjoyed by those who are prepared to provide shelter for the young trees, to take care of their moisture and nutritional needs and to protect them from rodents, insects and disease. In urban gardens, shelter from adjacent buildings is generally sufficient to protect the trees from drying winter winds. In the larger and often more exposed rural garden, windbreaks of hardy trees have to be set out except where shelter from natural trees or rising land is present.

In the farm garden, there is usually room enough to set out three or four rows of trees on the north and west boundaries of the orchard and a single row on the south side, leaving the east side open. The main purpose of such a shelterbelt is to cut down the force of wind to lessen its desiccating effect on the young branches and opening blossoms. It also catches snow, piling it in a warm blanket to insulate the tree roots against deep, penetrating frost. Furthermore, the trapped snow melts to add to the available moisture, vital in prairie gardens since the normal supply of rain is insufficient in most areas. On the broad plains where most of the cereal crops are grown, rainfall is never copious, seldom sufficient and often scanty.

Soil — In some parts of the prairies there are problem soils; some, being highly alkaline, need special preparation before fruit trees can be grown successfully. Other soils may be too sandy or too heavy. Where the soil is sandy and low in humus and nitrogen, growth is stunted, fruit small and the trees short lived. On the other hand, if the soil is heavy clay there may be a drainage problem. The ideal soil is medium loam, porous enough to allow the free drainage of excess water but with sufficient humus to ensure adequate moisture throughout a normal growing season.

Climate — If the site faces to the northeast, so much the better, for here there will be less fluctuation in the spring temperatures. Land that slopes in the opposite direction will be a poor choice for fruit trees, as the trees are exposed to bark injury caused by direct and reflected rays of the sun, particularly in the early spring. Sunscald can be a serious problem even in urban gardens when trees are planted on the southwest side of buildings with the trunks exposed to direct sunlight. Besides the danger from sunscald, trees near buildings often are excited into early growth only to have the flower buds damaged by spring frost. The number of days without frost varies from north to south by as much as twenty days but, even in the most favored areas, there is danger that a late spring frost will kill most of the flowers to ruin the crop of fruit. One thing *can* be depended upon — the long hours of sunlight, which are needed to ripen the wood before winter comes.

Hardiness — In selecting trees for a prairie orchard, hardiness is the first consideration. Unless the tree is suited to the climate, and this means it must be able to survive extremely low temperatures, excessive heat and drought and ripen the current year's wood before the first hard frost comes, it is of no use in a prairie garden. There are species of apples, pears, plums and apricots growing in countries with long, cold winters, short, hot summers and scant rainfall, such as we have in most of the prairies. It is from these hardy species that the most promising new varieties have been developed. The popular sorts of apples, plums and cherries seen in the markets are not suited to the prairie climate. The wise gardener will study the recommended fruit lists which are prepared by the provincial departments of agriculture in the three prairie provinces. Besides this, he will study the zone map and be guided by the recommendations for his particular area. In the most favored spots, where the rainfall averages about twenty inches and the number of frost-free days are about 120, it is possible to grow a wide selection of fruit trees. In some areas, however, there is little chance of success except with the hardiest crabapples.

When to plant fruit trees — In milder parts, the season for planting fruit trees starts in late autumn and continues through the winter months up until March. In the prairie regions, autumn planting is not recommended since, by the time the leaves are mature and ready to drop, hard frosts and sometimes heavy snowfall make planting risky or impossible. Plant in the spring as soon as the ground is dry enough to work. The planting dates may vary from year to year but, by the first week of May, the soil is usually ready for planting. The date on the calendar is not, however, so important as the state of the soil and the condition of the trees.

Choosing the stock — The best kind of tree is young; a one- or two-year-old plant will transplant with far less shock than an older tree and make more growth in the first few years. The best trees are produced by the prairie nurserymen; order them early so that you will have them on hand when the time comes to plant.

When the trees arrive, open the bundle to check the roots for moisture and to examine the bark for shrivelling. If the roots appear to be dry and the bark shrivelled, soak the roots in a tub of water overnight but no

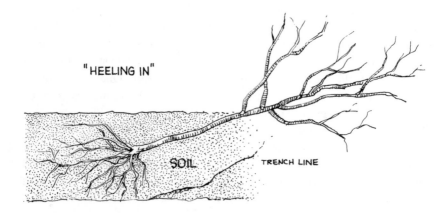

"HEELING IN"

SOIL   TRENCH LINE

longer, then bury the plants in a cool spot for a few days to plump up the stems and revive the roots. If the soil is too wet when the bundle arrives or if for some other reason planting must be delayed, the trees can be "heeled in" by laying them close together in a sloping trench, covering the roots and about one-third of the tree. Firm the soil and keep the roots moist while waiting for the time when the trees can be planted in their permanent quarters. It is better to wait a week than plant when the land is too wet.

Planting fruit trees — Fruit trees are intended to occupy space for a long time, so make sure they are planted properly. Dig a hole about two feet across and two feet deep, loosening the subsoil with a square-tined fork. The topsoil, which should be kept separate from the subsoil, is used to pack around the roots; the poorer subsoil will be spread around the surface. By adding a pailful of granulated peat to the topsoil, there will be sufficient soil to fill the hole without using the subsoil. Place a small mound of soil in the hole before you set the plant. See that the roots are fully extended and not doubled up. Any that are broken or ruptured should be shortened with a sharp knife or secateurs; make a diagonal cut, starting from the underside of the root to leave the cut portion facing downwards. Well-pulverized topsoil is worked in among the roots as the tree is shaken and gently pulled up to the planting depth. The right depth is about an inch deeper than it grew in the nursery; an inch or so deeper in sandy soil will not hurt but deeper planting in heavy clay soil will hinder the development of new roots. The soil is made very firm around the roots by tramping, starting when the hole is half full. By leaving a shallow depression around each plant, watering is made easier. Give each plant a pailful immediately, and more should the soil be very dry. Once the water has seeped away and before the surface soil dries, level the ground around the trees, leaving a shallow layer of loose soil.

Pruning apples — At planting time, young apple trees must be pruned. Pruning is necessary to restore a balance between the root system, which has been mutilated to some extent as the tree was dug out, and the top. One-year-old trees are called whips; they have a single slender stem which grew in one season from a bud inserted in the understock the previous summer. This stem should be cut back to about twelve inches. A newly planted, one-year-old tree, headed back to this height, will produce low branches to protect the main trunk from sunscald. The lowest branch is best pointed to the southwest to shade the area of the main trunk most liable to injury from sunscald. The main branches should be spaced about a foot apart, selecting those with the widest angles. Branches with narrow crotches are weaker and often provide an entry for disease organisms. A well-shaped tree has about six wide-angled branches and a single, upright leader or main shoot, with all surplus shoots pruned back flush with the branch or main trunk. The previous year's growth on an older tree is reduced by a third to a half, depending on the vigor of the tree. Branches that cross over other branches or head into the centre of the tree are cut out.

PRUNING AN APPLE TREE

The current year's shoots on the main, wide-angled branches are cut back to an outfacing bud to keep the tree growing upwards rather than allowing it to spread. Surplus shoots are pruned back flush with the main branch or trunk.

Clean cuts made with sharp tools heal rapidly; bad pruning leads to trouble when stubs die to provide an entry for disease. When branches an inch or more thick have to be cut, treat the wounds with tree paint. Special preparations are obtainable but a mixture of linseed oil and white lead, painted on wounds as soon as the pruning is done, will ensure rapid healing and keep out disease.

Sooner or later, apple trees get old and many will carry the scars of wounds suffered in storms or unseasonable frosts. There is no merit in coddling a worn-out tree; you are farther ahead to dig it out by the roots, burn it and plant a young tree in its place. It is a mistake to replant a young apple tree where an old one grew unless you first replace the old soil with well-enriched, new soil brought from another part of the garden. It has been shown in a number of root studies made at the East Malling Research Station, Maidstone, England, that young apple trees made less root and consequently less growth when planted in soil which had previously been used to grow apples. On the other hand, apple trees planted in soil which had previously grown plums made more roots and more growth.

Pruning plums — Young trees are headed back to two feet high when they are planted. Plum trees need different pruning techniques than those applied to apples. The main top branch should grow unrestricted for two or three years before it is pruned back by one third of its height, to induce the development of strong, wide crotches. After this, very little pruning is needed except to cut back stray branches, especially any vigorous basal shoots that are liable to wind damage.

Pruning cherry plums — The cherry plums bear the best fruit on one-year-old wood, much the same as do the black currants. Old, worn-out wood is cut back to ground level to encourage strong basal shoots to develop and produce fruit buds. Decrepit plants will not survive the winter as well as those with strong, vigorous branches. The pruning can be done as soon as the ground dries up in the spring.

Fruit bud initiation — Sooner or later, all fruit trees make flowers which, if fertilized, produce fruit. As a general rule, pears take longer than apples, and apples take longer than plums. Sandcherry hybrids bear fruit on young trees and it is not uncommon for three-year-old trees to bear a crop of fruit. There are several ways to speed up the process of fruit-bud initiation but none are infallible. Young apple trees in rich soil tend to make vigorous shoots and only leaf buds; similarly, fertilizing and irrigating stimulate vegetative growth of young trees and often delay blossoming. Root pruning is sometimes effective in slowing down vegetative growth to encourage the development of fruit buds. A trench two feet deep is dug around the tree; not closer to the trunk than the spread of the branches. The soil is replaced in the trench, made firm by treading and watering if it should be dry. The operation is best done in September or early October. Another method of slowing up growth is to remove a thin strip of bark from several branches at a point a few inches from the main trunk. This girdling is done around the middle of June when the tree is in lush growth and the bark peels back from the wood easily. The strip of bark should not be more than one-quarter of an inch thick, nor should more than three or four branches be girdled on a young tree. The desired results are not always obtained by these methods and it would seem that some trees cannot be induced to initiate flower buds simply by root pruning or girdling.

A single tree isolated from suitable pollinator trees may not carry a crop of fruit though it bears blossoms regularly. As a general rule, the cultivated varieties of apples and plums do not set fruit freely unless the blossoms are fertilized by pollen from another variety. In some instances, a variety is self-fertile and all that is needed is good weather and enough bees or other pollinating insects to work over the blossoms. The pollen of crabapples is compatible with the blossoms of apples. Selections and hybrids of the native plum usually bloom about the same time to pollinate each other. Triflora or salicina plums and the late-blooming sorts can be adequately fertilized by sandcherries. The backyard gardener may have no pollinating problem with his apples and plums if his neighbor is growing fruit trees and, if the weather is sunny and warm when the trees blossom, bees travelling miles to seek the nectar will transfer pollen in the process. **Summer care of fruit trees** — The seasonal growth of apple trees starts in May, continues through June and is completed in July. The amount and frequency of watering required during the first season will depend on the amount of rain. While it is important for the roots to be in well-moistened soil, it is possible to water too often and keep the soil so soggy wet that aeration is greatly reduced and new roots are slow in forming. Young trees should be watered in periods of drought, especially if they carry a crop of fruit after the June drop when unfertilized apples fall off. Those remaining will size up rapidly if there is plenty of soil moisture and nutrients. When the fruit has reached its full size, further watering is not necessary; in fact, it may prove harmful by delaying the ripening of the young wood. If the soil is dry in October, it is wise to give the trees a final watering to prevent them from drying out over winter.

Some fruit trees that tend to bear enormous quantities of fruit should be thinned or the weight will break down the branches. Thinning is done in late June or early July; later thinning has little if any benefit in sizing up the fruit that is left on the tree. It is usual to leave one fruit to a cluster but, if a large number of fruiting spurs have developed on a branch, you may remove some of them. One apple to each nine inches of branch will be a good crop. The fruit on overloaded trees will not only be small; it will exhaust the tree and lessen the chances of satisfactory winter survival.

Fertilizing fruit trees — Most of the soil in prairie gardens is suitable for fruit trees without special preparation, though in some areas certain elements may be in short supply. Healthy trees have large, dark green leaves and bear fruits typical of the variety. Yellowish leaves may indicate a deficiency of nitrogen; if the yellow leaves have prominent green veins, the trouble is likely to be a deficiency of iron. Small, dull green leaves that turn reddish bronze may indicate insufficient phosphorous. Potash deficiency is manifest in dull green and brown discolorations on the leaf margins. Deficiencies in minor soil elements are sometimes the cause of peculiar discolorations of the leaves.

No matter how well balanced the soil's supply of plant nutrients, over a period of time trees will exhaust the supply; when this occurs, supplementary nutrients must be added to maintain healthy growth. Either 16.20.0 or 11.48.0 can be used at the rate of one pound to a hundred square feet. Spread it evenly, starting at the outside branches, not close to the trunk. Early May is a good time to put it on, raking it in for the spring and early summer rains to make soluble. Fertilizing the trees in August or September is not recommended, as it tends to promote lush growth at a time when the wood should be hardening. If your trees show peculiar leaf discolorations, it is better to obtain professional advice to ascertain the cause of the trouble than to treat them with a fertilizer that may aggravate the very condition you are trying to correct.

In the farm orchard, cover crops may be used to maintain the fertility of the soil but, unless you have a supply of water, the trees make better growth in cultivated soil. A cover crop of fall rye, oats, barley or field peas will use up any excess moisture and help to harden the wood; moreover, it insulates the soil against deep frost penetration and holds a cover of snow. On the debit side, it encourages mice to winter in comfort near the trees where they can do a lot of damage by gnawing the bark.

Wintering fruit trees – Winter injury is manifest in a number of ways. Young shoots that were green and full of sap may have been caught by a hard frost in late September; when this occurs, they tip kill. Cultural practices should be adjusted to prevent this from happening by discontinuing the use of fertilizers and supplemental water in August. Late summer weeds may do more good than harm by sapping excess soil moisture to speed the process of ripening the young shoots of fruit trees. Sudden and severe frosts may split the bark of young trees if they are lush and green. Bark damage can lead to serious debilitation or death of the tree; repairs should be prompt and effective. Loose bark should be fastened firm with large-headed tacks or a heavy stapler before the wound is coated with grafting wax.

Since most, if not all of the trees sold by prairie nurserymen are budded on seedling understocks, there is naturally some variation in compatibility and hardiness. It is not uncommon for severe frosts to occur when the ground is bare of snow, to penetrate deep in the soil, killing or severely injuring the roots. The damage is first indicated the following spring when the leaves fail to develop normally and the flowers are blanched and emaciated; the leaves die because the roots no longer supply moisture. By season's end, the tree is dead and those who are unaware of what has happened will wonder why. Snow has tremendous insulating value, so it should be prevented from blowing to leave the soil bare around the roots of fruit trees. Snow fences, branches of deciduous trees or shrubs, evergreen boughs, corn stalks or garden trash will hold snow and may save a valuable tree. Before the ground freezes over in early November, see that fruit trees in dry soil are given a final watering. All else being equal, they survive the cold weather in better shape when there is plenty of moisture at the root.

Even in the best regulated orchards there is the chance of injury from unseasonable weather. Three nights of hard frost in mid-May 1946 did enormous damage not only to apple trees but to many ornamental shrubs in southern Manitoba. Good weather previously had advanced the fruit trees fully two weeks ahead of a normal season. On May ninth, many apple trees were in full bloom; on the twelfth, twenty degrees of frost destroyed most of the blossoms besides ruining plum and apricot crops. In 1942, a sudden frost of twelve degrees on the twenty-fifth of September had disastrous results, as young shoots on apple trees were caught in a green state. These abnormal temperatures are rare but, when they strike, the damage is enormous. Low and unseasonable temperatures can occur at either end of the growing season but spring frost is generally most damaging because it destroys the food-making potential of trees. New leaves take their sustenance from built-up reserves stored in branches and roots. When new leaves are killed by a spring frost, the tree is in shock until it has developed new leaves. It is not unusual for a tree to die the year following a severe, late spring frost.

Propagating fruit trees — Trees and other plants that have existed for countless generations can reproduce their kind by the natural process of seeds. The seedlings from these species plants maintain the character of the parent without change. Fruit trees and other plants which have been developed by man are usually hybrids of such mixed ancestry and complex make-up that their progeny differ, one from another. To perpetuate a particular variety requires that it be increased by one of several methods of vegetative propagation. To raise a large number of one variety, either budding or grafting is in general use.

Budding — The most common method of budding used in the production of fruit trees, roses and a number of other plants is the shield or T method. In dryland areas, where the use of the shield method may be restricted to a limited season or impractical because the bark adheres too tightly to the wood, another method known as plate budding can be substituted.

The process of T budding is not difficult if a few simple rules are followed. The understock on which the bud is to be inserted should be about pencil thickness, young and vigorous. One-year-old seedlings of crabapples lined out in the spring can be budded the same summer if they are not restricted in their growth by drought; old stocks or those that are too thick are difficult to work and the chances of success are greatly reduced. Budding begins about the middle of July and continues for several weeks if the weather is favorable and the bark separates easily from the wood. In dry weather, the bark is not so easily lifted and shield budding may be difficult or impossible.

The budwood is obtained from shoots of the current year's growth; old wood is not suitable. At the base of each leaf is a dormant bud or eye; the ones nearest the branch are more mature than those at the top of the shoot. The best kind of bud is located in the midsection of the shoot. The leaves are removed immediately, leaving a portion of the petiole or leaf stem as a handle. The budsticks must be kept moist in damp peat or wet sacking. A T-shaped cut is made low down on the seedling stock, deep enough to penetrate the bark. The bark is lifted carefully at the corners of the T shape cut in readiness to slide the bud into place. The bud is sliced off thinly with a sliver of wood attached. (It was once considered important to remove the sliver of wood before inserting the bud into the stock, but it has been shown in a number of tests that the removal of wood makes no difference to the success or failure of the operation. It is much more important to use a very sharp knife and cut the bud thin.) The bud is gently pushed down under the bark, then the top portion of the wood still attached to the bud is cut off flush with the horizontal cut in the understock to make a neat fit. Raffia or rubber bands are used to bind the buds to the stock; both materials are suitable, but rubber bands are quicker to put on and can be left to deteriorate and rot, whereas raffia has to be cut when scion and stock are joined in about three weeks.

"T" BUDDING

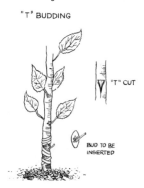

Plate budding, which may be necessary if the bark adheres too tightly to the wood, requires that a slice of bark be cut from the stock to be budded, making the cut an inch long and a quarter of an inch wide. You must leave a flap of bark at the base of the cut to hold the bud in place until you bind it with raffia or a rubber band. The bud is cut from the scion in the same way as described for the shield or T method. The buds are more likely to dry out when you use the plate method, so it is important to keep out the air by tying them tightly.

PLATE BUDDING

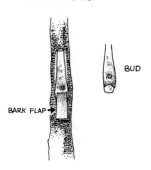

It is a good indication that scion and stock have united when the petiole or leaf stalk attached to the bud falls off at the slightest touch. The bud remains dormant through the winter but grows into a vigorous shoot the following spring. In May the stock is cut back, forcing all the plant's energy into the new shoot. By leaving a stub three inches long to which the young shoot is tied, it will not be necessary to use stakes. If the stock is cut back close to the union, leaving the new shoot without support, it may be blown out or accidentally broken off.

Grafting – Grafting is a method of propagation used by nurserymen and skilled gardeners to increase the number of a certain variety, to topwork an established tree and to repair trees that are damaged by rodents. Topworking is the placement of grafts on branches of established trees to change a poor variety to a good one. Root grafting is done to increase stock; the most commonly used method is the whip-and-tongue graft. To ensure the union of scion and stock, the narrow layers of cells underlying the outer bark of each have to be in contact. If scion and stock are the same thickness, contact can be made on both sides; otherwise, only one side can be united. This does not prevent a good union as long as the stock is vigorous and the scion wood plump and dormant.

To make a whip-and-tongue graft, the pieces to be united should be about the same thickness and not more than half an inch in diameter. A diagonal cut two or three inches long is made in both scion and stock. Starting in the centre of this cut another cut is made, extending two-thirds the length of the first cut. The scion, which is a piece of last year's wood with three or four buds, is cut in the same way, then the two are fitted together to interlock firmly. Before binding the graft with waxed thread or nurseryman's tape, check to see that scion and stock are in contact on at least one side. A coat of grafting wax is painted on to exclude air.

WHIP AND TONGUE GRAFTING

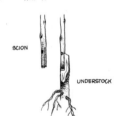

SCION

UNDERSTOCK

The narrow layers of cells lining the bark of both scion and stock must be in contact on at least one side.

A cleft graft is used when topworking apple trees, selecting suitable-sized branches spaced at equal distance throughout the tree. The branches are cut off square, then a cleft is made in the stub end. The scion is tapered, wedged into the cleft flush with the bark, bound with tape and waxed.

Bridge grafting and in-arching are used to save trees that have been girdled by mice. When bridge grafting, several scions are grafted into the trunk above and below the injured portion after ragged edges have been trimmed even. In-arching is a method of planting seedlings around the base of the injured tree and inserting the cut face of the seedling under the bark. Bridge grafting and in-arching are highly skilled techniques and, unless the backyard gardener has had considerable experience, he had best seek professional advice when faced with the problem of damaged trees. Young trees have tender bark that is more likely to be chewed by mice and, when these young trees are girdled, it is best to dig them out and plant another tree.

Fruit Trees for the Prairies

Apple – A number of hardy large apples have been introduced to the prairies as a result of breeding work done at prairie experimental stations and by private orchardists. The hardiest full-size apple is Heyer No. 12, which was raised by Adolf Heyer at Niverville, Saskatchewan. This variety fruits on young trees but the fruit deteriorates quickly and is limited in use to cooking. Battleford is another hardy apple with better keeping qualities. Goodland, a high-quality apple both raw and cooked, does well in some prairie gardens; it is not, however, fully hardy. Consult recommended lists for other varieties; crabapples suited to prairie gardens are described in chapter eight.

Pear – Pears are still something of a novelty in prairie gardens, though a few edible varieties are hardy and, if given the best of care, will bear fruit. Like the apple varieties from the milder parts, the well-known Bartlett and others of choice quality are of no use in a prairie garden. New varieties from the University of Saskatchewan give promise and others of proven hardiness, such as Golden Spice, Tail Dropmore, Pioneer No. 3 and Ohio, should be tried. The Ussurian pear *(Pyrus ussuriensis)* has no value except as a pollinator for the edible varieties. It makes a hardy tree, rather slow in flowering but handsome and attractive when in full bloom; the leaves turn ruby red in the fall.

Pears have an upright habit of growth, and some grow tall and slender unless headed back to encourage the branches to spread out. Cut back the terminal shoots of young trees by one third of their length when you plant a pear tree.

Fireblight is a devastating disease of pears, more so than apples, and no effective remedy has been found to control it. Infected trees appear to have been scorched; the leaves turn brown on apples and black on pears. It starts at the base of the current year's growth and works upwards. Doctoring the trees with streptomycin has not given satisfactory control.

Plum — Two species of plum are found growing wild in the eastern parts of the prairies, the Canada plum *(Prunus nigra)* and the American plum *(P. americana)*. Another prunus species called the western sandcherry *(P. besseyi)* is found in some parts of the prairies where the soil is sandy. All three species have contributed hardiness to the many hybrids suitable for planting in prairie gardens. The Japanese plum *(P. salicina)* offers promise in the development of hardy, high-quality plums. At the present time there are several good varieties offered by the prairie nurserymen.

The sweet cherries are much too tender for the prairies but some of the cherry-plum hybrids, which are hybrids between the sandcherry and plum, make acceptable dessert cherries.

In favored parts of the prairies, sour cherries have been tried with good results. The fruit is excellent for pies and jellies. The Mongolian cherry *(P. fruticosa)* is a better choice, as it is fully hardy all across the prairies and fruits regularly. It makes a bushy shrub with glossy, dark green leaves and attractive crimson fruit which is esteemed for making jelly.

Select strains of the Manchu cherry *(P. tomentosa)* are sweet and juicy dessert cherries. They make colorful preserves of high quality.

Apricot — Apricots are not generally considered reliable tree fruits for the prairies, although good-quality apricots are being grown in some parts. Heavy crops of Scout apricots have been harvested occasionally at the Morden Experimental Station, where this variety originated in 1935. More often than not, through winter injury of the dormant flower buds or a late spring frost, only a light crop is produced.

Like many plants from western Asia, the apricot is inclined to break its winter dormancy early but, when the trees escape frost, they are showy in bloom. They demand a well-drained soil; soggy soil will not be tolerated for long or the roots will die. Extreme heat and dry weather cause no distress, nor are the handsome dark green leaves attacked by insects. Some of the prairie nurserymen offer improved varieties of apricots for sale. Consult your recommended list for suitable kinds.

Small Fruits in the Prairie Garden

In the backyard garden, the small fruits, or soft fruits as they are called in England, are more important than the tree fruits. Good crops of strawberries, raspberries, currants and gooseberries can be grown in prairie gardens if the hardy, adaptable sorts are planted and given the proper care. Strawberries and raspberries are the most profitable and more popular than currants and gooseberries. The home gardener who can find room for a small plantation of strawberries and raspberries will harvest satisfactory crops if he is able to provide fertile soil, shelter from northwest winds and has a supply of water on tap. In the farm garden, where small fruits can be grown on a larger scale, shelter is most important. A belt of trees tempers the wind and traps snow to increase the moisture supply. In the summer, hot, drying winds are damaging to raspberries; windbreaks on the south side help to modify their effect.

Strawberries — There is no great difficulty in supplying the right kind of soil for strawberries. As a general rule, the rich prairie soil will grow excellent fruit with little preparation. The ideal soil is deep, rich and well charged with humus to hold water, yet porous enough to drain off any excess. Good strawberries can be grown in sandy soil by digging in plenty of well-rotted barnyard manure and supplying water in generous quantities in periods of drought. A heavy soil has the disadvantage of baking and cracking, though it is more likely to be rich in nutrients. Heavy soils are mellowed with sand and peat, dug in when the strawberry bed is prepared in the fall. Peat has very little plant food — about two percent nitrogen — but it will improve the physical texture of the soil. It is not good gardening to plant strawberries on land that was grass the previous year or there may be serious trouble from grubs. Grow a crop of potatoes first, then plant the strawberries the following spring.

When to plant strawberries — There is no question that the best time to plant strawberries is in the spring. Fall planting is not recommended, as plants that are set out late in the fall stand no chance of making new roots before winter comes, nor do they stand much chance of winter survival. As soon as the soil is dry enough to work in the spring, dormant plants can be set out. Nurserymen dig the plants in the fall, storing them over winter, or they dig the plants early in the spring before growth starts. Strawberries store up food reserves in the crown of the plant to be carried over winter. A rosette of leaves is also carried over, though the outer ones are usually dry when spring comes.

Planting strawberries — There are two main systems of growing strawberries; one is the matted row, the other, the hill system. In the matted row, the young plants are set a foot and a half apart in rows spaced at four feet and allowed to grow together to form a matted row about two feet wide. The runners, young plants which are produced from the old plants in July and August, are left to stand about six inches apart. The hill system is used in milder parts and is said to produce larger and earlier fruit. However, tests at experimental farms in Ontario show that matted rows have equalled or outyielded the double-row hill system where the young plants were planted in double rows a foot apart, allowing two and one-half feet between the double rows.

The depth of planting is important: if set too deep, the growing point may smother and rot off; if too shallow, the crown and a portion of the

STRAWBERRY PLANT WITH RUNNERS

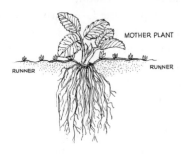

In about three years, the matted row becomes dense with new plants on the runners, which in turn produce their own runners, and the row should be dug up and replanted.

roots may dry out. The most efficient way to plant strawberries is for two persons to work together. One digs a hole deep enough to allow the roots to be fully extended and not doubled up; the other, who has the bundle of plants wrapped in wet burlap, sets the plant against the side of the hole. The plant is set so that the midpoint of the crown is level with the soil surface. The hole is filled in with well-pulverized soil and made firm around the roots by treading. By leaving a heel mark around the plant, watering is made easy; simply fill up the depression, then level the soil around the crown of the plant when the water has seeped away. A soluble form of quick-acting fertilizer will help to get the young plants away to a good start. It is made with a tablespoonful of 10.52.17 in a gallon of water; each plant is given a cupful.

Summer care of strawberries — Cultivation should begin as soon as the planting has been done, maintaining a fine tilth to keep down weeds, to conserve moisture and to provide a suitable bed for the new runners. Strawberries have shallow roots that can be seriously damaged by careless hoeing and, as the season advances, runners can be similarly destroyed.

The June-bearing varieties must have the first flower stems removed from plants set out in the spring or the plants will be weakened and the formation of runners delayed. The everbearing varieties, if allowed to develop flowers after early July, will produce a late summer crop if the plants are healthy and well supplied with moisture and nutrients. Everbearing strawberries were first discovered in 1898. They differ from the June-bearing sorts by producing a second crop of fruit in the fall.

In the backyard, where a small strawberry patch can be well tended, the runners can be spaced properly by pinning them down with bent wires or by setting a small stone or clod of earth on the vine. Each young plant should be spaced about six inches from its neighbor. Unless you sacrifice a number of runners by hoeing them off, the row becomes overcrowded, the fruit small and the season of fruiting is soon over.

Fertilizing strawberries — Young plants set out in the spring in well-prepared soil will need no supplemental fertilizer until the end of August, when a light dose of 16.20.0 will help the next year's fruit buds. Rake the fertilizer into the soil at the rate of two ounces to the square yard, then give the plants a soaking. As the roots of strawberries do not extend much beyond the area covered by the foliage, the fertilizer must be close to the plants to do any good. Fertilizers applied in the spring before the plants are set out should be raked into the soil evenly, using two ounces of 11.48.0 to the square yard.

Excess nitrogen applied to the plants in the spring of their fruiting year produces heavy foliage that interferes with flower development and pollination. A lush growth of leaves also causes heavy loss of water by transpiration in hot weather and, should the weather be damp and cool, fruit may rot under the wet leaves. In some instances, a light dose of nitrogen applied when the fruit has set may be of value. Use 16.20.0 at the rate of two ounces to the square yard, keeping it off the leaves and following up with a good soaking of water. While strawberries need rich soil to grow strong plants, the misuse of chemical fertilizers can be most harmful. It is better to err on the light side; rely on good soil preparation before setting out the young plants and see that water is supplied as required.

Watering strawberries — In prairie gardens, the normal rainfall is seldom sufficient to produce a bumper crop of strawberries. While it may be true that a wet June often produces a good crop, July and August are usually dry and it is at this time that plentiful moisture is needed to build strong crowns on existing plants and to grow runners. The time to water and the amount to put on is important. Excess water hinders normal growth as roots are unable to function to full capacity in soggy soil. Too much water leaches out plant food, especially nitrogen and, if large amounts of water are put on when the fruit is swelling, the berries are soft and may be insipid to the taste. However, strawberries have shallow roots and obtain nearly all their moisture from the top ten or twelve inches of soil. The sandy soils take water more frequently and, unless there is plenty of humus added, much of the water will drain away rapidly. It has been indicated by tests carried out by large commercial growers that strawberries return a greater profit from irrigation than any other crop. When the plants need water, soak the whole patch, putting on the equivalent of an inch of rain. If you use a garden sprinkler, put a straight-sided can in the middle of the strawberry patch to gauge the amount of water you put on. An inch of water in the can will indicate the equivalent of an inch of rain.

Wintering strawberries — Strawberries in the backyard garden, where shelter from buildings traps snow, usually survive the winter in good shape if given a light cover of straw. Out in the open, where the plants may be exposed to the northwest wind, a six-inch mulch of flax straw held in place with a layer of brush is recommended. Snow is the best insulator and every effort should be made to keep it from blowing off. It is important to put the mulch on before the plants are injured by early and hard frosts. On the other hand, plants may be injured when the mulch is put on too soon. When this is done the plant continues to grow, remaining soft and vulnerable to hard frost. A few nights of light frosts will harden the plants; when the hardening process has been completed, the mulch can be put on. In the southern part of the prairies the mulch is put on in early October, in northern areas a week or so earlier, but there is no hard and fast rule — good mulching depends upon the weather. If hard frosts occur in late September, it will pay to mulch the plants immediately following the frost.

The straw is generally removed in early May but, here again, the weather will be the governing factor. Warm weather in April may tempt the novice to take off the straw too early, exposing the plants to drying winds or to late frosts. Spring frosts can do enormous damage to strawberries when they are in bloom. In some instances the pistils are blackened and no fruit is formed. In other cases, when slight frosts occur, the berries are misshapen. Since the plants bloom over a period of two weeks or so, the late flowers will usually escape and go on to produce a crop of fruit, but it is the earliest flowers which produce the largest and earliest berries and these are the most likely to be frozen.

The selection of a site with good air drainage is one of the best precautions against frost injury. Lowlying areas where ground frosts settle should be avoided. By delaying the removal of the winter mulch for a week or so, the plants are retarded and frost damage may be avoided. The wise gardener removes the bulk of the straw in early May, the remainder by the middle of the month, keeping a little in reserve to provide a light protection against a late spring frost. Some gardeners remove the straw from the plants to the rows where it keeps down weeds, conserves moisture and keeps the fruit clean.

Strawberries for the prairies — Everbearing varieties differ from the June bearers in their fruiting habit. The June bearers form fruit buds in the cool days of the fall but the flowers do not appear until the following spring. The season of fruit lasts about three weeks, starting in early July. The everbearing sorts form fruit buds in midsummer to fruit in the late summer and in the fall. They also produce a crop of fruit in early July from buds that are formed the previous fall.

There is a good choice of both everbearers and June bearers. New varieties are introduced from time to time to replace older sorts that have served their purpose or have become infected with virus. A popular June bearer is Dunlap, an old reliable sort with large, good-quality fruit. Gem and Ogallala are two recommended everbearers. The best guide to suitable varieties will be the lists published by the provincial departments of agriculture and the catalogues of the prairie nurserymen.

Raspberries — Raspberries are second only to strawberries in popularity and, in some parts, they are grown more extensively. With proper care they can be the most profitable crop in the garden. A small patch of canes will yield enormous crops of fruit if you plant a suitable variety in a well-sheltered spot where the soil is rich in humus and well drained. Heavy soil that tends to be high in lime is not a good choice. Yellow leaves on weak plants indicate an unsuitable soil. Where the soil is heavy, badly drained and high in lime, yellow leaves with veins still green indicate an iron deficiency. By adding peat in sufficient quantity, the condition can be corrected. Like the strawberry, the raspberry needs plenty of humus in the soil; when this is supplied by adding peat, it serves to hold soil moisture and neutralizes the excess alkali. Large amounts of organic matter are needed in sandy soil; rotted barnyard manure and garden compost can be dug into the soil in the fall in readiness for lining out the canes in the spring.

Planting raspberries — Raspberries start growing new leaves quite early, so the plants should be set out as soon as the ground dries. It is most important to obtain healthy plants; stock that is certified to be free of virus is offered for sale by reputable nurserymen and is always the best investment. Many old patches of raspberries are infected with mosaic and leaf curl, two virus diseases that rob the canes of vigor and reduce the yield of fruit.

The hedgerow system for raspberries is recommended in prairie gardens, keeping the width to two feet by destroying unwanted suckers that are out of line and thinning the remaining ones to six inches apart. Overcrowding weakens the canes and reduces the size of the berries. The distance between the rows should be adjusted to suit the amount of available land and the amount of water that can be supplied. Where you have plenty of water on tap, the rows can be six feet apart and the young canes spaced at a foot and a half. In the farm garden where more land is available, water may be scarce and the raspberry patch will have to rely on rain. If such is the case, it is best to space the rows eight feet apart or wider to conserve moisture and permit the use of power cultivators.

The young canes are planted slightly deeper than they were growing in the nursery. Make a hole large enough to hold the roots without crowding. Well-pulverized soil is firmed around the roots and the plants watered if the soil is dry. The novice will hesitate to cut back the newly planted canes but they must be pruned to leave only two or three eyes at the base. Hard pruning will get the young plants away to a good start and all the plant's energies will be directed to the suckers. These are the next year's canes and will carry the first crop of fruit.

Fertilizing and watering raspberries — Raspberry canes must be kept vigorous to yield profitable crops of high-quality fruit. Thick, sturdy canes produce the best berries; thin ones should be cut out from overgrown patches. Rotted manure used as a mulch can be dug in after serving to keep down weeds and conserve moisture; it will improve the soil texture and release nutrients slowly. Ammonium phosphate (11.48.0) applied at the rate of two or three ounces to the square yard is beneficial.

Raspberries use large quantities of water when the plants are in full leaf and the crop is developing. The roots are shallow and spreading, so cultivating close to the canes can damage the roots. The top ten inches of soil should be always moist; the equivalent of an inch of rain weekly is needed to ensure large berries and a long season of fruiting. It is not uncommon for the period of fruiting to coincide with a period of dry weather; when this happens, the crop will be poor unless the plants are given a weekly soaking to carry them over the period of drought. It is good gardening to give the patch a good soaking if the soil is getting dry when the plants are in bloom, and another when the first berries show color.

Spider mites rapidly build up enormous populations on raspberry plants in dry weather. Control measures should be started as soon as the first leaves unfold.

PRUNING RASPBERRY PATCH

NEW SUCKERS

The old canes, having borne a crop of fruit, are cut out to ground level as indicated, leaving the suckers intact to produce new canes for next year's crop.

Pruning raspberry canes — After the crop is harvested, there comes a critical time for raspberries; instead of getting extra attention in the form of pruning, feeding and watering, the plants are often neglected. Once the canes have borne a crop of fruit they are of no further use, and the sooner they are cut out and destroyed, the better. Cut them back to ground level, gather them up and burn them. A well-established raspberry patch will produce an abundance of suckers to grow into a forest of canes. Some of these suckers can be removed with the old canes but the final thinning is best delayed until spring, as a good stand of new canes will hold a protective covering of snow. In the spring, surplus canes are cut out to leave the stoutest ones standing about six inches apart.

Supporting raspberry canes — In the backyard garden the raspberry canes may not require support but, where the canes are more exposed, they should be supported with wires attached to stout posts. The posts are set ten feet apart down the centre of the row. Wide rows may need a crosspiece attached to the posts or the canes may be drawn too close together. Stretch the wire from both ends of the crosspiece at three feet above the ground and, if the plants are very tall, it will pay to put on a second strand of wire to support the heaviest portion of the cane.

Wintering raspberries — In most parts of the prairies, the hardiest varieties of raspberries will survive the winter in good shape, though even they will suffer some injury occasionally. In problem areas such as southwestern Alberta, where chinook winds bare the ground of snow, the whole canes must be covered with a layer of soil. In other parts of the prairies, where the standard varieties are apt to suffer severe kill-back, the canes are bent over, pinning the ends to the ground by covering them with a shovelful of soil. Winter injury can be so severe that only the lower buds remain alive; when this occurs, it may be advisable to cut the damaged canes to the ground and hope for better luck next year.

Healthy canes, well ripened by a long period of sunny autumn days, stand the best chance of winter survival. Too much water late in the season and overdoses of high nitrogen fertilizer make soft plants that have to face winter before they are hardened off; the result, as a general rule, is heavy cane injury. Good shelter is most important, as the drying winter winds can cause severe injury by desiccation.

Fruit buds can be damaged by late frost if the canes have broken their dormancy. Canes that were mounded with soil in October are uncovered in late April, using a garden fork to free them from the soil. In a week or two, when they are growing in an upright position, check the tip growth for damage. There is nothing gained by leaving the top buds to develop into small, emaciated blooms that dry up before the set fruits. Cut the canes back to a strong bud, even if it means reducing the height of the plant by a foot.

Raspberries for the prairies — The old varieties, Chief and Latham, are still recommended as first-class raspberries. Chief has medium-sized fruits of good quality and the plants are dependably hardy across the prairies. Latham fruits over a long period, yielding large berries in great abundance. Boyne and Killarney are newer sorts that are proving to be hardy and highly productive. Redman, Muskoka, Madawaska, Fraser and several other sorts are available from the prairie nurserymen.

Black raspberries and other brambles — Black raspberries are offered for sale by some prairie nurserymen and, in favored areas where plants are well protected, they yield good quality fruit. The blackberries, found growing wild in the milder parts of the country, are much too tender for the prairies. The Himalayan berry is a vigorous blackberry with a trailing habit like the dewberry. In a suitable climate it makes tremendous growth; twenty feet in a single season is not unusual. It has been tested on the prairies but it killed out to the roots. The loganberry, youngberry and the boysenberry are all too tender for prairie gardens, though it has been reported that some enthusiasts have succeeded in bringing the plants through the winter and picked a little fruit.

Black currants — Black currants have long been popular in European gardens and are esteemed for their unique flavour and healthful vitamin C content. Certain hardy sorts are productive in prairie gardens and were widely planted in the farm garden by the early settlers. To grow a crop of high-quality black currants, you need a deep, medium-heavy loam, plenty of rotted barnyard manure and a supply of water. On sandy soil with poor water-holding capacity, and during periods when the supply of moisture may be uncertain, the plants will not thrive. On the other hand, heavy clay soil tends to bake and crack and this will not suit currants. To keep the roots cool and to conserve soil moisture, plant black currants on the north side of a hedge or group of shrubs and mulch the plants with manure.

Black currants break dormancy and leaf out early in the spring so, unless dormant plants can be set out in April or early May, it is best to wait until September. One-year-old plants set out in the spring should be cut back to six inches high at the time of planting. Those put out in September should not be pruned until the following April, cutting them back in the same way as recommended for the spring-planted stock. Black currants should be set a bit deeper than they were in the nursery and, by cutting the tops back to six inches, strong shoots will start from the base to make a fruitful plant.

Young plants need to be cultivated regularly to kill weeds and to keep the topsoil in fine tilth. The roots are near the surface and deep hoeing close to the plants will therefore damage them; frequent shallow hoeing will encourage sturdy growth which will yield fruit the following year.

Plenty of water is needed when the leaves are fully expanded and when the flower trusses develop.

The black currant bears most of its fruit on wood made the previous year, so a certain amount of old wood is cut out each year to encourage strong shoots to develop from low down on the bush. Pruning can be done as soon as the fruit is picked in the fall, or may be postponed until the following spring. If the hardiest sorts are planted in a well-sheltered garden, they survive the winter in good condition. Where heavy snow may break down the bushes, tie the branches at the top with strong twine.

Boskoop, Giant Kerry and Willoughby are black currant varieties offered for sale by prairie nurserymen. Boskoop has large fruit of good quality but is not so productive as Kerry. Willoughby is resistant to mildew and recommended where irrigation is not possible.

Clove or Missouri currants — Select forms of the native *Ribes odorata* are offered for sale by some prairie nurserymen, who recommend them for dry areas where the ordinary black currant has not thrived. The fruits are purple-black, large and juicy. The flavor is quite different to that of the black currant and is preferred by some.

Red and white currants — Red and white currants yield enormous crops of fruit if the hardy and well-adapted sorts are planted and properly cared for. They differ from the black currants in bearing their fruit on shoot spurs which develop on two- and three-year-old wood. The bushes require the same general care as outlined for the black currants and the soil should be rich and well drained. The main difference is in the pruning: shoots that are three years old or older are removed; new shoots are encouraged to replace the old ones and tall or straggly ones are cut back to keep the bush neat and trim. Red Lake and Stevens are two excellent varieties of red currants; White Grape is one of the best white varieties.

Gooseberries — The native gooseberry is found in a wide area of the prairies extending into the far north. Improved sorts can be grown profitably all across the prairies but gooseberries do best where summer heat is not excessive. It takes several years for the bushes to become established and fruitful but, with proper care, they can be maintained in health and vigor for many years. Gooseberries do well in heavy soil as long as it is well drained. Plants on the north side of a hedge, sheltered from the hot sun but not so close that they compete for soil moisture, will carry a heavy crop of fruit almost every year.

As the gooseberry is one of the earliest plants to leaf out, early autumn planting is recommended. The plants lose their leaves early; by mid-September, it is safe to transplant. One-year-old or two-year-old plants are best, set five feet apart in rows spaced at six feet or wider. Set the young plants a bit deeper than they grew in the nursery and tramp the soil very firmly around the roots. Cut them back to about nine inches to encourage young shoots to start from the base. Like the currants, the gooseberries will benefit from a mulch of strawy manure, which keeps the soil cool and conserves moisture.

If gooseberries are left unpruned, the bushes become a tangle of dense shoots and the fruit will be small. Branches that drag the ground should be removed and most of the wood that is three years old is pruned out in late fall or early spring. The centre of the bush is kept open to allow the free circulation of air; otherwise, mildew will be a problem. As the bush gets older, young shoots will take the place of the old. Surplus growth is cut out but the pruning should not be too drastic or the fruit may sunscald.

Pixwell is the standard hardy gooseberry for the prairies. The berries are of medium size, borne in enormous quantities on long stems. The fruit is acceptable for pies and, when the berries ripen, they can be eaten out of hand. There are a number of improved varieties offered for sale, some with quite large fruit. Occasionally they suffer serious winter injury but are worth a try in a well-sheltered garden.

Eighteen

The Rock Garden

Alpine and rock garden plants are the dwarfs of the plant kingdom; what they lack in size is more than made up for by a wide variety of bright colors and forms of intrinsic beauty. As the land rises to hills and mountains, the plants adapt to an environment of lean soil, sun and wind. The stems of flowering plants are short; the plants themselves are compact and inclined to make cushions that spread slowly, anchoring their new shoots to the ground with shallow roots. In the valleys, the plants are taller; as a rule, their flowers are not so showy but their leaves are much larger and their roots penetrate the soil more deeply.

On the flat prairies, rock gardens are more difficult to fit into the landscape than they are in the foothills of Alberta or on the west coast, where natural outcroppings of rock are likely to occur. While it may be difficult to make a rock garden part of the landscape plan of a prairie garden, we do have a suitable climate for growing alpines; in fact, our prairie climate is better for alpines than the wet, mild weather of the coastal areas. The flowers of the mountains are conditioned to intense light, dry air, a long dead season and a sudden transition from winter to summer and renewed life. In northern prairie gardens, where the summer nights are cooler than they are in the south and where snow generally comes early to cover the plants with a deep blanket, alpine plants will also grow well.

A rock garden provides year-round interest; it is here one finds the first signs of renewed life as the species tulips and other bulbs push their way through the warming soil in April. It is true the main show of color occurs in the spring and early summer but, when this is over, the different shades of green and the varying texture of the leaves will sustain interest for the rest of the growing season. The trailing plants — moss phlox, thymes and sedums — make mats among the stones that stay green and attractive; a few well-placed evergreens that are natural dwarfs will give season-long interest when used as spot plants in a rock garden. Even in the dead of December and January, the snow-covered rocks relieve a drab and otherwise flat landscape and give the rock garden winter beauty.

Designing and Building the Rock Garden

A small area made into a rock garden can be a home for a greater number of plants than can be accommodated in the herbaceous border or in any other part of the garden. You have a choice of hundreds, most of them blooming in the spring and early summer long before the annuals open their first flowers.

How does a novice gardener go about making a rock garden that will fit in with the rest of the landscape and not appear to be out of place? The site must be away from trees or their roots will interfere and, if the branches overhang the rock garden, the drip from rain will be ruinous to the plants. The ideal site is undulating, against a background of evergreens for shelter and pleasing effect. Since most alpines face the sun, the rock garden should be open to the southeast to ensure plenty of light and, at the same time, shelter from the drying northwest winds. The insulating value of snow is most important to certain alpine plants that must carry their evergreen tufts over winter. Without the deep cover of snow that a sheltered spot will provide, the leaves of these tiny plants are seared brown by the winter winds.

It is important that the plants be high and dry in the spring, when the snow melts to leave water in low spots. Alpine plants will not tolerate poorly drained soil, so take special care to see that the soil is well drained and that water from melting snow is not allowed to smother the plants.

If you have no choice of site except a level piece of lawn, start by striping off the turf and digging over the area a foot deep, burying the sod upside down. By adding granulated peat to a heavy soil and enough sand to make it porous, you will make it suitable for most alpines. For those plants that require a lean soil, add more sand; the soil for the acid-loving plants will need more peat. As most rock garden plants are modest in their nutrient needs, it is unnecessary and may be harmful to enrich the soil with barnyard manure or chemicals.

The rock garden enthusiast may buy suitable stones for his rock garden or he may make a field trip in search of them. The first choice is weathered limestone, not easy to come by, but in some parts of the prairies there are natural outcroppings and there may be suitable loose stones in upland meadows. Be on the lookout for good stones, avoiding the round granites and choosing the flatish limestones.

When you have gathered enough stones, they must be placed to the best advantage. Set them into the soil with the best side facing outwards — make sure you set them at about the same angle, to give the effect of a natural outcropping of rock. Bed each one firmly in soil; loose stones will be dangerous as you step from one to another tending the rock plants. Use rocks of different size but avoid brick-sized stones; a few well-placed large stones will give a pleasing and more natural look than a number of smaller ones. The amount of stonework should be in proportion to the size of the rock garden; it is better to have less than too much. As a rough guide, the amount of stone surface should not be more than one-third of the whole area.

If the area is large enough, a path of flat stones may be laid to divide the rock garden into two sections. In the pathway and between stones you can plant a variety of ground-cover plants; thymes are a good choice but they must be in well-drained soil.

The best time to make a rock garden is in the fall. The soil is usually dry; the gardening chores are not as pressing as they are in the spring and the cool weather of October makes the manual labor of moving rocks and soil into position exhilarating.

Planting the Rock Garden

As most rock garden plants bloom in the spring or early summer, it is best to plant them in August or early September. Later planting is not recommended as there is danger that the young plants will be heaved out of the soil by sudden and hard frost.

Many kinds of bulbs can be planted in October to give a show of bloom in May and June. It is best to cover them with a layer of flax straw to delay the deep penetration of frost until the bulbs have made good roots.

It is questionable whether shrubs have a place in the rock garden — certainly not in a small rock garden but, where space is not so limited, there may be room for a few dwarf evergreens. These are chosen for their special shapes — globe, pyramidal or creeping. It is well to keep in mind that alpine plants grow where woody plants cannot thrive, so fast-growing deciduous shrubs should not be considered.

You will find a good selection of rock garden plants in some prairie nurserymen's catalogues and more in the catalogues of specialized growers from the milder parts of Canada. The novice will be well advised to consult the recommended lists of rock plants put out by the provincial departments of agriculture.

The following lists of rock garden plants have been assembled after testing hundreds of varieties on the prairies. They are all fully hardy and will give interest from April, when the first bulbs bloom, until late in the fall when the leaves of some are still attractive.

Bulbs for the Rock Garden

Tulip *(Tulipa)* — There are numerous species tulips that are hardy and reliable when planted in the rock garden. Many come from Turkestan, where the climate is not unlike that of the prairies, with definite seasons of heat and cold. Bulb catalogues will provide an extensive list of suitable varieties, many of them rare and expensive, but the novice with a small home garden is wise to begin with the more popular sorts proven on the prairies.

The waterlily tulip *(T. kaufmanniana)* blooms early in May. The flowers have white petals tinged with pink on the outside and suffused with yellow at the base. There are a number of hybrids between the waterlily tulip and another species, *T. greigii*. Some have mottled leaves that spread over the ground; the flowers are large and may be red, yellow or pink.

One of the most popular tulips is a fosteriana hybrid called Red Emperor. It blooms so early it is often injured by spring frost. A dwarf form, *T. fosteriana princeps*, is only eight inches high and blooms a bit later; otherwise, it is much the same as Red Emperor.

T. tarda is a charming species from Turkestan, not more than six inches high with a profusion of starry flowers in early May. The petals are bright yellow, each with a white tip, and several are produced on a single stem.

Onion *(Allium)* — There are a number of flowering onions worth considering as rock garden plants. The lily leek *(A. moly)* grows a foot high with flattish leaves and dense umbels of yellow flowers in June. The Ostrowsky onion *(A. ostrowskianum)* grows only six inches high with heads of rosy pink flowers in June. It will not be out of place to plant a

ROCK GARDENS

Top: The annual border. Individual plants remain distinctive when planted in bold patches rather than as scattered specimens; note the dwarf marigolds, the snapdragons and the white stocks.

Centre: The rock garden. The desired effect of a natural outcropping is achieved by setting stones in the soil at about the same angle and providing an appropriate background.

Bottom: The May-blooming corydalis, with a flowering onion in the foreground.

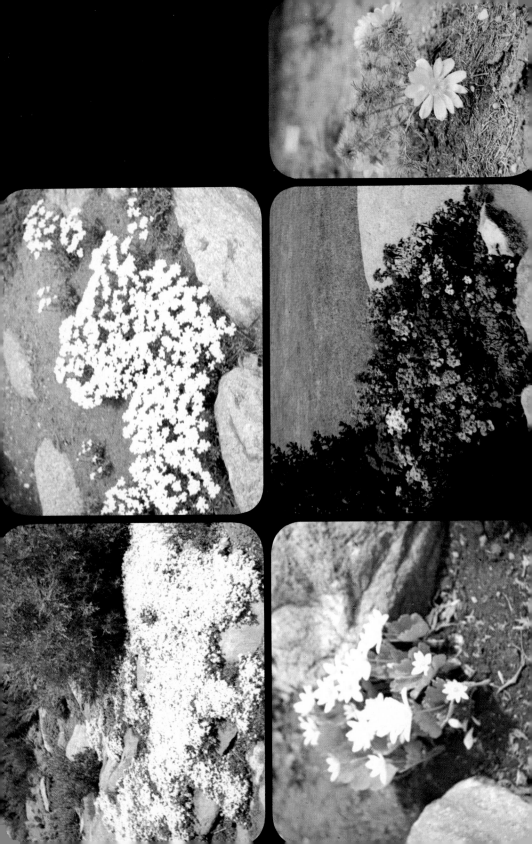

small patch of chives in the rock garden. The soft purple flowers are not unattractive and the leaves can be used in salads.

Crocus *(Crocus)* — The true crocus *(C. hybridus)* is not hardy in prairie gardens; the bulbs may survive for a year or two in a well-sheltered spot but they do not thrive as rock garden plants. The native prairie anemone *(Anemone patens)* often erroneously called crocus, will thrive in prairie rock gardens if given poor soil and full sun.

Squill *(Scilla)* — The Siberian squill *(S. sibirica)* is one of the hardiest and most satisfactory bulbs for the rock garden. Its nodding blue bells open as soon as the snow goes and are unharmed by frost. An improved form of the Siberian squill called Spring Beauty has darker blue flowers on taller stems than the original species. There is a white-flowered variety identical in every respect except that it bears white blooms.

A similar plant *(S. puschkinia libanotica)* is sometimes called the striped squill. It has white petals, each striped with blue. It makes an attractive rock garden plant and is just as hardy as the Siberian squills.

The English bluebell *(S. campanulata)* is not hardy; attempts to winter it have always ended in failure. Those who remember the drifts of misty blue under the beechwoods of an English countryside may be tempted to try to grow bluebells in a prairie garden but there is virtually no chance of success.

Fritillary *(Fritillaria)* — The Siberian fritillary *(F. pallidiflora)* and the northwestern species *(F. pudica)* make fine rock garden plants. The Siberian species grows a foot or so high with broad, blue green leaves and slender stems, each with several nodding, pale yellow flowers. *F. pudica* is only six inches high with narrow leaves and solitary blooms of pale yellow. Occasionally, a stem bears more than one bloom; the flowers are sometimes a darker shade of yellow.

Rock Garden Plants

Adonis *(Adonis)* — The spring adonis *(A. vernalis)* and the Amur adonis *(A. amurensis)* are choice, early flowering plants for the rock garden. The spring adonis has bright yellow flowers surrounded by dark green, ferny

ROCK GARDEN PLANTS

Top Left: Moss phlox

Top Centre: Perennial candytuft

Lower Left: The native bloodroot

Lower Centre: Nemesia produces bright flowers over a long period; it is an annual unlike the true alpine plants, but it will not look out of place in the rock garden.

Lower Right: The Amur adonis flowers in early May.

foliage. The Amur adonis has coarser leaves and larger flowers, somewhat paler than the spring adonis but otherwise much the same. Both grow about a foot high and bloom in early May.

Alyssum *(Alyssum)* — The goldentuft alyssum *(A. saxatile)* makes a leafy, compact plant a foot high with a profusion of bright yellow flowers in June. It grows best in a sunny spot where the soil is well drained and needs good snow cover to survive the winter.

Aster *(Aster)* — The alpine aster *(A. alpina)* is a fine rock garden plant with large mauve daisies in July. In well-drained soil where the plants are shaded from hot sun, they will survive with little attention. Several forms of Michaelmas daisies *(A. novibelgii)* that grow a foot high may be used in the rock garden. These dwarf plants bloom late in the fall when little else is in flower.

Bedstraw *(Galium)* — The yellow bedstraw *(G. vernum)* may not be a first-class plant for the rock garden but it blooms in July when most of the rock garden plants are out of bloom; for this reason, if for no other, it is valuable. The plants are a foot high with fine, dark green foliage and tiny yellow flowers.

Bellflower *(Campanula)* — Some of the bellflowers are good rockery plants; one of the most common is the Carpathian bellflower *(C. carpatica)*, which makes a spreading plant with roundish leaves and a profusion of flowers in June and July. The flowers are usually shades of blue but there are good white-flowered varieties. The native bluebell *(C. rotundifolia)* is sometimes cultivated on the prairies and may be used effectively in the rock garden, where it will continue to bloom from July until September if given a place in the sun. The lowcluster bellflower *(C. glomerata acaulis)* is a spreading plant six inches high with dense heads of purple flowers in July. It tolerates some shade and is not demanding in its soil requirements. The Sarmatian bellflower *(C. sarmatica)* is not so well known as the others, but it is fully hardy and makes an attractive plant with gray leaves and soft blue flowers in July. The plants are a foot high and they do best in full sun.

Bergenia *(Bergenia)* — The bergenias, once known to botanists as saxafragas and later as megaseas, are bold, low-growing plants with large leathery leaves. The heartleaf bergenia *(B. cordifolia)* and the strapleaf bergenia *(B. ligulata)* are two well-adapted species. Both grow about a foot high, spreading to make patches of greenery that change to purple in the fall. The dense heads of rosy purple flowers appear so early in May that they are sometimes damaged by spring frost.

Bleedingheart *(Dicentra)* — The well-known bleedingheart *(D. spectabilis)* has no place in the rock garden but the improved form of the Pacific bleedingheart *(D. formosa)*, Bountiful, is a dwarf plant with attractive grayish leaves and a long season of bloom. The plants are not more than a foot high and the flowers are a soft shade of pink.

Bloodroot *(Sanguinaria)* — The native bloodroot *(S. canadensis)* is one of the first spring flowers, often opening its snow-white blooms in early May. The plants are about nine inches high with large, roundish leaves of bluish green. It needs a deep moist soil in partial shade and a cover of dry leaves in the fall. A double-flowered form is available.

Bugle flower *(Ajuga)* — The ajuga or bugle flower makes a good ground cover with limited use in the rock garden. Both the Geneva bugle *(A. genevensis)* and the carpet bugle *(A. reptans)* will grow in either sun or shade. Winter survival depends on good snow coverage. If the rosettes of leaves are exposed to drying winter winds, they brown and die. Both kinds flower in June, making mats of misty blue.

Campion *(Lychnis)* — Most of the campions are found in the flower border but one or two can be used with good effect in the rock garden. The Arctic campion *(L. alpina)* is a foot-high plant with pink flowers in July. The clammy campion *(L. viscaria)* and its double-flowered form make compact plants with a show of cerise red flowers in July and August.

Candytuft *(Iberis)* — The perennial candytuft makes a fine plant for a sunny spot. The evergreen candytuft *(I. sempervirens)* and its improved sorts will grow about a foot high with narrow, dark green leaves and heads of white flowers in June. The plants are shrubby, so the tops must be protected from drying winds and the early spring sun or they brown and the flower buds die.

Columbine *(Aquilegia)* — Most of the columbines are too tall for the rock garden but the foot-high alpine columbine *(A. alpina)* is a fine plant for a half-shaded spot. It has short-spurred flowers of intense blue and the leaves are an attractive shade of grayish green.

Cranesbill *(Geranium)* — The cranesbill is not to be confused with the bedding geraniums, which are a different genus and tender to frost. Several hardy cranesbills make good plants for the rockery. The lilac cranesbill *(G. grandiflorum)* grows a foot high with deeply cut leaves and masses of lilac blue flowers in June and July. The Caucasus cranesbill *(G. ibericum)* is a bit taller with flowers of violet blue.

Deadnettle *(Lamium)* — The spotted deadnettle *(L. maculatum)* grows a foot high with dark green leaves, each with a silvery midrib. It will grow either in sun or in shade, producing dense heads of purple flowers in July.

Dryad *(Dryas)* — The Mount Washington dryad *(D. octopetala)* is one of the gems of the rock garden. It covers the ground with its attractive leaves; in June, it is showy with small white flowers on four-inch stems.

Gentian *(Gentiana)* — The gentians include some of the rarest gems of the alpine meadows. The flowers range from the palest shades of blue to deepest purple. Not many have been tried in prairie gardens but there is an excellent chance that, given good cover in the winter, many gentians would survive. The Purdom gentian *(G. purdomii)* is hardy if covered with snow for the winter. It has violet purple flowers on slender, six-inch stems. One of the most reliable gentians, the seven-lobed gentian *(G. septem-loba),* flowers in July and August. The flower stems are a foot high and the blooms are medium blue with darker spots. Another hardy gentian which is doing well in prairie gardens is the Hascomb gentian *(G. hascombensis).* It makes a low, spreading plant with trusses of deep blue flowers in July and August. A rock garden enthusiast will find many more worth a trial in prairie gardens. At the Morden Experimental Farm, a plant of the rare *Gentiana farrerii* bloomed for a number of years in the rock garden. Its slender, creeping stems were covered in September with tiny, sky-blue flowers.

Gypsophila *(Gypsophila)* — The common babysbreath *(G. paniculata)* is of no use in the rock garden but there are several dwarf kinds that are suitable if given a place in the sun where the soil is well drained. One called Rosenschleir (rosyveil) is a fine plant. It starts to bloom in July and continues through the summer well into the fall. The dainty pink flowers are produced in large panicles on low plants with grayish green leaves. The creeping gypsophila *(G. repens)* is a trailing plant with white flowers in July.

Iris *(Iris)* — The dwarf iris, sometimes called the Crimean iris, is a fine plant for a sunny spot. It grows about six inches high; some have white flowers, some yellow, some blue and some dark purple. Dwarf irises require the same general care as the bearded irises, but do not require transplanting so often.

Ladyslipper *(Cypripedium)* — The native ladyslippers are sometimes dug from the wildwood and transplanted to the garden; although they have been established in some prairie rock gardens, it is not a recommended practice. The chance of giving the plant a suitable home in a prairie garden is poor and most attempts will end in failure. The special requirements of this handsome orchid are difficult to provide, so it is best to leave it in its natural environment.

Lily of the valley *(Convallaria)* — The lily of the valley *(C. majalis)* should not be overlooked as a good plant for a shaded part of the rock garden. It increases slowly by underground stolens to make a dense mat of greenery through the summer and fall. The pure white, sweet-scented bells are freely produced on wiry stems in early June.

Lotus *(Lotus)* — The double-flowered deervetch *(L. corniculatus* var. *florepleno),* makes a green mat of tiny leaves covered in July with a mass of bright yellow flowers. It needs to be under snow in the winter or it may be injured by drying winds.

Moneywort *(Lysimachia)* — The moneywort or loosestrife is known to some gardeners as creeping jenny *(L. nummularia).* It spreads to cover the ground with pale green leaves on trailing stems that are studded with yellow flowers in June. It roots from every joint but is never too invasive and tolerates sun or shade.

Periwinkle *(Vinca)* — The common periwinkle *(V. minor)* survives under good snow cover but is likely to brown if exposed to drying winds. It has trailing stems with dark green leaves and tiny, sky-blue flowers in July. It prefers a shady spot where the soil is moist but well drained.

Phlox *(Phlox)* — Besides the moss phloxes *(P. subulata),* there are several other kinds particularly suited to the rock garden. Two of the best are the creeping phlox *(P. stolenifera)* and the amoena phlox *(P. amoena).* The creeping phlox has bright green leaves and tiny purplish flowers on six-inch stems in June. The amoena phlox grows about a foot high and flowers in May and early June.

The moss phloxes are excellent for creeping among the rocks; there are many named sorts in shades of blue and red. The Arctic phlox *(P. borealis)* has bright green leaves all the year around; in May and early June, the plants are covered with carmine rose flowers. *Phlox hoodii* has white flowers on plants that are similar to the moss phloxes. If the tops of moss phloxes are under snow, they will stay green through the winter; if exposed to drying winds, they turn brown and the flower buds die.

Pinks and carnations *(Dianthus)* — The large family of pinks and carnations provides some good rock garden plants. The maiden pink *(D. deltoides)* is one of the best known. It makes a mossy cushion of dark green leaves covered with tiny pink or red flowers in June and July. The evergreen leaves will be browned by winter winds, so it is necessary to cover them with boughs to hold the snow. Several kinds of grass pinks *(D. plumarius)* and related sorts will make useful plants for a sunny spot in the rock garden. The variety Shadow Valley grows well in some parts but frequently it suffers from a mysterious disease, manifest in purple markings on the stems and leaves, which stunts the plants. It produces large, double red flowers all through the summer if the plants remain healthy.

Plantainlily *(Hosta)* — Several species of the plantainlily should be considered for the shady spots in the rock garden where the soil can be kept moist. The blue plantainlily *(H. caerulea)* and fortune's plantainlily *(H. fortunei)* grow a foot high with large handsome leaves and pale mauve flowers in June and July.

Primrose *(Primula)* — There are a number of primulas rated as fully hardy in prairie gardens, and many more that have not been tried but may be suitable. Primulas prefer cool soil and shade from the hot sun; the low-level, north-facing aspects of the rock garden will be best. In periods of drought the plants should be watered.

The cortusa primrose *(P. cortusoides)* is able to stand more heat and dry weather than most primulas. It makes a neat plant with roundish leaves and slender stems of carmine rose flowers in May and June. The auricula *(P. auricula),* sometimes called dusty miller, is hardy and dependable in prairie gardens. It is a good plant for a half-shaded place in the rock garden where the soil is gritty. The leaves and flower stems are coated with a mealy substance from which the plant gets its common name. The plants are a foot high and produce sturdy stems of dark red or yellow flowers in May and June. The Siberian primrose *(P. sibirica)* has small, lilac pink flowers in May; it grows six inches high and, though it is not showy, it is worthy of a place in the rock garden. The English primrose and the polyanthus have been tried in prairie gardens without much success. Under a deep cover of snow, the plants sometimes survive to produce flowers in May and June but, more often than not, they die the first winter.

Rockcress *(Arabis)* — In some prairie gardens the wall rockcress *(A. albida),* both single- and double-flowered forms, grows fairly well. In other parts, where snow cover is not so certain, the plants will die out. The plant has grayish leaves and six-inch stems of white flowers in June. After blooming, it is best to cut off the flower stems and any straggly shoots.

Rockjasmine *(Androsace)* — The silvery green rosettes of the rockjasmine *(A. sarmentosa)* and its clustered heads of pale pink flowers on six-inch stems make it a choice rock garden plant. It flowers in June and is perfectly hardy if under a deep cover of snow.

Shooting-star *(Dodecatheon)* — The eastern shooting-star *(D. meadia)* is a rare native and worthy of a place in the rock garden, where it will thrive in moist shade. It grows a foot high and bears slender stems of rosy pink flowers in May. The petals are turned back in the manner of the cyclamen.

Siberian wallflower *(Erysimum asperum,* formerly *Cheiranthus allionii)* — The Siberian wallflower is never long lived in prairie gardens, but it is easily raised from seed to make a good plant for a sunny spot in the rock garden where the soil is poor, gritty and well drained. It produces a show of bright orange flowers in June and July on compact plants that grow about a foot high.

Snow-in-summer *(Cerastium)* — The common snow-in-summer *(C. tomentosum)* is hardly fit for the rock garden unless it can be given enough room to spread without encroaching on less rampant plants. Where it can be kept within bounds by regular and ruthless pruning, it is worthy of a place in the sun; it makes a mat of silvery gray leaves and six-inch stems of pure white flowers in July.

Soapwort *(Saponaria)* — The rock soapwort *(S. ocymoides)* is a creeping plant six inches high with small leaves and pink flowers in June. It thrives best in a sunny spot and is able to stand drought.

Speedwell *(Veronica)* — Several speedwells are creeping plants useful in sunny places in the rock garden. The comb speedwell *(V. pectinata)* is a low, spreading plant with tiny leaves of grayish green and spikes of deep blue flowers in July. The woolly speedwell *(V. incana)* is about six inches high with gray leaves and either blue or pink flowers in July; the pink-flowered variety is not so robust as the blue. The creeping speedwell *(V. repens)* has tiny leaves and bright blue flowers; it is liable to winter injury unless under a deep cover of snow.

Stonecress *(Aethionema)* — Sometimes called Persian or Lebanon candy-tuft but, correctly, stonecress, *A. pulchellum* makes a splendid plant for a sunny spot in the rock garden. It is rather difficult to transplant because of its wiry roots but, once established, it produces volunteer plants from self-sown seeds. The plants are six inches high with narrow, gray green leaves and tiny heads of carmine flowers in June and July.

Stonecrops *(Sedum)* — Some of the stonecrops make fine plants for a sunny place in the rock garden. One of the best is the evergreen stonecrop *(S. hybridum)*. It is a low, spreading plant with glossy, dark green leaves and masses of bright yellow flowers in July. The two-row stonecrop *(S. spurium)* has roundish leaves on spreading plants that grow six inches high. The pink or red flowers are produced in July. The orange stonecrop *(S. kamschaticum)* is one of the easiest plants to grow. The leaves are bright green, the flowers orange yellow and the plants are about six inches high. The goldust stonecrop *(S. acre)* is only three inches high with tiny yellowish leaves and yellow flowers. It spreads by volunteer seedlings and may be a nuisance when it grows in unwanted places.

Sundrop *(Oenothera)* — The Ozark sundrop *(O. missourensis)* is first choice as a long-season rockery plant. It has dark green, glossy leaves and large, primrose yellow flowers from July until October. It needs a place in the sun where the soil is well drained. The curious winged seed pods are useful decorations.

Thrift *(Armeria)* — The common thrift *(A. maritima)* grows abundantly in the seaside area of British Columbia, but it is not fully hardy in prairie gardens. It sometimes survives to produce its dense heads of pink flowers on foot-high stems in June.

Thyme *(Thymus)* — Plants that spread to make mats of greenery are useful in the rock garden and the thymes offer a good selection. You can interplant them with bulbs to give color in early spring and the thymes will follow with a show of bloom in July. The plants are evergreen as long as they are safe under a blanket of snow but they can brown badly if exposed to drying winds. The various forms of mother of thyme *(T.*

serpyllum) include those with white as well as pink flowers and leaves that are golden, green or grayish; some smell of lemon, some of caraway and some have the scent usually associated with thyme. All need a place in the sun with good soil drainage.

Viola *(Viola)* — A number of violas, or tufted pansies as they are sometimes called, are useful in the shaded parts of the rock garden. One of the hardiest is the altai violet *(V. altaica)*. It grows about six inches high and bears its soft yellow flowers from June until October. Various kinds of the horned violet *(V. cornuta)* survive in well-sheltered gardens and are useful rock garden plants. They need shade from hot sun, plenty of moisture and a deep cover of snow to survive the winter. They are not long-lived plants and it is best to raise new plants from seed sown indoors in February.

Wormwood *(Artemisia)* — The beach wormwood *(A. stelleriana)* and its variety Silver Mound are fully hardy and excellent gray-leaved plants for the rock garden. The beach wormwood has deeply lobed leaves on low, spreading branches that grow a foot high. The flowers are gray and not attractive, so cut them off as they appear. Silver Mound makes a neat plant with finely cut leaves of silvery gray. It seldom produces flowers but, should flower stems appear, they should be cut off.

Yarrow *(Achillea)* — Plants with silvery leaves give contrast to the all-over green of the garden. The silvery yarrow *(A. ageratifolia)* grows only six inches high, making a dense mat of silvery foliage from which rise heads of grayish white flowers in July. The flowers are not attractive and should be removed as they form.

Index